MONETARY FOUNDATIONS OF THE RAJ

In the administration of colonial finances, the monetary policy of the Imperial power relating to their dependencies had tremendous impact on the colonial economy. The British East India Company, in 1835 was able to introduce a universal currency in all its Indian possessions which proved to be a landmark in the economic consolidation of the British rule in India.

This volume presents an account of the monetary policies adopted by the British East India Company by which it was successful in securing full control over money supply – the life blood of a monetized economy. This, in turn, affected almost every aspect of India's colonial economy and played a crucial role in laying the foundation for its colonial subjugation.

In this unique anthology, published studies along with unpublished archival records have been integrated into an overall theme. Together with a comprehensive bibliography-cum-list for further readings this volume is aimed to serve as a veritable reference tool.

**Sanjay Garg** (b. 1965) is a numismatist and economic historian of international repute. He has extensive research experience in history of South Asia, with specialization in economic and monetary history, currency and coinage, historical architecture, and archival studies. His research findings have been widely published in print and multimedia, and include an edited volume of S.H. Holdivala's numismatic contributions, *Studies in Mughal Mint-Towns & Other Essays* (2014); and *Studies in Indo-Muslim History*, 2 vols. (2018).

At present Dr. Garg is posted as the Director, Swami Vivekananda Cultural Centre, Astana (Kazakhstan).

# MONETARY FOUNDATIONS OF THE RAJ

*Edited by*
SANJAY GARG

Routledge
Taylor & Francis Group
LONDON AND NEW YORK

MANOHAR
2019

First published 2019
by Routledge
4 Park Square, Milton Park, Abingdon, Oxon OX14 4RN

and by Routledge
605 Third Avenue, New York, NY 10017

First issued in paperback 2023

*Routledge is an imprint of the Taylor & Francis Group, an informa business*



*British Library Cataloguing in Publication Data*
A catalogue record for this book is available from the British Library

*Library of Congress Cataloging in Publication Data*
A catalog record for this book has been requested

ISBN 13: 978-1-138-28062-5 (hbk)
ISBN 13: 978-1-03-265246-7 (pbk)
ISBN 13: 978-1-315-27190-3 (ebk)

DOI: 10.4324/9781315271903

Typeset in Minion Pro 11/13
by Ravi Shanker, Delhi 110 095

MANOHAR

# Contents

## PART II: RECORDS

# Introduction to the Series

Themes dealing with both history and numismatics have rarely been integrated in the mainstream historiography of India. For Mughal India, a beginning was indeed made to bridge this gulf (*The Imperial Monetary System of Mughal India*, 1987). Sadly this noteworthy initiative had no takers amongst historians and numismatists dealing with post-Mughal and colonial India.

While excellent studies, both in the fields of economic, social and political history of India as well as on the contemporary coinage, its production technologies, and mint administration have appeared over the last one and a half centuries, seldom have these two streams intermingled or even intersected. Likewise the enormous historical material available in the form official records, personal narratives, and other contemporary accounts as well as in the archives of the British East India Company and later the Crown's representative government in India remains largely untapped in the numismatic writings dealing with this period. Though a beginning to fill this vacuum was made with the publication of *The Coins of the Bengal Presidency* (Stevens 2012) and *The Sikka and the Raj* (Garg 2013), many more studies are needed to evolve a better understanding of the monetary history of India.

This series, therefore, seeks to fill this vacuum by presenting comprehensive readers on the monetary history of India, covering the entire period for which written documentation is available (both from Indian and colonial authorities), i.e. from *c.* 1300 CE onwards. The individual volumes in this series would be a mix of the published and unpublished research papers as well as the archival sources on different topics, ranging from coinage and paper currency management, to coinage production and circulation, and its effects on financial health of the state, as well as the symbiotic relationship between currency and fiscal management, international trade and overall economy of a nation, to name a few. The actual ratio between the published studies and unpublished documentary sources would, however, vary in each volume and where necessary, translations of non-English sources would be provided. A fresh introduction would integrate these selections into the overall theme. A comprehensive bibliography-cum-list for further readings would be appended to each of these volumes so as to make them a veritable reference tool.

Sanjay Garg

# Preface

In the administration of colonial finances, the monetary policy of the Imperial power relating to their dependencies had tremendous impact on the colonial economy. The British East India Company, which gradually replaced the tottering Mughal Empire, inherited a chaotic currency system in which a large variety of coins were in concurrent circulation. These coins were of different kinds and denominations, minted at different places on different dates, and had no uniform system of weights and purity whatsoever. For a trading organization that was required to constantly transport money and goods from one part of India to another, and make heavy disbursements in the local currencies for its investments as well as for its numerous military campaigns, the establishment of a standard currency and regulation of its supply was of crucial importance.

The East India Company, therefore, adopted a policy of gradually subsuming the local currencies and replacing them with a uniform imperial currency. After passing a series of regulations dealing with the issues such as the metallic standards (monometallism vs. bimetallism), standard weight and purity of the Company's coins, regularization of the agio (discount), rates of exchange, reform of the coin-production techniques, etc., in 1835 the Company was able to introduce a universal currency in all its Indian possessions. This proved to be a landmark feat that laid the foundation of the monetary integration of India, which, in turn, provided the requisite economic prowess for consolidation of the British rule in India.

This volume presents an account of the monetary policies adopted by the East India Company to establish a uniform monetary regime in British India. The area of circulation of the uniform currency was subsequently enlarged with the expansion of territories that were acquired by the East India Company and simultaneous demonetization of the regional currencies. It demonstrates how passing through the stages of prohibition and permission of their minting activities by the Indian powers, the Company was able to secure full control over money supply – the life blood of a monetized economy – which affected almost every aspect of India's colonial economy. This, in turn, played a crucial role in India's subjugation by the colonial power.

The first part of the book presents fifteen essays by eminent historians, numismatists, and contemporary writers where various aspects of the evolving monetary policy of the British East India Company have been discussed and analysed. The second part includes a selection from the contemporary archival records and serves as source for many crucial markers discussed in this evolution process. Spellings, naming conventions and citation styles have been retained as in originals. Full references of the cited works along with additional reading list have been given in the Bibliography.

This volume does not in any manner claims to be an exhaustive reader on the subject as there is a rich repertoire of academic writings dealing, directly or indirectly, with the different aspects of the administration of colonial finances by a colonizing power, including its monetary policies. Likewise, the archival sources included here are only a 'tip of the iceberg', as millions of such sources, both official and non-official, still lie untapped in the muniment rooms across India and Europe. This reader, however, aims to present a connected and corroborative narrative of various forces that were at work in shaping the monetary policy of the East India Company as well as the process of monetary administration during the phase of Company's direct administration of its Indian empire.

It is hoped that this book will be able to rekindle the interest of the scholars as well as of the scholars-in-making to undertake further studies and illuminate some other obscure aspects of the monetary foundation of the English rule in India.

*New Delhi* SANJAY GARG
*Holi 2018*

# Acknowledgements

My primary debt in bringing out this volume is to all scholars whose valuable contributions have been included in the first part of this volume. These are:

Ambedkar, B.R., 'From a Double Standard to a Silver Standard', in *History of Indian Currency and Banking*, Thacker and Company (Bombay, 1947).

Anonymous, 'The Monetary System of British India', *BQR*, vol. 6.2 (1857), 249-64.

Dalrymple, A., *Observations on the Copper Coinage wanted for the Circars* (London, 1794).

Dayal Das, 'First Uniform Currency for India', *PIHRC* (Bhubaneswar Session), vol. 33:2 (1958), pp. 65-71.

Dodwell, Henry H., 'Substitution of Silver for Gold in South India', *IJE*, vol. 3:2 (1921), pp. 183-204.

Garg, Sanjay, 'Prinsep and the Currency Reform', *JAS*, vol. 43:3 (2001), pp. 40-55.

Mitra, Debendra Bijoy, 'Changing Monetary System in Bengal during the British Rule', in *Monetary System in the Bengal Presidency, 1757-1835*, K.P. Bagchi (Calcutta, 1991).

Perlin, Frank, 'Growth of Money Economy and Some Questions of Transitions in Late Pre-Colonial India', *Social Scientist*, vol. 10:11 (1983), pp. 27-38.

Ramachandran, C., 'Madras Currency under the Early British Rule', *IBR*, vol. 2:3 (1970), pp. 42-9.

Rothermund, Dietmar, 'Monetary Policy of British Imperialism', *IESHR*, vol. 7:1 (1970), pp. 91-108.

Sinha, J.C., 'Currency in Early British Days', *IJE*, vol. 7:3 (1927), pp. 166-75.

Sinha, J.C., 'Economic Theorists among the Servants of John Company (1766-1806)', *EJ*, vol. 35:137 (1925), pp. 47-59.

Stevens, P.J.E., 'Imperial and Colonial Coinage', *BNJ*, vol. 73 (2003), pp. 148-60.

Thomas, Edward, 'The Coinage of the East India Company at Bombay, under the Charters of Charles II, with a note on the Indian exchanges of the period', *IA*, vol. 11 (1882), pp. 313-19.

Thurston Edgar, 'Note on the History of East India Company Coinage from 1753-1835', *JASB*, vol. 62 (1893), pp. 52-84.

I am especially thankful to Profs. Dietmar Rothermund, D.B. Mitra, and Dr. Paul Stevens, who very willingly gave their consent for reproduction of their contributions in this volume. My sincere efforts to contact Prof. Frank Perlin failed and I was constrained to take the risk of inviting his displeasure for including his extremely informative article in this volume, which has also been subsequently reproduced in *The Journal of Peasant Studies*, vol. 11.3 (1984), pp. 96-107.

I am also grateful to Shri Ramesh Jain, owner of the Mahohar Publishers & Distributors, New Delhi who encouraged me to begin this series, and evinced great interest during the preparation of this volume.

My friends Prof. Syed Ejaz Hussain, Professor of History, Visvabharati University, Santiniketan, and Dr. Shailendra Bhandare, Assistant Curator, Ashmolean Museum, and Fellow, St. Cross College, University of Oxford, have always helped me with their valuable advice, comments, and even criticisms of my academic undertakings, and I owe my gratitude to them. I also gratefully acknowledge the help and encouragement that I have received from another esteemed friend, Prof. Jan Lucassen, Honorary Fellow, International Institute of Social History, Amsterdam, and also a member of the Netherlands Royal Academy of Arts and Sciences, in shaping this series.

Finally, I am indebted to my wife, Nurussaba, who has been, for over past two decades, my first audience, first reader, first editor and first critic of all my academic and literary writings.

SANJAY GARG

# Abbreviations

| | |
|---|---|
| *AER* | *American Economic Review* |
| *BNJ* | *British Numismatic Journal* |
| *BQR* | *Bombay Quarterly Review* |
| *CEHI* | *Cambridge Economic History of India:*<br>Vol. I (Raychaudhuri and Habib 1982)<br>Vol. II (Kumar 1983) |
| *EJ* | *The Economic Journal* [of Royal Economic Society, London] |
| FWIHC | Fort William India House Correspondence |
| IA | The Indian Archives |
| *IBR* | *Indo-British Review: A Journal of History* |
| *IESHR* | *Indian Economic and Social History Review* |
| *IJE* | *Indian Journal of Economics* |
| *IMB* | *Indian Museum Bulletin* |
| *INC* | *Indian Numismatic Chronicle* |
| *JAH* | *Journal of African History* |
| *JAS/ JASB* | *Journal of the Asiatic Society [of Bengal]* |
| *JASBom* | *Journal of the Asiatic Society of Bombay* |
| *JEEH* | *Journal of the European Economic History* |
| *JEH* | *Journal of the Economic History* |
| *JIB* | *Journal of the Institute of Bankers* |
| *JIH* | *Journal of the Indian History* |
| *JPE* | *Journal of Political Economy* |
| *JSS* | *Journal of the Statistical Society* |
| *MIQ* | *Medieval India Quarterly* |
| MSA | Maharashtra State Archives, Mumbai |
| NAI | National Archives of India, New Delhi |
| NC | Numismatic Chronicle |
| Num. Cir. | (The) Numismatic Circular |

| | |
|---|---|
| OC | Original Consultations |
| OIOC | Oriental and India Office Collection (now Asia, Pacific and Africa Collection), British Library, London |
| *ONSNL* | *Oriental Numismatic Society Newsletter* |
| OR | Original Receipt |
| *PIHC* | *Proceedings of Indian History Congress* |
| *PIHRC* | *Proceedings of Indian Historical Records Commission/ Committee* |
| TNSA | Tamil Nadu State Archive, Chennai |
| WBSA | West Bengal State Archives, Kolkata |

# 1

# Introduction

Sanjay Garg

The history of the British presence in India is conveniently divided into two halves – the period of administration of the English East India Company and that of direct rule by the British Crown, generally called the 'British Raj'. In this binary, the year 1858 acquires a salient significance in which the administration of the territories under the English East India Company was transferred to the British Crown and the last vestige of the tottering Mughal rule was removed from India's political scene, once and for all.

The success of the British Raj largely depended on the administrative structure, exploitative economy, and a regular army that was built by the East India Company over a century or so, roughly from 1757 onwards. In this process of converting India into a colony of the British Empire, the monetary policies of the Company played a crucial role. By gradually increasing its control over the currency supply, the Company assumed a commanding position which crippled the Indian economy and political system. For a trading Company that was always in a need of liquid cash for procurement of goods and its other commercial activities in India, control of the channels of money supply was crucial for its successful career. At the same time this was a subject that was linked with a number of internal and external factors. For example, the inflow-outflow of bullion through international trade resulted directly in the expansion-contraction of money supply, which in turn led to inflationary-deflationary price trends affecting the entire society. The Company's capacity to pay cash salaries to its troops contributed in the success of its military expeditions against a number of Indian powers, which resulted in large territorial acquisitions that formed the nucleus of its colonial empire. The Company's revenue collection from a large part of the country was able to finance not only its own investments in India, but it also opened up a regular stream of drain of wealth from India. Once again its capacity to realize this revenue in cash was determined by the state of currency in these regions. It was through its control over currency that the Company entered India's larger money market which during the pre-colonial regime supported a thriving economy through its remarkable credit and banking networks. These networks suffered a severe blow through the Company's sustained policy of supplanting them with the institutions fashioned on the European model.

The emergence of the East India Company as a 'dominant firm' (Kutty 1985: Ch. III – East India Company as a Dominant Firm: 61-175) in India chiefly depended on its ability to manipulate the money market, which it used to its benefit, and to establish a regime of exploitative and extractive 'mercantile colonialism' (as against settler colonialism) in which 'currency proved to be a vital weapon as it directly affected almost every aspect of economic life of the society' (Garg 2013: 16).

The currency, however, was 'the most supreme desiderata in the economy of the Indian people when they came, in the middle of the eighteenth century, under the sway of the British' (Ambedkar 1947: 2). During the early days of the East India Company's trade with India, the gold and silver imported by them was either sold to the bullion merchants situated in the port cities, or was taken to the imperial mints to be converted into the coins of the realm. Both the systems proved to be unsatisfactory to the English. While bullion merchants were always able to strike a deal which undervalued the metal being offered for sale; the mints, on the other hand, kept the treasure idle for some time, before it was converted into *sikka*. The English, who were always in the need of ready cash for their investment had, therefore, from the very early days aspired to appropriate to themselves, the minting rights in the land of their trade.

The minting rights that the English Company was initially able to obtain from the local rulers – from the Naik ruler for Armagaon (1626) and from the Raja of Chandragiri for Madraspatnam (1639) – made it clear to it that for a successful trading career in India, control over money supply was an essential prerequisite. The Company, thus, further consolidated its position in 1692, when it was able to obtain the authority from the Mughal Prince Kambaksh, to mint silver rupees at Madras, though initially, for use in its trade with Bengal. The Company further extended its control over the money supply in the Coromandel region by acquiring minting rights at Tegnapatnam (Fort St. David) from the Marathas (1690) and at Chindradipet from the Nawab of Arcot (1742).

On the Western coast, the Company's efforts to acquire minting rights were not as successful as they were in the Coromandel. A mint established in Bombay in 1672 under the authority of the Court of Directors did produce coins in gold, silver, copper and tin, but these had limited circulation owing to their English design and inscriptions. For its general requirement of cash for investment and trade in India, the Company was obliged to send its bullion to the Mughal mints at Surat and Ahmadabad, or to buy Mughal coins from the money changers, who charged a premium. Finally, in 1717, the Company obtained the permission from the Mughal Emperor, Farrukhsiyar (1717-19), to mint Mughal-style coins at Bombay that would pass current as all other *siccas* throughout the empire.

The English trading establishments on the Eastern coast of India usually met their requirements of coined money by importing coins from Madras and Surat, as also by getting their bullion coined at the Mughal mint at Rajmahal (Akbarnagar). Later, in 1717, though the Company was able to obtain a *sanad* from the Mughal Emperor, Farrukhsiyar to make use of the Mughal mint at Murshidabad for three days in a week to coin their bullion, the scheme remained on paper due to stiff opposition by the powerful Nawab of Bengal. Finally, here too, the Company was able to secure favourable concession from the new titular Nawab and establish its own mint at Calcutta in 1757 (Garg 1990).

Thus, by middle of the eighteenth century, the East India Company had established a fairly secure and dependable mechanism to partially meet its requirements of coined money. This scenario, however, rapidly changed once the nature of activities of the Company in India underwent a radical change following the Grant of *Diwani* (revenue-collection rights) of three important and rich provinces of Eastern India, namely Bengal, Bihar and Orissa, to it in 1765. In lieu of an annual payment of Rs. 2.60 million to the Mughal exchequer, the Company was now authorized to collect revenue in these provinces, and for this an elaborate system of government was required. The entire land revenue was now collected in cash, which, in turn, resulted in seasonal surge in the demand for silver specie. The cessation of silver imports from Europe after 1757, coupled with increased demand for money by the Company for investments in trade, military expenditure, tribute to England, funding of the China trade as well as other Presidencies lead to an unprecedented contraction in money supply. The resultant scarcity of silver coins in Bengal rendered the collection of revenue extremely difficult.

The problem posed by the scarcity of silver rupees – the principal monetary unit in much of Northern, Central, Western and Eastern India – would not have been so serious by itself had the money market was not inundated with a large variety of coins which were of different kinds, of different denominations, minted at different places, on different dates and had no uniform standards of weight and fineness whatsoever. The following estimate gives an idea of the multiplicity of coins in circulation in India around 1766:

> There were at that time [c. 1766] 139 different kinds of gold *mohurs*; 61 different kinds of gold pagodas or *huns*; 24 different kinds of *fanams*; and 59 different kinds of foreign gold coin; besides 556 different kinds of silver rupees and 155 different kinds of foreign silver coin in circulation. (Macleod 1899: 553)

The currency, thus, lost its velocity and became regional, even local, in nature. This proliferation of disparate coin types was linked with the collapse of the highly centralized monetary system of the Mughals, from the beginning of the eighteenth century during which the political ascendancy of various Indian as well as European powers was almost simultaneous. In this scramble for power, *Sikka*, or the right to coinage, became the 'right-most-cherished' by the Indian claimants as an expression of their de jure sovereignty. The European Companies, on the other hand, sought this right to expand their economic activities. As a result of the fall of the Mughal Empire, the number of mint-towns grew rapidly in India. As a result, the market was filled with a large variety of coins of different denominations, having different weights and purity – often debased and rudely fashioned, minted at different places on different dates and fetching differing values. 'For a trading organisation that was constantly trans-shipping money and goods from one part of India to another, and was in the position of having to make very large disbursements in local currencies, the multiplicity of rupees and other coins had very serious implications' (Chaudhuri 1978: 183).

The scarcity of silver rupees in Bengal was also accentuated by opening up of several regular streams of drain of its wealth and resources. Primary amongst these was 'tribute' sent to England, chiefly in the form of silver coins, as a result of which while Bengal faced a currency crisis, the economy of England was revolutionized with the influx of 'Indian treasure' which fuelled the Industrial Revolution. Another channel of 'drain' was export of Bengal to Canton to balance the tea-trade between China and England. Besides, the inflow of silver in bullion and specie from the Bombay and Madras presidencies also changed into reverse direction after 1757.

The contraction of circulating media and demand for more cash to fulfil Company financial obligations necessitated currency reforms in Bengal and between 1766 and 1771, within a short span of five years, the Company altered its monetary policy three times – by introducing bimetallism in 1766, abandoning it in 1768 and re-introducing it a year later, in 1769; and by passing a regulation to check by the menace of *batta* or discount charged by the money changers to exchange silver coinage of older mintage. None of these adventurist approaches was able to address the problem adequately which led to the adoption of a more professional approach by the Company to solve the monetary crisis in India.

By 1770, the Company's financial position had become quite precarious. After an 'artificial boom based upon wild exaggeration of [Bengal] province's wealth . . . the prices of Company shares [had] rocketed and there was a period of giddy speculation between 1767 and 1769. The bubble [however] was pricked by reports of the invasion of Karnataka by Haidar Ali and of the Bengal famine [1769-70]' (Lawrence 1997: 49-50). As Kuiters adds:

In order to meet their financial obligations, the Bengal Council decided to attract money from private individuals, first upon bonds and later, when this source proved to yield insufficient liquidity, by offering bills of exchange upon the Company in London. In the season 1769-70, they issued bills for four times the sum they had been limited to by Directors. As a result, the Company was confronted with a heavy drain of its cash reserves when those bills were presented to them for payment in London between 1771 and 1772.

To make matters worse, during the same period the annual income from the sales of goods in London fell. Tea lay at the heart of this problem. The increased investment of the Company in this article was not followed by a sustained growth in the sales of this commodity in London. Between 1768 and 1772, the stocks in the Company's warehouses more than doubled. At the latter date, when the Company's need for capital was acute, its stock of tea represented an immobilised capital of more than two million pounds sterling (Kuiters 2002: 64).

The Directors of the Company, quite alarmed by their rapidly growing financial liabilities, were driven to seek short-term loan from the Bank of England. On 15 July 1772, they applied for loan of £4,00,000 for two months. Within a fortnight, on 29 July, they applied for another loan of £3,00,000. The Bank, however, could not offer more than two-thirds of that amount. Unable to secure the money from the Bank of England, the Directors of East India Company, on 10 August applied for a Government loan of £10,00,000.

At the same time the Directors also contemplated sending a Special Commission of Supervision comprising a team of experts, including the noted Scottish economist, Adam Smith (1723-90), to India to examine the currency situation in Bengal. The idea of the Commission, however, never materialized as Parliament intervened and forbade any such Commissions to be sent at all. In early 1772, the East India Company approached Sir James Steuart (1712-80), another famous political economist, for his advice. Sir James never visited India, but stayed in London for three months (May-July) in 1772 to prepare his report. Originally styled as *Observations for the Court of Directors*, the report was eventually published in July 1772, under the title, *Principles of Money Applied to the State of Coin in Bengal*. It was the first authoritative study on Indian currency problems ever made and is the source book for several subsequent studies. However, it is not until 1774 that this report was sent to India for implementation of its recommendations (Garg 2013: 72-3).

Meanwhile, public opinion in England was increasingly becoming hostile towards the affairs of the East India Company in India and there was a rising clamour favouring government's intervention to rein in the Company which 'had become a sort of Frankenstein's monster, out of control and capable of wrecking havoc both in India and Britain' (Lawrence 1997: 49). Writing in 1771 John Scott Warring, who was very critical of the economic policies of the Company, observed: 'For these twelve or fourteen years past, a private body of merchants . . . have taken a principal part in the transactions of the great peninsula of India' (Warring 1771: 2). The critics dubbed the Indian possessions of the Company as 'an empire within an empire' [*imperium in imperio*] possessing vast resources and answerable to no one but its own shareholders (Lawrence 1997: 49). In January 1772, William Bolts published his *Considerations on Indian Affairs* in which he made scathing attack against the Company's flawed policies in India. This work is considered by Edmund Burke (1730-97), Irish statesman and a Member of British Parliament between 1766 and 1794, as the first book 'that turned the national attention to the state of our affairs in the East Indies' (quoted in Kuiters 2002: 65). It would be incorrect, however, to presume that the attention of the British Parliament was not drawn at an earlier occasion towards the chaotic affairs in India that were caused by the Company's flagrant abuses of its privileges and mismanagement of situation arising out of post-Plassey (1757) and post-*Diwani* (1765) developments. In 1766, Lord Chatham (William Pitt, the Elder), had 'toyed the idea of taking responsibility for the government of Bengal away from the Company and placing it in the hands of the [British] Parliament' (Lawrence 1997: 50). Later, in 1767, a Parliamentary Committee was appointed to consider 'whether the Bengal revenue belonged of right to the Company or to the State' (Lawrence 1997: 50). A 'deal', however, was later concluded between the Company and the government and by the East India Company Act, 1767, the Company agreed to pay an annual subvention of £4,00,000, in respect of the territorial acquisitions and revenues lately obtained in the East Indies. In theory, this sum 'represented payment for the assistance rendered by the [British] army and navy during the recent war [and] a contribution to the costs of the Royal Navy, which was India's first line of defence, and small garrison of British troops that supplemented the Company's army'. (Lawrence 1997: 50). The government, in turn, left the decision of the revenue rights unsettled, as a result of which the Company continued to appropriate the revenue collected by it as the *Diwan* of Bengal, Bihar and Orissa.

Thus, in 1771-2, when the attention of the British Parliament was drawn towards the Company's chaotic 'Indian affairs', Lord North, the Prime Minister of Great Britain (1770-82), was quick to seize the opportunity to establish Parliamentary control over the Company. On 13 April 1772, the House of Commons appointed a 31-member Select Committee under the chairmanship of General John Burgoyne, MP, 'to enquire into the Nature, State, and Condition of the East India Company and of the British Affairs in the East Indies'. The Committee was later scaled down and reappointed as 13-member Secret Committee in November 1772. The financial recommendations of the Select Committee included the grant of a Government loan of £1,400,000 at the rate of 4 per cent to the Company; reduction of the Proprietors' dividend to 6 per cent, and the postponement of the Government share of £400,000 per annum till the payment of the loan amount. The Company was forbidden to declare a dividend exceeding 6 per cent and was required to submit its accounts to the Treasury every six months. The recommendations of the Committee were accepted by the Parliament and the result was the passing of the Regulating Act of 1773. Its arrangements concerning the business at home commenced on 1 October 1773 while those concerning administration in India, on 1 August 1774. According to William Dalrymple, 'the world's first aggressive multinational corporation was saved by history's first mega-bailout – the first example of a nation state extracting, as its price for saving a failing corporation, the right to regulate and severely rein it in' (Dalrymple 2015).

In March 1774, the Court of Directors despatched a copy of the treatise prepared by Sir James Steuart to Bengal where, with a direction to pay immediate attention to the state of coinage and currency and endeavour 'to establish an equitable rupee' (Garg 2013: 79). Philip Francis (1740-1818), a prominent member of the newly appointed Council of the Governor-General of Bengal, carried out a detailed analysis of Sir James' treatise and prepared a detailed plan to ameliorate the ills of the monetary situation pervading Bengal. In his Minute dated 13 March 1775, Francis advocated silver monometallism, a principle which was finally adopted by the Court of Directors in 1806, and the induction of copper currency as the third tier of the currency system. He also recommended centralization of minting to a single mint in Bengal. Francis' plan, however, remained on paper as Warren Hastings (1732-1818), the Governor-General of Bengal, chose to propose a new regulation for reforming the ailing currency which was laid before the Board on 5 May 1777. This plan proposed new regulations for reforming the ailing currency, which included, among others, the closure of the mints at Patna, Dacca and Murshidabad and centralization of all the minting activities at Calcutta. The overall impact of closing of mints was further aggravation of the currency problems, as the Calcutta Mint could not cope with the work of four mints (Garg 2013: 83-5).

Among other measures planned by the government of Bengal

to ease the currency crisis was introduction of paper currency – a measure originally recommended by Sir James. Though in 1780 a plan was announced for the issue of paper currency and even an amount of 30 lakh *sicca* rupees was set aside as a security, the scheme remained abortive (Garg 2013: 86-7). The Bengal government also planned to ease the pressure on silver currency by farming out the minting of copper coins to one John Prinsep (1746-1830), a prominent government contractor who secured a lucrative contract to mine the copper ore in Rohtas and Monghyr districts of Bihar and use it to mint copper coins mint at Falta, a village 22 miles south of Calcutta, which the government was obliged to purchase for general circulation in the Province. This contract copper coinage scheme too was short lived (1781-3), and did not do any good to solve the currency problems faced in Bengal.

The monetary problems again led the Company to adopt an 'administrative' solution to what was essentially an 'economic' problem. Thus, on 25 September 1787, the Government of Bengal appointed a 'Committee for Enquiring into the Causes of the Scarcity of Silver Coin'. This was probably the earliest Currency Committee in India. The recommendations of this first ever enquiry Committee on currency reforms provided only ad hoc solutions. As the Committee itself admitted, 'that to decide fully, and with sufficient supply [of] precaution upon so great a question as the alteration of the coinage of a country, would require a much longer and mature deliberation'. The Government considered these recommendations in December 1787. Though no steps were immediately taken, practically all the recommendations were ultimately given effect to by Lord Cornwallis, who, in May 1792, decided to constitute a Mint Committee in Calcutta for superintending the mints and enquiring into the general state of coinage in Bengal, Bihar and Orissa.

Equipped with the expert advice of the Mint Committee, the Government now set forth to introduce various reform measures to streamline the currency. These included, enhancing the minting Capacity by re-opening of Dacca, Patna and Murshidabad mints and re-introduction of bimetallism (1792).

By the end of 1792, the Supreme Government at Bengal was not only fully seized of the nature and extent of the financial ailments, thanks to the findings of the official committees, but had also learnt a lot from the past experiments of currency reforms. The establishment of the Mint Committee of Calcutta in 1792 institutionalised the reforms process in Bengal and this Committee was frequently asked to consider and advice on various aspects of the currency and coinage reforms in the Madras and Bombay presidencies. The recommendations of this Committee provided the foundation for a series of legislations passed by the Bengal Government from 1793 onwards for a better currency administration. The process of legislative reforms in the currency administration was centred in the Bengal Presidency, and over a period of four decades (1793-1833), a uniform currency was established in all the territories of the East India Company. These reforms addressed the liquidity crisis faced by the Company in its multifarious activities ranging from revenue collection to military campaigns. With the establishment of a uniform standard (silver mono-metallism) and assimilation of weight and fineness of the principal currencies of different regions, the velocity of money was greatly enhanced which, in turn, helped the Company to meet the currency crunch in one region by mobilizing surplus money from other regions. These reforms also struck down the menace of discount (*batta*) charged by the money changers, which resulted in streamlining the rates of exchange between different species of rupees circulating in a particular region. In order to meet the large-scale demand for standard coins, technological up-gradation of minting process in India was started. Screw presses were introduced for the first time in Indian mints, which resulted in manifold increase in the output of these mints. This quantum leap in mint production greatly facilitated the replacement of various sorts of currencies in the region by the Company's coins. It also helped in meeting the demands of an expanding area of money use in the society.

Thus, by 1833 the East India Company was able to integrate the currencies of its dominions and secure the currency administration firmly into its hands. This provided to the Company a powerful tool which not only helped her transform from traders to full-fledged administrators – a role bestowed upon it by virtue of the Charter Act of 1833 – but also in establishing an imperial currency to serve as the facilitator of the imperial finances. John Crawfurd, writing in 1833, noted the conducive 'state of the money market in India' for extension of the presence of free British settlers in India (Carwfurd 1833: 9-10).

From 1833 to 1835 the currency measures of the East India Company were directed at establishing a universal coinage, which was not only of the same weight and standard but also bore the same device and impression, as the stamp of its sovereign authority. As early as 1818, the Mint Committee had recommended that 'it would be more consistent with the dignity of the British Government of India to authorise its own currencies by its own peculiar stamp and impression'. In 1824, the Court of Directors too had expressed their desire of having 'the most appropriate impression for the obverse and the reverse of the coinage of the new mint [at Calcutta]' (Garg 2013: 202). Finally, it was left to James Prinsep (q.v.) not only to convince the government about the expediency of adopting an English device on the universal coinage that he proposed for the British India, but also to employ Indian die-engravers to prepare the design for the new coins. In first of these – the Company Rupee coin – Prinsep saw a tacit declaration of 'the rule of British monarch without any assumption of a title which might be obnoxious to political discussion' and, in its larger role conceived it as a 'colonial currency', not only for India, but also for other British colonies, at its intrinsic value of two shillings (Garg 2013: 207). The new rupee, with its 'pictorial and essentially English' design, was also seen in the context of its larger role to serve as a universal colonial currency in other colonies of Britain. For this purpose the English name of its denomination – One Rupee – was inscribed on the coin, with no indication of the place of its minting.

The change of device for the new Company Rupee was approved by the Governor-General and a Resolution was passed on 27 May 1835. This Resolution pronounced the determination of the Government of India, 'to establish one uniform rupee corresponding in value, weight and standard with the present Farruckabad,

Madras and Bombay rupee, but of a new device, and to declare and make the same current in all the Presidencies and possessions of the British nation in India'. The provisions of the above mentioned Resolution were subsequently incorporated in Act XVII of 1835 which was passed on 17 August 1835 (Garg 2013: 212-13).

## II

In this volume several issues concerning the East India Company's currency management from the mid-eighteenth century to the end of its rule in India in 1858 have been discussed by some of the leading experts. Dietmar Rothermund (Part I: 1) studies the 'administration of colonial finance' through the lens of 'monetary policy of the imperial powers' and stresses upon the crucial role of the latter in 'agrarian relations, rural credit, revenue administration, the export of cash crops, and the pattern of foreign and indigenous investment' (p. 3). He points out to the prevailing economic doctrine of the nineteenth century that 'there was no monetary policy at all. The currency was regulated by economic forces and nobody was supposed to temper with it; the very idea of having a monetary policy was anathema to the orthodox economists' (p. 3). India's currency problems, especially from the mid-eighteenth century till mid-1830s, when a uniform currency and later, a uniform coinage was established throughout the territories of the East India Company, however, did see evolution of a monetary policy which was aimed at instituting a regulated currency regime, not only for India, but for other British colonies of in South-East Asia. The more apposite question, therefore, is whether the development of a monetary policy during the initial days of the Company's administration in India was a forced obligation on the administrators of colonial finance or was it a conscious effort to fulfil their wider economic and political agenda? Perhaps it was both, though at different points in time. When the English East India Company started its trading operations in India, there was a robust monetary regime established by the Mughals over a large part of the Indian subcontinent.

A dominant question that was being debated during early

years of Company's political ascendency in Bengal related to the adoption of a viable metallic standard for the principal currency. J.C. Sinha (Part I: 2) analyses this debate, which had raged both in India and England from the time of Company's acquisition of *Diwani* rights in 1765 till it was decidedly concluded in 1806 in favour of silver mono-metallism. Sinha points out as to why gold standard, 'which was almost an accomplished fact in Bengal, was out of question in Bengal', and why early experiments to introduce bimetallism in 1766 and in 1769 were unsuccessful due to mismatch between the official and market ratio for gold and silver. 'Economic laws', as Sinha rightly observes, 'have little respect for statesmen and administrators' (p. 22). In 1792, when the bimetallism was attempted for the third and final time in Bengal, the government had become wiser by its past experience. This time in addition to declaring the gold *mohurs* as 'legal tender in all public transactions throughout the country at the rate of sixteen sikka rupees', it also decided to levy certain charges on gold bullion sent to the government mint for coinage, so as to discourage the receipt of gold coins in preference to silver. Though this measure was able to reduce the currency crises in Bengal to some extent, the Court of Directors of the East India Company had by this time made up their mind to abandon bimetallism in all the three presidencies in India, and recommended the adoption of silver mono-metallism, with gold as optional currency (see Part II: 2).

Frank Perlin (Part I: 3) situates the debate on the 'growth of commercial capitalism on an international scale', which included international trade in coinage media. Thus, while he considers the imports of copper and cowries in India 'in terms of the need of economies growing in size and changing in their basic characteristics: becoming more specialised, more settled, more ruled and bureaucratized' (p. 43), he ascribes the 'large-scale export of taxed wealth' from Maharashtra's villages during the nineteenth century as one of the causes for the 'a relative demonetisation of local economy and a contraction (or whithering away) of those social, political and economic conditions characteristic of the old order, in which monetary exchange could flourish' (p. 43). The generalization of 'relative demonetisation' for the country of the size of India, or for that matter, for the entire region (Maharashtra) on the basis of a sample test of a few villages, however, is contrary to the evidence of increased monetization of the society, especially in the territories administered by the East India Company from the mid-eighteenth century onwards. B.R. Ambedkar (Part I: 5), has rightly attributed the shift of Indian economy from 'kind to cas' during the early years of the Company's rule, as a result of British system of revenue and finance. First of all, the British adopted a system where not only the land revenue, but also various other taxes such as customs, salt tax, *abkari*, *sayer* duties, etc., were collected in cash. As territory after territory came under the Company, 'first step taken was to substitute in place of rural militia of the feudatories a regularly constituted and a well disciplined army located at different military stations, paid in cash'. The civil establishment was also extended to these new acquisitions, by appointing 'a host of revenue collectors and magistrates with their extensive staff, all paid in current coin'. In addition, there were other charges such as 'Home charges' and 'Interest Public Debt', which were all realized on a cash basis. Thus, a cycle was formed which gave momentum to the monetization process.

J.C. Sinha (Part I: 4) compares the currency problems faced by the East India Company to 'an old enemy against whom the early empire-builders ... had fought in vain (p. 51). On the basis of the contemporary archival sources, he demonstrates the regional and even local character of different specie of silver rupees that had become established currency not only in different parts of Bengal but also for purchasing different commodities of daily use within the same district. Velocity, one of the prime features of a healthy currency, having thus lost, the coins circulating in one district were rendered bullion, whenever they crossed the threshold of the area of their circulation. Coupled with this problem was another one – that of the practice of charging discount on coins of older mintage. As many of the money-changers also controlled the supply of bullion to the mint, and receiving coined money, they practically controlled the entire chain of money supply, especially during the seasonal increase in demand for cash for making advance payments to the *aurangs* (or 'investments') for purchase or during collection of land revenue. The remedy lied in establishing a uniform currency and a uniform coinage throughout the territories of the East India Company.

Ambedkar contrasts the currency situation under the Company with that under the Mughal, and argues that due to maintenance of a standard weight of silver rupees throughout the empire, 'there was advantage, rather than danger in the plurality of mints' (p. 66). However, when this centralized control was lost with the disintegration of the Mughal Empire during the eighteenth century, the money market was flooded with multiple currencies of different weight and fineness, as a result of which, 'trade was reduced to barter, whether one looks upon barter as characterized by the absence of a common medium of exchange or by the presence of a plurality of the media of exchange; for in any case, it is obvious that the want of a "double coincidence" must have been felt by people engaged in trade' (p. 68). He compares this situation then prevailing in India to Lacedaemonia whose citizens were compelled by Lycurgus (800-700 BCE), 'to use iron money in order that its weight might prevent them from overmuch trading'. He rightly points out that in any economy, 'Diseased money is worse than want of money'. The latter at least saves the cost. But society must have money, and it must be good money, too' (p. 69). He then goes on to describe the process of 'evolving good money out of bad money' that was set in motion by the Court of Directors' despatch of 1806, and culminated in introduction of silver monometallism and a common currency for whole of India, as the sole legal tender in 1835.

On the basis of different official records of the Madras and Calcutta mints, Edgar Thurston (Part I: 6) presents a chronological summary of the coinage of the East India Company from 1753 to 1835. He also describes the circumstances in which the Company's mint at Calcutta undertook the coinage for its other colonies such as Mauritius and Singapore (pp. 111-12, 115-16). Though Thurston does not cite any references to the records from which he has quoted extensive passages, much of these materials could be found in later works (see Stevens 2012 and Garg 2013).

Among the later writers, Debendra Bijoy Mitra (Part I: 7) has dealt both exclusively and extensively with the changing monetary system in Bengal. While analysing the causes of decline in money supply in Bengal after 1757, he points out that there not only was 'cessation of the import of bullion, chiefly silver, from England after 1757', but also 'stoppage of the import of bullion by other foreign traders', coupled with 'decline in Bengal's trade with Persia and the Red Sea area after Plassey' (p. 132). On the other hand there was an increased demand for money during the corresponding period for 'investment', China trade, remittances to other presidencies, as well as to the Mughal king as part of the annual tribute, and military expenditure. He, however, counters the argument that the scarcity of silver currency in Bengal was also caused by unfavourable balance of trade between India and England, as 'the drain was chiefly in goods, for "to send silver into Europe would be to, send it from the best to the worst market"' (p. 135). After discussing various attempts at reforming the currency of the Bengal Presidency from 1766 to 1777, Mitra produces evidence from the proceedings of the Board of Trade to demonstrate that the uniformity of currency was still a distant dream and 'different varieties of coins were in circulation after 1777' (p. 152). The credit of the Bengal government to borrow money from the public also suffered due to 'the inability of the administration to discharge [its] debt obligations. . . . In November 1785, the [Government] bonds bore a discount of 24 per cent and few purchasers could be found' (p. 153). Before adopting some drastic measures for establishing a uniform currency all over the Bengal Presidency, a survey of the currency situation in different districts was conducted in 1789 by the Board of Trade, through its Commercial Residents (p. 157). The views communicated by these Commercial Residents on the currency situation then prevailing in Bengal, make an interesting reading. They favoured establishing one currency for the whole of presidency (p. 161). Accordingly, a new silver rupee – 19 *sun sicca* – was authorized in September 1790, which was later adopted as the principal currency of the Bengal Presidency by Regulation XXXV of 1793 (see Part II: 1). Mitra also discusses the third bimetallic experiment of 1792 and the difficulties faced by the government in popularizing the gold *mohurs*. An important aspect of Mitra's study is the incorporation of district-level inputs submitted by the Residents to the Board of Trade.

In the Madras Presidency, where gold and copper coins comprized the circulating media, the currency reforms were first advocated by Alexander Dalrymple (Part I: 8), who calls himself 'Company's old and faithful servant' (p. 184). In a Memorandum dated 28 March 1794 addressed to the Court of Directors of the East India Company, Dalrymple aimed to 'remove the calamities, to which the inhabitants of the *Circars* were exposed' by proposing a new copper coinage for this region (p. 185). The Circars, or more appropriately the Northern Circars, was a division of the Madras Presidency and consisted of four (later five) districts located on a strip of land on the eastern coast of India, in the present day Andhra Pradesh and Odisha. These districts were initially ceded by the Nizam of Hyderabad to the French in 1753, but were occupied by the British in 1758. In 1765, the British had formally obtained from the Mughal Emperor, Shah Alam II, a grant of the five Circars, but it was not until 1768 that the Nizam acknowledged the validity of Shah Alam's grant and resigned the administration of the Circars to the Company.

Dalrymple pointed out to the very volatile exchange rate that prevailed between the gold *pagoda* and the copper *dubs*, which sometimes altered to '24 *dubs* in the course of a day' (p. 185), which was equivalent to four days wages of a labour (p. 187). By a regulation promulgated in 1791, 'the currency was proposed to be 12 *fanams* to the rupee, of which 4 are reckoned to the Madras *pagoda*' (p. 186). While no exchange rate was fixed for the copper *dubs*, the prevailing rate went 7 *dubs* to one *fanam* and thus amounted to 336 *dubs* to the Madras *pagoda*. Dalrymple argued that this arrangement was flawed as '*fanam* in those Circars being only an *ideal* Money, [was] not a *real* coin and the rupee not the proper or necessary currency'. He, therefore, held that was impractical to introduce an imaginary denomination between gold and copper coins, and that their price should be determined by the price of copper, with the minting charges added to it to avoid destruction of the copper coins (p. 186). At the same time he emphasised the necessity of introducing new denominations of small copper coins so as to meet the monetary requirement of the poor. Citing the example of China, which, 'seem to have brought the matter of currency to the greatest perfection, as there is no other coin than copper, or rather a base metal, unapplicable to any common use' (p. 189), Dalrymple observes that 'A perfect knowledge of the subject, of copper coinage for India, requires an exact knowledge of the gold coin to which it is to bear a relation' (p. 191).

In this contribution we also come across a detailed description of the operations of the Madras mint during the late 1750s when Dalrymple served under the Assay Master of the mint. While no immediate steps were taken by the Company to adopt the recommendations made by Dalrymple to reform currency in 'the Madras Presidency, the matter could not be neglected for long and in 1798, the Madrag government appointed a Finance Committee to look into a variety of subjects including the core issue of currency reform. The Committee's Report, which was submitted to the Government on 26 March 1800, is considered as 'one of the important documents on the history of Madras Currency' (Garg 2013: 104).

H. Dodwell (Part I: 9) elaborates the history of shift of the monetary regime of South India from gold-base to silver-base during the Company's administration. As early as in 1749 the Company announced that rupees were to be current in the English settlement at the rate of 350 per 100 Star *pagodas* (p. 209). Though this attempt proved unsuccessful, largely due to undervaluation of gold, it did push large quantities of silver rupees in circulation. After 1757, when the Company had assumed a predominant position in Bengal, commenced the movement of gold and silver from Bengal to Madras, not only for trade and export to China and Manila, but also on account of several military campaigns such as Anglo-French War (1756-63), and Anglo-Mysore Wars (1767-69, 1782-84, 1790-92, and 1799) that the Company was obliged to carry in South India (p. 209). In 1760, the expenses of the army in the Madras Presidency were reckoned at two lakh rupees a month, which saw a sharp rise in the subsequent years (p. 210).

The failed experiments of introducing bimetallism in Bengal in 1766 and 1769, saw large-scale export of gold *mohurs* from Bengal to recoinage as *pagodas* in Madras. Though this transfer of precious metals from Bengal to the Madras Presidency was unable to induce any immediate change in the usage pattern of currency in South India, in the long run, it did play a catalytic role in the shift of the currency base in favour of silver in South India. As per one estimate, 'in the five years 1795-9, more than half the coin minted at Madras was principally silver, and in the five years which followed [1799-1804], more than three-quarters of it was silver' (p. 214). This shift was almost complete by 1806, when it was noticed that, 'while gold constituted the nominal standard at Madras, *silver formed the currency*' (emphasis added) (p. 214). Later in 1812, 'the Mint Committee had observed that silver had already became the standard of value in the countries dependent on Madras'. By 1818 the only region still possessing any considerable gold currency was the Northern Circars. Dodwell, however, concluded with the mono-causal simplification for this change: '. . . when both metals [gold and silver] are unlimited legal tender, gold can only be maintained in circulation by being overvalued as currency [as against bullion]. The currency of gold at Madras vanished with the disappearance of that overrating' (p. 218).

C. Ramachandran (Part I: 10) chronicles the history of currency in the Madras Presidency under the British rule. Carnatic – a region that lies in modern Indian states of Karnataka, Tamil Nadu, north-eastern Kerala, and southern Andhra Pradesh – came under the Company's rule as a result of the three successive Carnatic Wars (1744-48, 1749-54, and 1756-63). About the beginning of the eighteenth century, principal supply of the circulating media in the region came from nearly twenty-two mints under the Nawab of Arcot. In addition, the English, the French, and the Dutch East India Companies also operated their mints. There existed a rivalry between the mints of the Nawab and the European companies, in which 'by the year 1720, the Nawab's mint began to issue coins of lower touch' (p. 226). This was chiefly done 'in order to attract more people to their [Nawab's] mint and divert the flow of bullion from the Company's mint . . .'

(p. 226). This resulted in money-market gradually being flooded with 'coins of various types but inferior in standard'. Wholesale transactions that were earlier conveniently settled by sealed bags of usually 1,000 *pagodas*, were seriously hampered as now sealed bags contained *pagodas* of inferior value. The falling purity level in prevailing standard currency led the Company to issue a new denomination of the gold coin – the Star *pagoda* – in 1740 that had a purity of 8 *matt* instead of $8^5/8$ *matt* as in earlier issues. This became and remained the standard coin of the Madras Presidency until 1808 (Pridmore 1975: 26). In addition, other coin-types too had regional circulation. There were heavily alloyed gold coins called *fanam*, copper 'cash' or *kasu*, and silver rupees which were introduced in the Carnatic by the Mughals.

By the close of the eighteenth century the English East India Company was able to establish its direct rule over a large part of South India and 'these developments gave the right to the English to exact the needed legislation including the reform of currency for the acquired provinces' (p. 228). Ramachandran describes the role of the Finance Committee (1798-1800) that was set up by the Madras government to enquire the financial anomalies then prevailing in the region. One of the major recommendations of this Committee was 'the introduction of a uniform currency throughout the Carnatic with uniform weight and standard to overcome the evils of the day' (p. 229). The principles of currency reforms based on silver mono-metallism for the three presidencies of India that were subsequently enunciated in the famous Despatch of the Court of Directors in 1806 (Part II: 2), are said to have been greatly influenced by the recommendations of this Committee. It is notable that the Madras government was the first presidency to initiate action on the recommendations of the Court of Directors. A three-member Madras Mint Committee was then set up in 1808 'to suggest the steps required to implement the currency reforms recommended by the Court of Directors' (Garg 2013: 153). On the recommendations of the Madras Mint Committee not only the regular 'coinage of Rupees, halves and quarters of a standard and weight recommended by the Court of Directors' commenced in Madras in 1812, which, by 1818, 'became the standard circulating medium of the Madras Presidency, and retained its characteristics when it was assimilated in a general plan to establish a uniform currency for all the three presidencies of the East India Company in 1833' (Garg 2013: 156). This development later paved the way for establishing 'a common currency as against uniform currency' throughout British India, that was achieved through 'an Act of Imperial Government (XVII of 1835) [that] introduced a common currency for the whole of India as the sole legal tender' (p. 234).

Edward Thomas (Part I: 11) describes the coins issued by the Company's officials in the Island of Bombay, which was made over to the East India Company by the English king, Charles II (r. 1660-85), on 27 March 1668. The Bombay Mint (estb. 1672), produced coins in gold, silver, copper and tin, bearing English designs and legends out of which eight examples issued during the reign of Charles II and one specimen of Rupees of James II (r. 1685-8), have been described by Thomas (pp. 244-6). He also describes the monetary systems prevailing both in England and India, and of the relative value of gold and silver, over the years and puts forth a case for establishing a judicious exchange rate between the principal currencies of India and England, to counter 'the leech-like heavy charges of the present Home Government, which draws indiscriminately, for its own wants Bills in Rupee on its hapless dependency, in season and out of season, whether the balance of trade or metallic exchange is for or against them' (p. 253).

This contribution by Thomas, however, is confined only to the seventeenth century. The currency situation in the Bombay Presidency during the eighteenth and early nineteenth centuries, till the time when the East India Company was able to establish a uniform currency regime throughout its possessions in India in 1835, have not been studied in detail. The fact, however, remains that the situation in the Bombay Presidency during the eighteenth century was no better than in the other two presidencies. In 1717, the Company was able to obtain a *farman* from the Mughal Emperor, Farrukhsiyar (1713-19), to mint coins in the name of the Mughal ruler in their Bombay mint, which was partially able to offset their dependence on the Mughal mints at Surat and

Ahmadabad which they were obliged to use in order to convert their bullion into coins. By 1765, however, the scarcity of silver reached such an alarming level throughout the Island of Bombay that the Bombay government, drawing a parallel from the Bengal Presidency, tried to introduce bimetallism by issuing gold 'rupee' with its halves and quarters. (Garg 2013: 105-6). These 'rupees' had a fixed exchange rate of 15 silver rupees to 1 gold 'rupee'. Even after the design of these gold 'rupees' was altered in 1770, and even after their 1/15$^{th}$ denomination that was equivalent to one silver rupee, was issued to pass current in lieu of a silver rupee, these experiments failed and failed miserably. As a result, the Bombay Mint was practically shut down in 1778. In May 1800, the Company was able to secure the control of the Surat Mint, following which 'the Surat Rupee was adopted by the Company as the standard unit for Western India' (Garg 2013: 165). With a view to consolidating their minting activities in Bombay Mint, Surat Mint was abandoned in 1815 and all its minting operations were transferred to Bombay.

Thus, by the beginning of the nineteenth century silver currency has been practically established in all the presidencies of the East India Company – the Surat Rupee in Bombay, the Arcot Rupee in Madras and the 19 *sun sicca* Rupee in Bengal. There were also Lucknow 45 *sun sicca* Rupee circulating in the Ceded and Conquered Provinces in the north India, and the Benaras (*Machhlidar* – so called for carrying the symbol of a fish) Rupee circulating in the Benaras province.

The task of assimilating these disparate currencies into a uniform weight and fineness was deftly carried out by James Prinsep (1799-1840), who served as the Assay Master of the Calcutta Mint and the Secretary of the Mint Committee from 1833 to 1838. Various currency reforms pioneered by Prinsep are the subject matter of my chapter in this volume (Part I: 13). Right from the time when aged 21, he assumed the duties of the Assay Master of the Benaras Mint in 1820, Prinsep became seized of the currency chaos prevailing in the country. He started the reform process in Benaras in small measures, removing one obstacle at a time. Over a span of next five years (1821-6), he was instrumental in introducing three very important currency legislations, viz., Regulation V of 1821, Regulation II of 1824, and Regulation VII of 1826 (p. 280). First of these regulations, prescribed the rates at which Benaras and Farrukhabad rupees were to be received in payment of revenue; the second the Farrukhabad Mint was abolished and the minting of the Farrukhabad Rupee was confined to the Calcutta, Benaras, and to the newly established Saugar Mint. At the same time, the Farrukhabad Rupee was also declared legal currency of the recently acquired Saguar and Nerbuddah territories. Thus, a uniform coinage was introduced into the entire northern and central India. By the third Regulation the government transferred the control of the Benaras Mint from the Board of Revenue in Central Provinces, to a Local Committee, and appointed James Prinsep as its Secretary (p. 280).

Prinsep approached the dicey issue of currency reform first by harmonizing the prevailing measures of weight with the principal coin that formed the chief circulating medium. This was achieved in 1833, i.e. within a short span of two-and-a-half years of his return from Benaras. By Regulation VII of 1833, the weight of the Farrukhabad rupee was fixed at 180 grains troy by which measure it was also assimilated to the weights of the Surat rupee and the Arcot rupee – the principal coins of the Bombay and the Madras Presidencies respectively (p. 282).

The road to the introduction of a universal coinage for the British India was thus paved. Prinsep again lobbied hard, and with his irrefutable logic he was able to drive home the point that the device of the universal coinage should be altered, and that the new mint at Calcutta – which was fully commissioned by the end of 1833, with a total capacity of one crore thrity thousand pieces per annum – should only issue coins with the English design (p. 284). He then went ahead and got a number of designs prepared for the new coinage, of which the one depicting the head of King William IV (r. 1831-7) was finally adopted for the universal silver rupee, designated as the 'Company Rupee' (CR), that was commissioned by Act XVII of 1835. In the same year, by Act XXI of 1835, Prinsep was able to achieve the introduction of a uniform copper coinage, thus achieving the monetary integration of the British India.

The contribution of Dayal Das (Part I: 14) slightly overlaps the preceding one as far as the background of the introduction of Acts XVII and XXI of 1835 is concerned, but he brings out very interesting details from the contemporary archival sources about the reaction of the Court of Directors on these measures. 'They apprehended that the prevailing confusion due to the existence of different currencies in India would become worse still by the addition of one more and, an entirely new currency' (p. 297). According to Dayal Das, the anger of the Court of Directors was 'mainly directed against a change so extensive and important having been determined upon merely in anticipation of their approval and without waiting for their formal orders' (p. 297). Even with halting approval of the Court of Directors, the universalization of the British coinage in India was a *fait accompli*, which indeed laid the monetary foundation of the British Raj.

The anonymous contributor to this anthology (Part I: 12) draws a very interesting analogy of currency and human anatomy:

> The currency of a country may, to use a homely illustration, be aptly compared to the blood in the human body. If it circulate too rapidly, a state of feverish excitement is betrayed; if too slowly, a falling-off in social health or prosperity becomes quickly apparent. There may be too much or too little iron in the blood; so likewise there may be too much or too little paper in a currency (p. 257).

Originally published in 1857, that was penultimate year of the East India Company's rule in India, this paper sums up not only the long process of currency reforms undertaken by the Company that had finally culminated in the introduction of 'Company Rupee' as the principal currency for British India in 1835, it also makes a review of the impact of this measure on the economy in the subsequent years. The author also elaborates various new currency reforms that were being debated across India at that point in time. In Bombay, for example, the 'arithmetical convenience of a decimal currency' was advocated in an article published in the *Bombay Times* in May 1856 (pp. 259-60). The practical problem, apart from the heavy expenses involved in withdrawing the old copper coins from circulation throughout India and replacing them with the new ones based on the decimal system were estimated at *c.* 50 lakh rupees (p. 263). It was then argued that 'the gain which would be derived from a decimal currency would be simply arithmetical. The loss on the other hand which the change of system would entail would be real' (p. 264). Thus, considering the 'great and extensive . . . confusion and inconvenience' that it would entail, the introduction of the decimal coinage was considered 'almost impractical' in 1857.

The author also reopens the debate regarding the suitability of mono-metallism for Indian currency system, and whether that 'favored metal should be silver' (p. 264). Quoting extensively from the Earl of Liverpool's famous treatise addressed to king George III (r. 1760-1801), where he had put forward a strong case in favour of gold mono-metallism as 'the most suitable standard for Great Britain', the author holds that 'These grounds appear to be as really, if not in the same degree, applicable to British India' (p. 264). The force of this preference for gold in the mid-nineteenth century indeed came from 'the recent discoveries of auriferous deposits in California and Australia' (p. 267), which gradually started 'displacing silver as a standard of property throughout Europe and America' and prompted the author to raise the question whether it is 'advisable that the standard coin of India should continue of a different metal from that of the rest of the world?' (p. 267). He finds 'silver currency is too slow, too cumbrous, for extensive mercantile dealings, and is utterly unsuitable for government purposes, especially in periods of emergency or difficulty; ... and its value too indefinite and precarious to justify its extended use, or its ever being adopted authoritatively into the currency of the country' (p. 268). He, therefore, suggests that gold coin should be made the 'the standard of property in British India' and that the British coin, the sovereign, be declared legal tender in India (pp. 271-3).

The author also expresses his reservation about the idea that bank notes should be used to fill in the void in circulation of metallic currency and that there notes 'should be issued solely by Government'. 'Bank notes', according to him, 'have hitherto been only tolerated by, and will never be a favorite currency with, the people of India' (p. 270). It is another matter that within a few years of the beginning of the British Raj, the Government of India passed the Indian Paper Money Act, 1861, and became the sole issuers of the paper currency in India.

Paul Stevens (Part I: 15) devotes considerable space to India in his review of the British imperial and colonial coinage across continents – from Europe to Asia, Africa to Americas, and across Australia – not only because India was the 'jewel in the Crown' of the British Empire, but also because of 'the complexity of coinage associated with the British' in India. After describing various features of the principal coins of the three presidencies and the related numismatography, Stevens, based on the studies on the subject published by Doty (1998) and Pridmore (1975, 1979), outlines the history of modernization of the Company's mint in 1820s as well as of coinage produced at modern mints at Soho, near Birmingham, for Company's use in India (pp. 306-15). Stevens also presents a survey of British colonial coinage in Ceylon, which has become its colony around the same time when English mintage of coins for use in India was being experimented (p. 315). Together with the regular coins, tokens formed a parallel series of monetary transactions in specific areas such as plantation areas in Ceylon or penal settlements in the Andaman Islands. A large-scale mintage of coins circulating in other territories under the British Empire points towards the larger schema of colonial monetary policy pursued by the British.

## III

The in-depth studies on various aspects of the monetary policy and related currency reforms included in this volume are suitable supplemented by *in-extenso* reproduction of archival texts ranging from legislations to commentaries and from communications to analytical notes by Company officials.

The most important piece of legislation that laid the foundation of the currency reforms, initially in the Bengal Presidency but eventually in the whole of British India, was Regulation XXXV of 1793 (Part II: 1). It was aimed at giving a wide circulation to the

Company's coins – 19 *sun sicca* rupee, and the 19 sun gold *mohur*. The revenues in Bengal were not only to be assessed in terms of the *sicca* rupees but also to be realized in that specie only which was obtainable only from the mint at Calcutta. However, as sufficient quantity of the 19 *sun sicca* rupee was not yet pushed into circulation, the farmers were permitted to make their payment in older species of rupees at a fixed rate of exchange. This measure was aimed at drawing all coins issued from non-Company mints to the government mint for re-coinage into 19 *sun sicca* rupees.

By Act XVII of 1835 (Part II: 5a), a universal rupee, denominated the 'Company's Rupee (CR)' was established within the territories of the East India Company. By another enactment, ACT XXI of 1835 (Part II: 5b), a universal copper coinage was established within the Presidency of Bengal while all other copper coins were demonetized within the territories of the East India Company, after 20 December 1835. By Act XIII of 1836 (Part II: 5c), Calcutta *sicca* rupee was demonetized and was declared to cease to be a legal tender with effect from 1 January 1838. The holders of Calcutta *sicca* rupees were allowed to pay it in General Treasury of Calcutta till 1 January 1838 at the rate of 16 New or Company Rupees for every 15 Calcutta *sicca* rupees of due weight (Part II: 5d). The Act XIII of 1836 also partially demonetized copper coins. The legal tender status of the pice struck at the mints of Benares and Farrukhabad throughout the provinces of Bengal, Behar, and Orissa was abolished and now these pice were to circulate only within the provinces and places for which they were respectively coined. The receipt of Trisoolee pice of Benares was allowed at Calcutta Mint till 1 July 1837 at the rate of 720 pice of proper weight for 640 new Company pice, coined under Act XXI of 1835 (Part II: 5e).

Within two years of the issue of new gold and silver coins bearing the image of King William IV, the British sovereign died on 20 June 1837 and was succeeded by Queen Victoria. As the change in the coin design could not be effected immediately, the relevant clause in the ACT XVII of 1835 which provided that the rupee/*mohur* 'to have the head of the reigning Sovereign of the United Kingdom of Great Britain and Ireland' had to be temporarily suspended. This necessitated the enactment of ACT XXXI of 1837 (Part II: 5f) by which the depiction of the 'Head of his late Majesty William the Fourth' on the rupees and *mohurs* was allowed to continue. It was not until 1840 that rupees bearing the head of Queen Victoria were ushered from Indian mints. This anomaly in the depiction of the reigning sovereign of the Great Britain on silver rupees and gold *mohurs* issued from the Company's mints was finally removed by two Proclamations, date 11 November 1840 (Part II: 5j) and 13 January 1841 (Part II: 5m) respectively and the coins now bore the head of Queen Victoria. The old coins, however, were to remain legal tender.

By Public Notices dated 21 March 1838 (Part II: 5g) and 9 May 1838 (Part II: 5h) the Mint Master of Calcutta was authorized to receive Bombay, Farrukhabad and Madras rupees or any other rupee issued from the mint of the British government, for re-coinage, without seignorage. In the same year, the government enacted another legislation – Act XXI of 1838 (Part II: 5i) – through which it authorized the issue any fractional silver coin of the standard prescribed for Company rupee, vide Act XVII of 1835. These fractional coins were to have devices, inscriptions and embellishments as prescribed in Acts XVII of 1835 and Act XXXI of 1837.

The universalization of copper coins was also eventually established – first by demonetization of Trisuli Pyce with effect from 1 August 1844 by Act XIII of 1844 (Part II: 5n), and later by Act XXII of 1844 (Part II: 5o) by which the provisions of Act XXI of 1835 were extended to 'all the territories of the East India Company'. This latter Act also authorized the issue of three new denominations of copper coins – pice (100 grs.), Double pice (200 grs.), and pie (1/12 anna = 33 1/3 grs.) – which were to circulate all over British India. Another denomination, that of half pice (50 grs.), was added to this series of universal copper coinage by Act XI of 1854 (Part II: 5r). The design for this new denomination (half pice) was authorized by a Notification dated 24 March 1854 (Part II: 5s).

Other legislative measures included in this volume pertain to removing certain anomalies faced in implementation of previous measures. Thus, certain defects in the penal provision for fraudulent practices involving current coins that were prescribed in the Criminal Law (India) Act, 1828 [Statute 9 Geo. IV, c. 74], were remedied by Act No. XXXI of 1839 (Part II: 5j).

At the same time the government was keen to ensure the circulation of silver coins issued from the Company's mints. A Notice issued on 13 January 1841 (Part II: 5l), declared that Government treasuries would not demand seignorage on silver coins of Government mints that are defaced provided these were of proper weight, or within the time allowed for their circulation.

Two Acts – Act VI of 1847 (Part II: 5p), and Act XVII of 1855 (Part II: 5t) – dealt with the copper currency in the Company's settlements of Penang, Singapore and Malacca, in the Straits. It is interesting to note how the supply of colonial currency was facilitated from the Company's mints in India.

By the Notification dated 22 December 1852 (Part II: 5q), the legal tender status of the gold coins was declared to cease from 1 January 1853. The famous economist Macleod calls this declaration 'the most astounding *coup de finance* in the history of the world' (1898: vi), as an estimated gold coins worth £120,000,000 immediately went out of circulation.

One of the very last legal remedies adopted by the East India Company by a Notification dated 17 March 1856 (Part II: 5u) was aimed at removing anomaly between Sections 3 and 5 of Act XVII of 1835, relating to the receipt of fractional silver coins.

Thus, the currency reforms carried out by the East India Company greatly facilitated the exploitation of Indian economy by the British, which the later colonial government under the British Crown, continued and raised to its alarming levels from 1858 till the independence of India in 1947.

## IV

The East India Company was the most powerful multinational corporation the world had ever seen. 'Imagine a company with the influence of Google or Amazon, granted a state-sanctioned monopoly and the right to levy taxes abroad – and with MI6 and the army at its disposal' (Ruggeri 2016). William Dalrymple finds the mightiest mega-corporations of the present day, mere 'tame beasts' in comparison to the East India Company: 'For all the power wielded today by the world's largest corporations – whether ExxonMobil, Walmart or Google – they are tame beasts compared with the ravaging territorial appetites of the militarised East India Company' (Dalrymple 2015).

The secret of much of this unprecedented financial success of the Company lay in its currency management in its colonies. 'The unprecedented change of the monetary system . . . is the strongest underlying impetus to financialisation' (Luo 2017: 41). Scholars tend to think of financialization (financial development) not as occurring exclusively within the economic system of capitalism but as existing throughout an entire human history filled with numerous financial innovations. 'Financialization is the unintended consequence of a change in the monetary system from commodity money to credit money' (Luo 2017). Post-1858 developments in the currency administration of India were aimed at this exploitative finacialization of the British Raj at the cost of India. The introduction of fiduciary paper money by the government in 1861 is one such example.

Perlin (p. 37) ascribes the widespread processes of monetization affecting a number of Asian societies, and especially India, as one of the more remarkable but neglected features of the growth of commercial capitalism on an international scale from the sixteenth century onwards. It is hoped that this volume would be able to do its bit in filling in this void and addressing this neglect.

# PART I
# STUDIES

# 1

# The Monetary Policy of British Imperialism*

Dietmar Rothermund

The administration of colonial finance and the monetary policy of the imperial powers for their dependencies made an impact on the structure of the colonial economy. This impact has not yet been studied adequately. Critics of British-Indian finance have paid attention to the 'Drain of Wealth' and some economists have studied currency problems in detail,[1] but they have not tried to relate monetary policy to agrarian relations, rural credit, revenue administration, the export of cash crops, and the pattern of foreign and indigenous investment. This neglect of the wider context of imperial monetary policy can be traced back to the dominant economic doctrine of the nineteenth century. According to this doctrine there was no monetary policy at all. The currency was regulated by economic forces and nobody was supposed to tamper with it; the very idea of having a monetary policy was anathema to the orthodox economists. These economists have influenced the interpretation of the events of this period. For all those who followed them it was difficult to prove that a policy existed in practice although it did not exist in theory.

*Earlier versions of this paper were read at the Fourth International Conference on Asian History, Kuala Lumpur 1968, at a staff seminar of the Gokhale Institute of Politics and Economics, Poona, and a seminar at the Delhi School of Economics. The author wishes to thank his colleagues, especially H.C. Rieger, for their criticism and suggestions, whatever errors of judgement remain in the text are, of course, entirely his own.

## The Currency Principle and Monetary Policy

The dominant doctrine of the nineteenth century with regard to money and banking was the currency principle which was based on the assumption that a currency consisting of precious metal would always establish an automatic equilibrium of all economic transactions. The advocates of this principle, following their master Ricardo, reduced everything to this metallic model. Their assumptions were challenged by economists who believed that the evolution of banking and credit did not fit into this static model; the doctrine was called the banking principle. But throughout the nineteenth century the advocates of the currency principle remained the dominant party whereas, those who believed in the banking principle remained a heterodox minority whose views were appreciated only in the twentieth century, particularly in the era of Keynesian economics.[2]

In keeping with its basic assumptions the orthodox school could not admit the existence of a monetary policy, but in the late nineteenth century this school was affected by a development which led to partisan quarrels within its own ranks and forced the different parties to advocate certain policies. In the last quarter of the nineteenth century the rapid increase of the world production of silver caused a discrepancy of the gold-silver ratio which had shown a remarkable stability at a rate of about 1:15 over centuries. The experts debated for some time whether they were faced with an appreciation of gold or a depreciation of silver, but they were all aware of the alarming proportions of this development. Soon they split into various camps of gold or silver monometallists and of bimetallists who hoped to keep both metals in circulation by adjusting the exchange rate by means of international agreements. The debates about these issues were of a curious kind, the interests of those who produced silver and those who sold it were deeply involved, expediency was often the final arbiter of the policies adopted, but the various parties advanced arguments so as to establish the orthodoxy of their respective proposals. The flexibility of these arguments enabled the British experts to adhere to the gold standard at home and to defend the maintenance of a silver standard elsewhere, as British bankers and merchants were eager to export America's new production and Europe's demonetized stock to the East.

India was the main victim of this 'double standard' which was defended with such orthodox rigour. Since 1835 silver had been the only legal tender in India. The mints of Bombay, Calcutta, and Madras were open to the free coinage of silver. According to the currency principle the seigniorage was limited so as to pay only for the operating cost of the mints, it was not supposed to be used as an instrument of monetary policy which would have enabled the government to control the flow of silver. The government could, of course, close the mints but this would have been an even more radical violation of the currencv principle than increasing the seigniorage. Under these circumstances the world's depreciating silver could pour into India unchecked. In 1876 the first drastic fall in the exchange alarmed the Government of India, but the home authorities did not permit any remedial measures.[3] In 1877 India absorbed about 84 per cent of the world production of silver[4] and the exchange continued to fall. There was a conflict of interests between the home authorities and the Government of India. The revenues of India were collected in silver but the home charges had to be paid in gold. With every fall in the exchange the Government of India found it more difficult make both ends meet. Its main sources of income – land revenue, opium, and the salt tax – were fixed and could not be enhanced easily. The Government of India, therefore, thought of various measures such as closing the mints or regulating the exchange rate by raising the seigniorage or adopting a gold standard. Even proposals for a gold-exchange standard, i.e. a standard based on gold but not necessarily implying the circulation of a gold currency, were made at that time, anticipating the proposals which were finally adopted at the end of the century. But at this early stage of the depreciation of silver none of these suggestions found favour with the home authorities.[5]

The mints remained open, on principle, and a cold standard was denied to India, not on principle, but for practical reasons. India had an important function in supporting the world price of silver and it was not permitted to cut into the scarce resources of gold. Those who defended the British approach to this problem argued that monetization in India required an adequate supply of currency, and that India would have found it difficult to expand its currency if it had adopted a gold standard.[6] But they deliberately neglected the fact that India paid a high price for this kind of expansion of its currency by absorbing a rapidly depreciating commodity. Absorbing silver was like riding a tiger – it was difficult to stop it after having started it. If India would have decided to demonetize and to sell its silver after having absorbed a major part of the world production it would have had to sell this silver at a great loss which would have been magnified by its own decision, because the price of silver would have fallen even more the moment India stopped absorbing it. British monetary experts did not mind India's ride on the silver tiger, they were even proud of this feat which was performed under their guidance,[7] but if anybody would have told them that theirs was a clever monetary policy they would have denied it and would have maintained that they simply adhered to the currency principle. A modern economist has observed that the bankers had good reasons for subscribing to the currency principle, because it provided them with a convenient shield against closer scrutiny. By claiming that their operations were regulated by the currency principle they could deny the responsibility for their actions.[8] This could also be said about the arbiters of India's monetary fate who invoked their orthodox creed whenever they were faced with suggestions for a new monetary policy for India.

In explaining the Indian case contemporary economists gave a dialectical twist to the currency principle. Walter Bagehot set an example in writing on the depreciation of silver in 1877 and making a plea for keeping the Indian mints open.[9] He ardently defended India's silver monometallism, and criticized all attempts at restricting the free flow of silver to India. He adhered to the orthodox axiom that trade is nothing hut an exchange of goods which cannot be affected by the rate of exchange in the long run as the automatic equilibrium will always restore itself. However, he did admit that a falling exchange constituted an export bonus and a fine on imports into India. But he reconciled this admission with the general orthodoxy of his views by pointing out that the export bonus would lead to a further flow of silver to India which would help to support the silver price and thus lead to a new equilibrium. Similar views were expressed by British delegates at international conferences which were convened so as to reach a bimetallist compromise. The British did not show any genuine interest in bimetallism but presented their own double dealing monometallism – gold for Britain, silver for India – as the ideal contribution to a better monetary world.[10]

## The Expansion and Depreciation of the Indian Currency

India's mints remained open due to this stand taken by the British authorities, and the Indian currency expanded very rapidly. The total active circulation of rupees amounted to 1,250 million in 1876, 1,500 million five years later, and 1,850 million in 1891.[11] At the same time the silver rupee depreciated by about one-third within 18 years. In 1874 the rupee stood at 1s 10d, in 1892 at 1s 2d.[12] In this way the vastly expanded currency of 1893 was worth about as much in terms of gold as that of 1876. The total stock of money at the beginning and at the end of the period could be roughly compared in terms of 2 : 3, and as the total stock depreciated by one-third its gold value remained the same.[13]

In this period the quantity theory of money had not yet been superseded by modern theories which attribute equal importance to the velocity of the circulation of money. According to the quantity theory both the growth of the population and the increase of economic transactions would justify an expansion of the currency. The advocates of non-interference, therefore, made much of the need of India's growing population for an increase in the circulation of money. But a scrutiny of the respective figures shows that the expansion of the currency was several steps ahead of the growth of population throughout this period. The population of

India was 254 million in the census year 1881, the growth rate of the population was rated at about 1 per cent per annum at that time. Ten years later the next census showed a total population of 287 million. This meant an increase of 13 per cent in a decade which would correspond to an average increase of about 1.23 per cent per annum.[14]

If the velocity of the circulation of the currency is assumed to be more or less the same throughout this period the increase of the currency should correspond to the growth of the population. But in India the increase of the currency outpaced the growth of the population by at least 2:1, because the currency expanded at the rate of about 4 per cent per annum for the first five years after 1876 and then at about 2.3 per cent for the following ten years whereas the population grew at the rate of 1 per cent in the earlier period and about 1.23 per cent in the subsequent years.[15]

It is difficult to get a precise idea of the increase of economic activity in this period, and, therefore, it cannot be estimated to what extent the expansion of the currency was justified by this increase rather than by growth of the population. If we look merely at the growth of the population we may state that the currency expanded at a rate which was about 1 per cent higher than the rate which would have been justified by that growth. At the same time prices rose in India by about 1 per cent per annum during the last decades of the nineteenth century.

While prices were actually rising in India there was a rapid decline of gold prices for agricultural produce in the world market. Experts praised the remarkably stable export prices of Indian produce.[16] The expansion and depreciation of the silver currency explains this 'stability'. If one thinks of the silver imported by India as a commodity for which it had to export agricultural produce which was frequently in great demand inside the country and if one considers that the imported commodity was subject to a rapid depreciation these 'stable' export prices may appear in a different light. The fact that people had to die of famine in India when a surplus of agricultural produce caused a glut in the world market and prices fell everywhere except in India should pose a question to all those who held that the free flow of silver was of great benefit to India and could stimulate its economic growth.

## Export Bonus and Indirect Projection

The contemporary Indian nationalists, for reasons of their own, also believed in the benefits of the free flow of silver. They blamed the British revenue policy for the famines and as far as the currency was concerned they echoed the orthodox doctrine emanating from London. However, they attached unorthodox importance to the export bonus aspect of the flow of silver to India. Unlike the British experts who saw in the export bonus only a temporary phase in the restoration of the automatic equilibrium, the nationalists emphasized the advantage which India had when selling goods to gold standard countries and the indirect protection which Indian manufacturers enjoyed against the competition of those who had to pay the cost of production in gold. They stressed the incentives to investors, the relief of debtors and – in the British-Indian context of an inflexible system of taxation – even the relative reduction of the burden of land revenue. They mentioned the growth of the Indian textile industry in this period, and they resented just as much as William Jennings Bryan the 'Cross of Gold' which they considered to be a common burden for the Indian peasant and the American farmer of those days.[17]

In reasoning along these lines most Indian nationalists did not raise the question whether the export of agricultural produce actually benefited India or not. Some had noticed that the area under cash crops had expanded even in famine periods when one would have expected a shift towards food grain, and they knew that the Indian peasant was not free to decide what he should grow beacause he was dependent on his creditors.[18] But they did not consider the wider context of this problem so as to find out about the adverse effects of the 'export bonus'. The indirect protection which India enjoyed due to the falling exchange may have been of some benefit to the tiny industrial sector but for the huge agricultural sector indirect production became a means of direct exploitation.

## Flushing out India's Produce: The Discrepancy of External and Internal Prices

Keeping in mind that the gold value of the total stock of money in India remained more or less the same throughout this period of a rapid expansion of the currency we begin to realize how depreciating silver was used to flush out India's produce. At an earlier time the Dutch had adopted a deliberate method of extracting cash crops from Java by circulating a large amount of worthless copper coins.[19] In India the British did not have to do this deliberately because by simply keeping the mints open to the free flow of depreciating silver they got practically the same result. The management of credit facilitated the extraction of cash crops. By advancing money to the peasants who grew cash crops for export the British and their agents pre-empted the productive capacity of India's agriculture. The area under cash crops expanded even at a time when food grain for home consumption would have fetched a better price. Wheat grown for export has to be rated as a cash crop in this context. The depreciation of the currency and the pre-emption of the productive capacity of vast parts of the country combined so as to achieve the miracle that India could export produce at 'stable' export prices even at a time when severe famines tormented the country. By absorbing silver and exporting wheat at the lowest price India served as the buffer at the base of the world economy of the late nineteenth century. India was linked to the world economy in a most unfair manner. The 'export bonus' provided by the depreciating currency imposed a pattern of trade on India which was not to its advantage.

The discrepancy of external and internal prices for India's agricultural produce was quite striking. The late nineteenth century witnessed a sensational fall in the gold prices of agricultural produce.[20] This led to a large scale reconstruction of the rural economy in Europe and America and to a nev international division of labour. India was shielded against all that by its depreciating silver currency which provided it with its remarkably 'stable' export prices. These stable prices referred only to the main export commodities like wheat and to the established export channels which were not necessarily linked with the whole internal economy of the country. Internally there was on the average a slow but steady trend of an increase in prices throughout this period.[21] Famine years and good harvests caused considerable fluctuations but the overall trend was nevertheless quite obvious. The combined impact of population growth and continuous depreciation and expansion of the currency helped to maintain the rise in prices. The trading practices of Indian grain dealers supported this trend beause they knew how to hold the price line even in years with a good harvest.[22] Due to the sufficient flow of money the system was not subjected to deflationary pressures which might have started an avalanche of falling prices.

## Investment and the Emancipation of Debtors: A False Hope

Those who relied on the positive effect of the flow of silver, like the Indian nationalists who praised the export bonus, also hoped for the emancipation of debtors and the increase of investment generally associated with easy money. In other words, they hoped that the slightly inflationary trend would benefit the structure of the Indian economy. This trend and the prospect of growing export should have encouraged investment in agricultural production and freed the Indian peasant from his burden of indebtedness. But this did not happen. The increasing monetization enabled the rich to buy control over land without investing much in the improvement of its productive capacity. Population growth guaranteed that the control over land was worth buying because it meant that it would always be possible to exploit the man who tilled the soil rather than the soil itself. In keeping with this point of view the Indian creditor was not interested in the emancipation of the debtor. But unlike the conservative creditor elsewhere who insists on a stable currency in order to recover his money the Indian creditor had adjusted to the depreciating and expanding currency by perfecting his own methods of getting his pound of flesh. He saw to it that the debtor could never pay back his capital but would get caught in a web of compound interest so that he could never extricate himself from his bondage. The system of usufructuary mortgages was best suited to this kind of relationship, the creditor became a de facto landlord and the debtor a permanent serf.[23]

It is easy to condemn the viciousness of this system and to deplore the depraved attitude of the Indian creditor who shirked the duties of a bona fide capitalist and investor and seemed to display the atavistic instincts of a petty usurer. However, we should not forget that the colonial regime and the development of the currency to a large extent predetermined this deviant behaviour. Even the richest men of India were excluded from the really substantial financial transactions which were based on the gold standard and controlled by the bankers of London. The easy access of the British-Indian Empire to the capital market of the metropolis which has often been praised as a boon to India's economic development was nothing but a curse in disguise. India's silver capitalists could not dare to enter the charmed circles of advanced imperial capitalism and they spent much of their money on landed property.[24] The often lamented Indian weavers who were driven back to the land by the powerlooms of Lancashire[25] have not been such a burden to Indian agriculture as the Indian capitalists whose attentions were diverted to the land by the City of London.

## Gold and Silver Capitalism: The Double Standard and the Dual Economy

The Indian economy of the late nineteenth century developed a dual pattern of gold and silver investments. The loans raised directly by the British-Indian government in the London money market or the investment of the British firms to whom the government guaranteed a minimum profit belonged to the gold sector. The debt service for these loans became a burden for the Indian economy because the interest had to be paid in terms of the gold standard and the increasing depreciation of the Indian currency practically produced the same effect as the compound interest of the usurer.[26] However, only the gold standard provided a stable foundation for long-term credit; the depreciating silver currency was as unsuited as quicksand for such a foundation. The silver capitalist was therefore forced to concentrate on short-term profit made in trading ventures or in moneylending of the kind which is not geared to long-term investment.

The rupee and the sterling debt of the Government of India are of some interest in this context. In 1876 this debt consisted of 719 million rupees and 55.2 million pound sterling, Indians held only 142 millions of the rupee debt, the lion's share was in British hands. In the following years the rupee debt increased by about 30 million per year until 1884, when it reached a total of 931 million and remained more or less at that level for some years. In the meantime the sterling debt had shown a steep increase from 59 to 69 millions pounds in 1879, had remained at that level until 1884 and then began to rise continuously from about 74 million in 1885 to 114 million in 1893. The interest rate on the sterling debt was usually about 1 per cent less than that on the rupee debt, which increased from about 3 to 4 per cent from 1876 to 1893 whereas the interest on the sterling debt increased from about 2.5 to 3.5 per cent.[27] These interest rates were, of course, very low compared to those which Indian moneylenders would charge, and, therefore, this kind of investment would not attract much Indian capital.

The dualism of gold and silver capitalism was not conducive to indigenous capital formation and economic growth which could only be based on a constant process of syphoning off capital accumulated by the agriculturist and investing it in industry. Monetization which is a prerequisite for this process does not necessarily induce the process if the currency is not sound and stable credit is available elsewhere. A slow inflation and indigenous investment based on an Indian money market could have gone a long way towards establishing a foundation for India's economic growth in the late nineteenth century, but the dual pattern of gold and silver capitalism under a colonial regime frustrated these hopes.

## Exchange Banks and Council Drafts

India had to pay her colonial rulers for the services which they rendered to the subject nation and this payment had to be made in gold. In addition to these so-called home charges there was the ever increasing debt service for the loans raised in London. These obligations forced India to export more and to import less. The depreciation of the silver currency meant that more and more silver had to be committed to the payment of these charges. This was the real 'export bonus' which India obtained due to the free flow of depreciating silver.

The home charges were transferred by means of so-called Council Drafts which the Secretary of State sold against sterling in London and which were cashed by the Government of India. Theoretically the Secretary of State should have been able to sell these drafts to the highest bidder but in practice he sold them through a small group of exchange banks which were not interested in outbidding each other. These banks combined so as to keep the rate of exchange comfortably low and they were even prepared to ship more silver to India if they could keep the exchange rate down in this way. They could thus claim more rupees for the gold which they paid to the Secretary of State. In other words they inflated the Indian currency in order to make a profit on the exchange rate.[28] Their business was booming as the increasing depreciation of the Indian currency made it necessary for the Secretary of State to sell more and more Council Drafts. In 1873-4 the Government of India remitted 140 million rupees in this way, in 1892-3 it had to remit 265 million rupees.[29] The sale of Council Drafts was immediately reflected in the relationship between exports and imports. More drafts meant more export, a suspension of the sale of drafts invariably led to in increase in imports.[30]

The whole system operated so as to inject inflation into the Indian economy and to extract a flow of cheap agricultural produce. It served the colonial power well and could have been perpetuated if it had not strained the resources of the Government of India which depended on a limited revenue.

## The Closing of the Indian Mints: Fiscal Expediency

The government of a prosperous country can find ways and means for raising a revenue which is in keeping with the general rate of economic growth. The Government of India, however, could not do so and its main income was derived from such items as the land revenue and the opium and salt monopoly which were more or less static and inflexible.[31] Taxes like excise, sales tax, export and import duties would have enabled the government to ride the tide of inflation, but most of these taxes were explicitly denied to the Government of India because they did not fit in with the doctrines of free trade and the vested interests of Britain. The Government of India was after all a dependent government in a poor country and, therefore, its powers and resources were severely limited. The total home charges increased from 13.5 million in 1876 to 15.8 million in 1893. In the same period the land revenue, the largest single item in the British-Indian budget increased only very slowly from about Rs. 200 to 250 million, and the gross customs revenue actually declined from an average Rs. 25 million per year during 1876-88 to Rs. 10 million in 1884 and was still as low as Rs. 16 million in 1893. The total gross customs revenue for 1876-92 amounted only to about Rs. 300 million whereas the loss of exchange incurred by the Government of India during this period was more than Rs. 770 million.[32] When, therefore, the task of collecting taxes in depreciating silver and paying the home charges in gold became more and more burdensome to the Government of India, it had to think of contracting and deflating the Indian currency by closing the mints.[33]

This radical step was taken only after a long period of prevarication. During the 1880s the Government of India had shared the universal hope for an international settlement of the currency question in terms of a bimetallist compromise.[34] It was only when the hope for an international settlement receded and when the American government proved to be unable to contain the flood of silver produced in its country by buying a large share of it at a fixed price that the British-Indian government resorted to the radical measure of closing the mints. This was done in 1893 and it had an immediate impact on America. Britain was pressed by America for a reopening of the Indian mints and there were many voices in Britain and India which echoed this demand.[35] Critics pointed out that the artificial appreciation of the currency which resulted from the closing of the mints amounted to a devaluation of Indian silver metal savings and to the imposition of an indirect tax on land revenue payers.[36] But as the government was in fact interested in an indirect tax it did well not to answer its critics and keep the mints closed.

## A Gold Exchange Standard for India

Those who believed in the virtue of a gold standard would have liked to synchronize the closing of the mints to the free coinage of silver with the introduction of a gold currency. It was not easy to dispel the notion that a gold standard implied a gold currency. But the financial position of the Government of India precluded all hasty experiments with a gold standard and a gold currency and necessitated a pragmatic approach to the management of the currency. Even the introduction of a gold exchange standard at the time of the closing of the mints would have been hazardous as it would have committed the government to the establishment of a fairly substantial gold reserve and it was anybody's guess what this reserve should be. Therefore, the government followed the safer course of simply watching the deflationery effect of the closing of the mints and waiting until the rupee had reached the exchange rate of 1s. 4d. at which the government wanted to stabilize it.[37]

The contraction of the currency took some time. In the few years immediately following the closing of the mints silver continued to pour into India and the exchange rate fell somewhat more but did not drop as much as the metal itself.[38] Soon the contraction was felt and the exchange rate rose and by 1898 reached the point where it could be supported by a gold reserve at the rate of 1s. 4d. The, sale of Council Drafts could now be employed as a device for the management of the currency.[39]

Putting the development of the currency into reverse gear was certainly necessary but it inevitably caused a great deal of distress. The cash commutation of rents in kind, the land revenue assessment of the peasant, the relation of creditor and debtor in the rural areas which had all been shaped by an expanding and depreciating currency were affected by the contraction and deflation which set in after 1894.[40] Two years of bad harvests added to this calamity and famine spread in India. The contraction of the currency was paralleled by a contraction of population growth.[41] After having been drowned in a sea of silver India was now nailed on a 'Cross of Gold'.

## The Effect on India's Economic Structure

India was shielded against the effects of the world agrarian crisis behind the wall of its depreciating silver currency. Therefore, it did not have to adjust and modernize its agricultural modes of production. It was only partially exposed to the forces of an emerging world economy. It was used as a buffer and it did not get into the mainstream. At the time when the world agrarian crisis subsided at the end of the nineteenth-century India was pushed into a deflationary phase for purely fiscal reasons. It was subjected to severe strain in order to achieve what British contemporary observers considered to be a sound economic basis, because they looked at it from a monetary point of view, but it did not gain any structural benefits from this new phase either. The banking principle and the currency principle provided the guiding lines for partisan arguments about Indian economic affairs at that time and the Indian economist Mahadev Govind Ranade who was groping for structural modes of analysis[42] was a lone sentinel whose voice was not heard in the councils of those who determined India's fate in the interest of British imperial policy. In the twentieth-century India suffered from this heritage of the nineteenth-century and could not overcome the handicap of a hidebound agricultural sector and of a stunted capitalism which was tied to trade and usury at a time when it should have laid the foundation for India's future economic growth.

## Notes

1. See, e.g., C.N. Vakil and S.K. Muranjan, *Currency and Prices in India*, Bombay 1927, and Sir J.C. Coyajee, *The Indian Currency System, 1835-1926*, Madras, 1930.

2. Sir John Hicks, *Critical Essays in Monetary Theory,* Oxford University Press, 1967, here especially pp. 155 ff: 'Monetary Theory and History - An Attempt at Perspective'.
3. Coyajee, op. cit., pp. 54 f.
4. Fred Atkinson, 'Rupee Price in India', in *Journal of the Statistical Society,* vol. LXVI, 1903, p. 116.
5. Vakil and Muranjan, op. cit., pp. 78 f.
6. Waller Bagehot, *On the Depreciation of Silver,* London, 1877.
7. Coyajee, op. cit., pp. 56 ff.
8. Hicks, op. cit., p. 168.
9. Bagehot, op. cit., see also the summary af Bagehot's views in Coyajee, op. cit., pp. 53 f.
10. Vakil and Muranjan, op. cit., p. 53.
11. Atkinson, loc. cit., 1903, S. 110-12.
12. Government of India, *Reports of the Currency Committees,* Calcutta, 1931, pp. 19, 87.
13. The total active circulation as calculated by Atkinson (see n. 11) was 1,890 million rupees in 1893, if reduced by 36 per cent this would amount to about 1,186 million, the total active circulation in 1876 was 1,250 million.
14. See *Census of India 1881* and *Census of India 1891.*
15. For the data on the expansion of the currency, see Atkinson, loc. cit., 1903, S. 110-12.
16. On India's stable export prices see Fred Atkinson, 'Silver Prices in India', in *Journal of the Statistical Society,* vol. LX, 1897, p. 117.
17. For his argument see Dwijendra Tripathi, 'The Silver Question: India and America', in *Journal of Indian History,* vol. XLIV, pt. III, December 1966, pp. 789-98.
18. G.V. Joshi, *Writings and Speeches,* Poona, 1912, pp. 606 ff.
19. In his provocative study *Agricultural Involution: The Process of Ecological Change in Indonesia* (Berkeley, 1963) Clifford Geertz points out how the colonial rulers 'skimmed cash-crops off the surface of an immobilized agrarian society'. But Geertz does not mention the monetary policy of the Dutch. This policy is described by N.P. van den Berg, *Munt Credieten Bankwezen, Hantel en Scheepvaart in Scheepvaari in Nederlandsch lndie,* The Hague, 1907.
20. For the fall in gold prices see the index numbers of Augustus Sauerbeck published in his article 'Prices of Commodities and the Precious Metals', in *Journal of the Statistical Society,* vol. XLIV, 1886, reprinted in E.M. Carus-Wilson, ed., *Essays in Economic History,* vol. III, London, 1902, pp. 68-127.
21. See Atkinson, loc. cit., 1903, p. 105.
22. Atkinson, 'Rupee Prices in India', in *Journal of the Statistical Society,* vol. LXXII, 1909, p. 566.
23. See Note on Land Transfers in Govt. of India, Dept. of Revenue and Agriculture, Land Revenue, October 1895, Pro. nos. 72-3.

24. Ibid.
25. See R.C. Dutt, *The Economic History of India under Early British Rule*, London (8th impr.), 1956, pp. 256 ff, on the Decline of Industries.
26. See R.C. Dutt, *The Economic History of India in the Victorian Age*, London (7th edn.), 1956, pp. 592 ff., on Finance and the Indian Debt.
27. C.N. Vakil, *Financial Development in Modern India, 1860-1921*, Bombay, 1924, pp. 576-7 (Table showing the composition of the Indian debt).
28. See Fred Atkinson, *The Indian Currency Question*, Allahabad, 1894, p. 23.
29. Govt. of India, *Reports of the Currency Committees*, p. 1.
30. See the note of H. Waterfield prepared for Lord Farrer in Farrer Collection, vol. III, Item no. 68, British Library of Political and Economic Science, London.
31. See Dutt, *The Economic History of India in the Victorian Age*, p. 373.
32. Vakil, op. cit., pp. 583 f. (Tables showing the loss of exchange, revenue, etc.).
33. Govt. of India, *Reports of the Currency Committees*, pp. 1 ff. (Lord Herschell's Committee).
34. David Barbour, *The Standard of Value*, London, 1912, pp. 178 ff.
35. See Tripathi, loc. cit., pp. 794 ff.
36. See the remarks of Mr. Moses in the Bombay Legislative Council, quoted in Govt. of India, Dept. of Revenue and Agriculture, Land Revenue, December 1901, Proc. 26-7.
37. See Barbour, op. cit., pp. 207 ff.
38. Ibid., p. 208.
39. Ibid., pp. 217 ff.
40. See Note on Land Transfers (n. 23).
41. See *Census of India 1901*.
42. See M.G. Ranade, *Essays on Indian Economics*, Madras, 1920.

# 2

# Economic Theorists among the Servants of John Company (1766-1806)*

J.C. Sinha

When the British first came into power in Bengal, in 1765, the first economic problem that faced them was the currency of the country. Diverse kinds of rupees were then in circulation, in various stages of debasement. In framing their schemes of reform, the servants of the East India Company were naturally guided by the economic doctrines then current in England, subject to modifications due to the peculiar social and economic condition of Bengal.

Expert economic opinion in England was at that time opposed to bimetallism. In the very year of the battle of Plassey, 1757, Harris, in his *Essay Upon Money and Coins,* condemned bimetallism.[1] He considered silver to be the fittest material for money, as being less subject to fluctuations than gold. But neither silver nor gold monometallism was then practicable in Bengal. The silver standard, though it had long been in existence in the province,

* This article is mainly based on the Public Department Records of the English East India Company from the year AD 1766 to 1800, preserved in the Imperial Record Office, Calcutta. I have consulted in this connection the District Records recently published by the Government of Bengal, Seton-Karr's *Selections from the Calcutta Gazette* (vols. I and II), MacGregor's *Commercial Tariffs,* and the writings of Verelst, Sir James Steuart, Colebrooke, Harrington, Prinsep, Wilson, Hunter and Thurston. Earlier this article was published in *The Economic Journal,* vol. XXXV, no. 137, March 1925, pp. 47-59.

had broken down on account of shortage of the metal. The gold standard, which was almost an accomplished fact in England at the time, was out of the question in Bengal, where even the silver rupee was of too high a denomination for ordinary transactions.

Clive was therefore obliged to adopt bimetallism in 1766. But from its very inception the plan was foredoomed to failure, as the official ratio between gold and silver was much higher than the market ratio.[2] Clive and the members of his Council seem to have had no idea of the economic consequences of this divergence between the two ratios, and they issued the following notice on 30 June 1766 :

> Notice is hereby further given that any person or persons discovered in attempting to make a variation of the exchange here settled between gold and silver or in obstructing the currency of a new coin by refusing to accept it in payment, if natives they will be punished with the utmost severity, if Europeans they will forfeit the Company's protection and be sent to England forthwith.

But this stringent order proved quite ineffective. Economic laws have little respect for statesmen and administrators. It was no wonder that silver gradually disappeared from circulation. Where it circulated at all, it commanded a premium; in other words, gold *mohurs* passed at a discount, which rose to about 38 per cent even in Calcutta within a year and a half.

Verelst, who succeeded Clive as the Governor of Bengal, had sounder knowledge of economic theory. He ascribed the breakdown of bimetallism to the over-valuation of gold. In his Minute of 1 September 1768, Verelst observed that the gold currency of 1766 had encouraged the import of gold 'by putting a current value upon it considerably above its real one'. The gold *mohurs* of 1766 were withdrawn from circulation, and on 20 March 1769, the official ratio between gold and silver was reduced from 16.45 to 14.81.[3] Even this new ratio was 5.71 per cent higher than the market ratio. The result was that this second attempt at bimetallism also failed.

Neither the Court of Directors in England nor the Company's servants in India could find a correct solution of the currency problem of this province. The matter was therefore referred to Sir James Steuart, who embodied his views in his *Principles of Money.* In this book he explained at great length that bimetallism could succeed only if the ratio between gold and silver coins was frequently adjusted to keep it 'exactly in proportion to their value as metals'. It was better in his opinion to have a mixed standard with coins of both metals 'in the same mass' instead of ordinary bimetallism. He was therefore one of the earliest economists to suggest a scheme like symmetallism. 'Were mankind all philosophers,' he explained, 'I should propose to mix the gold and silver together in the same mass, according to the market proportions of the metals, and to make the coin out of this mixture. I am not so extravagant as to propose so great an innovation. I throw it out merely as a hint.' The remedy he actually proposed was the introduction of paper money. A great banking institution like the Bank of England, with branches in different districts, was to be started and controlled by the Company, which was to issue notes upon some specified kinds of security. This was then regarded as too far in advance of the time.

The failure of two successive attempts at bimetallism and Sir James Steuart's condemnation of the double standard converted the Company's servants to silver monometallism. Thus Francis, Clavering and Hastings,[4] although differing in their plans for the establishment of a stable standard of value, were unanimous on this point.

Francis, however, recognized the suitability of gold for large payments. He recommended the issue of gold *mohurs* at the rate of Rs. 16 per *mohur.* These were not to be made legal tender, but 'that the paying or receiving of them be left to a voluntary agreement between the parties'. The use of gold coins as optional currency with silver as the standard of value was also advocated by Locke, Harris and many other English writers.

Clavering was also a strong monometallist. But he differed from Francis on one point. The latter proposed that the existing weight of the sicca[5] rupee was to be maintained, while its fineness was to be reduced to the English standard[6] to make it more suitable for circulation. Clavering's plan was that the amount of pure silver should remain unaltered in the sicca rupee, but its fineness was to be reduced to the English standard. This would, of course, increase the weight of the rupee and thus raise the standard of weight in the country. Clavering held the currency theory that the value of all things depended on the bullion value of the standard coin. He also recommended stopping the circulation of gold altogether. He was thus a more uncompromising monometallist than Francis or Hastings. Francis, as we have seen, advocated the issue of gold *mohurs* as optional currency. Hastings, though he would stop future coinage of gold, did not demonetize the existing gold *mohurs*.

By his Regulations of 29 May 1777, Hastings set up a kind of limping standard by suspending gold coinage. This continued for three years, but the mint was again opened for the coinage of gold for the next eight years, up to December 1788. In a notification of 17 September 1777, it was laid down that gold *mohurs* would 'universally pass in circulation at the usual value of 16 sicca rupees each, and be received and issued at the public treasuries at the same rate'. But the fate of this notification was no better than that of the previous ones on the same subject. Gold *mohurs*, the currency of which was practically confined to Calcutta, began to circulate even there at a discount. The *batta*[7] for exchanging gold *mohurs* into rupees, which was only 5 annas per Rs. 100 in March 1787, rose to Rs. 3 in the course of five months.

On 26 September 1787, Cornwallis therefore appointed a committee to inquire into the cause of the scarcity of silver coins'. The committee at first analysed the causes of depreciation of gold *mohurs* and then went on to discuss the causes of the premium on rupees. They failed to realize that these two were not really different but merely the two aspects of the same problem. In their opinion, the depreciation of *mohurs* was due to their limited demand, combined with increased circulation of paper. 'The accumulation of any specie in one place', said the committee, 'must cause great plenty of that article. This plenty, whatever extent it has in itself, is, as it were, increased by the paper, which is in circulation at the Presidency.'

The committee ascribed the scarcity of silver in Calcutta to numerous causes. They pointed out the increase in the remittance of revenue through bills for the last two years, during which period, out of a total remittance of 7½ crore, 3¾ crore had been sent in bills, 1¾ crore in sicca rupees and the rest in gold. The stringency of silver in Calcutta had been very acute from April to August 1787. This, continued the committee, was mainly due to the drain of silver to the *aurungs*[8] to provide for 'investments', with no return of rupees to Calcutta in the shape of land revenue during these months.

These were temporary causes of the scarcity of silver, but a more permanent cause was the general diminution of silver in the province on account of its reduced import from Europe for the last thirty years and its increased export to other presidencies and to China. Besides these, there was another cause, observed the committee, 'and perhaps not the least of those already adduced, of the diminution of the silver coin in Calcutta', viz., 'the too high value of the gold coin compared with that of silver'.

The Committee pointed out the danger of fixing the ratio between gold and silver in this country by looking at the ratio ruling in England. In the opinion of the committee, 'the medium proportionate value of the two metals in Europe may be taken at 15 of silver for 1 of gold; in India, they may be estimated at 12, or at least 13, to 1'.[9] 'In lowering the value of the gold coin, by raising that of silver, to the natural relative values they seem to bear to each other in India, silver coins would, we think, increase and occupy that place in the circulation which is filled with the superabundance of gold.' Thus the committee, after considerable circumlocution, traced the real economic cause of the disappearance of silver and suggested the correct remedy.

In the report of the Committee we find also the following interesting remarks on the salt tax in Bengal:

The profits arising from this monopoly certainly operate as a tax upon the public equal to the whole amount of the enhanced price thereof, and as salt constitutes an article of living that cannot be dispensed with, bears particularly hard on the lower orders of the community, the ryot, the weaver and others, whose ingenuity and industry is their only fortune and which barely suffices to procure them subsistence. It is not, therefore, an equable assessment, where every man should contribute to the exigencies of the State according to his means, nor is it felt by the rich in circumscribing their luxuries and enjoyments, but is, in fact, a tax upon industry. This must lessen the ability of the ryot to pay his rent, increase the price of the manufactures by raising the value of labour and consequently reduce the quantity.

This passage may easily be mistaken for an extract from the last book of the *Wealth of Nations,* where Adam Smith discusses the question of tax on necessaries. The members of the committee of 1787 must have been conversant with Adam Smith's ability theory of taxation and his idea that a tax on necessaries becomes a tax on labour.

The government did not take any immediate action after the publication of the Report. The first step was to stop the coinage of gold *mohurs* by an order of 3 December 1788. Two months later, Cornwallis took another step in the right direction. The official rate of exchange was reduced[10] to 15 siccas and 1 Arcot rupee[11] for a gold *mohur,* and an order similar to Clive's notification was issued on 18 February 1789. This order seems to have been enforced only in Calcutta and led there to a series of prosecutions of the shroffs for charging illegal *batta* on *mohurs.* Motte, the Superintendent of Police, in his letter dated 16 March 1789, described how he carried one 'Govinram Poddar to the Burrabazar, and with the tomtom declared his crime'.

The next step taken by the government was to discontinue the seigniorage of 1 per cent on the coinage of silver by a regulation of 20 February 1790. But this measure hardly brought any relief in the shape of increased supply of rupees. The war with Mysore was going on and draining Bengal of its silver. The government was, therefore, compelled to reopen the mint for the coinage of gold. It was notified on 21 July 1790, 'that from and after the 1st of the next month, gold bullion would be received and coined without any charge to individuals'. Thus the policy of raising the value of the gold *mohur* by suspending its coinage was abandoned after a year and a half. The supply of *mohurs* became relatively abundant and the *batta* on gold coins again ruled high. The government was sorely perplexed at this state of affairs. Harris, the Mint Master in Calcutta, in his letter quoted in the Public Proceedings of 22 September 1790, observed, 'that the present high *batta* in exchanging gold into silver is not caused by a disproportion of the metals is evident, because there is no *batta* on the Moorshedabad and Patna gold *mohurs*, which are known to the shroffs to be from 2 to 6 per cent worse than that of the Calcutta coinage'.[12]

G.C. Meyer, the Superintendent of Police, seems to have grasped the real cause of the currency trouble better than the currency experts of the government. In his letter of 3 November 1791, he declined to take any coercive measure against the shroffs on the following economic grounds.

His first reason was that gold and silver coins under the existing circumstances should be treated 'simply as commodities of which one was to be bartered for the other, and not as the standard or measure of value of other commodities'. Consequently, 'the exchange value or price of each would be determined by the same principles which regulated the price of every other commodity that comes into the market', viz., by the 'ratio between the demand for that commodity and the quantity of it forthcoming to supply such demand'.

His second argument was that the adoption of coercive measures would 'only aggravate the evil complained of'. 'The quantity of fine gold in the *mohur*,' he continued, 'is confessedly not of equal value in the market to the quantity of fine silver in one Arcot and fifteen sicca rupees.' If the shroffs were compelled to exchange the gold *mohur* into rupees at the official rate, it

> would exchange for more silver in coin than it would purchase in bullion. The consequence of this would be that if the difference were considerable enough to bear the expense of freight, insurance, etc., etc., the silver would be exported to foreign markets and there exchanged for gold, which would be brought back in order to be exchanged for silver, which would be again exported as long as it yielded any profit.

But even if it were not profitable to export silver, it would pay to melt it down and sell the bullion for gold coin. In any case, a large amount of silver 'would be withdrawn from circulation, to which it could not be restored without a constant and heavy charge on the Public Treasury'.

These arguments convinced Cornwallis of the futility of coercive measures against the shroffs, and in a notification of 18 November 1791, it was declared that in future the sale of gold and silver coins would be as free and unrestrained as that of gold and silver bullion. Thus the relation between gold and silver currency, which existed in Mughal times, was restored after twenty-five years.

Some eight months before the publication of the notification of November 1791, there was an acute stringency of money in Calcutta. On 12 March 1790, the chiefs of the leading Agency Houses of Calcutta wrote to Cornwallis:

> The quantity of specie now in circulation is inadequate to the current business of the settlement, and . . . the value of money has in consequence risen and that of the Company's paper has sunk in so great a degree that whereas money might have been borrowed to any amount by persons of adequate credit at 10 per cent on personal security only so lately as November last, and at 8 or 9 per cent when a security of Company's paper was given, it cannot now be borrowed on any security at legal interest,[13] and whereas the Company's paper then bore a premium, the same paper now sells, when it can be at all sold, at discount from 10 to 12 per cent.

We find here an instance of the rise in the market rate of interest causing a fall in the price of securities. In ascribing, however, this dearness of money to the decrease in the quantity of specie in circulation, these European merchants were simply repeating the erroneous theory of John Locke and many other seventeenth-century English writers. As every student of economics knows, the rise in the rate of interest takes place when the demand for loanable capital outstrips the supply. If the quantity of money in circulation declines, the price level would ultimately fall, and this would bring down the rate of interest. It is true that a sudden drain of money from a country may bring about a contraction of credit, and this would ultimately raise the rate of interest. But this reduction of credit is only the natural sequence of a trade boom. The drain of money only hastens the crisis, which would have arisen, sooner or later.

The chiefs of the Agency Houses suggested that in order to meet the stringency of money the government should print promissory notes to the extent of ten lakhs of rupees, and undertake to receive these notes in all payments due to it. These papers were to be lent to the European merchants at an interest of 8 per cent,[14] and there was to be a moratorium of all payments to the government until these notes were ready and the loan tendered. The signatories of the above letter undertook to receive such notes in all payments among themselves.

In reply to this representation, Cornwallis pointed out that the promissory notes, if they were issued, would immediately bear a discount, as there was no plan for redeeming them, and thus the scheme would be unworkable. 'It is incident to all paper currency,' continued his lordship, 'that its full value cannot be upheld longer than the paper can be converted into cash at the option of the proprietors.'

More than a year and a half after the monetary stringency of March 1790, there was a financial panic[15] in Calcutta. In November 1791 there was a run on the two European banks in Calcutta. During the eight days from 20 to 27 November, the Bengal Bank[16] paid out more than 8 lakh sicca rupees. On 28 November, Benjamin Mee of the Bengal Bank applied for a loan of 5 lakh rupees in specie for three months at the rate of 12 per cent per annum upon depositing Company's paper to the full value as security. A similar application was made also by T. Redhead of the Bank of Hindustan for a loan of 1½ lakh of rupees on practically the same conditions.

In spite of the positive orders of the Court of Directors not to engage in any pecuniary transaction with the private banks of this country, the Government of Lord Cornwallis granted the applications of the banks on their depositing Company's paper 25 per cent. above the advance they required.[17] In their minute of 29 November 1791, the Board remarked that 'the rejection of the application before us would tend to depreciate government securities'.

It is not necessary to discuss here the recommendations of the Mint Committee of 1792, as they do not refer to any interesting economic theory. The Report, however, is an important landmark in the currency history of Bengal. It forms the basis of the government resolution of 21 November 1792, and of the currency reform of 1793. In the latter year bimetallism was again attempted in Bengal.

Harrison writes[18] that on this occasion the government erred on the other side and slightly undervalued gold in terms of silver. This statement, however, is not confirmed by the papers in the Public Department of the Imperial Record Office. We do not come across any instance of the disappearance of gold from circulation which would have been quite a striking phenomenon in those days, and would have found at least a passing mention in the records of the period. On the other hand, we find Caldecott, the Accountant-General of Bengal, in his letter of 21 February 1794, alluding to the discount on *mohurs.* In this letter Caldecott suggested that *mohurs,* their halves and quarters, should be sent to the *mofussil* to reduce the disproportion between gold and silver coins in Calcutta. But 'it appears to admit of some doubt,' he added, 'whether the *batta* can be done away (with) without making such an addition to the quantity of pure gold in the *mohur* as is requisite to render its intrinsic value equal to the intrinsic value of sixteen sicca rupees.'

A fluctuating *batta* on gold *mohurs* continued almost up to the end of the century. On 1 January 1800, Meyers, the Accountant-General, however, reported that the discount on gold *mohurs,* which had become as much as Rs. 4-3 as. per cent in March 1796, had ceased to exist since September 1799. This was mainly due to the large importation of silver at that time.[19] This influx of silver by reducing its value brought at last to a parity the market and the mint ratios of the two metals. Another reason was the increasing use of gold coins in the *mofussil,* except in some backward parts. By the end of the century the currency difficulties of Bengal were well-nigh over. The year 1795 saw the final establishment of the nineteenth *sun* sicca rupee[20] as the standard coin of the province in place of a variety of old and light coins of different weight and standard, which had so long been in circulation. The method of coinage had also improved, making clipping and counterfeiting more difficult. The *batta* on *mohurs* which had been troubling the Bengal government since the days of Clive had at last come to an end, at least in Calcutta. But the Court of Directors had made up their mind to abandon bimetallism in all the presidencies.

In their famous Dispatch[21] of 25 April 1806, the Court of Directors observed:

It is an opinion supported by the best authorities, and proved by experience, that coins of gold and silver cannot circulate as legal tenders of payment at fixed relative ratios . . . without great loss; this loss is occasioned by the fluctuating value of the metals of which the coins are formed.

They therefore recommended the adoption of silver monometallism with gold coins as optional currency, which 'should not be forced into circulation at a fixed value in silver coin, but left to find its own level'. The subsequent history of the currency system of Bengal is well known. The circumstances under which the government definitely abandoned bimetallism and adopted a rupee of uniform weight and fineness as the standard coin throughout British India, and how they ultimately stumbled upon the gold exchange standard, have been told by many writers.

Thus the official records left by the Company's servants throw interesting sidelight on the economic thought in England during the latter half of the eighteenth century. We find, in the writings of these busy officials, who were anything but economic experts, fairly accurate ideas about bimetallism and Gresham's Law. Some of the Company's servants appear to have also realized the possibility of a concurrent circulation of gold and silver on the principle of limitation of supply. This economic theory, which was later on developed by Ricardo and formed in the nineteenth century the basis of the limping standard, seems to have influenced the suspension of gold coinage by Hastings in 1777 and by his successor eleven years later.

It may therefore be naturally asked, why did the Company's servants fail repeatedly in their attempts at establishing bimetallism in this province? The answer is that it was very difficult in those days to fix the mint ratio in such a way as to correspond exactly with the market ratio between the two metals. Bitter experience soon taught the Company's servants that the market ratio varied not only from province to province, but also from district to district. Bengal in those days was not a single economic unit. Different kinds of rupees, more or less debased, were in circulation in different parts of the province. It was hardly possible to fix the accurate ratio between the gold *mohur* on the one hand and the different kinds of rupees on the other. It is not, therefore, surprising that bimetallism attempted under such conditions failed.

But does the record of this failure establish a case against gold currency in India? It is a matter of common knowledge that during the latter half of the eighteenth century, England was passing from silver to gold standard by an accidental overvaluation of the yellow metal. Does the limited circulation of over-valued gold coins in Bengal during the same period prove the unsuitability of gold currency in this country at the present day? Such historical inference is hardly fair. It is true that during the latter half of the eighteenth century the prices of all important commodities rose in this province. But Bengal was even then a land of low incomes and low prices, and naturally the gold *mohur* and its subdivisions could have only a limited circulation.

It may, on the other hand, be argued that just as in those days *cowries*[22] were being replaced by silver, the latter metal will in turn yield its place to gold, in view of the rapid rise in prices. But to establish a case for gold currency in this manner is equally unsound. It is, of course, now possible to introduce gold currency, but whether it is more desirable than the gold exchange standard is quite a different question.

The chief advantage of gold currency is that it is less subject to corrupt or foolish practices on the part of governments than the gold exchange standard. But under ideal conditions the latter is certainly the more desirable currency system. Unfortunately, what we now have is a travesty of the gold exchange standard. The truth is that the currency trouble of John Company has now reappeared in a more acute form. With the official rate of the sovereign fixed at Rs. 10, it is now passing hands for more than Rs. 16. The present *batta* is therefore twenty times the maximum rate in the days of Cornwallis ! This is all the more regrettable, for what the Company's servants with their imperfect knowledge of economics and with their political and commercial preoccupations failed to carry out, has not been accomplished in our more enlightened days.

## Notes

1. Harris, *An Essay Upon Money and Coins,* 1757, pt. I, pp. 57-8.
2. Sir James Steuart, *The Principles of Money applied to the Present State of the Coin in Bengal* (1772); and Harrison, 'The Past Action of the Government of India with regard to Gold', *Economic Journal*, vol. III.
3. Steuart, loc. cit., p. 34.
4. Governor-General of India from 1774 to 1785. Sir Philip Francis, believed to have been the author of the *Letters of Junius,* and General Clavering were Members of the Council of Warren Hastings. Both Francis and Clavering were influenced by the economic theories of Sir James Steuart. Francis in his Minute on Coinage, dated 13 March 1775, quoted a passage from the *Principles of Money.*
5. Newly-coined silver currency of the Mughal Emperors struck in Bengal.
6. The English standard for silver was then, as it is now, 92.5 fine, while the siccas were at that time 98 fine. The weight of the sicca rupee was 179.666 grains (troy), approximately equal to 1 *tola,* the unit of weight in Bengal.
7. *Batta* literally means the premium or discount for exchanging different kinds of coins. Properly speaking, the *batta* on *mohurs* at that time consisted of two distinct elements. The smaller portion of the charge represented the rate for converting one kind of currency into another. But there was another and more important element in the *batta,* which represented the over-valuation of gold in terms of silver. In fact, it was this element which, instead of driving out undervalued silver, kept it in circulation.

   With regard to the *batta* on *mohurs,* there was no unanimity of opinion among the Company's servants. The more intelligent of them considered it to be due to the divergence between the mint and market ratios of the two metals. Others ascribed it to the intrigue of the shroffs (money-changers), although it was really the consequence of the economic blunders of the government. An interesting parallel is to be found in the outcry against profiteering during the war. This was the natural *result* of rapidly increasing prices due to the inflationist policy of governments and not the *cause* of high prices, as was popularly supposed.
8. Places of manufacture.

9. On the margin of this line of the Report of the Committee in the Imperia Record Office, Calcutta, there is the following interesting remark: 'Vide Smith's *Wealth of Nations*, vol. I, p. 265'. From the character of the handwriting, it is clear that this note must have been inserted at the time of writing of the Report. This fact gives an instance of the tremendous influence of Adam Smith's epoch-making book, which was quoted only eleven years after its publication in a government report in this country.
10. It is assumed by all writers that the official rate of exchange between gold and silver coins, viz. 16 siccas per *mohur*, remained unchanged throughout. But it is clear that there was a temporary reduction. The old rate was, however, restored by the year 1792.
11. Originally, this rupee was struck by the Nawab of Arcot in the Madras Presidency. By 1740 the English, French and Dutch secured the privilege of coining Arcot rupees. After the establishment of the Calcutta mint, the English East India Company began to coin Arcot rupees there, mainly for circulation in Dacca and Cuttack districts. The amount of fine silver in the Arcot rupee was generally 7 per cent less than the sicca rupee.
12. It is difficult to see how this could have been.
13. By a regulation of 28 March 1780, 24 per cent per annum was declared to be the legal rate of interest when the principal did not exceed Rs. 100, and 12 per cent per annum when the principal exceeded Rs. 100.
14. The chiefs of the Agency Houses thus wanted for a certain period (six months) a loan at less than the current rate of interest. Their trouble was therefore really due to the contraction of credit as a result of their over-trading and speculative transactions for some time past, and not due to the insufficiency of money in circulation.
15. I have not been able to trace the cause of this panic. Could it be due to rumours of British reverses in Mysore?
16. This should not be confounded with the Bank of Bengal, recently merged into the Imperial Bank of India.
17. The panic soon subsided. In his letter of 30 November 1791, Mee thanked the government for the liberal offer of assistance, which, he added, was no longer necessary.
18. *Economic Journal*, vol. III, p. 54.
19. As the editor of the Calcutta *Gazette* wrote on 28 November 1799, 'the amount of silver only, imported by sea within the last four months, (was) near one orore of sicca rupees, or about one million two hundred thousand sterling'. About one-half of this amount had been on government account. For the first time, after an interval of forty-one years, the Company imported to Bengal £99,699 of bullion in 1798.
20. That is, sicca rupee bearing the date of the 19th *sun* or year of the reign of Emperor Shah Alum. The reason for putting this invariable date on coins minted in different years was that the shroffs charged discount on old coins, even though they had not deteriorated at all.

21. There is some confusion regarding the date of the introduction of this clever measure for outwitting the shroffs. According to the Mint Committee of 1792, the date was 1773. This has been repeated by all subsequent writers, including Harrison. But as Shah Alum succeeded his father as Emperor in 1759, the nineteenth year of his reign could not possibly be 1773. I made a reference to Foster, who searched the India Office Records of 1773, but could not find the order referred to by the Mint Committee. Mr. Allan, the well-known expert on Indian coins, was kind enough to examine for me the complete set of coins at the British Museum. He did not find any 19th *sun* sicca rupee before 1778. For fuller details, reference may be made to a paper on 'Some Currency Reforms of Hastings 'read by me before the Indian Historical Records Commission in January 1924, and subsequently published by the Government of India.
22. The whole of this dispatch is printed in the House of Commons Return, No. 127 of 1898.
23. *Cowries,* or shells, were used as small tokens in many parts of Bengal only a generation ago. But during the middle of the eighteenth century, *cowries* were in some cases used for large monetary transactions also. As late as 1791, even the land revenue in the outlying district of Sylhet was paid in *cowries.*

# 3

# Growth of Money Economy and Some Questions of Transitions in Late Pre-Colonial India

FRANK PERLIN*

One of the more remarkable but neglected features of the growth of commercial capitalism on an international scale from the sixteenth century, consists of widespread processes of monetization affecting a number of Asian societies, and especially India. This was in turn connected with commercialization of both agrarian and urban economy, and the development of markets and manufactures. By the middle of the eighteenth century, this development had become distorted through increasing European intervention in both trade and manufacture, in this respect colonial occupation was both a culmination of earlier processes, and the means (through political monopoly, use of violence, control over the taxation system) for the East India Company to destroy competition and drive prices downwards in an increasingly competitive world. The corollary was that till the mid-nineteenth century at least India's integration into a colonial empire was marked by a broad-based process of underdevelopment of which deindustrialization was merely part, and including a process of relative de-monetization.[1]

In the following pages, I shall begin by presenting the problem in terms of the unprecedented international flow and subcon-

* The author thanks Sulabha Brahme, Sudhir Bedekar, Ram Bapat, S.D. Kulkarni and others at the Shankar Brahme Samaj Vidayana Granthalaya, Pune, for stimulating and critically discussing the arguments in this paper in February 1981.

tinental use of monetary media which took place between the sixteenth and early nineteenth centuries. Then I shall consider the implications of these phenomena for an understanding of the development of commercial capitalism during this crucial period, first, within India itself, and second, within a broader international context. Finally, I end with some statements concerning the implications of this hypothesis for an understanding of the early colonial period. The result is to place India firmly on the map of developments affecting the world more generally, long before colonialism.

## The Trade in Coinage Media

This paper begins with two problems. The first concerns the remarkable international trade in coinage media, both precious and of a more humble kind, which developed from the sixteenth century. The second concerns the extent to which monetary relationships had developed in the hinterland economies of the same period. There are indications that these had developed to a remarkable degree, surely not equalled during the nineteenth century.

The trade in precious metals, especially silver, is well known, not the least the international division of labour upon which it depended at an early stage in the growth of commercial capitalism, and also the steady drain of valuable payments-media into Asia, and especially India and China (e.g. Vilar 1976; Chaudhuri 1978; Furber 1976; Atwell 1977). But the trade in humble payments-media, like copper and cowries, was even more remarkable, not only because they also formed a vital, long-term lynchpin of international exchanges during this period, but also because of their implications for the receiving economies.

Copper formed one of the basic commodities of the inter-Asian trade, beginning with the Portuguese and continuing through the Dutch and English East India Companies (Glamann 1958; Furber 1976; Vilar 1976; Magalhaes-Godinho 1969).[2] Prices paid in Asian markets were remarkably high when compared to those for other industrial metals or those paid in Europe, and except for brief periods such as in the crisis-ridden 1630s and at the turn of the eighteenth century, such high prices were remarkably stable. Later, we shall see how significant were those conjunctures of widespread crisis and low copper prices.

By the later seventeenth century, the most important Asian source of the metal was Japan. Other parts of Asia were also substantial importers of copper, while European states also began to import or produce substantially greater quantities of the metal than they had done hitherto (the major European source became Sweden after Central European sources had become insufficient to meet increasing demand). The significant period of accelerated growth in these copper dealings begins in the sixteenth century, both in Europe and in Asia (Parker 1974, on Europe).

Cowries were by far the most important of a number of non-metal and base-metal currency media of much lower value than copper, and a reconstruction of international movements in the commodity forms a remarkable but little-known aspect of the development of a world market and division of labour, but one whose implications have not yet been properly appreciated.[3]

Produced mainly in the Maldives, they were a major commodity for both Asian and European traders, while European ports like London and Amsterdam acted as major entrepots for their exchange between company and company, and between private traders, on their way towards West Africa. By the early eighteenth century, the annual total shipment can be measured in hundreds of millions.[4]

In the seventeenth century they were found widely distributed as a means of payment in many parts of the Indian subcontinent. By the eighteenth century an important change had taken place, little documented, and only discussed, to my knowledge, in an enigmatic paragraph in Furber, where he notes that copper tended to displace cowries in many regions (Furber 1976). The areas where they had originally circulated and where they remained important in the eighteenth century included Burhanpur, Agra and Bengal, while in the seventeenth century bitter almonds (*badam*) were brought from Persia for use in south and central Gujarat, including Surat. What marks these areas is the fact that they were regions characterized by a widespread development of manufacturing in both countryside and town.

Also, by the early eighteenth century, cowries were being shipped to major new markets outside Asia (new, less in the sense that cowries had not been used before, than in the fact that they were now integrated into new patterns of international exchange and that their use occurred on a much vaster scale than ever before).

West Africa, in particular, became the chief destination, while ports in the Indian Ocean and East Indies became major entrepots for their further shipment westwards. When we add to this list ports such as London, Hamburg and Amsterdam we begin to reconstruct the complex web of commodity exchanges which enabled cowries to become the payments medium par excellence for the developing Atlantic export of slaves from West Africa to the Caribbean and Americas. European companies could be found purchasing cowries in India, while Asian and European private traders re-exported cowries from Surat (having been brought there from ports in the Indies, or directly from the Maldives) to entrepots such as Mocha.[5]

Scattered evidence suggests that European companies became increasingly interested in purchasing cowries in the interior of India and directing them westwards towards Europe (for West Africa). This was the case in the mid-seventeenth century when Dutch traders sought cowries around Burhanpur, a major area of textile manufacturing at this time. By the early eighteenth century, the Dutch East India Company (VOC) was issuing reports on the cowrie trade and giving orders for cowries to be redirected away from their major source of demand in Bengal, to VOC factories in Ceylon and elsewhere from where they would be shipped onwards.[6]

Finally, West Africa and Bengal were indeed the major markets for cowries, but they or a number of other more unusual types of currency medium, such as lead, iron and bitter almonds, also seem to have been used elsewhere in Asia, such as Thailand.

What were the reasons for these extraordinary developments? Why did African, Indian and other Asian economies absorb these vast quantities of payments media? What were the conditions which permitted an elaborate international exchange of commodities to develop, both of payments media and of goods more generally? On what developments elsewhere did the growth of Europe's own international trade and internal economic growth depend?

First, let us note that we have been reticent about the use to which copper was put. With cowries the doubts concern their nature as a form of money,[7] while with copper the question is whether armaments or coinages were the most significant long-term destination of the metal. However, the fate of prices during the widespread crises, alluded to above, is symptomatic of the real priorities: the great crisis at the turn of the eighteenth century was also a period of intense warfare in the Deccan, yet demand appears to have dropped dramatically until the agrarian economy picked up in the 1720s (Glamann 1951).[8]

Copper coinages were first introduced into Europe in the sixteenth century (Parker 1974). They were used largely by ordinary people (peasants and manufacturers, say – thus my term 'humble currency media'), whose low value 'black money' coins are well known to historians. This was also the period when financial institutions, commodity exchanges and domestic manufactures – in a word, the various components of commercial capitalism – experienced rapid growth and became the dominant forces in European economy. Many historians have described the manner in which urban capital was invested in the countryside of the sixteenth, seventeenth and eighteenth centuries, peasants losing their land and becoming caught up in credit dependencies and money relationships.[9] At the same time populations were increasing (if unevenly) and husbandry was becoming more intensive. This is the European context for increased copper imports and production.

## Growing Monetary Exchanges

Now for the hypothetical dimension of my paper. What happened in the rest of the world to stimulate these developments? In the West African case there has already been a good deal of stimulating and enlightening discussion and research. A great phase of state development begins in the sixteenth and seventeenth centuries, one especially well-documented example being that of eighteenth and nineteenth century Asante (Wilks 1975). These developments, embracing the growth of new forms of power, of lordships, bureaucratic mechanisms and new conquest states, coincide with the growth of the slave trade. Slavers traded mixed packets of commodities, including Indian textiles, to the coast, to which unit values were given, but of primary importance were cowries (Johnson, 1970: I, and Johnson, Hogedorn and Lynch, I). Hopkins has argued that the epoch of the slave trade only affected a narrow elite of traders and rulers (in contrast to the growth of peasant cash cropping for an international market during the nineteenth century) and had little economic significance of a developmental kind (Hopkins 1973). But Johnson had, earlier, rightly pointed out that the vast import of cowries, fairly steady price levels, and their deeper and deeper penetration into the West African hinterlands, must themselves have been predicated upon burgeoning economies and exchanges in that hinterland (Johnson 1970, I). We may add the further point that cowries, used as a means of exchange, seem to imply a numerous population involved in many, small but frequent exchanges.

The last pre-colonial centuries also seem to me to constitute a unique phase of Indian history. Not only the Mughal Empire, but other states in the subcontinent were characterized by the growing sophistication of their administrative apparati, and by the increasing monetization of taxation, by the wide range of new measures undertaken to survey, assess and levy the demand. It was a time when commercial cropping and domestic manufacturing were also increasing on a wide scale for both export and home markets. Bengal's production, for example, was destined for upcountry markets in Bihar, what is now UP and Nepal, as well as for overseas markets in Asante, South America and England (Marshall 1976). Further, we also find that goods were moved over large distances, both by sea and land: Bengal rice for Maldives cowries, cotton from Nagpur, Oudh, and the upper Ganges for Bengal, or on a smaller scale, around Patna, to take a few examples. All are cases of an increasingly elaborate regional and occupational division of labour embracing both city and countryside, hinterland and littoral. Similarly, in Gujarat, a concentrated nexus of manufactures and financial and commercial activities, distributed in a number of small but vigorous towns, together with a countryside producing grains for export and for urban consumption, and industrial crops for manufacturing, formed the essential economic hinterland lying behind the much-studied ports of Broach, Surat and Cambay.[10]

Finally, I want to suggest that peasant settlement and population levels increased apace during the period, so that growth in commerce, manufacturing, administration, and money tax demand could be set against the development of agrarian setteled societies themselves, of objects to be ruled and exploited (for example, argued in Perlin 1981, and by Moosvi 1973 and 1980: 31).[11]

This means that the import of copper and cowries can be explained in terms of the need of economies growing in size and changing in their basic characteristics: becoming more specialized, more settled, more ruled and bureaucratized. The local corollary of this is that a study of eighteenth century Maratha documents reveals a remarkable involvement in monetary relationships by humble people, not only to service the revenue demand but to pay rents, to exchange products in local markets and, through their receipt of day and monthly wages for soldiering, household service, agricultural labour, and craft production, all in money forms.[12]

By contrast, in the nineteenth century, after occupation by the English East India Company, the displacement of local elites from the countryside, the more ruthless and efficient exploitation of peasant populations and the large-scale export of taxed wealth, left Maharashtra's villages suffering a relative demonetization of local economy and a contraction (or whithering away) of those social, political and economic conditions characteristic of the old order, in which monetary exchange could flourish.[13]

This view of late pre-colonial society and economy should be seen as the context for state interventions in monetization, especially where taxation was concerned: administrative economy operates within the context of the broader economy of the old 'mode of production'. To argue, as does Habib, that money economy was dependent upon the central organization of the Mughal state – that whatever form of capitalism we identify in the seventeenth century was *parasitic* on the form and energies of the ruling organization (so that decline in the latter spelled the decline of capitalistic relationships before colonialism) – is to fail to sec that monetized tax demands could only occur in wider contexts of monetary relationships, and that India's late pre-colonial commercial capitalism far transcends the Mughal experience.[14]

We can begin now to understand the reasons for the import of currency media into the subcontinent, not just to service an elite-oriented silver economy of traders and rulers, confined to great trade routes, the coast and the big towns, which largely ignored the peasant, but one which worked in depth through the whole of society, mediating India's complex economic and political institutions.[15] Nor were cowries merely a question of a ritual exchange medium used by people who possessed no conception of 'modern economic' concepts such as 'profit' and 'exploitation'.[16] Cowries were used because of the need for an exchange medium of extremely low relative value and in types of economic relationship which can be precisely documented.

## The Shift to Copper Coinage

The shift to copper coinage in many hinterland regions can be understood through two mechanisms:

(i) There is reason to think that copper became more suitable than cowries as a medium of humble exchanges in regions like Maharashtra, due to a gradual fall in costs of production and also in the prices of raw and minted copper relative to prices more generally in India.

(ii) In addition, the organization of international trade, and the' priorities governing the major movements of commodities, required that cowries be rerouted towards West Africa, and, accordingly, in spite of the continued existence of a strong demand for cowries in regions such as Bengal, supply appears to have become constrained by major policy decisions taken by the dominant international carriers of the commodity (the English and Dutch East India Companies).

So far as the retention (and increased use) of cowries in Bengal is concerned, this region was the centre of the most dramatic development of domestic manufacturing over an extensive countryside in the eighteenth century, and of an inter-regional and international trade in food grains. In the later eighteenth century, under the East India Company rule, we find documented evidence that they were using cowries in local markets, in dealings concerned with the manufacture of textiles destined for export. Moreover, it has been shown that in the late eighteenth century the use of cowries could be made compulsory through the kinds of exploitative relationships to which manufacturers were subject (Hossain 1979; see also Bhadra n.d.). Whether or not compulsion was the rule before colonial occupation (and we must remember that numerous major occasions of payment, such as rents and taxes, were the subjects of enforceable demands, even in so far as type of payment was concerned), use of cowries can be understood merely by reference to some basic and well-known facts: Bengal was well known in the late seventeenth and early eighteenth centuries for its cheap labour and food grains. Prices were notably lower than elsewhere in India (Marshall 1976). Second, domestic manufacturers were characterized by their near ubiquitous poverty: prices of labour in the textile industry in Bengal were notably lower than prices of agricultural labour in the Western Deccan. Yet, it was precisely these people who were most conspicuously integrated within an international and inter-regional market of considerable complexity, cowries serving them in their numerous, tiny purchases and sales, as copper coins did in the Deccan. The use of cowries thus seems to have marked those areas where commercial capitalism showed its most precocious developments and to have most clearly influenced structural changes in the nature of production relations.

This last remark requires serious qualification, because I believe that the character of peasant production, even when engaged in basic food crop production in relatively poor ecological conditions such as that characterized Maharashtra, displayed similar developments in this period.[17] We can observe the strength of this view if we consider the institutional apparati which made all these monetary relationships possible, which integrated the peasant, the ruler, the banker and the merchant in a single exchange/production nexus, and which indeed were so fundamental in the organization of society and polity in this period, that if we imagined a state of affairs in which they were absent, we would have to conceive of societal types of a much more simple, and completely different character to those actually existing.

I am referring to banking, credit and other forms of finance, to money remittances, *hundi* transactions and currency dealings, and to the extensive use of credit production relations, in both agriculture and manufacture, throughout the subcontinent, institutions which knit together region and region, town and countryside, producer and noble, and transcended particular regions, dynasties and polities.[18] The peasant, manufacturer, ruler, noble, state administration, and the East India Company were generally dependent upon prior financing of the season's production. Moreover, the 'official' administrations treated in the textbooks were totally dependent upon, and complemented by a further administration, hidden behind the priorities and categories of our documents, but one which handled the actual movements of grains and moneys, the amazing network of remittances, transfers, and money payments which were necessary to mediate a complex and flexible social organization with an inflexible geography and property system.[19] Finally, consider the fundamental role of money as a value and payments medium in facilitating the creation of such socio-political forms of organization as the Mughal *mansabdari* system (ranks translated into value terms and payments made to nobles whose movements were subject to frequent transfer across the subcontinent).[20]

Returning to the question of financial institutions, what is remarkable is the strong degree of control which financiers had over a dispersed production and marketing system. By the eighteenth century, to take a single example from among many well-known cases, banking firms were financing the production and marketing of raw cotton in the Eastern Deccan for the Bengal market (Guha 1972), and a similar commercial/financial centralization of decision-making and economic, power existed in the case of Bengal's manufactures (Hossain 1979; Marshall 1976).

## Commercial Power and Industrial Capitalism

This is the special mark of commercial capitalism. The use of money is only an *aspect* of developing systems of production whose major characteristic lay not in investments in fixed capital but in highly flexible investments in the relationships of production, thus in development of the institutions needed to mediate such relationships.[21] They are also typified by pauperization of the producer and by a low technological base. The generation of stagnation, as much in peasant production as in manufacturing, is the necessary corollary of the growth of early forms of capitalistic economy.

The same phenomena can be seen throughout Europe, during the same period, where domestic manufacturing expanded throughout many peasant-agricultural hinterlands, east and west, from the sixteenth/seventeenth centuries on, but where industrialization took root in only a small handful of highly specific and strategically placed locations (see for example Mendels 1972; Levine 1977 and Medick 1976, Supple 1959, being especially useful, however). In such locations, commercial profits, accumulated from the production of manufactures in Prussia, Bengal, Bohemia and Gujarat (to take a few examples) were re-invested. Thus the growth of commercial manufacturing in town and country does *not* imply that India would have industrialized if colonial domination had not occurred. It seems instead that the growth of an international division of labour led to stagnation in the very regions where pre-industrial manufacturing had also developed, and at the same time to accumulation by those who increasingly dominated the commercial power structure, thus by outside interests, in England and Holland by the later eighteenth century. In turn, this implies, when seen in an international context, that India's political economies were developing in particular directions antipathetical to an indigenous industrialization.[22]

In short, India was one of a small number of centres of developing commercial capitalism in the Early Modern period, but its particular development became increasingly distorted through the institutional character of these same processes, and the growing hegemony over international exchanges gained by Europe's once dependent but ruthless traders. Even 'remote' hinterland politics in western India must be seen as part of this broad international theatre of activities, changes and influences. Money, and the international trade in currency media, are prima facie indicators of these portentous developments. At the *same time*, new currencies and money exchanges performed a vital structural role in the latter. It is this structural role – its nature and detail, and its chronological and regional variations – that remains the fundamental research task of the future, one that will alter the entire character of our knowledge of late pre-colonial societies.

One last word: this is a very different scenario from that recently elaborated by Wallerstein, and one that has important implications (although, it is true, I favour his basic structural approach). His 'world system' turns out to be only a special and relatively local development within a much vaster, and originally, much more spontaneous *system* of exchanges and production relations, developing from the fifteenth/sixteenth centuries onwards in different parts of the world (Wallerstein 1974 and 1980).[23] The transition to industrial capitalism (but here we have some complex chronologies to work out) occurs together with the growing coincidence of these two types of 'world system'. Money economy and humble currency media were fundamental tools in these processes of transition.

## Notes

1. The central hypotheses, upon which this discussion paper is based, is worked out in detail in my articles in *Past and Present* and the volume edited by Richards (Perlin 1983 and 1987).

2. Glamann and Furber are unusual in the attention they give to copper.
3. Most secondary sources ignore cowries, and indeed their low value is generally taken as implying complete lack of significance. The economic anthropologists are the exception, but this paper departs radically from their standpoint.
4. Johnson 1970; and Johnson, Hogerdorn and Lynch, forthcoming, for the following details on cowrie trade within Europe and to West Africa.
5. Information conveyed by H. van Santen who is researching Dutch trade with western India in the seventeenth century.
6. Information on current research provided by J. Hogerdorn.
7. Polanyi's 'substantivist' interpretation is representative and increasingly fashionable. According to it, cowries were part of archaic exchange systems, autonomous economies, not conversant with market economy as it has developed through 'the great transformation'. See Polanyi, Arensberg and Pearson, 1957. The concept of *jajmani* so popularized by anthropologists, is also substantivist.
8. The warfare was caused by the last bitter phases of Mughal attempts to subdue the southern portion of the subcontinent.
9. Kamen 1971, gives a graphic account of these processes.
10. The criticism implied here is that big ports like Surat are studied in isolation of the wider local economic context which they serviced. We have many studies of particular ports, but none on the growth and character of south Gujarat's urban and rural 'industrial' economy. However, Gokhale in 1964/5 and 1968/9 has many interesting remarks on this question.
11. The problem lies in a framework of assumptions that in the past has prevented us from accumulating evidence.
12. These remarks are based on the results of my research in 1975 and 1976 on eighteenth century archives of Maratha families, kept in the Bharat Itihas Sanshodhak Mandal, Pune.
13. Which I formulate elsewhere as the probable creation *by colonial rule* of the very object identified by colonial administrators as pre-colonial, and which has become the classical anothropological image of the 'traditional' village.
14. Habib 1969, who also maintains the dominant approach to pre-colonial India, treating its characteristics and changes in essential isolation of those occurring in the rest of the world.
15. Besides contradicting dualistic conceptions in general, this particular formulation is phrased in disagreement with Das Gupta 1970.
16. Polanyi's influential 'substantivist' hypothesis, is itself part of a broad current of anothropological thought. See note 7.
17. In Europe as well as in South Asia.
18. Although a great deal of incidental information on these institutions exists in the secondary literature, and a small number of articles describes their modes of operation, they are only now beginning to get the detailed study

they deserve. Their full implications for understanding the nature of the old order has not yet been recognized.

19. Observed all over India. See for example Sharma 1979.
20. Ali 1968, for organization of the Mughal nobility.
21. Supple (1959: Introduction) and Chapman (1973) describe these characteristics of commercial capital in the symptomatic case of contemporary Europe.
22. This argument implies that the deindustrialization debate rests on a much too narrowly formulated set of problems, on which see my article in *Past and Present*, 1983.
23. Wallerstein's conception of a capitalism only generated in Europe in the sixteenth century, from whence it expands, is thus Eurocentric, and it is symptomatic of this that he neglects the modern literature on pre-colonial Asia and does not argue the case in comparative terms.

# 4

# Currency in Early British Days

J.C. SINHA

The bark of Indian currency has sometimes sailed through calm waters but has oftener than not been tossed in stormy seas. The captains have been many. The most recent skipper is Hilton Young, who was preceded by Chamberlain and Babington-Smith in the present century, Mansfield, Herschell and Fowler in the nineteenth and Herbert Harris in the eighteenth. The name of the last captain is not so well known as it should be, for he combined in him the double offices of the Mint Master and that of the Chairman, as did the Chairman of the earliest Currency Committee appointed in 1787. But the currency problem was even at that time an old enemy against whom the early empire-builders beginning from Clive had fought in vain.

It was partly a legacy left behind by their predecessors but the evil was much aggravated under their *regime.* In Mughal times, although the revenue was reckoned in copper *dams,* silver rupees formed the chief currency of the country. *Mohurs* were struck mainly for making presents and receiving tributes but no legal ratio was fixed between gold and silver. It was in southern India alone that gold *hun* or *pagoda* was the standard coin. Cowries were used for subsidiary currency specially in Bengal. Occasionally, however, they were used in large payments also. As late as 1803, a feudatory chief of Orrissa agreed to pay 12,000 *kahuns* of cowries as his annual tribute.

With the break-up of the Mughal Empire after the death of Aurangzeb, every adventurer assumed the power of striking coins as the easiest and most incontestable emblem of sovereignty. The result was a multiplicity of currency in various stages of debasement. But the quasi-independent *nawabs* of Bengal such as Murshid Quli and his successors, did not tamper with currency in any way. They could not, however, stop the import of debased coins from the various provinces of India for liquidating the favourable balance of trade of Bengal. Even the *sicca* rupees coined by them did not circulate at par, if they bore different dates, notwithstanding the fact that they had not been worn out through use. As Verelst writes, 'at the expiration of three years, when these sicca rupees then called *sunats,* at 111/116 parts of the original denomination, they are carried to the mint, chiefly by shroffs, who receive them back recoined and consequently raised in value to 116, the first and the highest denomination, deducting the expenses of coinage, amounting to something more than 2 per cent. By this operation, the shroffs gain nearly 3/116, parts upon the value of the coin every third year.' The result was the triennial recoinage of *sicca* rupees, which seldom lost their original purity.

Long before the East India Company had come into power in Bengal, there had been a mint at Madras, which converted 89½ oz. of dollar silver into 218 rupees. These rupees were accepted not only in southern India but also in the north, for the purpose of remitting Imperial revenues to Aurangzeb, who spent his last days in the Deccan. With the retransfer of the Mughal Court to northern India, the provincial satraps no longer required Madras rupees and their value fell in consequence.

The Company's chief import at about this time was silver not only in Bengal but also in other parts of India. As the import of Madras rupees was no longer profitable, they were anxious to start a mint in Bengal. A *farman* was secured from Farrukhsiyar, granting the privilege of using the *nawab's* mint at Murshidabad free of charge three days in the week. But this was not recognized by Murshid Quli. It was also opposed to the powerful interests of Jagat Seth, who was the sole purchaser of all the bullion imported into the province. With the passing of the political power in the hands of the British, all difficulties regarding the establishment of a mint at Calcutta were over and the first rupees was struck on 29 August 1757.

But the acquisition of territorial revenues of Bengal after the grant of the Dewani in 1765, rendered further imports of silver by the English East India Company unnecessary. The other European companies reduced also considerably their respective imports of silver, as they were supplied with ample funds by the English Company's servants anxious to remit home their fortunes through these companies. The business of making and unmaking *nawabs* was so profitable that within eight years of the battle of Plassey more than five million pounds was obtained by the Company and its servants as compensation and 'presents' – presents comparable to tudor benevolences! The 'Plassey drain' did not stop only with this decline in the import of silver. Large quantities of bullion were exported out of Bengal to China and to other British settlements in India.

This depletion of currency caused such a grave economic distress that even Clive's attention was diverted from the congenial task of shaking the Indian *pagoda* tree. On 2 June 1766, he prescribed gold *mohurs* weighing 179.66 grains 20 carats fine as legal tender. To encourage the flow of gold to the mint, the official rate for gold in terms of silver was fixed at 17½ per cent. above the market rate and most stringent orders were passed against the export of gold. The inevitable happended. Silver disappeared from circulation. When it circulated at all, it commanded a high premium. This depletion of the already depleted currency caused a grave financial crisis. At last, matters came to such a pass that the leading European merchants of Calcutta petitioned to Governor Verelst in 1769 pointing out that 'at present the distress is so great that every merchant in Calcutta is in danger of becoming bankrupt or running a risk of ruin by attachment on his goods, which would sell for half their value, it being impossible to raise a large sum at any premium or bond'. The gold *mohurs* of 1766 were therefore withdrawn from circulation and on 20 March 1769, the official ratio between gold and silver was reduced from 16.45 to 14.81. Even this new ratio was 5.71 per cent higher than the market ratio. The result was that this second attempt at bimetallism also failed.

Apart from this disparity between market and official ratios with gold, silver currency was in a state of hopeless confusion. There were four mints in Bengal – at Calcutta, Murshidabad, Dacca and Patna, coining rupees of varying weight and fineness. These rupees again were in various stages of debasement and circulated at different *batta* or discount. Gradually different species of rupees became the established currency in the different parts of the province as shown in the following table, compiled from contemporary official records:[1]

| *Parts of Bengal* | *Species of rupees* | *Used for* |
|---|---|---|
| Dinajpur | (1) Sonauts of different *suns* | Rice and other grains |
| | (2) English and French Arcots. | Ghee, jaggery, etc. |
| | (3) Sonauts but the buyer leaves (?) (this portion of the record is illegible) half-an-anna *batta*. | Cloth. |
| | (4) French Arcots | Hemp, gunnies, etc. |
| Purnea | Patna Sonauts | |
| Nadia | Siccas | |
| Rungpur | French Arcots. The revenues were collected in Narayani[2] rupees. | |
| Birbhum | Murshidabad Sonauts | |
| Malda | Murshidabad Sonauts | |
| Hugly | Siccas | |
| Ghoraghat (a district in North Bengal) | (1) Siccas | Rice and other grains, chunam, cocoanut, etc. |
| | (2) French Arcots | Cloth, salt and betelnut. |
| | (3) Murshidabad Sonauts | Sugar and jaggery. |
| Jessore | (1) Siccas | Rice, grain, betelnut, sugar and jaggery |
| | (2) Murshidabad Sonauts | Cloth, ghee, oil, long-paper, turmeric, etc. |
| | (3) French Arcots | Salt. |
| Bishnupur | (1) Sonauts | Granin, bamboo, jaggery, etc. |

| | | |
|---|---|---|
| | (2) Old Dusmasha | Oil, ghee, brass and other metals |
| | (3) Arcots | Cloth |
| Futty Sing, Khergong Barbucksing, and Cutlabpore. | Murshidabad Sonauts | |
| Chandelhey (comprising portions of present Maldah and Rajshahi districts). | (1) Siccas | Grain, bamboo, ghee oil, jaggery and sugar |
| | (2) Dusmasha | Cloth, brass and other metals |
| Barbezu | French Arcots | |
| Atteah (sub-division north of Dacca | (1) French Arcots | Grain, ghee and oil |
| | (2) English Arcots | Cloth |
| | Viziery[3] and Benares rupees | |
| Pachette | French and English Arcots | |
| Dacca and Tipperah | In the city of Dacca its own siccas were current | |

Thus not only were different kinds of rupees in circulation in different districts but even in the same district different commodities had to be exchanged with different kinds of rupees. A greater chaos in currency cannot be imagined! The Court of Directors, realized the enormity of the situation created in Bengal only when trade became almost impossible. But as usual their greed for gain outran their good intentions. Thus they opposed the regulation passed on 26 August 1771 abolishing the *batta* between *sonauts* and *siccas* because that would involve a loss of revenue amounting to Rs. 13 lakh every year. Nor were they prepared to bring all *sonauts* to the *sicca* standard by systematic recoinage on an adequate scale.

It was this desperate condition of currency on the one hand and the divi-hunting policy of the Court on the other that Warren Hastings had to contend against as the Governor of Bengal. He rightly realized the difficulties of having four mints coining different kinds of rupees. But instead of bringing them under the same control to secure uniformity, he closed the mints of Patna and Dacca within a year and a half. The result was that bullion had to be carried through long distances either to Calcutta or to Murshidabad at great risk and expense. The Murshidabad mint was also closed on 30 April 1777.

Another measure of currency reform introduced by Hastings similarly failed. As stated, above, *sonauts* circulated at a *batta* in spite of the fact that they might be full weight coins. To outwit the *shroffs,* Hastings put an invariable date, viz., the nineteenth year of the reign of Shah Alum on all coins beginning from 1778.[4] But as the correct *Hizra* year was continued till 1792, the measure failed in its purpose.

Some time before this in August 1776, Hastings had addressed a circular letter to the different provincial Councils calling for a report on the various kinds of rupees in circulation and inviting suggestions. The replies stated that the *sicca* rupee was generally coming into general use and should be the standard coin in Bengal. Fortified with the support of the 'men on the spot' Hastings carried a number of resolutions through the Council, which unfortunately was a divided family. Bimetallism was abandoned, with a single mint in Calcutta undertaking to coin without any profit *sicca* rupees which were to pass current without any *batta* by weight and not by tale. In other words, the impression on each coin was meant to certify fineness alone and no more. No uniformity of currency could be expected until all the specie in circulation was coined into *siccas* for which the Company had neither the money nor the resources.

Another currency measure of Hastings was the introduction of copper currency for small payments in the place of time-honoured cowries. But unfortunately it was overruled and tended to return from circulation. As late as 1 July 1783, the Postmaster-General complained that so much copper was received in payment of postage that he could not change it into silver except at a discount of 20 per cent. Five years later, in April 1788, the merchants of Calcutta complained to the government that 'copper pice are [*sic*] generally refused by the natives because the nominal value exceeds the real value so much that it occasions a very heavy loss'.

But the Currency reform with which the name of Hastings is associated in contemporary state records, although not in later accounts, is his scheme of paper currency. It is true that as early as 1772 Sir James Steuart, to whom the bewildering problem of Bengal currency was referred by the Court of Directors, gave it as his considered opinion in his treatise on *The Principles of Money applied to the present state of coin in Bengal* that here was no escape from the prevailing chaos except by a system of paper currency. He advocated the gradual introduction of notes not directly by the government but by a bank enjoying government patronage. Hasting's scheme was, therefore his own, being a state issue pure and simple. The form of the note as published in an advertisement issued in pursuance of his minute of 1 May 1780 is given below:

> Seal of the Company.
>
> No. Calcutta th, 1780.
>
> We, the Governor-General and Council of Fort William do, on behalf of the United Company of Merchants of England trading to the East Indies—promise to pay at our Treasury in Calcutta on Demand to............................ or Bearer[5] the sum of Current Rupees ............ for value received.

This scheme did not materialize. Thus we see that all attempts at currency reform made by Hastings failed for one reason or other.

Cornwallis had therefore to begin his administrative reforms with currency. Complaints against high *batta* charged by shroffs, for changing gold into silver which began early in 1786, became loud and insistent when Cornwallis assumed charge, and could no longer be ignored when *batta* rose to as much as 3 per cent in August 1787. On 25 September, Cornwallis appointed a 'Committee for enquiring into the causes of the scarcity of silver coin'. The terms of reference were 'to ascertain the cause of the present discount in the exchange of gold mohurs into silver'and to 'propose in consequence whatever measures may appear . . . best calculated to obviate the conveniences arising therefrom which are now so generally complained of.'

There were six members: Herbert Harris, the Mint Master (Chairman), Richard Johnson, the Accountant of the Revenue Department, C. Cockerell, the Postmaster-General, William Harding the Company's *Buxey*, John Burgh, probably a non-official expert and A. Lambert, the Secretary. The Committee finished its work in the course of two months. The enquiry was not perfunctory, *gomastahs* or agents of the principal indigenous banking houses were orally examined. Written memoranda were called for from the Treasury, the General Bank of India, Bengal Insurance Company and other well-known firms of the time. The report was not unanimous, Cockerell writing a note of dissent.[6]

The recommendations of the Committee were not immediately given effect to. In course of six months, the *batta* almost doubled itself and rose to as much as 6½ per cent in April 1788. The matter was taken up in the *Calcutta Gazette* and was also pressed before the government in petition signed by the leading merchants of the time, both Indian and European. To alleviate the distress, Cornwallis ordered on 13 August the issue of bills payable in silver at the various *aurungs* against, gold tendered to the Treasury at Calcutta. *Batta* on *mohurs* paid in respect of government dues was definitely abolished These measures were partially successful for towards the close of November, Messrs. Shaw Gopal Doss and Monohur Doss and twenty-four other *Kothiwals* (i.e. indigenous bankers) sent an 'address of thanks' to Cornwallis for the steps taken by him.

On 1 January 1789, Cornwallis reduced the seigniorage on the coinage of silver from 3³⁄₆₄ to 1 per cent. Shortly afterwards the official rate of exchange between gold and silver was brought more nearly to a parity with the market rate. In order to make this rate effective, severe punishment were inflicted on all delinquents, In a letter, dated 16 March 1789, the Superintendent of Police, Calcutta, described how he carried one 'Govinram Poddar to Burrabazar and with tom-tom declared his crime'. About a year later, on 20 February 1790, even the reduced seigniorage of 1 per cent, on silver coinage was done away with but this measure failed in its purpose, for all the available silver had to bo sent to the south, to prosecute the war with Tippo. In course of another year,

the futility of coercive measures against shroffs to stop the *batta* was brought home to Cornwallis who decided on 18 November 1791 that 'in future the sale of gold and silver coins' would 'be as free as that of gold and silver bullion'. The result was that the fiction of legal rate was definitely abandoned.

Having thus given up the idea of forcing gold into circulation, Cornwallis directed his attention towards establishing the *sicca* rupee as the standard coin throughout Bengal. To facilitate recoinage, the three mints at Patna, Dacca and Murshidabad were re-opened. But as the progress was too slow, he appointed a peripatetic Committee to study conditions locally and suggest remedies. The recommendations are embodied in the Public Department resolution, dated 24 October 1792 which definitely laid down the 19th *sun sicca* as the sole legal tender currency of Bengal. This coin was sought to be protected from debasement by improved methods coinage such as milling, and to be standardized by having similar dies for all the four mints. Certain administrative measures such as unity of control of all the four mints were also adopted for greater efficiency and uniformity.

In their zeal for the rccoinage of all current coins into *siccas*, the government forgot to make up for the loss in the total volume of currency, due partly to the annual wear and tear of coins and partly to their export to the south. The result was an acute shortage of currency, specially when large quantities of silver were held up for coinage at the various mints. To alleviate the distress due to such dearth of currency, bimetallism was adopted lor the third time in 1792. In the resolution, dated 23 November, gold *mohurs* were declared legal tender at a rate which rendered gold overvalued as before but not to the same extent.

The *batta* therefore remained and formed the subject matter of one of the most interesting minutes drawn up by Share. He pointed out that it had a periodic rise in April, May and June, although it continued throughout the year. This seasonal fluctuation he ascribed to the flow of rupees from Calcutta to the *aurungs* for the purchase of 'investments', which trickled back only after some time, He suggested the adoption of two measures during the summer months to obviate this difficulty. One was the holding

of a stock of rupees in advance at the various *aurungs* before the commencement of the busy season. The other measure was the payment of half of each disbursement by the government in gold in order that it might circulate throughout the province. These measures achieved their object in less than a year.

But the permanent *batta* continued almost till the end ot the century, i.e. till the market rate came to a parity with the official rate on account of large imports of silver.[7] It was not till 1806, however that the Court of Directors finally decided to abolish *batta* by giving up bimetallism, in their famous Despatch of 25 April 1806, they observed,

> It is an opinion supported by the best authorities, and provided by experience, that coins of gold and silver cannot circulate as legal tenders of payment at fixed relative ratios . . . without great loss; this loss is occasioned by the fluctuating value of the metals of which the coins are formed.

More than hundred and twenty years have elapsed after this Despatch was written but we are still as far off from the safe haven of a satisfactory ratio between the rupee and gold as before. The old problem of *batta* seems to have re-appeared in another form and the immediate problem before the country is the question of 16 pence *versus* 18 pence rupee. Hut the ultimate issue is clear. It is the adoption of the gold standard with gold currency which will solve the problem of *batta*, by making the rupee definitely a token coin. The latest skipper Hilton Young has proposed to move the bark of Indian currency to gold by what he has called the gold bullion standard. This is another form of the gold exchange standard which failed us in the last storm of war. The quest for a safe haven begun so long ago is not yet ended.

## Notes

1. O.C. (Original Consultatiors) 3 (b), 12 April 1770, I.R.D.
2. Named after Nar Narayan, a famous king of Cooch Behar.
3. The Vizieries were the rupees of the Vizier or Nawab of Oudh.
4. The date of this measure is generally started to be 1773. But see my paper on 'Some Currency Reforms of Hastings' read before the Sixth Meeting of the Indian Historical Records Commission, held in Madras in January 1924.

5. 'Or order' in case the Note was payable to Order.
6. For further details see my paper on the 'Earliest Currency Committee in India (1787)', read at the English Meeting of the Indian Historical Records Commission, held in Lahore in November 1925.
7. *Calcutta Gazette*, 28 November 1799.

# 5

# From a Double Standard to a Silver Standard

B.R. AMBEDKAR

Trade is an important apparatus in a society, based on private property and pursuit of individual gain; without it, it would be difficult for its members to distribute the specialized products of their labour. Surely a lottery or an administrative device would be incompatible with its nature. Indeed, if it is to preserve its character, the only mode for the necessary distribution of the products of separate industry is that of private trading. But a trading society is unavoidably a pecuniary society, a society which of necessity carries on its transactions in terms of money. In fact, the distribution is not primarily an exchange of products against products, but products against money. In such a society, money therefore necessarily becomes the pivot on which everything revolves. With money as the focusing-point of all human efforts, interests, desires, and ambitions, a trading society is bound to function in a regime of price, where successes and failures are results of nice calculations of price-outlay as against price-product.

Economists have no doubt insisted that 'there cannot . . . be intrinsically a more significant thing than money', which at best is only 'a great wheel by means of which every individual in society has his subsistence, conveniences and amusements regularly distributed to him in their proper proportions'. Whether or not money values are the definitive terms of economic endeavour may well be open to discussion.[1] But this much is certain, that without the use of money this 'distribution of subsistence, conveniences and amusements', far from being a matter of course, will be distressingly hampered, if not altogether suspended. How can this trading of products take place without money? The difficulties of barter have ever formed an unfailing theme with all economists, including those who have insisted that money is only a cloak. Money is not only necessary to facilitate trade by obviating the difficulties of barter, but is also necessary to sustain production by permitting specialization. For, who would care to specialize if he could not trade his products for those of others which he wanted? Trade is the handmaid of production, and where the former cannot flourish the latter must languish. It is therefore evident that if a trading society is not to be out of gear and is not to forego the measureless advantages of its automatic adjustments in the great give-and-take of specialized industry, it must provide itself with a sound system of money.[2]

At the close of the Mogul Empire, India, judged by the standards of the time, was economically an advanced country. Her trade was large, her banking institutions were well developed, and credit played an appreciable part in her transactions. But a medium of exchange and a common standard of value were among others the most supreme desiderata in the economy of the Indian people when they came, in the middle of the eighteenth century, under the sway of the British. Before the occurrence of this event, the money of India consisted of both gold and silver. Under the Hindu emperors the emphasis was laid on gold, while under the Mussalmans silver formed a large part of the circulating medium.[3] Since the time of Akbar, the founder of the economic system of the Mogul Empire in India, the units of currency had been the gold *mohur* and the silver rupee. Both coins, the *mohur* and the rupee, were identical in weight, i.e. 175 grs. troy[4] and were 'supposed to have been coined without any alloy, or at least intended to be so'.[5] But whether they constituted a single standard of value or not is a matter of some doubt. It is believed that the *mohur* and the rupee, which at the time were the common measure of value, circulated without any fixed ratio of exchange between them. The standard, therefore, was more of the nature of what Jevons called a parallel standard[6] than a double standard.[7] That this want of ratio could not have worked without some detriment in practice is obvious. But it must be noted that there existed an alleviating circumstance in the curious contrivance by which the *mohur* and the rupee, though unrelated to each other, bore a fixed ratio to the *dam*, the copper coin of the Empire.[8] So that it is permissible to hold that, as a consequence of being fixed to the same thing, the two, the *mohur* and the rupee, circulated at a fixed ratio.

In southern India, to which part the influence of the Moguls had not extended, silver as a part of the currency system was quite unknown. The *pagoda*, the gold coin of the ancient Hindu kings, was the standard of value and also the medium of exchange, and continued to be so till the time of the East India Company.

The right of coinage, which the Moguls always held as *Inter jura Majestatis*,[9] be it said to their credit, was exercised with due sense of responsibility. Never did the Mogul emperors stoop to debase their coinage. Making allowance for the imperfect technology of coinage, the coins issued from the various Mints, situated even in the most distant parts of their Empire,[10] did not materially deviate from the standard. The table below of the assays of the Mogul rupees shows how the coinage throughout the period of the Empire adhered to the standard weight of 175 grs. pure.[11]

| *Name of the Rupee* | *Weight in pure grs.* | *Name of the Rupee* | *Weight in pure grs.* |
|---|---|---|---|
| Akbari of Lahore | 175.0 | Delhi Sonat | 175.0 |
| Akbari of Agra | 174.0 | Delhi Alamgir | 175.0 |
| Jehangiri of Agra | 174.6 | Old Surat | 174.0 |
| Jehangiri of Allahabad | 173.6 | Murshidabad | 175.9 |
| Jehangiri of Kandhar | 173.9 | Persian Rupee of 1745 | 174.5 |
| Shehajehani of Agra | 175.0 | Old Dacca | 173.3 |
| Shehajehani of Ahamedabad | 174.2 | Muhamadshai | 170.0 |
| Shehajehani of Delhi | 174.2 | Ahmadshai | 172.8 |
| Shehajehani of Delhi | 175.0 | Shah Alam (1772) | 175.8 |
| Shehajehani of Lahore | 174.0 | | |

So long as the Empire retained unabated sway, there was advantage rather than danger in the plurality of Mints, for they were so many branches of a single department governed by a single authority. But with the disruption of the Mogul Empire into separate kingdoms these branches of the Imperial Mint located at different centres became independent factories for purposes of coinage. In the general scramble for independence which followed the fall of the Empire, the right to coinage, as one of the most unmistakable insignia of sovereignty, became the right most cherished by the political adventurers of the time. It was also the last privilege to which the falling dynasties clung, and was also the first to which the adventurers rising to power aspired. The result was that the right, which was at one time so religiously exercised, came to be most wantonly abused. Everywhere the Mints were kept in full swing, and soon the country was filled with diverse coins which, while they proclaimed the incessant rise and fall of dynasties, also presented bewildering media of exchange. If these money-mongering sovereigns had kept up their issues to the original standard of the Mogul emperors, the multiplicity of coins of the same denomination would not have been a matter of much concern. But they seemed to have held that as the money used by their subjects was made by them, they could do what they liked with their own, and proceeded to debase their coinage to the extent each chose without altering the denominations. Given the different degrees of debasement, the currency necessarily lost its primary quality of general and ready acceptability.

The evils consequent upon such a situation may well be imagined. When the contents of the coins belied the value indicated by their denomination they became mere merchandise, and there was no more a currency by tale to act as a ready means of exchange. The bullion value of each coin had to be ascertained before it could be accepted as a final discharge of obligations.[12] The opportunity for defrauding the poor and the ignorant thus provided could not have been less[13] than that known to have obtained in England before the great re-coinage of 1696. This constant weighing, valuing, and assaying the bullion contents of coins was, however, only one aspect in which the evils of the situation made themselves felt. They also presented another formidable aspect. With the vanishing of the Empire there ceased to be such a thing as an Imperial legal tender current all through India. In its place there grew up local tenders, current only within the different principalities into which the Empire was broken up. Under such circumstances exchange was not liquidated by obtaining in return for wares the requisite bullion value from the coins tendered in payment. Traders had to be certain that the coins were also legal tender of their domicile. The Preamble to the Bengal Currency Regulation XXXV, of 1793, is illuminating on this point. It says:

The principal districts in Bengal, Behar and Orissa, have each a distinct silver currency . . . which are the standard measure of value in all transactions in the districts in which they respectively circulate.

* * *

In consequence of the Ryots being required to pay their rent in a particular sort of rupee they of course demanded it from manufacturers in payment of their grain, or raw materials, whilst the manufacturers, actuated by similar principles with the Ryots, required the same species of rupee from the traders who came to purchase their cloth or their commodities.

The various sorts of old rupees, accordingly, soon became the established currency of particular districts, and as a necessary consequence the value of each rupee was enhanced in the district in which it was current, for being in demand for all transactions. As a further consequence, every sort of rupee brought into the district was rejected from being a different measure of value from that by which the inhabitants had become accustomed to estimate their property, or, if it was received, a discount was exacted upon it, equal to what the receiver would have been obliged to pay upon exchanging it at the house of a shroff for the rupee current in the district, or to allow discount upon passing it in payment to any other individual.

* * *

From this rejection of the coin current in one district when tendered in payment in another, the merchants and traders, and the proprietors and cultivators of land in different parts of the country, are subjected in their commercial dealings with each other to the same losses by exchange, and all other inconveniences that would necessarily result were the several districts under separate and independent governments, each having a different coin.

Here was a situation where trade was reduced to barter, whether one looks upon barter as characterized by the absence of a common medium of exchange or by the presence of a plurality of the media of exchange; for in any case, it is obvious that the want of a 'double coincidence' must have been felt by people engaged in trade. One is likely to think that such could not have been the case as the medium was composed of metallic counters. But it is to be remembered that the circulating coins on India, by reason of the circumstance attendant upon the diversity in their fineness and legal tender, formed so many different species that an exchange against a particular species did not necessarily close the transaction; the coin must, in certain circumstances, have been only an intermediate to be further bartered against another, and so on till the one of the requisite species was obtained. This is sufficient indication that society had sunk into a state of barter. If this alone was the flaw in the situation, it would have been only as bad as that of international trade under diversity of coinages. But it was further complicated by the fact that although the denomination of the coins was the same, their metallic contents differed considerably. Owing to this, one coin bore a discount or a premium in relation to another of the same name. In the absence of knowledge as to the amount of premium or discount, everyone cared to receive a coin of the species known to him and current in his territory. On the whole, the obstacles to commerce arising from such a situation could not have been less than those emanating from the mandate of Lycurgus, who compelled the Lacedaemonians to use iron money in order that its weight might prevent them from overmuch trading. The situation, besides bring irritating, was aggravated by the presence of an element of gall in it. Capital invested in providing a currency is a tax upon the productive resources of the community. Nevertheless, wrote James Wilson,[14] no one would question

that the time and labour which are saved by the interposition of coin, as compared with a system of barter, form an ample remuneration for the portion of capital withdrawn from productive sources, to act as a single circulator of commodities, by rendering the remainder of the capital of the country so much the more productive.

What is, then, to be said of a monetary system which did not obviate the evil consequences of barter, although enormous capital was withdrawn from productive sources, to act as a single circulator of commodities? Diseased money is worse than want of money. The latter at least saves the cost. But society must have money, and it must be good money, too. The task, therefore, of evolving good money out of bad money fell upon the shoulders of the English East India Company, who had in the meanwhile succeeded to the Empire of the Moguls in India.

The lines of reform were first laid down by the directors of the Company in their famous Despatch, dated 25 April 1806,[15] to the authorities administering their territories in India. In this historic document they observed:

17. It is an opinion supported by the best authorities, and proved by experience, that coins of gold and silver cannot circulate as legal tenders of payment at fixed relative values . . . without loss; this loss is occasioned by the fluctuating value of the metals of which the coins are formed. A proportion between the gold and silver coin is fixed by law, according to the value of the metals, and it may be on the justest principles, but owing to the change of circumstances gold may become of greater value in relation to silver than at the time the proportion was fixed, it therefore becomes profitable to exchange silver or gold, so the coin of that metal is withdrawn from circulation; and if silver should increase in its value in relation to gold, the same circumstances would tend to reduce the quantity of silver coin in circulation. As it is impossible to prevent the fluctuation in the value of the metals, so it is also equally impracticable to prevent the consequences thereof on the coins made from these metals. . . . To adjust the relative values of gold and silver coin according to the fluctuations in the values of the metals would create continual difficulties, and the establishment of such a principle would of itself tend to perpetuate inconvenience and loss.

They therefore declared themselves in favour of monometallism as the ideal for the Indian currency of the future, and prescribed:

21. . . . that silver should be the universal money of account (in India), and that all . . . accounts should be kept in the same denominations of rupees, annas and pice. . . .

The rupee was not, however, to be the, same as that of the Mogul Emperors in weight and fineness. The proposal that

9. . . . the new rupee . . . be of the gross weight of—

| | |
|---|---|
| Troy grains | 180 |
| Deduct one-twelfth alloy | 15 |
| And contain of fine silver troy grs | 165 |

Such were the proposals put forth by the Court of Directors for the reform of Indian currency.

The choice of a rupee weighing 180 grs. troy and containing 165 grs. pure silver as the unit for the future currency system of India was a well-reasoned choice.

The primary reason for selecting this particular weight for the rupee seems to have been the desire to make it as little of a departure as possible from the existing practice. In their attempts to reduce to some kind of order the disorderly currencies bequeathed to them by the Moguls by placing them on a bimetallic basis, the governments of the three presidencies had already made a great advance by selecting out of the innumerable coins then circulating in the country a species of gold and silver coin as the exclusive media of exchange for their respective territories. The weights and fineness of the coins selected as the principal units of currency, with other particulars, may be noted from the summary table on the next page.

To reduce these principal units of the different presidencies to a single principal unit, the nearest and the least inconvenient magnitude of weight which would at the same time be an integral number was obviously 180 grs., for in no case did it differ from the weights of any of the prevailing units in any marked degree. Besides, it was believed that 180, or rather 179.5511 grs. was the standard weight of the rupee coin originally issued from the Mogul Mints, so that the adoption of it was really a restoration of the old unit and not the introduction of a new one.[16] Another advantage claimed in favour of a unit of 180 grs. was that such a unit of

TABLE 1: PRINCIPLE UNITS OF CURRENCY

| *Issued by the Govern-ment of* | *Territory in which it circulated* | *Date and Authority of Issue* | *Silver Coins* | | | *Gold Coins* | | |
|---|---|---|---|---|---|---|---|---|
| | | | *Name* | *Gross Weight Troy grs.* | *Pure Contents Troy grs.* | *Name* | *Gross Weight Troy grs.* | *Pure Contents Troy grs.* |
| Bombay | Presidency | | Surat Rupee | 179.0 | 164.740 | *Mohur* | 179 | 164.740 |
| Madras | Presidency | | Arcot Rupee | 176.4 | 166.477 | Star *Pagoda* | 52.40 | 42.55 |
| Bengal | Bengal, Bihar and Orissa Cuttack | Regulations XXXV of 1793 XII of 1805 | *Sicca* Rupee (19th *Sun*) | 179.66 | 175.927 | *Mohur* | 190.804 | 189.40 |
| | Ceded Provinces Conquered Provinces | XLV of 1803 | Furrukabad Rupee (Lucknow *Sicca* of the 45th *Sun*) | 173 | 166.135 | – | – | – |
| | Benares Provinces | III of 1806 | Benares Rupee (Machhlidar) | 175 | 168.875 | – | – | – |

currency would again become what it had ceased to be, the unit of weight also. It was agreed[17] that the unit of weight in India had at all times previously been linked up with that of the principal coin, so that the *seer* and the maund weights were simply multiples of the rupee, which originally weighed 179.6 grs. troy. Now, if the weight of the principal coin to be established was to be different from 180 grs. troy, it was believed there would be an unhappy deviation from the ancient practice which made the weight of the coin the basis of other weights and measures. Besides, a unit of 180 grs. weight was not only suitable from this point of view, but had also in its favour the added convenience of assimilating the Indian with the English units of weight.[18]

While these were the reasons in favour[19] of fixing the weight of the principal unit of currency at 180 grs. troy, the project of making it 165 grs. fine was not without its justification. The ruling consideration in selecting 165 grs. as the standard of fineness was, as in the matter of selecting the standard weight, to cause the least possible disturbance in existing arrangements. That this standard of fineness was not very different from those of the silver coins, recognized by the different governments in India as the principal units of their currency, may be seen from the following comparative statement (Table 2).

It will thus be seen that, with the exception of the *sicca* and the Benares rupees, the proposed standard of fineness agreed to closely with those of the other rupees that the interest of obtaining a complete uniformity without considerable dislocation overruled all possible objections to its adoption. Another consideration that seemed to have prevailed upon the Court of Directors in selecting 165 grs. as the standard of fineness was that, in conjunction with 180 grs. as the standard weight, the arrangement was calculated to make the rupee eleven-twelfths fine. To determine upon a particular fineness was too technical a matter for the Court of Directors. It was, however, the opinion of the British Committee on Mint and Coinage, appointed in 1803, that[20] 'one-twelfth alloy and eleven-twelfths fine is by a variety of extensive experiments proved to be the best proportion, or at least as good as any which could have been chosen'. This standard, so authoritatively

TABLE 2: DEVIATIONS OF THE PROPOSED STANDARD OF FINENESS FROM THAT OF THE PRINCIPAL RECOGNIZED RUPEES

| *Silver Coins recognized as Principal Units and their Fineness* | | *Standard Fineness of the Proposed Silver Rupee Troy grs.* | *More valuable than the Proposed Rupee* | | *Less Valuable than the Proposed Rupee* | |
|---|---|---|---|---|---|---|
| *Name of the Coin.* | *Its Pure Contents Troy grs.* | | *In grs.* | *By p.c.* | *In grs.* | *By p.c.* |
| Surat Rupee | 164.740 | 165 | – | – | .26 | .157 |
| Arcot Rupee | 166.477 | 165 | 1.477 | .887 | – | – |
| Sicca Rupee | 175.927 | 165 | 10.927 | 6.211 | – | – |
| Farrukabad R. | 166.135 | 165 | 1.135 | .683 | – | – |
| Benares Rupee | 169.251 | 165 | 4.251 | 2.511 | – | – |

upheld, the Court desired to incorporate in their new scheme of Indian currency. They therefore desired to make the rupee eleven-twelfths fine. But to do so was also to make the rupee 165 grs. pure—a content which they desired, from the point of view stated above, the rupee to possess.

Reviewing the preference of the Court of Directors for monometallism from the vantage-ground of latter-day events, one might be inclined to look upon it as a little too short-sighted. At the time, however, the preference was well founded. One of the first measures, the three presidencies, into which the country was divided for purposes of administration, had adopted on their assuming the government of the country, was to change the parallel standard of the Moguls into a double standard by establishing a legal ratio of exchange between the *mohur*, the *pagoda*, and the rupee. But in none of the presidencies was the experiment a complete success.

In Bengal[21] the government, on 2 June 1766, determined upon the issue of a gold *mohur* weighing 179.66 grs. troy, and containing 149.52 grs, troy of pure metal, as legal tender at 14 *sicca* rupees, to relieve the currency stringency caused largely by its own act of locking up the revenue collections in its treasuries, to the disadvantage of commerce. This was a legal ratio of 16.45 to 1, and as it widely deviated from the market ratio of 14.81 to 1, this attempt to secure a concurrent circulation of the two coins was foredoomed to failure. Owing to the drain of silver on Bengal from China, Madras, and Bombay, the currency stringency grew worse, so much so that another gold *mohur* was issued by the Government on 20 March 1769, weighing 190.773 grs. troy and containing 190.086 grs. pure gold with a value fixed at 16 *sicca* rupees. This was a legal ratio of 14.81 to 1. But, as it was higher than the market ratio of the time both in India (14 to 1) and in Europe (14.61 to 1), this second effort to bring about a concurrent circulation fared no better than the first. So perplexing seemed to be the task of accurate rating that the government reverted to monometallism by stopping the coinage of gold on 3 December 1788, and when the monetary stringency again compelled it to resume in 1790 the coinage of gold, it preferred to let the mohur and the rupee circulate at their market value without making any attempt to link them by a fixed ratio. It was not until 1793 that a third attempt was made to forge a double standard in Bengal. A new *mohur* was issued in that year, weighing 190.895 grs. troy and containing 189.4037 grs. of pure gold, and made legal tender at 16 *sicca* rupees. This was a ratio of 14.86 to 1, but, as it did not conform to the ratio then prevalent in the market, this third attempt to establish bimetallism in Bengal failed as did those made in 1766 and 1769.

The like endeavours of the Government of Madras[22] proved more futile.than those of Bengal. The first attempt at bimetallism under the British in that Presidency was made in the year 1749, when 350 Arcot rupees were legally rated at 100 Star *pagodas*. As compared with the then market ratio this rating involved an under-valuation of the *pagoda*, the gold coin of the Presidency. The disappearance of the *pagoda* caused a monetary stringency, and the government in December 1750, was obliged to restore it to currency. This it did by adopting the twofold plan of causing an import of gold on government account, so as to equalize the mint ratio to the market ratio, and of compel' ling the receipts and payments of government treasuries to be exclusively in *pagodas*.

The latter device proved of small value; but the former by its magnitude was efficacious enough to ease the situation. Unluckily, the case was only temporary. Between 1756 and 1771 the market ratio of the rupee and the *pagoda* again underwent a considerable change. In 1756 it was 364 to 100, and in 1768 it was 370 to 100. It was not till after 1768 that the market ratio became equal to the legal ratio fixed in 1749 and remained steady for about twelve years. But the increased imports of silver, rendered necessary for the prosecution of the second Mysore war, once more disturbed the ratio, which at the close of the war stood at 400 Arcot rupees to 100 Star *pagodas*. After the end of the war, the Government of Madras made another attempt to bring about a concurrent circulation between the rupee and the *pagoda*. But instead of making the market ratio of 400 to 100 the legal ratio, it was led by the then increasing imports of gold into the Presidency to hope that the market ratio would in time rise to that legally established in 1749. In an expectant mood so induced it decided, in 1790, to anticipate the event by fixing the ratio first at 365 to 100. The result was bound to be different from that desired, for it was an undervaluation of the *pagoda*. But instead of rectifying the error, the government proceeded to aggravate it by raising the ratio still further to 350 to 100 in 1797, with the effect that the *pagoda* entirely went out of circulation, and the final attempt at bimetallism thus ended in a miserable failure.

The Government of Bombay seemed better instructed in the mechanics of bimetallism, although that did not help it to overcome the practical difficulties of the system. On the first occasion when bimetallism was introduced in the presidency,[23] the *mohur* and the rupee were rated at the ratio of 15.70 to 1. But at this ratio the *mohur* was found to be over-rated, and accordingly, in August 1774, the Mint Master was directed to coin gold *mohurs* of the fineness of a Venetian and of the weight of the silver rupee. This change brought down the legal ratio to 14.83 to 1, very nearly, though not exactly, to the then prevailing market ratio of 15 to 1, and had nothing untoward happened, bimetallism would have had a greater success in Bombay than it actually had in the other two presidencies. But this was not to be, for the situation was completely altered by the dishonesty of the *nawab* of Surat, who allowed his rupees, which were of the same weight and fineness as the Bombay rupees, to be debased to the extent of 10, 12, and even 15 per cent. This act of debasement could not have had any disturbing effect on the bimetallic system prevalent in the Bombay Presidency, had it not been for the fact that the *nawab's* (or Surat) rupees were by agreement admitted to circulation in the Company's territories at par with the Bombay rupees. As a result of their being legal tender the Surat rupees, once they were debased, not only drove out the Bombay rupees from circulation, but also the *mohur*, for as rated to the debased Surat rupees the ratio became unfavourable to gold, and the one chance for a successful bimetallic system vanished away. The question of fixing up a bimetallic ratio between the *mohur* and the rupee again cropped up when the Government of Bombay permitted the coinage of Surat rupees at its Mint. To have continued the coinage of the gold *mohur* according to the Regulation of 1774 was out of the question. One Bombay *mohur* contained 17738 grs. of pure gold, and 15 Surat rupees of the standard of 1800 contained 247.110 grs. of silver. By this Regulation the proportion of silver to gold would have been 247.11/177.38, i.e. 13.9 to 1. Here the *mohur* would have been much under-valued. It was therefore resolved to alter the standard of the mohur to that of the Surat rupee, so as to give a ratio of 14.9 to 1. But as the market ratio was inclined towards 15.5 to 1, the experiment was not altogether a success.

In the light of this experience before them, the Court of Directors of the East India Company did well in fixing upon a monometallic standard as the basis of the future currency system of India. The principal object of all currency regulations is that the different units of money should bear a fixed relation of value to one another. Without this fixity of value, the currency would be in a state of confusion, and no precaution would be too great against even a temporary disturbance of that fixity. Fixity of value between the various components of the currency is so essential a requisite in a well-regulated monetary system that we need hardly be surprised if the Court of Directors attached special importance to it, as they may well have done, particularly when they were engaged in the task of placing the currency on a sound and permanent footing. Nor can it be said that their choice of monometallism was ill-advised, for it must be admitted that a single standard better guarantees this fixity than does the double standard. Under the former it is spontaneous, under the latter it is forced.

These recommendations of the Court of Directors were left to the different governments in India to be carried into effect at their discretion as to the time and manner of doing it. But it was some time before steps were taken in consonance with these orders, and even then, it was on the realization of those parts of the programme of the Court which pertained to the establishment of a uniform currency that the efforts of the different governments were first concentrated.

The task of reducing the existing units of currency to that proposed by the Court was first accomplished in Madras. On 7 January 1818, the government issued a Proclamation[24] by which its old units of currency – the Arcot rupee and the Star *pagoda* – were superseded by new units, a gold rupee and a silver rupee, each weighing 180 grs. troy and containing 165 grs. of fine metal, Madras was followed by Bombay six years later by a Proclamation[25] of 6 October 1824, which declared a gold rupee and a silver rupee of the new Madras standard to be the only units of currency in that Presidency. The Government of Bengal had a much bigger problem to handle. It had three different principal units of silver currency to be reduced to the standard proposed by the Court. It commenced its work of reorganization by a system of elimination and alteration. In 1819, it discontinued[26] the coinage of the Benares rupee and substituted in its place the Furrukabad rupee, the weight and fineness of which were altered to 180.234 and 135.215 grs. troy respectively. Apparently this was a step away from the right direction. But even here, the purpose of uniformity, so far as fineness was concerned, was discernible, for it made the Furrukabad rupee, like the new Madras and Bombay rupees, eleven-twelfth fine. Having got rid of the Benares rupee, the next step was to assimilate the standard of the Furrukabad rupee to that of Madras and Bombay, as may be seen from the following table (Table 3).

TABLE 3: UNIFORMITY OF COINAGE AT THE END OF AD 1833[27]

| *Issued by the Government of* | *Silver Coins* | | | *Gold Coins* | | | *Legal Ratio* |
|---|---|---|---|---|---|---|---|
| | *Denomination* | *Weight* | *Fineness* | *Denomination* | *Weight* | *Fineness* | |
| Bengal | *Sicca* Rupee | 192 | 176 or 11/12 | *Mohur* | 204.710 | 187.651 | 1 to 15 |
| | Furrukabad Rupee | 180 | 165 or 11/12 | – | – | – | – |
| Bombay | Silver Rupee | 180 | 165 or 11/12 | Gold Rupee | 180 | 165 or 11/12 | 1 to 15 |
| Madras | Silver Rupee | 180 | 165 or 11/12 | Gold Rupee | 180 | 165 or 11/12 | 1 to 15 |

Thus, without abrogating the bimetallic system, substantial steps were taken in realizing the ideal unit proposed by the Court, as may be seen from the following table (Table 3).

Taking stock of the position as it was at the end of 1833, we find that with the exception of the *sicca* rupee and the gold *mohur* of Bengal, that part of the scheme of the directors which pertained to the uniformity of coinage was an accomplished fact. Nothing more remained to carry it to completion than to discontinue the *sicca* rupee and to demonetize gold. At this point, however, arose a conflict between the Court of Directors and the three governments in India. Considerable reluctance was shown to the demonetization of gold. The Government of Madras, which was the first to undertake the reform of its currency according to the plan of the Court, not only insisted upon continuing the coinage of gold along with that of the rupee,[28] but stoutly refused to deviate from the system of double legal tender at a fixed ratio prevalent in its territories,[29] notwithstanding the repeated remonstrances addressed by the Court.[30] The Government of Bengal clung to the bimetallic standard with equal tenacity. Rather than demonetize the gold mohur, it took steps to alter its standard[31] by reducing its pure contents[32] from 189.4037 to 187.651 troy grs., so as to re-establish a bimetallic system on the basis of the ratio adopted by Madras in 1818. So great was its adherence to the bimetallic standard that in 1833 it undertook to alter[33] the weight and fineness of the *sicca* rupee to 196 grs. troy and 176 grs. fine, probably to rectify a likely divergence between the legal and the market ratios of the *mohur* to the rupee.[34]

But in another direction the government in India wanted to go further than the Court desired. The Court thought a uniform currency (i.e. a currency composed of like but independent units) was all that India needed. Indeed, they had given the governments to understand that they did not wish for more in the matter of simplification of currency and were perfectly willing to allow the *sicca* and the *mohur* to remain as they were, unassimilated.[35] A uniform currency was no doubt a great advance on the order of things such as was left by the successors of the Moguls. But that was not enough, and the needs of the situation demanded a common currency based on a single unit in place of a uniform currency. Under the system of uniform currency each Presidency coined its own money, and the money coined at the Mints of the other presidencies was not legal tender in its territories except at the Mint. This monetary independence would not have been very harmful if there had existed also financial independence between the three presidencies. As a matter of fact, although each Presidency had its own fiscal system, yet they depended upon one another for the finance of their deficits. There was a regular system of 'supply' between them, and the surplus in one was being constantly drawn upon to meet the deficits in others. In the absence of a common currency this resource operation was considerably hampered. The difficulties caused by the absence of a common currency in the way of the 'supply' operation made themselves felt in two different ways. Not being able to use as legal tender the money of other presidencies, each was obliged to lock up, to the disadvantage of commerce, large working balances in order to be self-sufficient.[36] The very system which imposed the necessity of large balances also rendered relief from other presidencies less efficacious. For the supply was of necessity in the form of the currency of the presidency which granted it, and before it could be utilized it had to be re-coined into the currency of the needy presidency. Besides the loss on re-coinage, such a system obviously involved inconvenience to merchants and embarassment to the government.[37]

At the end of 1833, therefore, the position was that the Court desired to have a uniform currency with a single standard of silver, while the authorities in India wished for a common currency with a bimetallic standard. Notwithstanding these divergent views, the actual state of the currency might have continued as it was without any substantial alteration either way. But the year 1833 saw an important constitutional change in the administrative relations between the three presidential governments in India. In that year by an Act of Parliament[38] there was set up an Imperial system of administration with a centralization of all legislative and executive authority over the whole of India. This change in the administrative system, perforce, called forth a change in the prevailing monetary systems. It required local coinages to be replaced by Imperial coinage. In other words, it favoured the cause of a common currency as against that of a mere uniform currency. The authorities in India were not slow to realize the force of events. The Imperial Government set up by parliament was not content to act the part of the *dewans* or agents of the Moguls, as the British had theretofore done, and did not like that coins should be issued in the name of the defunct Mogul emperors who had ceased to govern. It was anxious to throw off the false garb[39] and issue an Imperial coinage in its own name, which being common to the whole of India would convey its common sway. Accordingly, an early opportunity was taken to give effect to this policy. By an Act of the Imperial Government (XVII of 1835) a common currency was introduced for the whole of India, as the sole legal tender. But the Imperial Government went beyond and, as if by way of concession to the Court – for the Court did most vehemently protest against this common currency in so far as it superseded the *sicca* rupee[40] – legislated 'that no gold coin shall henceforward be a legal tender of payment in any of the territories of the East India Company'.[41]

That an Imperial Administration should have been by force of necessity led to the establishment of a common currency for the whole of India is quite conceivable. But it is not clear why it should have abrogated the bimetallic system after having maintained it for so long. Indeed, when it is recalled how the authorities had previously set their faces against the destruction of the bimetallic system, and how careful they were not to allow their coinage reforms to disturb it any more violently than they could help, the provision of the Act demonetizing gold was a grim surprise. However, for the sudden *volte-face* displayed therein, the Currency Act (XVII of 1835) will ever remain memorable in the annals of the Indian history. It marked the culminating-point of a long and arduous process of monetary reform and placed India on a silver monometallic basis, with a rupee weighing 180 grs. troy and containing 165 grs. fine as the common currency and sole legal tender throughout the country.

## Notes

1. Cf. W.C. Mitchell, 'The Rationality of Economic Activity', *Journal of Political Economy,* vol. XVIII, 1910, pp. 97 and 197; also 'The Role of Money in Economic Theory', by the same, in the *American Economic Review* (Supplement), vol. VI, no. 1, March 1916.
2. For the whole of this discussion, cf. H.J. Davenport, *The Economies of Enterprise,* 1913, Chapters II and III.
3. J. Prinsep, *Useful Tables,* Calcutta, 1834, pp. 15-16.
4. Robert Chalmers, *History of Colonist Currency,* 1893, pp. 336, 340.
5. P. Kelly, *The Universal Cambist,* 1811, p. 115.
6. *Money and Mechanism of Exchange,* 1890, p. 95.
7. P. Kelly's view is that they circulated at their market ratio (loc. cit.). On the other hand, Sir R. Temple says: 'In ancient and mediaeval India the relative value of the coins of each metal was fixed by the State, and all were legal tender virtually without any formal limitation' ('General Monetary Practice in India', *Journal of the Institute of Bankers,* vol. II, p. 406). On another occasion he said: 'The earliest Hindu currency was in gold with a single standard. The Mohammedans introduced silver, and in later times up to British rule there was a double standard, gold and silver' (ibid., vol. XV, p. 9). In contrast to this it may be noted that die Preamble to Currency Regulation XXXV of 1793 and other Currency Regulations of early date make it a point to emphasize that under pre-British regime there was no fixed ratio between the *mohur* and the rupee.
8. Cf. S.V. Venkateswara, 'Mogul Currency and Coinage', in the *Indian Journal of Economics,* July 1918, p. 169; and F. Atkinson, *The Indian Currency Question,* 1894, p. 1.
9. According to the Mohammedan historian, Khafi Khan, it enraged the Emperor Aurangzeb when the East India Company in 1694 coined some rupees at Bombay 'with the name of their impure king' (*Imperial Gazetteer of India,* vol. IV, p. 515).
10. It is stated in the *Imperial Gazetteer of India* (vol. IV, p. 514), that in the early days of the Mogul rule, there was only one Mint - at Delhi - which struck the Imperial coins. The Emperor Sher Shah was the first to introduce a plurality of Mints for coinage purposes - practice continued and extended by the later emperors until between the reigns of Akbar and Bahadur Shah II the Mints numbered about 200. From the *East India Moral and Material Progress Report* for 1872-3 it is clear that not every Mint was open to the coinage of all three metals, gold, silver and copper; but that some Mints coined only gold, others silver, and the rest copper (see Report, pp. 11-12).
11. Prinsep, op. cit., p. 18.
12. It was this necessity for ascertaining the true bullion value of the debased coins which gave rise to that class of money-changers known as shroffs, who

specialized in the business of evaluating the coins at their proper discount from the standard purity by means of the dates and other characteristics engraved upon them.

13. It is stated that Dr. Roxburgh, who was an eye-witness, was so much impressed by the sufferings of the poor owing to the bad state of the currency that he urged upon A. Dalrymple, in a letter dated 30 June 1791, to give prominence to the evils by inserting a paper in his *Oriental Repertory* (2 vols., London, 1808), 'on the current coin in circulation over the Company's territories which might be productive of the most solid and lasting advantage to the Governing and the Governed,' and added, 'You may be able to correct the evil, by which you will certainly go to heaven, if the prayers of the poor avail, and I may get a step nearer paradise.' *Observations on the Copper Coinage wanted in the Circars*, by A. Dalrymple, London, 1794, p. 1.
14. *Capital Currency and Banking*, 1847, p. 15.
15. H. of C. Return 127 of 1898.
16. Cf. The Despatch, op. cit., para 8.
17. Cf. paras. 26-8 of the letter from James Prinsep to the Calcutta Mint Committee, printed in the Appendix to the *Indian Tables* by John Muller, Calcutta, 1836.
18. Ibid., para 28. How the English and the Indian systems of weights were made to correspond to each other may be seen from the following:

| *Indian* | | | | | *English* | |
|---|---|---|---|---|---|---|
| 8 | ruttees | = | 1 massa | = | 15 | troy grs. |
| 12 | massas | = | 1 tola (or sicca) | = | 180 | troy grs. |
| 80 | tolas | = | 1 seer | = | 2½ | troy pounds. |
| 40 | seers | = | 1 maund (or mun) | = | 100 | troy pounds. |

19. Attention may be drawn in this connection to the dissenting opinion of Captain Jervis on the project of 180 grs. troy as the unit of weight for the rupee. Cf. his most exhaustive treatise called *The Expediency and Facility of establishing the Metrological and Monetary Systems throughout India on a Scientific and Permanent Basis, Grounded on an Analytical Review of the Weight, Measures and coins of India . . .*, Bombay, 1836, pp. 49-64.
20. Cf. The despatch, op. cit., para 9.
21. F.C. Harrison, 'The Past Action of the Indian Government with regard to Gold', in *Economic Journal*, vol. III, p. 54 *et seq*. Alto Minute by Sir John Shore, in Bengal Public Consultations, dated 29 September 1796.
22. H. Dodwell, 'Substitution of Silver for Gold in South India', in *Indian Journal of Economics*, January 1921.
23. Report of Dr. Scott on the History of Coinage in the Bombay Presidency, with Appendices, Public Consultations (Bombay, dated 27 January 1801).
24. Cf. Fort St. George Public Depart. Consultation, no. 19, dated 7 January 1818.

25. Cf. Bombay Financial Consultations, dated 6 October 1824.
26. Bengal Regulation XI of 1819.
27. Bengal Regulation VII of 1833.
28. The Court of Directors were willing to permit the coinage and circulation of gold *unlinked* to the rupee, for they had observed in their Despatch:
'16. Although we are fully satisfied of the propriety of the silver rupee being the principal measure of value and the money of account, yet we are by no means desirous of checking the circulation of gold, but of establishing a gold coin on a principle fitted for general use. This coin in our opinion should be called a gold rupee and be made of the same standard as the silver rupee.'
29. Cf. Fort St. George Public Consultations of 19 August 1817, particularly the letter of the Accountant-General entered thereon.
30. Cf. The Public Despatches to Madras dated 6 March 1810; 10 July 1811; and 12 June 1816.
31. Preamble to the Bengal Regulation XIV of 1818.
32. It, however, increased its weight from 190.895 to 204.710 troy grs.
33. Bengal Regulation VII of 1833.
34. It may be that this alteration was also intended to make the *sicca* rupee eleven-twelfths fine.
35. Cf. Despatch to Bengal dated 11 March 1829.
36. The Accountant General of Bengal, in a letter to the Calcutta Mint Committee, dated 21 November 1823, wrote:
'Para 32. The amount of the balance must also necessarily depend upon the state of the currency. If the Madras, Bombay, and Furrukabad rupees instead of differing in weight and intrinsic value were coined of one standard weight and value bearing one inscription and in no way differing, the surplus of one Presidency would at all times be available for the deficiency of another, without passing through the Mint, and the balance of India might be reduced in proporion to the increased availability of currency for the disbursements of the three Presidencies' (Bombay Financial Consultations, 25 February 1824).
37. The evil of the system had already made itself felt in Bombay, where the government had been obliged by a Proclamation dated 9 April 1824, to declare the Furrukabad rupee of 1819 standard as legal tender within its territories on a par with the Bombay rupee, in order to facilitate the supply operation from Bengal. Cf. Bombay Financial Consultations, dated 14 April 1824.
38. 3 & 4 Will, IV, c, 85.
39. Cf the sentiments of Tucker in his *Memorial of Indian Government* (ed. Kaye), 1853, pp. 17-19.
40. Cf. their Financial Despatch to India, no. 9, dated 27 July 1836.
41. Section 9 of Act XVII of 1835.

# 6

# Note on the History of the East India Company Coinage from 1753-1835

Edgar Thurston

When I was engaged in collecting material for my *History of the Coinage of the Territories of the East India Company in the Indian Peninsula, and Catalogue of the Coins in the Madras Museum*,[1] the records of the Madras Mint were placed at my disposal by the Madras government, and I expressed a hope that someone would eventually explore the archives of the Calcutta and Bombay Mints with a view to clearing up many obscure points in the history of the coinage of the Company, which constitutes a complicated branch of modern numismatics.

My headquarters having, by the fortune of service, been temporarily transferred from Madras to Calcutta, the opportunity has been taken advantage of to examine the records of the Calcutta Mint; and facilities for carrying out the research in my spare moments were courteously given some by Colonel Baird, F.R.S., Master of the Mint, to whom I have to express my great indebtedness.

The Calcutta Mint Committee Proceedings which are preserved in the Calcutta Mint, commence with the year 1792 (more than thirty years after the establishment of the Calcutta Mint), and are, with very few exceptions, continuous to 1835, where my investigations ceased, as the history of the Company's coinage after that year, in which a general British currency was established, is no longer veiled in doubt and obscurity.

Of the Calcutta Mint Records from the establishment of the

Mint in 1760 to 1792, I have been unable to find any trace, and this is the more to be regretted, since the history of the coinage during this period is beset with difficulties, the problem being, as pointed out by Dr. Stanley Lane-Poole[2] to determine where the native coinage ends and the Company's begins.

## Calcutta

1753. In a despatch to the Court of Directors dated 12 February 1753, it is mentioned that 'the utmost secrecy was necessary with reference to the establishment of a mint at Calcutta, as any attempt to effect an arrangement with the *nawab* would be immediately overset by Juggut Sing'. A *vakil* was entrusted and consulted, who said that his master, Hackem Beg, had a son in great power at Delhi, who might be able to get a phirmaund from the king; but that this would be attended at least with the expense of 100,000 rupees, and that, on the arrival of the phirmaund at Cossimbazar, it would cost another 100,000 rupees to the *mutsuddys* and *diwans* of the *nawab* to put the phirmaund in force.

1759-60. The establishment of a, mint at Calcutta finally took place in 1759 or 1760, and the following is a translation of the *parwana*:

> To the noblest of merchants, the English Company, be the royal favour. In Calcutta a mint is established. You shall coin gold and silver of equal value and fineness with the ashrafees and rupees of Murshidabad in the name of Calcutta. In the suburbs of Bangala, Bihar, and Orissa, they shall be current, and no person shall demand or insist upon a discount upon them. Dated the 11th of the moon Zihada in the 4th year.

## Bengal

1792. In 1792 a Committee was constituted in Calcutta by order of the Governor-General, Earl Cornwallis, for superintending the mints and enquiring into the general state of the coinage in Bengal, Bihar, and Orissa. Among the instructions given to the Committee were:

1. To enquire particularly into the cause of the little progress which had been made towards the establishment of the general currency of the *sicca* rupees.

2. To ascertain the causes of the *batta* or discount that had frequently been levied on the exchange of a gold *mohur* for silver.

3. To report whether it would be advisable to declare the gold *mohurs*, and the multiples thereof, legal tender of payment in the three provinces in all transactions, public and private, at the value at which they were then received and paid at the general treasury and in all private transactions.

4. To enquire into the state of the copper coinage.

5. To state their sentiments on the practicability and expediency of coining the gold *mohurs*, rupees and pice, or either of those coins, with machinery of similar construction to that in use in the mints in Europe.

## Patna, Murshidabad

On 14 May 1792, the Mint Master informed the Committee that he had received orders from the Governor-General to establish mints at Patna and Murshidabad, to facilitate the conversion of the various species of silver coins current in the Bengal districts into *sicca* rupees.

A new gold *mohur* and *sicca* rupee of the current coinage were laid before the Committee, who were of opinion that the size, shape, and impression of the *mohur* were perfect, and equal, if not superior, to the newest English guinea, or any of the gold coins in Europe, the die being precisely the same size as the coin, which consequently bore the whole legend, the letters being cut flat, and the coin being difficult to drill without defacing it, owing to its being milled and of proper thickness. With respect to the rupee, the Committee considered that it was very defective both with regard to its size, thickness, and impression, which was struck with a die of twice the circumference of the coin, so that only a part of the impression appeared on the coin. The letters were considered to be too prominent, and liable to injury from common wear and filing, and the thickness of the coin and absence of milling rendered it liable to be easily filed, bored, and defaced. The Committee, therefore, recommended that the rupee should be coined in every respect in the same manner as the gold *mohur*.

## Benares

In the Calcutta Mint Committee's Proceedings, 1792, the following historical sketch of the Benares mint (concerning which great confusion exists) by Mr. Barlow, who had been deputed in 1787 to enquire into the trade and coinage of Benares, is placed on record.

A mint was first established at Benares in the 15th year of the reign of Muhammad Shah (1734). The assay of the rupee was fixed at 22 *chauwals*, but, by the connivance of the Superintendents of the mint, it was debased to 32 *chauwals* at different periods before the 30th and last year of the reign.

During the first three years of the reign of Ahmad Shah (1748-50) the mint was under the charge of Raja Balwant Singh, who increased the duties on the coinage by attaching the fees of the officers of the mint, and establishing new ones to the same amount. In the 1st year the assay was kept up to 22 *chauwals*, but in the 2nd and 3rd years the Raja farmed the mint to one Nandram who, to increase his receipts, debased the coin to 24 and 82 *chauwals*. The mint records were burnt by Balwant Singh, and no records were kept in the mint until the 17th year of the reign of Shah 'Alam (1776). The farmers carried away their books in order to conceal the profits they reaped from debasing the coins. The system of farming out the mints, first adopted by Ratan Chand, Diwan to Farrukhsiyar, at length introduced the custom of changing the value of the rupee every year. Those who had payments to make were consequently obliged to carry their old rupees to the mint to have them re-coined into *siccas*, the name given to the rupees of the current year. Previous to the 10th year of the reign of Shah 'Alam (1769), the new coined *sicca*, rupee, after circulating twelve months, fell 3 per cent, and at the expiration of two years 2 per cent more, at which value it continued under the denomination *sanwat*. On 6 August 1771, this usage was abolished by the

British Government, who resolved that the *siccas* coined in the 10th year of the reign should be considered as *sanwats*, and that those coined in the 11th and all subsequent years should pass in payment at the same value as the *siccas* of the current year.

From the beginning of the 4th to the end of the 6th and last year (1754) of Ahmad Shah the mint was under the charge of Agha Asad Beg, Kiladar or Governor of the Fort of Chunar. The assay of the rupees was from 26 to 32 *chauwals*.

At the commencement of the reign of 'Alamgir II (1754) the mint fell to the Vizier Shuja'ud-daulah. During the 1st and 2nd years the assay of the rupees was from 26 to 28 *chauwals*. In the 3rd year Shuja'ud-daulah made over the mint to his brother-in-law, Mirza 'Ali Khan, who farmed it to Subhaw Chand. The assay of the rupees was from 24 to 32 *chauwals*. In the 4th year the mint was farmed to the agent of an eminent Benares banker, and the rupees were debased to 64 *chauwals* and, for the first time, half a rati in weight. Raja Balwant Singh refused to receive them into his treasury. In the 5th year the rupees were raised to their proper weight of 9 *mashas*, 7 *ratis* (or 632 *chauwals*), but continued at the debased standard of 40 and 48 *chauwals*. In the 6th and last year of the reign the rupees were debased to 100 *chauwals* assay (i.e. 535/630 silver and 95/630 alloy) and half a *rati* in weight.

In the 1st year of the reign of Shah 'Alam, Shuja'ud-daulah appointed a person on his own part to superintend the coinage, and the rupee was restored to its former weight (9m. 7r.) and to 26 *chauwals* assay. During the 2nd to 8th years the assay remained at 40 *chauwals*. In the latter year (1767) Shuja'ud-daulah, at the recommendation of Lord Clive, resolved to reform the coin. The Benares mint was, accordingly, committed to the care of Mirza Hasan, who engaged to restore the rupees to their proper weight and standard. A Delhi rupee of the 18th year of Muhammad Shah was sent as a sample for the new coinage. This rupee was 22 *chauwals* fine, but, being worn had lost 2 *chauwals* in weight. The new rupees were, in consequence, 2 *chauwals* deficient, and from that time the Benares rupees continued at 9m. 6r. 6 ch., being 2 *chauwals* less than the original weight of 9m. 7r. In the 9th year the mint was farmed to Monsieur Gentille, the French Agent at Shuja'ud-daulah's court, and the same assay (22 *chauwals*) was continued until the 15th year (1774). A considerable portion of the rupees issued in the 16th year contained only 5½ oz. of silver, to 10½ oz. of copper.

In the 17th year of the reign of Shah 'Alam (1776) the mint was transferred by the Company to Chait Singh, who engaged to coin rupees of 9m. 9r. 6 ch., weight and 18 *chauwals* fine, and to continue the die of the 17th san, in order to put an end to the confusion in the currency occasioned by the constant alteration of the value of the coin. 'All rupees, therefore,' the Records state, 'coined in the Benares mint since the 17th year of the present reign, ought to be of the same weight and standard, and to pass current as *siccas*[3] of the present year. The rupees current in the district of Benares may, therefore, be classed as *sanwat* and *sicca*, the former coined under the Mughal Princes, and the latter since the 17th year of the reign of Shah 'Alam, when the mint was ceded to the Company by the Vizier, and by them transferred to Chait Singh.'

Table 1 gives information as to the assays, weights, and names of the rupees coined at the Benares mint from its establishment to 1782.

The fact is incidentally mentioned that, when the Shahzada (Shah 'Alam) invaded Bihar, the mint accompanied him, and a large quantity of Benares rupees were melted down and coined into *rikabees* (*rikab*, a stirrup) which were 1r. 2ch. deficient in weight, and of 64 *chauwals* assay, but were made to pass in the camp as *siccas* of the established weight and fineness. It is also noted that two lakh of rupees were annually melted down for the manufacture of the laces and rich stuffs for which Benares was celebrated.

From Mr. Barlow's sketch the following account of the coinage of copper has been derived.

The pice current in the city and district of Benares previous to the establishment of the mint, were mostly coined at Gorakhpur in Oudh from copper brought from the northern hills. The first coinage of pice at Benares was in the 23rd year of the reign of Muhammad Shah (1742), when 100 maunds weight were struck with the die of the *sicca* rupee. From that period till the 4th year of

Table 1: Assays, Weights, and Names of the Rupees Coined at the Benares Mint from its Establishment to 1782

| *Reign* | *Assay* | *Beneras Weight* | | | *Calcutta Weight* | | | *Remarks* |
|---|---|---|---|---|---|---|---|---|
| | | *M.* | *R.* | *Ch.* | *M.* | *R.* | *Ch.* | |
| Muhammad Shah | | | | | | | | |
| 15th to 22nd years | 22 | 9 | 7 | – | 10 | – | – | |
| 23rd to 28th years | | | | | | | | |
| 29th to 30th years | 22 | | | | | | | |
| Ahmad Shah | | | | | | | | |
| 1st year | | | | | | | | |
| 2nd to 4th years | 24 | | | | | | | |
| | 32 | | | | | | | |
| 5th year | 32 | | | | | | | |
| 6th to 7th years | 26 | | | | | | | |
| ‘Alamgir II | | | | | | | | |
| 1st and 2nd years | 26 | | | | | | | |
| | 28 | | | | | | | |
| 3rd year | 24 | | | | | | | |
| | 32 | | | | | | | The rupees of the 4th to 6th years of ‘Alamgir II were called Trisulis from having the *trishul* or Hindu trident stamped upon them. |
| 4th year | 64 | 9 | 6 | | 9 | 7 | 4 | |
| 5th year | 40 | 9 | 7 | | 9 | 10 | | |
| | 48 | | | | | | | |
| 6th year | 64 | 9 | 6 | 4 | 9 | 7 | 4 | |
| | 100 | | | | | | | |

*(contd.)*

Table 1 (*contd.*)

| | | | | | | | | |
|---|---|---|---|---|---|---|---|---|
| SHAH 'ALAM | | | | | | | | |
| 1st year | 26 | 9 | 7 | | 10 | | | The rupees of the 1st to 7th years were called Thumka Goharshahis; *thumka* signifying small, and Gohar Shah being the name of Shah 'Alam previous to his accession. |
| 2nd to 7th years | 40 | | | | | | | |
| 8th to 10th years | 22 | 9 | 6 | 6 | 9 | 7 | 6 | Called Chaura or broad Goharshahis[4] to distinguish them from the Thumka or small ones, which Shuja'-ud-daulah, at the desire of Lord Clive, ordered to be discontinued. |
| 11th year | | | | | | | | |
| 12th year | | | | | | | | |
| 13th to 14th years | | | | | | | | Called Jhardar from a mark or branch € marked on the coin. |
| 15th to 16th years | | | | | | | | |
| 17th to 28th years | | | | | | | | *Sicca* rupees of the same weight and fineness and which ought to pass current at the same value. They are distinguished also by the appellation of *machhlidar* from the head of a fish being stamped upon them. |

the reign of Shah 'Alam (1762), no pice were coined in the Benares Mint. In the 5th year the farmer of the mint purchased some English copper, and coined it into pice of 10 *mashas* stamped with the die of Gorakhpur. The number exchanged for a rupee was 45 to 48. The coinage of pice was again discontinued until the 17th year (1776), when it was re-established by permission of Raja Chait Singh. The new pice were 10m. 3r. in weight, and passed current at about 50 or 51 to the rupee. In the following year a, quantity of copper was brought to Benares from Calcutta, and the coining of pice and exclusive privilege of buying and selling copper in Benares granted to one Kashmiri Mall for Rs. 5,000. The weight of the coins continued to be 10m. 3r. and they passed in the bazar at about 52 or 53 per rupee. In the 19th and 20th years the coinage was declared free, and those who brought copper received pice in return, after paying duties. In the 21st year (1779) a considerable revolution took place in the copper coinage. The Nawab Vizier issued orders to the officers of the Allahabad Mint to reduce the weight of the pice to 9m. 2r. The merchants, finding that their maund of copper yielded 8,650 pice at Allahabad and only 3,250 at Benares, carried all their copper to the former place. The coinage of pice was, consequently, at a stand still, only 29 mannds being coined during the year. Large quantities of the new Allahabad pice were brought by merchants to Benares. Raja Chait Singh at first refused to authorize their currency, but at length gave his consent, and the Allahabad pice of 9m. 3r. were declared current, and ordered to be received in payment in common with the old pice of 10m. 3r. The result was that the bankers contrived to lower the value of the pice altogether, and were assisted in so doing by large importations from Allahabad. In the 22nd year Raja Chait Singh ordered pice to be coined of the same size and weight as the Allahabad pice, and this contributed early to overstocking the circulation. In the 23rd and 24th years, after the expulsion of Chait Singh, the same weight (9m. 2r.) was continued, and the price of pice continued to fall until the famine in the next year, when they sold at thirteen for a rupee. In the 27th year the Resident at Benares ordered that no pice should be issued from the mint under 10m. 3r. and that Gorakhpur pice, weighing 10m. to 10m.

3r. and Benares pice, weighing 10m. 3r. should pass at the same value. The price immediately rose to 58 per rupee. In the 28th year (1787), when it was supposed that sufficient new pice had been coined for the city of Benares, the Gorakhpur pice were forbidden, and only the new Benares pice stamped with a *trishul* (trident), and weighing from 10m. to 10m. 3r. and the Gorakhpur pice, re-stampcd and not under 10m. in weight, were declared current.

As regards the gold coinage at the Benares mint, it is stated that the gold was assayed there by touch on a species of the *salgram*[5] stone so celebrated in the *shastras* of the Hindus. Upon comparing the Calcutta with the Benares gold *mohurs*, it was found (1787) that the former was about Rs. 2-1-6 better than the latter, i.e. Rs. 1-14-9 in weight and As 2-9 in assay. It was suggested, therefore, that the Benares *mohur* should be raised to the same weight and standard as the Calcutta *mohur*.

## Dacca, Patna, Murshidabad

1792. On 26 June 1792, the following regulations were submitted, among others, for the consideration of the Governor-General:

1. That the rupees coined throughout Bengal, Bihar,[6] and the district of Benares, be of the same weight, standard, size and impression (the rupee of the 19th san then coined at Calcutta).

2. That the mints of Dacca, Patna and Murshidabad be re-established.

3. That one species of copper coin be declared current throughout the Company's dominions.

In August 1792, it was notified that directions had already been given by the Governor-General for the re-establishment of the mints at Dacca, Patna, and Murshidabad; and in the same month, the following propositions were, among others, made by the Calcutta mint Committee, with a view to drawing the old and light coins into the mints, and establishing the general currency of the *sicca* rupee:

1. That after 10 April 1794, only the san 19 *sicca* rupees be received at the public treasuries, or issued therefrom;

2. That public notice be given that government, with a view to enabling individuals to get their old coin or bullion converted into *sicca* rupees without delay, have established mints at Dacca, Patna, and Murshidabad in addition to the mint at Calcutta;

3. That the rupees coined at Dacca, Patna and Murshidabad, be made precisely of the same shape, weight and standard as the 19 san *sicca* rupees coined at Calcutta, in order that the rupees struck at the several mints might not be recognizable from each other, and might be received and paid indiscriminately;

4. That the dies be made of the same size as the coin, and that the coins be milled;

5. That the *hijrah* year be omitted, as the insertion of it, by showing the year in which the rupees were struck, would defeat the object of Government in continuing the 19th san upon the coins.

### *Dacca*

The earliest weekly account of the new Dacca Mint which I have been able to find, is dated 11 August 1792, on which day the Assay Master also submitted to the Calcutta Mint Committee the accounts of the preceding three months, and promised in future to forward a weekly account.

### *Murshidabad*

On 23 October 1792, the Assay Master of the Murshidabad mint reported that he was erecting workshops, etc., at the Dutch Factory, and hoped to begin coining by the end of the following week. The opening of the mint was announced to the Governor General in in a letter dated December 1792.

### *Patna*

1793. On 24 February 1793, the Assay Master of the Patna mint announced to the Calcutta Mint Committee that everything would be ready by the end of the month for the coining of five lakh monthly.

## Bengal

In 1793 a regulation[7] was passed, by which the gold and silver coin in Bengal, Bihar, was reformed, and the currency of any gold or silver coin in these provinces, but the 19th san gold *mohur* and 19th san *sicca* rupee, and their respective divisions into halves and quarters, was prohibited.

1795. In a minute dated 2 October 1795, the defective state of the copper coinage in Bengal was dealt with, and the principles upon which the copper currency was regulated under Native administration, and the rules that had been prescribed regarding it by the British government were noted. 'Under the Mogul administration,' the minute states, 'the silver coin was the only measure of value and legal tender of payments. Gold mohurs and pice were struck at the mints for the convenience of individuals, who carried gold or copper to be converted into those coins. But the Government never fixed the number of pice which should be equivalent to a rupee, any more than the number of rupees which should pass in exchange for a gold mohur. From the year 1772, when the mints at Dacca, Patna, and Murshidabad were withdrawn, no pice were coined in the Provinces until 1783, when a contract was concluded with Mr. Prinsep for coining pice on account of the Government. These pice were of four descriptions, viz., whole or pucka, weighing 20 annas, half pice, quarters and eighths. These pice were issued by the Government at the rate of 32 pucka pice, 64 half, 128 quarter pice, and 256 eighth pice for the *sicca* rupee.'

At a council, over which Sir John Shore, Governor-General, presided, held on 2 October 1795, it was considered expedient that there should only be two descriptions of copper coin, a whole and half pice, to pass at the value of a quarter and an eighth of an *anna* respectively. It was, accordingly, resolved that a Regulation should be framed, and published for the establishment of a new copper coinage[8] for Bengal Bihar, and Orissa. Among the provisions of this Regulation were:

1. That people in all parts of the country be apprised of the value at which the coin was issued by government, and to be received and paid by the public and individuals;

2. That the value be inscribed on one surface in Persian, Bangali and Nagari – the characters used in business in the provinces;

3. That the coin be declared legal tender of payment for fractions of half a rupee;

4. That the coin be struck at the Calcutta mint, and not at the three city mints.

The Governor-General approved of samples of the new pice and half pice in November 1795, and orders were issued to coin an equal value of the two coins, until it was ascertained which was likely to be in the greatest demand. A week later, however, the Governor-General, understanding that the relative values of the whole and half pice would be best understood by the Natives, especially the lower orders, by substituting *ek pai sicca* and *adha pai sicca* for *paun ana* and . . . (the inscriptions originally ordered) resolved that instructions for altering the inscriptions be issued to the Mint Master.

## Dacca, Patna, Murshidabad

Towards the end of 1795 trouble was caused by the debased quality of the gold *mohurs* issued from the Dacca, Patna and Murshidabad mints, and by the rupees issued from the Patna and Murshidabad mints being below *sicca* standard. It was, after enquiry into the matter, resolved that the coinage of gold at the Patna mint should be for the time discontinued, and that, for the present, no more coins should be struck at the Murshidabad mint. In the course of the correspondence relating to the debased coinage, reference is made to the distinguishing marks of the three mints, but, for precautions sake, the nature of these private marks (recognizable with a lens) is not mentioned.

## Bengal

1796. In February 1796, it was resolved that all the gold bullion sent to the Calcutta mint should, until further orders, be coined into quarter *mohurs*, inasmuch as these coins were in much greater request among the lower orders than the gold coins of higher value.

In April 1796, in. consequence of a report from the Mint Master, that considerable loss would be sustained annually if government adhered to their original intention of coining the whole pice at 16 *annas* and the half pice at 8 *annas sicca* weight, government was reduced to the alternative of relinquishing the establishment of the new copper coinage altogether, or reducing its value. It was accordingly resolved that the coining of whole pice of 12 *annas* and half pice of 6 *annas sicca* weight, be commenced immediately. The Mint Master, however, reported that dies could not be made for pice of smaller diameter than those than in use, as there would not be a sufficient body of metal to yield a bold impression. It was thereupon ordered that, in the event of its appearing impracticable to insert the whole of the inscription, the Persian portion should be omitted instead of the Nagari as suggested by the Mint.

## Dacca, Patna, Murshidabad

1797. The coinage of money at the Dacca and Patna mints ceased on 31 January 1797, and 31 December 1796, respectively. The date of the closing, of the Murshidabad Mint I have not been able to find, but the records of 1799 make reference to 'assaying materials which may be deposited in the late mint at that station, and to the best means of disposing of the building which was formerly used for a mint at Murshidabad'.

## Benares

1800. In a letter dated 12 December 1800, on the subject of the irregularities at the Benares Mint, the Collector of that city suggested the advisability of a European being placed in charge of the mint and of having rupees coined there of the same standard as the Bihar *sicca* rupees.

1801. In April 1801, a Committee was appointed to enquire into the state of the Benares Mint, and report on the expediency of continuing it. From the Committee's report it appears that, since the abolition of the Residency, the mint had been left without the superintendence of a European official, and that the same species of gold, silver, and copper coins continued to be struck as at the time when Mr. Barlow reported on the mint (p. 54). In recommending a continuation of the mint, the Committee stated that 'a connexion has always subsisted between the mint and the manufacturers of gold and silver wire and thread, and the weavers of rich cloths and embroideries made at Benares, on which the prosperity of the trade in these articles appears so much to depend that, in the event of the abolition of the mint, the manufacturers might require some similar establishment to supply its place'. In reviewing the report of the Committee, the Governor General did not think it advisable either to abolish the mint, or to alter the mode in which the coinage had been hitherto conducted, but ordered that the Agent of the Governor-General, the Magistrate of the city, and the Collector of the Province of Benares be constituted a permanent Committee for the superintendence and control of the mint.

## Bombay, Madras

1802. In 1802 letters were received from Madras and Bombay, from which it appeared very necessary that a general reform of their coinage should be carried out, and greater uniformity introduced, so as to relieve the public and individuals from the inconvenience arising from so great a variety of coins, and from so frequent fluctuations in their values. The following plan of a new coinage was submitted by the Calcutta Mint:

1. That the gold and silver coins of Madras, Bombay, and the Ceded Districts, be of the same standard and weight;

2. That the gold *mohur* (gold rupee) weigh 180 grains troy, and contain 168 grains of gold and 12 grains of alloy;

3. That the silver rupee weigh 186 grains troy, and contain 173 grains of silver and 13 grains of alloy;

4. That fourteen rupees be equal to, and pass for the gold mohur.

5. That the *mohur* and rupee of Bombay be divided into halves, quarters, and eighths (which last could be milled and stamped without trouble);

6. That the Madras quarter *mohur* pass for 42 silver fanams, and the Madras rupee for 12 *fanams.*

In this proposed coinage the quarter gold *mohur* was of the same intrinsic value as the Madras star *pagoda*, but the rupee was nearly 4 per cent. better than the Madras Arkat rupee. The proposed new rupee was more than 5 per cent better than the Bombay rupee, which had been adopted from the Surat Mint.

## Baraili, Allahabad

In a, letter dated July 1803, stating that the Governor-General had it in contemplation to establish a coinage of the same weight and standard throughout the provinces ceded to the Company by the Nawab Vizier, it was announced that a Committee had been appointed for the superintendence of the mints established at Baraili and Allahabad, which were to report to government their suggestions for the improvement of the coinage in the ceded provinces. I have not been able to ascertain how long the coinage of the Allahabad mint continued, but reference is made in December, 1805, to 'base coin issued from the mint at Allahabad a short time previously to the coinage at that place'.

## Gorakhpur

1803. In May 1803, the Collector of Gorakhpur stated that

it is the opinion of some sensible shroffs that, in the course of the ensuing year, it may be advisable to establish a mint at the town of Gorakhpur. In this case it is my opinion that the Lucknow *sicca* rupee of the 28th san should be gradually introduced as the standard currency of Gorakhpur. On the other hand, the shroffs would greatly prefer the Gorakhpur rupee because of the advantages always derived from the fluctuation of batta on rupees of different standards.

## Farrukhabad

By Regulation XLV, 1803, it was enacted that:

(Sect. II) A silver coin, to be denominated the Lucknow *sicca* rupee of the 45th san, struck in the mint of Farrukhabad, corresponding in weight and standard with the *sicca* rupee at present struck at Lucknow, in the dominions of the Nawab Vizier, and thence denominated the Lucknow rupee, is hereby declared to be the established and legal silver coin in the provinces ceded by the Nawab Vizier to the English East India Company.

(Sect. IV) A mint shall be established at, or in the immediate vicinity of Farrukhabad, in which Lucknow rupee of the 45th san, and of the prescribed weight and standard, and half and quarter rupees of the same standard and proportionate weight, will be coined.

(Sect. V) The Lucknow 45th san *sicca* rupee, as established by this regulation shall be of the same size and form as the 19th san *sicca* rupee struck in the mint at Calcutta, and shall bear the following impression:

| *Obverse* | *Reverse* |
|---|---|
| اله حامی دین محمد<br>سای فضل شا عالم بادشا<br>سک زد بر فت کشور [9] | میمنت مانوس<br>سن ۴۵ جلوس<br>ضرب فرخ آباد |

(Sect. VI) The half and quarter rupee shall be proportionately less than the rupee, and bear the same impression as the rupee.

(Sect. XII) The Mint Master at Calcutta shall cause a private mark to be put on all dies which may be prepared for the mint at Farrukhabad, but in such a manner as not to be distinguished by the naked eye, or by persons unacquainted with it.

## Cuttack

1804. In 1804 the Commissioner of Cuttack pointed out that great inconvenience was experienced in the Province of Cuttack from the want of a current coin of small value, especially for the use of the troops, and pilgrims resorting to the temple of Jagannath, and proposal that the coin should bear on one face the figure of Jagannath, and on the other the value of the coin in Persian and Uriya, and the date. This coin was never struck.

## Benares

In this year the Assay Master of the Benares mint expressed a wish that

> a coining, milling, and laminating machine may be sent up to Benares to enable me to ascertain by experiments what advantage there might be in introducing the mode at present used in Calcutta, or in containing the native method of coining with the hammer only, though the whole figure of the die is not impressed on the rupees that are made in any of the native mints. The Riwa rupees, though of inferior value, have to an inexperienced person very much the aspect of Benares rupees, and are sometimes passed as such.

## Baraili, Allahabad

The Mint Committees in the Ceded Provinces (Baraili and Allahabad) were called on, in 1804, to report their views as to the introduction of a new copper coinage. The Allahabad Committee recommended that a new copper coinage should be issued, bearing the same impression as the Lucknow rupees struck at Allahabad. 'There are,' the Committee stated, 'two kinds of copper coinage in currency. The average exchange of the first is two to an anna, and of the second four to an anna. We recommend that, for the present, the new coinage be limited to the first sort.'

## Baraili

In their report the Baraili Committee gave the following details concerning the history of the copper coinage era at that mint.

> At Baraili no copper coinage was known until about sixteen years ago, when it was introduced by Mahdi 'Ali Khan, the amil, who coined pice called shamsher shahi from their having the figure of a sword stamped

upon them. They were generally coined out of old pice or copper utensils. This coinage continued two years, after which the same amil substituted another species of pice called machhlidars from their having the figure of a fish stamped upon them. A few years after an improved coinage was introduced by the then amil of Rohilkhand, whose pice were termed katar shahis from their being stamped with a dagger. After that, when Mahdi 'Ali Khan became amil for the second time in 1205 (1790), though the name and appearance remained the same, the weight was reduced from 18, 10, 17 and even 16 mashas. In their diminished state the coinage of the katar shahis continued until the cession of the provinces to the Company in November, 1801. They are still current in the southern and eastern parts of Rohilkhand, but never obtained circulation equal to that of the najib khanis, which are current at Rampur.

The opinion expressed by the Committee was that there were no special circumstances of a local nature which urgently demanded the introduction of a copper coinage, but that it appeared advisable, on general principles, to introduce a sort of pice which would be intrinsically valuable from its purity, and difficult of imitation, and which should bear the same proportion to the local silver currency which the pice in the Lower Provinces bore to the Calcutta *sicca* rupees.

It appears from a report by Mr. Seton that the system of farming the Baraili mint was abolished in 1802. No alteration was introduced into the standard of the rupee, except that, to mark the period at which the change of system took place, the Persian letter ح (the first letter of the late Subah Hussain 'Ali Khan) was discontinued, and و (W) substituted in compliment to the Lieutenant-Governor.

## Farrukhabad

1805. In February 1805, the authorities of the Farrukhabad mint recommended the coinage of milled in place of hammered money as a measure tending to correct several existing abuses and imperfections. In July a letter from government stated that

The Governor General in Council has determined on the immediate introduction of a new silver coin into the provinces ceded by the Nawab

Vizier to the English East India Company, and into the conquered Provinces of the Nawab and on the right bank of the river Jumna, including the Zillah of Bundelkhand, to be denominated the Lucknow *sicca* rupee of the 45th san, struck at Farrukhabad, corresponding in weight and standard with the *sicca* rupee at present struck at Lucknow in the dominions of the Nawab Vizier; and has it in contemplation to establish a new copper coin in the provinces above-mentioned, of an uniform weight, to consist of pure copper.

## Benares

1806. In 1806 the Mint Master at Benares, in a report on the copper currency of the Benares Province, stated that 'there is no regulation for the weight, size, or impression of pice that can be the least check on any person making them privately without fear of detection. A great part of the pice now in circulation have been made in Oudh, the Riwa Raja's country, and other places, and smuggled into circulation.' He, accordingly, suggested for the consideration of government a new copper coinage (of which specimens were forwarded) to consist of:

| *Value* | *Number to the rupee* | *Weight: Grains troy* | *Diameter, inches* |
|---|---|---|---|
| Double Pice | 32 | 240 | 1¼ |
| Single Pice | 64 | 120 | 1 |
| Half Pice | 128 | 60 | ¾ |
| Quarter Pice | 256 | 30 | 6/10 |

'If,' the Mint Master wrote, 'the machinery of the Calcutta Mint could be used in laminating the derabs, it would greatly reduce the expense of making the pice, but I would by no means advise the impression being stamped in Calcutta, as the prejudices of the Natives in Benares should be conceded to.'

## General

In a letter dated 10 December 1806, the Governor-General, in forwarding a letter from the Court of Directors concerning a plan for one general coinage for the Company's possession, expressed his opinion that the coins should be struck in the name of the king of Delhi, and not of the Company with their arms, as proposed by the Court. In the letter referred to, of which the following is a *precis*, the Court of Directors wrote as follows:

We think the Earl of Liverpool[10] has established the principle that 'the money or coin which is to be the principal measure of property, ought to be of one metal only.' In applying the argument to a coin for general use in India, there cannot be any doubt, in our opinion, that such coinage must be of silver. The standard weight of the silver coins issued from the mints of our several Presidencies we find to be as follows:

| | | |
|---|---|---|
| Calcutta *sicca* rupee. Troy grs. | ... | 179⅔. |
| Madras Arcot rupee. Troy grs. | ... | 176⅖. |
| Bombay rupee. Troy grs. | ... | 179 |

We think it would answer a good purpose to fix the gross weight in whole numbers, and should prefer the weight of 180 grs. troy. The British standard for gold coins is $^1/_{12}$ alloy and $^{11}/_{12}$ fine. There is no doubt that $^1/_{12}$ alloy of copper would be equally proper for silver coin, and we are of opinion that this proportion should be adopted, in which case the new rupees would have 165 grains of fine silver and 15 grains of alloy. Should the new rupee be ultimately adopted, there may be coined also:

| | | |
|---|---|---|
| Half rupee weighing troy grs. | ... | 90 |
| Quarter rupee weighing troy grs. | ... | 45 |
| Anna rupee weighing troy grs. | ... | 11¼ |

A copper coinage should also be determined on for general circulation, and it is our opinion that it should consist of 6 pice or half anna, 3 pice or quarter anna, and 1 pice pieces.

We are desirous of establishing a gold coin on a principle fitted for general use. This coin should, in our opinion, be called a gold rupee, and be made of the same standard as the silver rupee, *viz.*, 180 grains gross weight and 165 grains fine, and be divided into halves and quarters. The quarter gold rupee appears well fitted to supply the place of the Madras star pagoda in the payment of the Madras army.

We have thought the adoption of a new coinage for British India a fit opportunity for giving a new impression to our currency, and the most appropriate, in our esteem, is the Company's arms with an inscription 'English East India Company,' as also the denomination and value of the coin with the year of coinage, and for the reverse a Persian inscription expressing the English one on the obverse with the date of coinage and value and denomination of the coin. If the smaller gold and silver coins (perhaps all below the half rupee) do not present surface sufficient for a clear impression, it would be proper to substitute for the Company's arms the Company's crest, the inscriptions to remain alike in all.

## Farrukhabad

1807. A letter from the Mint Master at Farrukhabad dated 24 October 1807, asks for new milling dies for rupees, and states that the mint had not yet been furnished with dies for the half and quarter rupees, the expediency of introducing which had been suggested by the Mint Committee.

## Madras

In this year, and early in 1808, proclamations were issued by the Government of Madras respecting a new coinage for the Madras Presidency, of which the following is a *résumé*.

### A. Silver Coinage

All the silver coins of the Presidency coined at the Madras mint shall be coined direct from dollars when imported, and be of dollar fineness.

The double rupee will contain double the quantity, the half rupee half the quantity, and the quarter rupee a quarter of the pure silver which the rupee contains.

There are also coined and issued the following small coins:

| | | | | |
|---|---|---|---|---|
| Five fanams, | on which is inscribed their denomination in English, | Persian, | Gentoo (Telugu), and | Malabar (Malayalam). |
| Three[11] | » | » | » | » |
| Two | » | » | » | » |
| Single | » | » | » | » |

### B. Copper Coinage

The Governor-General in Council has been pleased to issue a new coinage of the following numbers, values, etc.

| | | |
|---|---|---|
| Double Dubs | ... | 24 to the rupee |
| Single Dubs | ... | 48 to the rupee |
| Half Dubs | ... | 96 to the rupee |
| Quarter Dubs | ... | 192 to the rupee |

In case the above coins are issued at the Presidency, etc., they are to measure with the star pagodas:

| | |
|---|---|
| 84 | double dubs to one *pagoda* |
| 168 | single dubs to one *pagoda* |
| 336 | half dubs to one *pagoda* |
| 672 | quarter dubs to one *pagoda* |

There are also issued the following coins with their denomination inscribed on them in English, Persian, Gentoo, and Malabar: 40 cash, 20 cash, 10 cash, 5 cash.

In this Proclamation, which is dated 22nd August, 1807, it is stated that 'the Governor in Council has also deemed it expedient to issue a silver coinage of half and quarter pagodas of dollar fineness'.

This Proclamation was repeated on 28th November, 1807, with the addition of a 2½ cash piece as being 'also issued'.

### C. Gold Coinage

The Governor in Council, having deemed it necessary to establish a new gold currency, has resolved to coin a gold pagoda of 22 carats fine, and a double pagoda of the same fineness, with English, Persian, Gentoo, and Malabar inscriptions.

## Benares

In August, 1807, the mint master at Benares received a letter from Calcutta respecting a new copper coinage for the province of Benares, which was to be prepared in the Calcutta Mint. This coinage should, it was thought, consist of:

| | *Number to a rupee* | *Calcutta sicca weight* |
|---|---|---|
| Double pice | 32 | 1-1-6 |
| Single pice | 64 | 0-8-9 |
| Half pice | 128 | 0-4-4½ |

1809. By Regulation X, 1809, the Calcutta Mint was directed to coin pice for the province of Benares, valued at 64 per rupee.

## Madras

1810. In a letter dated 11 September 1810, reference is made to 'London made copper coins at Fort St. George, of which there is stated to be 80,000 *pagodas* in store, and which cannot be brought into circulation at that Presidency. We are of opinion that the 20 cash pieces might be circulated here at the value of one and a half of the Bengal pice, and that, in the present scarcity of copper, it would be advisable to send the whole of them to Bengal.

## Benares

1811. A letter dated 16 September 1811, states that

> Government having been pleased to determine that no change shall be made in the local currency of the province of Benares, but that it shall be recognised as the legal currency of that portion of the Company's territories, we entirely concur as to the expediency of placing the mint of that province under the immediate control of the Supreme Government, and of assimilating it in every respect to the mints of Calcutta and Farrukhabad, by which means the coin which may hereafter be struck in the Benares mint will be much improved in point of fabrication and appearance. The same letter states that 'the quantity of gold which has been coined in the Benares mint since 1782 only amounted to 121,949 *mohurs* or about 1,768,260 rupees, whilst, during the same period, the silver coinage has amounted to rupees 51,631,000, and it is accordingly proposed by the Board of Commissioners that the Benares mint shall not be open for the coinage of gold bullion in future.

A Regulation for the future management of the Benares Mint (the date[12] of which is not given in the records), has, among its clauses, the following:

Preamble. Whereas it has been deemed advisable to continue the mint at Benares, and to assimilate the internal management of it to the rules already in force in the Mints of Calcutta and Farrukhabad, the following rules have been enacted to be in force from their promulgation:

1. The silver coin now current in the Benares province under the denomination of the *machhlidar* rupee, commonly called the Benares rupee, shall continue to be the established coin of the province, and shall be received as such in all public and private transactions.

2. The Benares rupee is to continue of the following weight, and half and quarter rupees are to be ·coined of the. same standard and proportionate weight:

| | |
|---|---|
| Troy grains | 175 |
| Pure silver | 168.875 |
| Alloy | 6.125 |

3. The Benares rupee shall hereafter be struck of the same size and form as the 19th san rupee struck in the mint of Calcutta, and shall bear the same impression as is now in use;

4. The half and quarter rupee shall be proportionately less than the rupee, and shall have the same impression as the rupee;

5. The edges shall be milled, and the dies (to be cut in the Calcutta mint) shall be made of the same size as the coin, so that the whole impression may appear;

6. The mint master at Calcutta shall cause a private mark to be put upon all the dies which may be prepared for the Benares mint.

## Java

1812. In 1812 the Lieutenant-Governor of Java asked that a supply of copper coinage might be sent from Bengal to Batavia, as the want of a small currency was felt throughout the colony. The coinage, it was suggested, should consist of 165 coins to one Dutch pound weight, and the device be either the figure of a buffalo or elephant, and on the reverse JAVA and the date.

## Madras

In April 1812, the Madras Mint Committee recommended that, in conformity with the orders of the Court of directors, the coinage of half and quarter *pagodas* and of pie, two, and single *fanams* be discontinued, and that the coinage of rupees, half, quarter, and eighth rupees be commenced; and that the half and quarter *pagodas* and five *fanam* pieces be re-coined into rupees as fast as possible, leaving the double and single *fanams* to remain in circulation until the fractions of the rupee were fully established.

## Benares

1818. In 1813 it was pointed out that, since the *tirsoolee* paisa was originally established as the copper currency of Benares, no measures had been adopted to renew it, and the inscription had, by process of time, become more or less indistinct, and the shroffs had reduced the value of pice in which the *trishul* was defective by reducing it 11 per cent in current value for no other reason than the defectiveness of the *trishul*.

## Ceded Provinces

By a Resolution dated 7 August 1813, the Governor-General, anticipating great convenience and advantage from the establishment of an uniform coinage throughout, the ceded and conquered provinces, including the districts dependent on Delhi, resolved that the coinage to be carried on henceforth at the Delhi Mint be confined to new Farrukhabad rupees of the weight and standard of the coin issued from the Farrukhabad Mint, and bearing the same inscription. The Governor-General also expressed his opinion that there could be no objection to coining at the Delhi Mint, a limited number of rupees bearing the name and title of his present Majesty, Akbar Shah, these rupees being only intended to be presented to His Majesty on the anniversary of his accession for the purpose of being distributed as complimentary presents.

## Benares

In 1813 a Regulation for establishing a copper coinage in the Province of Benares was passed, among the clauses of which were the following:

1. A copper coin weighing 100 grains troy, and consisting of pure copper, shall be established in the province of Benares (the coin to be fabricated at the Benares mint);

2. The form, size, and impression of the copper coin shall correspond with those prescribed by Sect. XII, Reg. II, 1803, for the Benares rupee, but the edges shall not be milled or have any mark or impression.

## Bombay

In November 1813, the Court of Directors expressed their opinion that the coinage for the Bombay Presidency should be executed in the Calcutta Mint, and forwarded a number of coins as showing their views with respect to manner in which the coinage should be executed.

## Farrukhabad

1816. In September 1816, the Board of Commissioners, Farrukhabad, pointed out that for some time only a small quantity of silver had been brought to the mint by individuals for coinage, and suggested the expediency of employing the establishment in the coinage of copper pice on account of government. The following draft Resolution was submitted by the Commissioners:

1. That Sect. XLIII, Reg. XLV, 1803, prescribing a specified weight for the copper pice to be struck at Farrukhabad be rescinded;

2. That such copper coin be struck at Farrukhabad, weighing 200 grains troy for the whole, or double pice, and 100 grains troy for the half or single pice;

3. That such copper coin shall be issued from the mint at the rate of 32 whole and 64 half pice for each rupee.

## Mauritius

In November 1816, the Mauritius government wrote to the Governor-General that this Colony is subject to considerable inconvenience and difficulties, especially since the great fire, from the want of a small money for the ordinary daily transactions of common life. It would, therefore, be most desirable to obtain from the mint of the Supreme Government a coinage for the use of this land. A decimal division of the Spanish Dollar, which coin is here equivalent to two *sicca* rupees, would be the most convenient money for accounts. The books of the merchants and traders being kept in livres, ten of which are in this Colony equal to the Spanish Dollar, it would be desirable that each of the silver coins should be marked ONE LIVRE.

## Bengal

By Regulation XXV, 1817, it was enacted that:

1. The copper pice struck at the Calcutta Mint shall be of pure copper, and of the weight of 100 grains troy;

2. The inscription shall be on one side 'one pie *sicca*' in Bangali, Persian, and Nagari, and the date on the obverse;

3. That the pice shall be issued from the mint and public treasuries at the rate of 64 to 1 *sicca* rupee . . . , and be legal tender at the rate of 64 to a rupee of the local currency throughout the provinces subject to the Presidency of Fort William.

## Benares, Farrukhabad

4. The pice struck at the mints of Benares and Farrukhabad, agreeably to the provisions of Regulation X, 1809, Reg. VII, 1814, and Reg. XXI, 1816, shall be also considered as circulating equally with the pice of Calcutta coinage throughout the above-mentioned provinces, and shall in like manner, be received as legal tender in payment of the fractional parts of a rupee of the local currency at the rate of 64 pice for each rupee.

## Farrukhabad

By Regulation XXVI, 1817, it was enacted that:

1. Whereas it may from time to time be found expedient to coin rupees of the weight and standard of the Farrukhabad rupee at the

mints of Calcutta or Benares, it has seemed advisable to rescind so much of section II of Reg. XLV, 1803, as tends to limit the coinage of Farrukhabad rupees to the mint of Farrukhabad, and to direct that the following enactment be henceforth in force.

2. The silver coin denominated the Farrukhabad rupee, and of the weight and standard prescribed by section II of Reg. III, 1806, struck at the mints of Calcutta, Farrukhabad, or Benares, or at any other mint established by order of the Governor-General in Council, is hereby declared to be the established and legal silver coin in the ceded and conquered provinces.

## Calcutta

In 1817 the weight of the pice struck in the Calcutta mint was fixed at 100 grains, and they bore the inscription 'one pie *sicca*'.

## Delhi

1818. In June 1818, the Vice-President in Council expressed his concurrence with the Resident at Delhi as to the inexpediency of maintaining the Delhi Mint, and the Resident was accordingly directed to discontinue its operations, still causing, however, such a number of coins to be struck as might be necessary for the purpose of satisfying the feelings of the king.

## General

In August 1818, the Calcutta Mint Master submitted for the consideration of government specimen coins of the weight and standard of the proposed new currency, and stated that, as the difference in size and weight of the new coins might not be considered sufficient to enable all persons to at once distinguish them from the old ones, he had thought it expedient to affix such further distinctive marks as would be obvious to the most ordinary observer. The specimens, which were distinguished from the existing currency by a raised rim and perpendicular milling, were adopted as the pattern for the new coinage.

In 1818 the Calcutta Mint Committee stated that they were not aware of any objection to the inscription on the rupee undergoing an alteration, and that it would be more consistent with the dignity of the British government of India to authorize its own currencies by its own peculiar sta.mp and impression; and suggested that, if any alteration was made, no date should be inserted, as an arbitrary *batta* on coins of various issues would thus be obviated without having recourse to any fictitious inscription.

## Benares, Farrukhabad

1819. By Regulation XI, 1819, it was enacted that:

1. The coinage of the Benares rupee shall be discontinued;
2. The Farrukhabad rupee shall be considered the legal currency of the province of Benares;
3. The Farrukhabad rupee shall be a legal tender in all the territories under the Bengal government, with the exception of Bengal, Bihar, and Orissa, whether struck at the mints of Calcutta, Benares, or Farrukhabad, or any other mint that may be hereafter established within the aforesaid limits under the authority of the British government;
4. The Farrukhabad rupee to be struck at any of the mints before mentioned, shall be of the value of the present Farrukhabad rupee, and of the standard of the present Calcutta rupee, viz.:

| | | |
|---|---|---|
| Weight | Troy grs. | 180.234 |
| Pure silver | Troy grs. | 165.215 |
| Alloy | Troy grs. | 15.019 |

## Ajmere, Sagar

In addition to the substitution of the new Farrukhabad rupee, the Mint Committee recommended the temporary establishment of mints at Ajmere and Sagar, to convert the existing currencies into the new coin. The Sagar mint was at that time issuing rupees called 'Saugor or Balashaie'. The government expressed their opinion that the recommendation of the Committee was judicious. I can find no further reference to the Ajmere Mint in the records.

## Bombay

1821. The Bombay coinage consisted in 1821 of the following:

| | | *Troy grs.* |
|---|---|---|
| Gold | Mohar | 180 |
| " | Panchia (5 rupees) | 60 |
| " | Rupee | 12 |
| Silver | Rupee | 180 |
| " | Half Rupee | 90 |
| " | Quarter | 45 |
| " | Eighth | 22.5 |
| Copper | Anna | 400 |
| " | Half Anna | 200 |
| " | Quarter | 100 |
| " | Pice | 33.33 |

## Mauritius

In this year the Mauritius government being put to inconvenience by the use of paper money for the small change of the colony, asked that the Calcutta mint might coin for them small tokens to the value of 100,000 *sicca* rupees. The wish of the Mauritius government was acceded to.

## Singapore

1824. In 1824 an application was made by the Resident at Singapore for a supply of small coins to be struck at the Calcutta mint for the use of that settlement. In the Resident's letter it is stated that the small money in circulation throughout the Malay countries consisted of copper Dutch duyt and pice of Prince of Wales' Island, the brass coin of China, and of silver Dutch 2, 6, and 9 silver (stiver?) pieces, and the guilder or florin commonly called by the natives the rupee. The most universally used coins were the duyt and two stiver piece. The duyt was the real money of the most remote and unfrequented parts of Sumatra and Borneo, and the two stiver piece was the true circulating medium of the

Celebes, the Spanish dollar being only used in foreign commercial transactions. It was suggested that the duyt and two silver piece should be struck with the Borneo inscriptions, viz., the value in the English, Chinese, Malay and Bugies languages, and on the reverse the crest of the East India Company without the supporters, and with the date and motto of the Company beneath.

## Sagar

By Regulation II, 1824, it was decided that the Farrukhabad rupees, to be coined at the Sagar mint of 180 grains, 165 fine and 15 alloy, should be the legal currency of Sagar and territories on the Narmada (Nerbudda).

## Bombay

A letter from the Bombay Mint Committee, dated 27 September 1824, refers to a communication received from the Supreme Government, desiring that immediate steps be taken for the coinage of a new rupee of the Madras standard, and asking for their opinion on the measures to be adopted for a general reform of the currency. The Committee suggested, with reference to the first point, that a proclamation should be issued, announcing the alteration of the standard, and declaring the new rupee current at par with the old. They also recommended the division of the anna into sixteen instead of twelve pice, so that the copper currency would consist of:

| | *Troy grs.* |
|---|---|
| Anna | 400 |
| Half Anna | 200 |
| Quarter Anna | 200 |
| Double Pice | 50 |
| Single Pice | 25 |

A draft proclamation was submitted by the Committee, announcing the alteration of the mint standard, the sanction of which by the Supreme Government is not recorded in the Records.

## General

1825. In 1825 various suggestions for a change of impression on the currency were made, and the following extract is from an able report by Lieutenant Forbes, who was superintending the construction of the new Calcutta Mint, and who, before proceeding to England in 1820, had been instructed by the Bengal government to bring the subject of the device for the coin to the notice of the Court of Directors.

'It is observed,' Lieutenant Forbes wrote,

that the impression chosen by the king of Oudh for his new currency shows that in reality no prejudice exists against the representation of animals on coins. The common practice of putting Coats-of-Arms on coins having led to the adoption of those of the Hon. Company as a device for some of their copper coins executed in England, the propriety of employing them on the money to be struck for the general circulation of India came first to be considered. From the minuteness of the scale to which they must be reduced on a coin, it was found that the Royal Arms situated in the upper left quarter of the Company's shield became undecipherable, and that, as its plain was otherwise blank, the total effect of the piece was feeble and unmeaning. With the intention of enriching the design, two large lions (the supporters), and a little one (the crest), were introduced. The portion of surface occupied by such a number of animals in the rampant and strange attitudes adopted in heraldry, now left so little space for the shield that the Royal Arms, diminished to a peg, became utterly undistinguishable. The unanimous opinion of artists that such a device would appear inelegant and barbarous was strikingly confirmed by the specimens produced on the money executed at Soho for transmission to Penang and the islands to the eastward. Although some of the dies were engraved by artists of considerable talent, no effort of skill or ingenuity could prevent the little odd lion of the crest from being mistaken for a monkey, nor obviate the misapprehension of common observers in conceiving the figures used as supporters to be ill-designed cats. A praiseworthy attempt to correct such serious defects by the introduction of lions modelled from life brought the question of the Arms to its final issue. It then appeared that the animals with which heraldry is conversant under the denomination of lions are not 'real lions,' and that correct similitudes of the animal himself, placed in the splay-footed position, required as supporters, had a ludicrous effect.

I was induced to propose the simple emblem of the Company, a solitary lion, as a devise for the Indian coins. As an appropriate type of sovereignty, and as an emblem known and respected wherever British rule has been extended, I suggested that the ease, dignity, and strength which he so nobly personified on some of the coins of ancient Greece would be still more consistent and characteristic when applied to India. Moreover, I suggested that he might be completely localised by the ever-flourishing Palm, an Asiatic though ancient tasteful emblem of perpetuity.

I have to solicit the attention of the Committee to a model of this devise executed after a drawing by Flaxman.

It was agreed that this device was well adapted for one face of the new coin, and suggested that either the head of the King (George IV), or the designation of the coin within a wreath, should be placed on the other face.

## Delhi

1826. In 1826 the Collector of Delhi expressed his opinion that a proposal to establish a mint for copper coinage at Delhi would be productive of good to the people, and a check to the impositions practised by the shroffs, whose source of livelihood consisted in the exaction of discount on the various current copper coins.

## Calcutta

1823-7. A volume of the records, 1823-7, is devoted to details connected with the construction of the new Calcutta Mint.

In a report on the regulations for the conduct of the coinage subsequently to its transfer to the new Calcutta Mint it is recorded that:

1. It was the intention of the Hon. Court that the scale of the new mint machinery and establishment should be such as would permanently enable it to supply two-thirds of the coin required for the circulation of India;

2. It was their design that the remaining third should be supplied by similar apparatus of half the power to be sent to Bombay;

3. The new Calcutta Mint would immediately or eventually have to perform the work of the Calcutta Mint, and of the mints of Benares, Farrukhabad, and Sagar;

4. The Hon. Court held in view that the Calcutta and Bombay mints would, at any period found convenient, afford the means of equalising the coins, and of rendering uniform the coinages of India.

## Bombay

1827. In a letter dated 28 August 1827, the Mint Master of the 'new mint', Bombay, expressed his opinion that the Bombay division into rupees, quarters, and reas was preferable to the rupees, *annas*, and pie of the other side of India, and that the division of the gold *mohur* into fifteen parts was decidedly superior to the Calcutta division into sixteen.

## Spelter Money

1829. In 1829 it was suggested that the new Calcutta Mint might be usefully employed in coining spelter money, which would be very useful to the poorer classes as a substitute for cowries, and which might be called the quarter or *pao* pice.

## Delhi

The question of the re-establishment of the Delhi Mint for the coinage of pice only was re-opened.

## Benares

1830. In a, letter dated 2 February 1830, the Calcutta Mint Committee was informed that the Governor-General authorized the discontinuance of the establishment of the Benares Mint, and the disposal of the machinery, apparatus, and other property of that mint.

## General

In May 1830, a, letter was submitted by the Calcutta Mint Committee on the subject of the impression of the new coinage, and reiterating their opinion that the British Indian currencies should bear impressions characterizing the authority by which they were issued either in the form of a head, emblem, or coat-of-arms. The Committee, in the same letter, expressed their opinion that, until this question was settled by the Court of Directors, the Bombay coinage should continue to bear the same impression as it did at present. In a further letter, submitting specimens of two Franc pieces, the Committee stated that the French milling could not be advantageously introduced with the existing milling machinery, and recommending that a plain milling should be adopted.

## Calcutta

In August 1830, the Calcutta Mint Committee submitted specimens of copper pice with a, request that government would sanction their coinage, as they seemed to be preferable to those in circulation at that time.

In December of the same year the Calcutta Mint Master suggested that a copper coinage might with advantage be carried out at the new mint for the Madras Presidency and the settlements to the eastward (Singapore, etc.) in which latter the demand for copper coin was at that time very urgent.

## Sagar

1831 A letter dated 11 January 1831, stated that it had been resolved to abolish the mint at Sagar.

By an order dated 25 February 1831, it was notified that 'an alteration in the Calcutta *sicca*, and Farrukhabad rupees was authorised by the Governor-General in Council under date 13th July last, and that these currencies will in future be struck at the Calcutta mint with a plain flat milling only'.

## Bengal

In August 1831, the Calcutta Mint Committee submitted the following draft of a Regulation for legalizing the circulation of the sub-divisions in the copper currency authorized to be coined by government:

1. That, besides the copper pice now current, which shall remain unchanged, there shall be coined a copper half-*anna* piece, and a copper pie or twelfth of an *anna*;

2. The copper half *anna* pie shall weigh twice the weight of the present pice, or 200 grains troy, and shall bear on one face the legend 'Half anna' in Persian, and Nagari, and on the other the same in English and Bangali. The exchangeable value of the coin shall be two for one *anna*, or one for two pice;

3. The twelfth of an *anna* piece on one pie shall weigh troy grains 33.333, and shall bear on one face the legend 'One pai' in Persian and Nagari, and the same on the other in English and Bangali. The exchangeable value of the coin shall be twelve for one *anna* or three for one pice.

4. These coins shall be current at the above rates in all the provinces under the Bengal Presidency.

## Rupee Coinage

1833. In a letter from the Assay Master of the Calcutta mint (Mr. Prinsep) in April, 1833, some general information is given with reference to rupee coinage. 'It has ever,' he says,

> been the expressed desire of the Hon. Court of Directors to equalise the coin of the whole of the Indian possessions both in weight and standard. In this they have but followed the laudable practice of the Muhammadan Governments of India, which, while they arrogated to themselves the prerogative of coining, appear to have maintained with care and good faith the weight and purity of the circulating medium until the Empire was distracted with internal commotions, land the Viceroys of the Crown and tributary states assumed to themselves the control of the various mints, reserving a mere nominal subjection to the sovereign in the legend impressed upon their coin.

The silver rupee was introduced, according to Abul-fazl, by Sher Shah, who usurped the throne of Delhi from Humayun in 1542. It had a weight of 11¼ *mashas*, which, at the rate of 15½ grains per masha, is equal to 174.4 grains of pure silver. This standard was adopted by Akbar, and accordingly we find coins of his reign weighing from 170 to 174 grains.

The Murshidabad rupee was adopted for the coinage of the Company's subah of Bengal, and has accordingly remained unchanged as the present *sicca* rupee.

The Surat rupee was also adopted as the currency of the Bombay Presidency under the treaty with the Nawab of Surat, who retained the privilege of coining; but in 1800 its pure contents were found to have sunk to 164.79 grains, when, to prevent further depreciation, the Government assumed charge of the mint, and the rupee was then fixed at the later valuation of 164.7 grains pure.

The Delhi rupee struck at the Fathgarh mint by the Vizier of Oudh, in like manner, gradually diminished to 165.2 grains pure, when, by cession of the Duab to the English, it was there arrested, and by a, Regulation of 1806, was assumed as the standard currency of the Western Provinces. It was afterwards introduced into the Benares Provinces, where (that mint having come earlier into our possession), the depreciation of the rupee has not reached the same extent: pure contents 169.2.

The Arcot rupee in 1788, according to the assay tables, still retained 170 grains of pure silver. When adopted, however, as the standard rupee of the Madras Presidency, it had fallen to 165 grains, and there of course it has since remained.

The alteration of the standard to $^1/_{12}$ of alloy in 1818 did not affect the proportion of pure metal, but the facility of equalising the three coins (Bombay, Madras, Farrukhabad) had been observed both in England and India; and, when the Sagar mint was established in 1825, it was ordered to coin new Farrukhabad rupees of 180 grains weight, the same as the standard of Madras, or containing 165 grains pure. The Bombay mint was ordered to assimilate its coin to the same in 1829. The Benares rupee alone continued to coin Farrukhabads of 180.234 grains until its abolition in 1829; and the Calcutta mint has since coined them of the same weight, although a good opportunity was afforded by the promulgation of the new system in Bombay to have effected a simultaneous reform here.

In the letter under notice Mr. Prinsep recommended (and government saw the expediency of adopting the recommendation)[13] that:

1. The weight of the Farrukhabad rupee struck at the Calcutta mint be 180 grains troy instead of 180.234 grains; and that the weight of the Calcutta *sicca* rupee be 192 grains instead of 191.916, corresponding alterations being made in the half and quarter-rupee.

2. The *sicca* weight (contra-distinguished to the *sicca* rupee) be equalized with the weight of the Farrukhabad rupee.

## Calcutta

In October 1833, Mr. Prinsep recommended that the armorial bearings impressed on both the Bombay and Madras copper coins, should be immediately adopted at Calcutta and that on the reverse should be the value in English, Nagari, and Persian, enclosed in a wreath. 'The determination of this point,' Mr. Prinsep said, 'is the more urgent as it is now in contemplation to issue a large copper coin to replace the tirsoolee pice.'

## General

1834. In April 1834, the following recommendations were submitted for the consideration of government:

1. That there should be a common device for the coins of the three Presidencies;

2. That this should differ on the three metals, so as to fully distinguish them from one another, and prevent fraud and imposition by gilding or silvering;

3. That the device should be pictorial and essentially English, as among other reasons, the adoption of such a device would entitle the government to claim from the Colonial governments of the Crown a recognition of the coin or India as a national money entitled to circulate at its intrinsic value in all the possessions of the Crown. The rupee in its present form is not so considered beyond the limits of the Company's authority.

4. That the gold *mohur* of Bengal should in future be equalized with that of Bombay and Madras;

5. That the coinage of the *sicca* rupee should be discontinued from the commencement of the new Charter, so as to prevent all confusion from the two coins being permitted to circulate together.

A specimen coin, executed by a native named Kashinath, was submitted with the letter. The obverse bore a facsimile of the king's head on the English Sovereign, and the legend GULIELMUS, IIII. D.G. BRITANNIANUM, REX. F.D., and the reverse a laurel wreath with ONE RUPEE. 1834. in the centre, and the same in Persian, Bangali, and Nagari in the margin. This device, with the substitution of *MOHUR*, was recommended for the gold coinage. Mr. Prinsep had already suggested that the copper coins should bear on the obverse the Company's Arms, and on the reverse a wreath with the designation of the coins in lieu of the word 'adil' of Bombay or 'ek falus panch kas ast' of Madras. 'The recommendations of the Committee were referred to the Court of Directors.

Various designs for the new coinage by Mr. Prinsep's were also submitted, viz.:

1. Britannia from the English penny;
2. A lion from an ancient Greek coin;
3. An elephant (from the Ceylon coin) ;
4. A ship;
5. A British senator, between a Hindu and Mahommedan, presenting the charter;
6. An emblematical figure of Justice and Plenty;
7. Typical figures of Britannia and India;
8. The Pipal tree (*Ficus Indica*), from the seal of the Royal Asiatic Society of London.

## General

1835. Early in 1835 engravings were prepared of the head of the king with the simple legend 'WILLIAM, IIII. KING, instead of the titles in Latin, and an impression in pure gold of the King's head with the lion as the reverse (proposed as a double *mohur*) was submitted.

In April 1835, the Calcutta Mint Committee was informed that the rupee having on one side the inscription EAST INDIA COMPANY, with the nominal value of the coin in English, Persian, and Nagari, and the representation of a lotus flower and myrtle wreath had been approved by the Governor-General as the model for the future coinage of rupee. The Committee were requested to communicate with madras, Bombay, and Sagar mints with the view of effecting a change in the rupee currency throughout British India with all convenient expedition. In a subsequent letter, however, it was resolved that on the obverse of the new silver coinage the title of the king should be simply WILLIAM, IIII. KING, and that on the reverse should be engraved the denomination of value on English and Persian only.

## Madras

In June 1835, it was resolved by the Governor-General to abolish the Madras mint in conformity to the orders of the Court of Directors, and the Madras government was desired to forwarding to Calcutta or Bombay such parts of the mint machinery as, if publicly sold, might be employed on fabricating coins.

## Sagar

In September of the same year, it was resolved that the Sagar Mint should be abolished, as it was no longer considered necessary for supplying coin of the new legal currency with reference to the capability of the Calcutta and Bombay mints for the whole coinage of India.

## Bengal

In October the Calcutta Mint Committee submitted specimens of a device which they thought suitable for the copper coinage of Bengal, i.e. on the obverse the Company's Arms as on the pice of Bombay and Madras enclosed in a wreath, and the title of the Hon'ble Company on the margin in correspondence with the device of the new rupee. This device was adopted.

## General

A letter from the government, dated 25 November 1835, states that

under the circumstances represented, from which it appears that it would lead to considerable further delay to prepare and execute a new device for the gold coin proposed to be issued (with the name of the coin in English within a wreath instead of the lion) whereas the coinage of double mohurs can be immediately, commenced if the die cut with the device according to the design of Flaxman be adopted, the Governor-General has been induced to waive his objection to the representation of an animal upon the gold coin of India, and to approve the adoption of this device.

The details of the now coinage were finally laid down by Acts XVII and XXII 1835.

## Notes

1. Madras Government Press, 1890.
2. *Catalogue of Coins of the Moghul Emperors*, 1891.
3. Previous to the time of Farrukhsiyar all rupees coined under the reigning king were considered as *siccas*, and passed at their original value during his life. At the accession of a new king, the rupees of the former reign were subject to a *batta* and were not received into the royal treasury.
4. Regulation V, 1821, refers to 'Ghurshahee or Tirsoolee rupees'.
5. *Salagrama* stones are fossil ammonites, which, as worshipped by the Hindus, are commonly perforated by holes behoved to have been made by Vishnu.
6. I have, for convenience, adopted a uniform spelling of the names, of places, e.g. Bihar and Murshidabad instead of Behar and Moorshedabad.
7. See Prinsep, *Indian Antiquities*, and Thurston, *History of the Coinage of the East India Company*.
8. The existing piece was known as the Calcutta, or Prinsep's pice.
9. The above is quoted from the text of the Regulation. Mr. Rodgers (*JASB*, vol. LVII, part I for 1888) gives a slightly different version. – Ed.

10. Letter to the king on the coins of the realm.
11. The five *fanam* pieces are now very scarce. Double and single *fanams* are fairly common. The three *fanam* pieces I have never seen, and have met with no other reference to them. I am inclined to think that the mention of them is a mistake.
11. It was probably 1810, as it refers to 'From and after the first day of 1811'.
12. Reg. VII, 1833. See Thurston, op. cit.

# *BENGAL*

# 7

# The Changing Monetary Systems in Bengal during British Rule

D.B. Mitra

To the English after 1757 the currency situation in Bengal appeared most chaotic and confused. When the British arrived in India, they encountered a variety of currencies in this country. More than a thousand kinds[1] of gold and silver coins with different standards of weight and fineness were in circulation. Within Bengal there were mints in Calcutta and Dacca, Patna and Murshidabad but the coins struck at these hunts did not exchange at the same value. The *sicca* rupees became sonauts every third year and became subject to a *batta*, though the intrinsic value remained the same as before. Since the rupee which were struck during the regimes of the previous Mughal emperors were still in circulation and each rupee differed from the other in respect of weight and fineness, Bengal easily became the shroffs' paradise. 'For a trading organisation like the East India Company that was constantly transhipping money and goods from one part of India to another and was in the position of having to make very large disbursements in local currencies', observes K.N. Chaudhuri, 'the multiplicity of rupees and other coins had very serious implications. Unless, a procedure for standardisation was found, its accounts and trade were likely to be in a permanent state of confusion'.[2] The British administrators beginning with Clive took a number of measures to solve the problem once for all. The most serious problem that Clive had to face immediately after 1757 was acute scarcity of silver rupees which was the Common medium of exchange. There were several reasons to account for this scarcity.

## Causes of Declining Money Supply

The most important cause of the declining money supply in the market was the cessation of the import of bullion, chiefly silver, from England after 1757. It has been estimated that during the period from 1708 to 1756, the English Company had imported into Bengal bullion worth £ 64,06,023.[3] But the import of gold and silver was altogether stopped after 1757. The English East India Company no longer felt it necessary to import bullion to finance its 'investment' after 1757. Immediately after 1757, the Company acquired a great fortune in the form of presents and compensations for the losses suffered by them. But the chief reason why they did not have to import bullion any more was the grant of Diwani in 1765 which brought the Company a huge surplus of territorial revenue which could be utilized for their 'investment'. The stoppage of this annual inflow of specie adversely affected the total volume of money in circulation in Bengal.

Shortage of money supply was also due to the stoppage of the import of bullion by other foreign traders, European as well as Asian.[4] Since, the Dutch and the French could tap the wealth of the English Company's servants by remitting their illicit fortunes against bills of exchange paid in Europe, they too ceased to import bullion into Bengal. In the ten years previous to 1767 the import of bullion into Bengal averaged 90 to 100 lakh a year. This included 36 to 40 lakh by the Dutch, who were the greatest importer's of silver, some 12 to 14 lakh by the English and some small amount each by the Danes, Austrians and Prussians. All this had practically ceased.[5]

Another factor contributing to the low supply of money was the decline in Bengal's trade with Persia and the Red Sea area after Plassey. The reasons were primarily political disorder in those regions and the loss of bullion for Bengal from this source alone was worth about £ 50,000 to 2,50,000 per year.[6]

## Increasing Demand for Money

The shortage of currency led to an increasing pressure on the available money supply. There took place a phenomenal increase in the English Company's Investment' after 1767. The invoice amount of the English Company's investment from Bengal in 1766 was £ 4,37,511. In 1767, it rose to £ 5,65,461.[7] Thereafter investment rose steadily though the rate of increase was not uniform. There was a sharp rise from 1777 when the total exports amounted to £ 10,82,233. The upward trend was maintained and in 1780 it reached the figure of £ 12,54,958.[8] The consequences of the increase of investment without any corresponding increase in the import of bullion from England on the monetary life of the Presidency were fully realised by the Governor and Council and they repeatedly drew the attention of the Directors[9] to this problem with little result. Commenting on the evil consequences, Verelst wrote

> now the whole amount of the Lands is swallowed up in one Gulph, your treasury, nor does any part of it return into the circulation, except the sum issued for our Investment, so that there ensues an annual loss to the currency equal to the difference between the aggregate of the investments and disbursements and the total of the Revenues. This, if continued, must in time draw in all the specie.[10]

Another constraint on the resources of Bengal was that in the late eighteenth century bullion had to be sent annually from Bengal to China. The East India Company was in need of funds at Canton to balance the tea trade between China and England. The trade between India and China was carried on in the form of British 'Country trade'. After some abortive atternpts to take part in this trade, the East India Company decided to leave it to the private merchants both Indian and British who were to conduct it under licence from the company. This has been described by Michael Greenberg as a 'chink in the wall of monopoly'.[11] The growth of a triangular trade between India, China and England necessitated the export of a huge amount of silver from Bengal to China. Verelst calculated that in the five years following the grant of the Diwani, the sums exported in silver from Bengal to China amounted to 12,84,008 Sterling and the practice of sending silver from Bengal to China had commenced as far back as the year 1757 and continued, without remission to the year 1770.[12] By 1773, it was decided that money remitted to Canton must largely be provided by private individuals and a number of scheme were devised. In 1776, the Council gave bills on London for £ 105,129 in exchange for bullion subscribed by individuals in Calcutta for shipment to Canton.[13] In 1781, the Company sent two ships from Calcutta to Canton loaded with opium which had been bought with money advanced by individuals in return for bills on London worth £ 2,00,000.[14] Though the sale of opium was officially forbidden by the government in China, the clandestine traffic in Bengal opium continued. It was sold without much difficulty at Macao and Canton. The men responsible for bringing money from Calcutta to Canton were the Calcutta shipowners. Individuals who wanted to remit their fortunes to London via Canton lent money on respondentia to a shipowner who used it to buy a cargo for China. When the cargo was sold, its proceeds were offered to the company's agents at Canton in exchange for bill in London Between 1770 and 1783, bills worth £ 30,00,000 were issued at Canton for money received from India.[15]

The council in Calcutta had on an earlier occasion drawn the attention of the Court of Directors to the adverse effects of such remittances of specie but the directors ordered the president and Council to provide in concert with the other presidencies at least 24 lakh of rupees annually for the China investment adding 'we positively direct that you do not under any pretence whatsoever omit to supply them with that sum'.[16] Thus the large exports of silver to China which brought no imports in exchange became a great burden on the currency of Bengal.[17]

A large sum of money had to be sent annually from Bengal to the other presidencies and settlements. It has been calculated that between 1761 and 1771, Bengal remitted to other settlements in India, a net amount of £ 23,58,298.[18] About £ 1,00,000 a year was regularly sent out to China and £ 1,60,000 a year on an average to Bombay.[19] Madras required an almost constant supply of specie from Bengal to the amount of 20 lakh per year to provide for its investments as well as to meet the costs of wars. The council wrote 'The great demands which have been made on this Presidency for supplies of money have reduced the Treasury to a very low state.'[20] But still these presidencies and settlements had to be given with financial assistance and the Court replied 'You must continue to supply our other presidencies with such sums as they may apply to you for, to answer their various demands.'[21] This became a systematic feature in Bengal's monetary life. Verelst calculated that from the reduction of Chandernager in 1757 to 1766 (the year of the adoption of gold coinage), Bengal had lost by deficiency in the usual imports of bullion and the exportation of silver more than eight millions sterling.[22]

In the same context, one should take into account the immense treasure in specie and jewels which Mir Kasim carried off from Bengal amounting, according to the 'fairest calculations' of Verelst, to five crore of rupees.[23] Besides, the tribute of six lakh of rupees paid to Shah Alam passed out of Bengal every year and no return was ever received in exchange. The disbursements for the Third Brigade stationed at Allahabad required more than 20 lakh[24] per year. The expenditure incurred on this item rose sharply and for the years from 1766 to 1768 it was actually found to be more than 80 lakh of rupees.

## Effects of the Export of Bullion on the General Economy

How the massive export of bullion affected the general economy of Bengal is a question worth examining. The impact of such a large outflow of bullion has not been correctly understood. It has been argued that every year, tribute to the Delhi Emperor had to be sent and this amounted to at least 1¼ million sterling. After this despatch of tribute, there hardly remained any currency in Bengal with which to carry on trade and commerce.[25] Hence, the annual export of bullion was there even before the English came and so far as Bengal was concerned, the despatch of tribute to Delhi and the sending out of bullion to China or to other presidencies made very little difference. There is some truth in this argument but what is more important is to ascertain whether the excess of exports over imports to England consisted of commodities or species. Actually the drain was chiefly in goods, for 'to send silver into Europe would be to, send it from the best to the worst market'. Some remittances were made in diamonds. In a recently published book,

P.J. Marshall has shown that the transfer of fortunes to Britain has only *indirectly* contributed to the shortage of species. He notes that only a minute part of the private remittance produced a *physical transfer of specie* out of Bengal. The great bulk of remittances were made by bills of exchange for money advanced in Bengal. Thus the transfer of fortunes to Britain 'certainly contributed *indirectly* to the shortage of specie about which there were so many complaints in Bengal from the late 1770s, in that British and foreign companies would have been obliged to import more silver with which to pay for their exports, if private British money had not been available in Bengal for bills'.[26]

However, it is beyond doubt that there was severe shortage of silver rupees in Bengal throughout the period. The most crucial factor responsible for the acute scarcity of silver was the cessation of the import of bullion and since Bengal did not possess silver mines; its supply could not be replenished within a given period of time.

## Clive's Remedy

### *Bimetallism of 1766*

Clive tried to solve the problem of scarcity of silver by introducing bimetallism. Taking shortage of silver as a given fact, he wanted to reduce the pressure on it by the adoption of gold coins side by side with silver. The Court of Directors did not see eye to eye with, the Governor[27] and entertained doubts about the chance of success of the new measure but did not straightaway oppose the move.[28] In introducing bimetallism Clive disregarded the common prejudices of the people against any innovation. He was of the opinion that a substantial quantity of gold had been hoarded in the previous regime and that people would be induced to bring gold to the mints for coining. He wanted to go ahead with his plan which was made public in 1766.

The Regulations of 2 June 1766 declared that gold *mohurs* would be struck and this *mohur* would be issued in the sub-divisions of halves, quarters and eighths to facilitate small transactions. The coin would be of the fineness of 20 carats. The weight of the *mohurs* already in circulation was fifteen *annas* weight. The weight of the new *mohurs* was fixed at sixteen *annas*. The proportion between one gold *mohur* and the silver rupee would be at the ratio of 1 : 14 and in all payments gold and silver would be acceptable.

To enforce these regulations, Clive issued strict orders on 30 June 1766 to the effect that if anybody was found trying to disturb the ratio between gold *mohur* and silver fixed by the government, he would be, if a native, punished with the utmost severity. If the offender happened to be a European he would forfeit the Company's protection and be sent back to England forthwith.[29] Refusal to accept the gold coins would be punishable.

## *Effects of the Experiment*

The Council, not being in possession of the requisite amount of bullion to start coining gold *mohurs*, had hoped that these regulations would have the effect of drawing out more gold to the mints for coining. But what happened was the opposite of what had been expected. Although the official rate between gold *mohur* and silver rupees was fixed at 1 : 14, the intrinsic worth of the gold *mohur* of 1766 in terms of silver was a little more than 11½ *sicca* rupees.[30] When in the official rate, the value of the gold *mohur* in relation to silver was raised as high as 14 *sicca* rupees, it exceeded the market rate by 17½ per cent of their value ill silver.[31] Cearly gold was substantially overvalued in terms of silver. One consequence was that silver was withdrawn from circulation and could not be got by fair means in exchange of gold. The fixing of the value of the new coin by the council had made it , 17½ per cent more profitable to make payment in gold but it had only done it by rendering it 17½ per cent less profitable to pay in silver.

The greater part of the silver rupees, then in circulation, the actual figures of which could not be ascertained, was hoarded and melted down because more gold could be obtained for it. Thus hoarding, melting and exporting of silver instead of gold became profitable.

Clive and the other members of his Council could not fully grasp the problem that might arise out of a difference in the official value and the market value of the two metals. The Governor and Council had overvalued gold in the hope that it would bring out in the open hidden hoards of gold. With more people bringing gold to the mints for coining the famine of specie in circulation would be somewhat relieved. But the result was quite different. Through the inexorable operation of the Gresham's law good money (Gold *mohurs*) was driven out by bad money (Silver *sicca*). The doubts expressed by the Court of Directors in their letter of 16 March 1768 were confirmed. They had argued that it was wrong to expect that hidden hoards of gold would be brought into circulation, Granting that there were large hoards of gold in private possession, 'no man would part with his gold but for a consideration and that consideration could be only silver, therefore, the effect was that there was so much silver hoarded up instead of gold, not only the hoardes changes from gold to silver, but all the neighbouring, provinces would undoubtedly pour in their gold for your silver'.[32] The Court of Directors strongly felt that the Governor and Council have been guided by some private individuals and those 'who took the lead in these matters must have secretly bought up large quantities of gold'.[33]

The net result was that there was acute scarcity of silver in circulation so much, so that 'internal traffic ceased'.[34] During 1767-8, the entire population, English as well as native, implored the government to move one way or the other in the matter. The leading European merchants of Calcutta in a petition to Verelst, who became the Governor after Clive, intimated that money could not be procured even at a high premium. They appealed to the Governor to take immediate measures to solve the impasse.[35] They argued that gold is likely to be successful as a coin in Calcutta but not in the whole of the province because in the interior the shroffs would surely play a crucial role in upsetting the ratio fixed by the government. The American mercants doing business in Calcutta wrote to the Governor

The necessity of coin now felt in this capital, amongst the many intolerable evils arising from it, affects every individual to that degree, that the best houses, with magazines full of goods are distressed for daily provisions and that not only a general bankruptcy is to be feared but a real famine in the midst of wealth and plenty.[36]

They suggested 'the immediate recoinage of *mohurs* with all their divisions to one *anna*, sixteen *sicca* value of pure gold' as universal legal tender throughout the province. The English merchants had proposed by way of remedy the prosecution of all who hoarded silver and would not give it in exchange for the gold coins at rates fixed by the government. The sufferings of the people reached a point when they refused to make payment's in a currency that had been depreciated to the extent of 17½ per cent and preferred instead to send it abroad either in exchange for gold or for the purpose of trade. A similar situation occurred in England in the early seventeenth century. The English currency system was one of bimetallism. The ratio between the two metals, gold and silver, had been disturbed by the rapid fall in the value of silver due to its influx from America in large quantities and consequently compared to the ratios established elsewhere gold in England became undervalued in relation to silver. This led to an outflow of gold to other countries, where it could be exchanged for a greater quantity of silver than in England.[37] The only difference was that in England it was gold that was undervalued whereas in Bengal, it was silver which lost in value. In Bengal only a few individuals who had gold in their possession could benefit from the new situation. Hunter observed 'The gains of the fortunate few who held gold had to be paid a thousand fold by the unfortunate many who held silver.'[38] There was confussion all around giving rise to what has been called the 'General Evil'.[39] The trade of the country was interruipted and the merchants 'laboured from the great scarcity of Silver and high price it bore'.[40]

### *Actual Character of the Bimetallic Experiment of 1766*

An analysis of Clive's system shows that it was in fact a form of duometllism rather than bimetallism. It had introduced a double price system – the same commodity might have one price in gold and another in silver and duometallism was most cumbersome.[41] According to theory a duometallic standard with two monetary units and two price systems could really be changed into a bimetallic standard with one monetary unit and only one price system, provided certain requirements were fulfilled. These requirements were first, that both gold and silver coins were legal tender; second, that there existed free coinage for both metals, so that anyone bringing gold or silver bullion to the mint, would receive the same weight in gold or silver coins of the desired denominations and finally, that there existed a fixed legal ratio between gold and silver.[42] Furthermore, for the bimetallic standard to operate properly, it was also necessary that the

> market ratio be equal to the legal ratio or in other words, that the price ratio between gold and silver ingot's or bars in the bullion market be the same as that established by the mint. As long as this requirement is fulfilled, it is indifferent to a debtor whether he effects payment in gold or silver coins, because they have the same value in bullion as in currency. For this reason, both kinds of currency will remain in circulation and one will not have the tendency to drive the other out.[43]

The system introduced by Clive was in flagrant violation of the theory of bimetallism. There were differences between the market value of gold and silver and their official value. In fixing the value of the gold coin, the Council had made it 17.5 per cent more profitable to pay in gold but it had only done it by rendering it 17.5 per cent less profitable to pay it in silver. The experiment of 1766 was thus foredoomed to failure.

Disappointment with the attempted establishment of a gold currency led to a change of policy. The Governor and Council decided to put an end to this experiment and in this they were supported by the mint master.[44] Gold coins were withdrawn from circulation and the establishment for converting gold into coins was abolished. The number of gold coins received into the treasury amounted to 1,20,161 out of a total of 1,28,728.[45] These had to be paid for in silver. Anticipating the payment of land revenue in silver, the Council paid these *mohurs* by interest notes payable at the expiration of twelve months for all sums above and of the value of 1,000 rupees paid into the treasury within the space of fifteen clays after the publication of this resolution.[46] Thus the gold currency of 1766 was abandoned.

The withdrawal of the gold currency did not improve matters at all. On the contrary, it worsened it. Silver became more scarce and became difficult to procure. The Council reported that under the circumstances even the most reputable of their servants found it very hard to obtain silver.[47] The Governor and Council agreed that something had to be done to ease the situation.

At their meeting of 20 March 1769, the Council after considering the petitions of the European and American merchants came to the conclusion that the scarcity of specie was neither accidental and fictitious nor confined to Calcutta alone and that it was bound to increase every year.[48] Beside the continued drain of silver to China and other settlements, only a part of the total revenue necessary for investment and current expenses came back into circulation. The difference between the amount of the revenues and the sum of the investment and disbursements was an annual loss to the currency.[49] The merchants expressed surprise how the country had so long supported itself in this state of affairs.

## Second Experiment of Bimetallism, 1769

After prolonged deliberations, Verelst and his Council decided once again to experiment with bimetallism but this time with greater safeguards than before. Having consulted all the bankers, banians and merchants the council in accordance with their wish adopted the new gold currency in June 1769 on the following basis.[50]

(i) The value of the gold *mohur* would be sixteen *sicca* rupees;

(ii) The *mohur* would weigh 17 *sicca anna's* and would be of the old Delhi standard;

(iii) The *mohur* would be sub-divided into halves, quarters, eighths, sixteenths so that the value of each sixteenth would be one *sicca* rupees;

(iv) Every piece of gold with the equivalent weight of 100

*mohurs* delivered into the mint would be coined into 25 *mohurs*, 36 halves (*adhelis*) 72 quarters (*sikis*) 144 eighths (*yakanis*);

(v) For the prevention of fraud, officers would be appointed to superintend on behalf of the Company as *diwan* to the *subah*, the assay of all gold received in the mints of Patna, Murshidabad and Dacca jointly with the assay masters of the *nizamat*. The gold that was not jointly assayed by the officers of the company and the *nawab* would not be made into coins;

(vi) A small fee equivalent to the actual cost of coinage would be fixed. No other duty would be charged on behalf of the *nizamat*, the company, the Governor or the Mint Master;

(vii) No Mint Master or other official would refuse to receive any gold for coinage or assay. The Assay Master would assay every quantity of gold brought to him or give the proprietor a certificate specifying the assay;

(viii) The new gold coinage would be. issued and received in all public and private disbursements and receipts.

Being wiser by the mistakes of the previous administration. the Governor and Council bought to 'observe equitable proportion between the value of gold and silver which is nearly equal to what it bears in all the countries of the world'. The authorities expected that the following advantages would result from the enforcement of these measures. In the first place, the depleted currency would vastly increase and the small gold coins would gradually take the place of the silver coins. In the second place, large quantities of gold coins would gradually take the place of the silver coins. Third, it was hoped that as the

Proportion of 1⁄16 of sixteen *sicca annas* of gold to one *sicca* rupee was as near as possible to relative value, the new currency would be enforced everywhere notwithstanding any combination or artifice on the part of the shroffs and in the event of the future withdrawal, the company would sustain little financial loss.[51]

But in this experiment too, there was a divergence between the legal ratio and the market ratio of the price of the two metals, gold and silver. In the new ratio, gold was overvalued in terms of silver by about 5.25 per cent. The events of 1766, therefore, repeated themselves in a mitigated form. The phrase 'nearly equal' is a clue to the ultimate failure of this experiment as well. Immediately after the adoption of the second gold coinage people brought out their hoarded gold to the mint for coining and the council believed that they had taken a step in the right direction. Very soon, however, they realized that while the value of the gold *mohurs* had been artificially enhanced by 5.25 per cent, the value of silver rupees was depreciated to an equal degree. The inevitable result was that men withheld silver from circulation on a large scale, and gold coins could not fill the void created thereby trade and commerce gradually came to a halt and before the end of the year 1769 the Council found their treasury empty. They complained that the merchants had deserted their trade and were locking up their fortunes in their treasure sheets.[52]

In a bimetallic system it is difficult to maintain the indentity between the legal and the market ratio for a considerable length of time. It is possible only when the mints use up the bulk of the gold and silver bullion offered on the market. In such a case the mint price (that is the amount of currency supplied by the mints in exchange for a given weight of bullion) tends to dictate the market price and the bimetallic system becomes stable at least for the time being. It is difficult, however, to make the system work smoothy.

If there should be an appreciable change in the production of either one of the two metals, or in the tastes of the public for jewellery and plate, or in the preference of hoards for gold or silver, or in the demand for gold rather than for silver coins, then the market ratio would tend to deviate from the legal ratio.[53]

For example, while silver remains fixed at 1 to 15½, gold might rise to 1 to 16 or drop to 1 to 15. In the first case gold would be worth more as bullion than as coin. Silver being overvalued by the mint, will surely be delivered by the public to be coined. The silver coins thus obtained would be exchanged for gold at the legal ratio of 1 to 15½. This gold would then be resold at a profit in the bullion market, with the result that the gold coins would soon disappear from circulation yielding place to silver coins. In the second case, silver instead of gold is at a premium and is worth more as bullion than as coin. Therefore, silver is likely to be hoarded or exported or sent to the melting pot. Gold coins would remain in circulation but these would be most inconvenient for small transactions. Complaints would be heard about the scarcity of small change. 'Thus the bimetallic standard is bound to become an alternating monometallic standard, swinging from gold to silver and from silver to gold, to the great annoyance of the public.'[54]

To prevent these swings the theory of bimetallism provided two safeguards. One of them was the seignorage. It was to a certain extent a check against the practice of belling coins in circulation for their value as bullion whenever the market price of bullion exceeded the mint price. But seignorage is effective only up to a certain point. The other device to maintain the bimetallic standard was 'to change the legal ratio in accordance with the variations of the market ratio'.[55] But this device is rather clumsy and difficult to use. It involved recoinage either of all the gold or of all the silver in circulation and if fluctuations of the market ratio were frequent and appreciable, 'one recoinage would follow on the heels of another and the currency would always be In a state of flux and confusion'.[56]

Serious difficulties were caused by repeated increases and decreases in the silver content of the real basic coins by the introduction of new real basic coins. If the authorities reduced the weight of silver in the basic coin and imposed a new weaker groat with its divisions and multiples as the basis for the current money of acount,

> they would actually debase the money of account and if the old heavier groats were not. allotted a higher money of account rate – and usually they were not – they become officially undervalued and in accordance with Gresham's Law, they would disappear from circulation into the royal or seignorial mint, which attracted them by a higher silver price so as to recast them into the new weaker coins at a profit.[57]

There was also the possibility that these coins would be drawn off abroad. The men in the street would not bother his head over these subtle difference but the money changers, merchants, dealers in money and not least the authorities could derive advantages from them.[58] The converse situation occurred when the authorities decided to increase the weight of silver in the basic coin and in its multiples and divisions. The money of account, in such a case, would rise in value. The upward adjustment of the current money of account implied a drop in the rate of the gold coins and large silver coins. The old silver basic coins in so far as it was kept in circulation with divisions and multiples, had likewise to be reduced in rate. If the authorities keep the old basic coins in circulation they made a point of reducing them to a rate lower than necessary, the object being to ensure their automatic supersession by the new basic coins.

But resistance to a heavier basic coin and as a result, of a heavier current money of account, was usually strong. Not only did force of habit react in the local economy to such a brusque change in the real basic coin and in the value of the unit of account, but the revaluation aggravated the indebtedness of many of those in a small way of business.[59]

Moreover, the new basic coins would not be immediately available in sufficient quantities and hence a period of toleration of the old circulation often had to be permitted. 'There would ensue a hectic repayment of debts from which only people of substance could profit. Not infrequently such revaluations consequently gave rise to dangerous riots and revolts.'[60]

The experiment of 1769 had overvalued gold in relation to silver be only 5.25 per cent, It was expected that the slighest overvaluation would not affect the relative value of gold and silver seriously. But just the opposite of what was expected had happened. The divergence between the legal ratio and the market ratio of the two metals, gold and silver, introduced a double price system and this experiment also failed like that of 1766. The bimetallic scheme of 1769 was according to Nandalal Chatterjee an improvement on that of 1766 inasmuch as the legal value now fixed was not so far above the market value as in 1766.[61] Yet it is clear that the efforts of the authorities to avoid the errors of the previous scheme proved abortive. There was no doubt that the authorities had not been able to collect the necessary data and hence gold was slightly (5.25 per cent) over-valued in relation to silver and whatever silver there was disappeared from circulation because of this over valuation. 'In short' as N.L. Chatterjee rightly remarks, 'the effects of the old currency reappeared in a less severe form' and 'the well meaning currency reform of Verelst being of a palliative nature failed to deliver the goods.'[62]

In such a situation, the Court of Directors wanted to pursue the traditional policy of having only one specie of rupees current in Bengal.[63] They held that silver *sicca* rupee was to be the only coin and wanted that steps be taken to prevent the annual fall in the price of rupees. To achieve this object the Court of Directors had suggested the reform of the coinage. The president and Council issued regulations in 1771 which provided that the *sicca* rupees coined in the 11th year of Shah Alam's reign would not fall in value but would pass on the same footing as the *siccas* of the present and every future year throughout the provinces and that whenever new *siccas* of any future year should be issued, they should not reduce the *siccas* of the former years as far back as the 11th sun to the state of sonauts but that they would all be considered and pass in payment at the same value as the *siccas* of the current year.[64]

The *sicca* rupee was thus made the only standard coin of the country by which the value of other coins were to be determined and consequently by ridding this standard of its annual; fluctuations, the most essential part of the plan of the court of Directors was implemented.[65] The coins issued earlier than 1770 were liable to *batta* but all subsequent coins were exempted from this hazard and in this way, the council hoped to secure uniformity in the coinage of Bengal. But this was not approved by the Court of Directors and this regulation had to be revoked within a very short time. The Court of Directors argued that their troops suffered financially because, in the money market, *sicca* rupees were worth very little more than sonaut rupees of full weight and can only be passed at their nominal value by means of an arbitrary power which the court was anxious to avoid.[66] Their main argument was that 'the loss upon the revenue's is alarming. The rents are ascertained in *sicca* rupees but the amount of the revenues paid specifically in that coin will be nearly 13 lakh per annum less than if paid in Sonaut rupees.'[67] They desired that any scheme of reform of coinage should take into account the interests of all persons, and that the President and Council be guided by the recommendations made by Sir James Steuart in his book *The Principles of Money Applied to the Present State of the Coin of Bengal.*

The argument of Sir James Steuart was that by this regulation all the coins struck since the 12th year of the reign of Shah Allam would be brought at par with the current *siccas*. 'Would this not mean a raising of the denomination of all the coin and consequently a debasing of the value of the current rupee from $^{100}/_{100}$ to $^{100}/_{116}$?[68] A section of clever people, he argued, would take advantage of this regulation by buying up all depreciated coins at a lower value and again selling these at an advanced value of 3 per cent.[69] Again, after the regulation was known, the 10 sun *siccas* which were to become sonaut would fall in their price 2 per cent upon which they might also be bought up by those in power and by a stroke of hammer be turned *siccas* of the 12 sun. Steuart recommended the revocation of the regulation outright. It has already been pointed out that the regulation of 1771 remained ineffective.

## The Nature of the Problem during Warren Hastings and his Remedial Measures

Thus stabilising the currency was yet unachieved when Warren Hastings took over as Governor-General of Bengal. What appeared to him to be the most important thing was to maintain uniform weight and fineness in the coins struck in the four mints of the province. The second problem was to stop *batta* on the coins. With a view to achieve the first objective, he closed down the mints of Patna and Dacca. The result was that bullion had to be carried to Calcutta and Murshidabad and this involved expenses and also risks. The Murshidabad Mint was also shut down on 30 April 1777. Hastings next tackled the problem of *batta*. The shroffs exacted this *batta* on sonaut coins. Hastings ordered that all coins struck since 1778 would bear the same year, i.e. the 19th regnal year of Shah Alam and hoped that the shroffs would not be able to make out which coins had become sonauts because all these would bear the same year. However, the correct

Hijra date was to be inscribed on the coins and this defeated the very purpose for which it was introduced. The shroffs could easily determine in which year one particular coin was struck and hence they continued to demand *batta* on the coins of the previous years. It is surprising that Hastings missed this simple point and hence the currency picture remained as ever before marked by the continuance of *batta* and the predominant influence of the shroffs in the economic life of the province.

Something had to be done to remove the confusion and the Court of Directors took initiative to tackle the problem. In their letter of 30 March 1774 they wrote 'there is not any object before you which more immediately claims your attention than the state of the coinage and currency of Bengal'.[70] Before embarking upon any concrete steps Hastings sought the opinions of the members of the council whereupon Francis submitted his masterly minute of 13 March 1775.

Francis had read the book of Sir James Steuart and wanted to be wiser from his conclusions. According to Steuart, the main cause of the failure of the two attempts at bimetallism in 1766 and 1769 was the over-valuation of gold in terms of silver. He was of the opinion that 'bimetallism could succeed only if the ratio between gold and silver was frequently adjusted to keep it exactly in proportion to their value as metals'.[71] Steuart held that what was of the greatest importance was that 'the intrinsic worth of this denomination which is the standard unit in all accounts be properly ascertained and preserved invariable'.[72] Verelst sharply contradicted Steuart and pointed out that if by these expressions, he meant that the unit should express a certain quantity of the precious metals and that the denominations of all coins should conform to that unit, according to their intrinsic value, it was sufficient to say that the same thing is effected by giving a certain denomination to a certain quantity of silver as in the *sicca* rupees which was the sole coin legally current in Bengal. But since Steuart had remarked on the supposed variation in the relative value of gold and silver, in which case, Verelst argued, the same denomination of value can no longer express the same quantity of the respective metals as it did before.[73] Further, it was impossible that the unit or money of account should be itself a standard or should have any other significance than to express a certain quantity of current coin.[74]

Keeping all these conflicting arguments and counter-arguments in mind, Francis laid down three broad principles. First, coins should be struck of one metal and that metal should besilver, Second, the difference between the intrinsic value and the face value should be no more than would cover the expense of sound and efficient minting. Finally there should be only one mint.

On these principles, Francis based his concrete proposals. A new rupee was to be struck in Calcutta which would bear the name of Shah Alam, the year and place of coining. The standard of this new rupee would be of the standard of England. It should be of a fixed weight. Ten per cent *batta* on Calcutta rupee would continue until the entire circulating coins had become the coins struck in Calcutta. The coins struck in the 11th and 12th years would continue in circulation at a fixed *batta* for one year after which these coins would be treated as bullion and only bought and sold as merchandise. After one year all receipts and payments would be made in Calcutta rupees. Half and quarter rupees would be struck of a compound mass of silver and copper in such a way that intrinsic value should nearly correspond to the face value. Pice might also be coined of pure copper. Gold *mohurs* might be struck and would pass for 16 silver rupees.

Pending discussions on these proposals of Francis, the first step that Hastings had to take was to re-open the mints of Dacca and Patna. The closing of these mints had caused much hardship to the people especially to those residing at a very considerable distance from Calcutta. The people found it difficult to procure *sicca* rupees coined either in Calcutta or Murshidabad and consequently *sicca* rupees acquired a scarcity value in Bihar and Eastern Bengal. In 1775, the *sicca* rupee at Dacca commanded a premium of as high as 17½ per cent over Arcots which were the established currency of Eastern Bengal.[75] The Board of Trade strongly recommended the opening of the mint's and hoped that it would be of great convenience to all and would enable the people to convert bullion plate or foreign coins into *siccas*.[76] They also pointed out that by the proposed move to use the same stamp on rupees coined at these four mints the shroffs would be prevented from exacting *batta* on the rupees of the several mints.[77]

As a result of the acquisition of 90 lakh of rupees from Shujah-ul-Dowlah and the savings made by the president and council, the financial position of the company improved a great deal and the Court of Directors wanted 'to discharge great part of their debt at interest in Bengal, and to reduce the *batta* on *siccas*. They, therefore, directed that

> for one hundred sonaut rupees paid into the company's treasury, the subscriber shall be entitled to one interest note for one hundred and eleven current rupees and in proportion thereunto for a larger amount and for one hundred Arcot rupees, the subscriber shall be entitled to one interest note for one hundred and eight current rupees and that the *sicca* rupees shall not be received at a higher *batta* than sonaut rupees unless there shall be a difference between the intrinsic value of the *siccas* and sonauts.[76]

Francis criticized this measure on the ground that there was hardly any logic in reducing the value of the *siccas* from 116 to 111 current rupees. It was nothing but a breach of faith on the part of the government and the possessors of the *sicca* rupees would lose 5⁄116 part of their possessions. Second, the land revenue would be paid in depreciated coins and thereby, the company would lose 5⁄116 on the entire collection. Moreover. the favourable balance of trade against the other settlements would be paid in *siccas* and not in other commodities since the *siccas* had been depreciated in value.

By this time, Warren Hastings had considered it necessary to ascertain the opinions of the different councils of revenue and issued a circular letter to each of these. They were asked to offer their opinions on the proposed move to establish *sicca* rupees as the only currency of the province without any *batta* or discount. All the provincial councils agreed and promised their full support to stabilize the *sicca* rupees as the only currency of Bengal. All the councils agreed that it would be beneficial for the people who would not have to pay *batta* on various rupees. The Chief and

Council of Dacca intimated that in Dacca division Arcot rupee was the only currency accepted in payments. No doubt. there would be certain difficulties at least at the initial stage if *sicca* rupee was made the only currency there, but for the sake of convenience of the whole of the presidency, the Dacca council accepted the proposal.

Thus with the strong support of the 'men on the spot', Hastings put forward his proposal for currency reform before the Board. He was fully supported by Barwell. Even Francis mostly accepted his proposals. Clavering was opposed to Hasting's ideas but ultimately gave his conditional assent and all the original proposals were passed with certain amendments by the Council on 29 May 1777. Notice was given that the new regulations would be effective immediately all over the Bengal Presidency.[79]

There was to be only one mint for the purpose of coinage and that would be the mint in Calcutta. Only the *sicca* rupees of the present standard would be struck and gold coins would not be coined after 31 May 1777. As an inducement for the people to bring bullion to the mint the existing duty of 4½ per cent on coinage was abolished. The charges were to be exacted from the owners. To encourage the owners of bullion it was provided that all such bullion as would be tendered to the mint after being assayed would be received into the Company's account. and the value would be immediately paid to the owners from the public treasury on production of the receipt of the mint master for the weight of the bullion received and the certificate of the Assay Master of its value in *sicca* rupees.

These regulations were welcomed by many. The contemporary newspaper *Bengal Gazette* appreciated the intentions of Hastings and commented that except for the money-changers whom it compared with 'sweaters and clippers of coins in Europe', everybody else would be benefited.[80] The striking feature of the currency reform of Hastings was the closing of all the other mints except that of Calcutta. There was to be only one mint at Calcutta. Second, by the regulations, it was stipulated that the new *sicca* rupee would be the only standard coin accepted in use. But how was this to be enforced ? The mere passing of the regulations would not have brought about the desired change. What Hastings should have attempted was the wholesale recoining of all the existing coins into new *siccas* but since this was extremely expensive Hastings was not prepared to take that step. It was improbable that the people, living in the remotest corners of the province would bring the depreciated coins in sufficient quantity to Calcutta for recoining. It was expensive and hazardous to bring specie to Calcutta for recoining from the distant parts of the province. Hence the owners of older coins had no incentive to bring out what they possessed for recoining and continued to use coins struck in previous years with the result that these depreciated coins gained currency in very many districts.

The regulations of Hastings thus could not bring about uniformity in currency. There is plenty of evidence to show that different varieties of coins were in circulation after 1777. At Lakhipur only the Arcot rupees were acceptable to the artisans. The Board of Trade in a letter to the Governor-General and Council expressed its inability to make the people of Lakhipur accept any other coin. One member of the Board of Trade who had lived in Lakhipur for quite some time confirmed that the artisans would not accept anything but the Arcots as it was 'the practice of their forefathers' and this feeling was so general that it would be difficult to overcome it and if the Company's advances were made in *siccas* the Company's 'investment' would become 8 per cent dearer.[81] At Sonamukhi, the Sonaut rupees were in circulation and the Provincial Council of Burdwan informed the Board of Trade in April 1778 that numerous difficulties would arise in case the advances were not made in this particular currency (Sonaut rupees).[82] Charles Bentley, the Commercial Resident of Patna, wrote in 1780 that the Sonaut rupee was the established currency and the saltpetre assames sufferered heavily when paid in Calcutta *sicca* rupees. The circulation of this particular kind of money was strongly opposed by local bankers and shroffs.[83] French Arcot Rupees were accepted in Rangpur and E.E. Pote the Commercial Resident thought that if advances were made in *sicca* rupees, he would suffer great loss because *siccas* could be exchanged for French Arcots at great *batta*.[84] Francis Law from Dacca wrote that he lost heavily in exchanging *sicca* rupees for Arcots and desired that advances should be made in Arcot rupees.[85] For the district of Dinajpore advances had to be made in French Arcot rupees. The collector of Dinajpore informed that if advanced were made in other coins, the Resident would have to exchange it in French Arcot rupees and the *batta* was much higher than the rate fixed by the government. If Rs. 100 was advanced in *sicca* rupees, he would get in exchange only 105 French Arcot rupees though in all the company's dealings, the difference was 9.25 per cent.[86] Thus we find that Warren Hastings failed in his most important object of establishing the *sicca* rupee as the standard coin of the province. Coins of different varieties continued in use and with it the nuisance of *batta*. At times even gold *mohurs* were used to relieve the famine of silver rupees. The Board of Trade in July 1784 admitted that they had not become successful in establishing the *sicca* rupee as the general currency.[85]

The condition of the money market as a whole tended to deteriorate from the closing years of the administration of Warren Hastings. The Maratha and Mysore wars had seriously affected the market and had greatly diminished the total amount of money in circulation in Bengal. Moreover, the depletion of the treasury and the inability of the administration to discharge debt obligations caused a fall in its credit. This state of affairs continued for some years during which the government papers were at great discount. In November 1785, the bonds bore a discount of 24 per cent and few purchasers could be found.[88]

The various steps taken by Macpherson in 1785 to discharge the debt regularly (mainly by the certificate plan) must have raised the government's credit. The plan to transfer Indian debt to England[89] might also have added up to it. In September 1787, the average rates of discount on the Company's papers ranged between 1 and 6 per cent according to the proximity of discharge.[90] Towards 1789, the bonds were selling at a small premium in the market. The money market was very favourable and the only problem that claimed the attention of Cornwallis was that of maintaining a standard between gold *mohurs* and silver rupees.

## The Problem during the Time of Cornwallis

The problem of maintaining a fixed standard between gold *mohurs* and the silver rupees demanded the attention of Cornwallis. The *batta* on gold *mohurs* was steadily rising. John Bebb, the Agent of Santipur, informed that by exchanging 200 gold *mohurs* for *sicca* rupees, he had incurred a loss of Rs. 65-1-6 or 2 to 1/16 per cent.[91] Herbert Harris, the contractor of Khirpai complained that scarcity of silver had become so acute in his area that silver rupees could not be usually procured in exchange for gold *mohurs*. The shroffs demanded 3 to 4 per cent *batta* on gold *mohurs*.[92] Evidently the *batta* on gold *mohurs* rose from 5 *annas* for every one hundred rupees in March 1787 to 3 to 4 rupees in August of the same year. But next year, the *batta* reached a record high. The Resident of Radhanagar reported that silver had become so scarce that a *batta* of one rupee per *mohur* was demanded in his area.[93]

In September 1787, Cornwallis appointed a Committee for investigating the causes of the scarcity of silver coins. The Committee was asked 'to ascertain the cause of the present discount in the exchange of gold *mohurs* into silver and to propose what measures were to be adopted to obviate these in consequence'.

The Committee found that the scarcity of silver was the result of a number of factors. In the years 1785 and 1786 there was acute shortage of silver in Calcutta because the land revenue collected in the different districts had been used up in purchasing commodities for 'investment' and very little was sent in to Calcutta in silver rupees. But the moist important cause, according to the committee, was the reduced import of silver from Europe and the increased exports to the other presidencies and China. The presidencies of Bombay and Madras depended a great deal upon Bengal for necessary funds not having enough resources themselves. Their financial dependence increased as wars became frequent in the last thirty years of the eighteenth century. Not only were the Anglo-Maratha and Anglo-Mysore wars financed from Bengal, but provision had to be made for enhanced military budget in both the presidencies in the few years of uncertain peace intervening between the wars. Silver species had to be sent regularly to China to finance the Company's tea investment. Every year Bengal had to furnish Canton with Rs. 17,97,378, Bencoolen and Penang with CRs. 5,00,000 and Bombay and Madras with twenty-five to thirty lakh each.[94] The Committee also found that the excessively high value of gold coin was the cause of disappearance of silver from circulation.

On the basis of these findings, the Committee recommended that three measures should be adopted by the government. The government should receive all the rupees without any distinction and *batta* and recoin them. These rupees should be subdivided into halves, and quarters. Duty on coinage was to be abolished. One gold *mohur* should pass for 16 silver rupees and the government should punish those trying to disturb this ratio.

The recommendations of the Committee were not immediately given effect to. The *batta* on gold *mohurs* had already doubled itself. The *Calcutta Gazette* remarked: 'The tricks in raising the *batta* on gold called for redress. This extortion, which has prevailed in despite every representation and even the security of the Committee of Enquiry continues to gain ground and is now as high as 6 per cent.'[95] It hoped that the government would take immediate steps to stop the evil otherwise 'trade must sink under the pressure of usury'. The leading merchants of Calcutta, both European and native, complained that their loss on gold *mohurs* had been quite considerable and they suggested that this could be stopped if, in all government payments, particularly in land revenue payments, gold *mohur* was accepted without discrimination for 16 silver rupees. If the cultivator could pay his rents in gold, he would have no objection to accepting gold as the price of his grain. The editor of *Calcutta Gazette* hoped that the high premium on silver which had risen to 7 per cent, would soon decline and disappear ultimately.[96]

Cornwallis was not in a position to decide whether or not to issue orders that land revenue could be accepted in gold *mohurs*. He, therefore, chose to seek the opinion of the members of the Board of Revenue. The members of the Board, however, failed to give an agreed opinion. Some Suggested that the receipt of gold *mohurs* would reduce the *batta* but others thought that gold was too valuable a metal for use in the remote districts. Cornwallis, therefore, postponed the idea for the time being. But to reduce the *batta* on gold *mohurs*, Cornwallis ordered (13 August 1788) that gold *mohurs* would be received for the payment of the bills which were formerly paid in silver and *batta* on *mohurs* paid in respect of government dues was definitely abolished. This measure seemed to have checked the evil at least partially for we find that Gopal Doss, Monohar Doss and other twenty-four leading bankers of the time sent an 'address of thanks' to Cornwallis or reducing the *batta* on *mohurs*.

Cornwallis next stopped the coining of gold *mohurs*. He also reduced the seignorage on the coinage of silver from 4 to 1 per cent. He felt the necessity of readjusting the proportional value of gold and silver coins so as to bring it nearly at par with the market value. The official rate of exchange now became the 15 *sicca* rupees and one Arcot rupee for one gold *mohur* instead of 16 silver rupees as before. Steps were taken to punish those who tried in any way to disturb this proportion and as a matter of fact, some were prosecuted.[97] Cornwallis next ordered the abolition of seignorage of even 1 per cent on silver coinage. But in spite of all these measures it was difficult to get silver in exchange for gold and petitions were sent by individuals to the Superintendent of Police requesting him to compel the shroffs to furnish silver in exchange for gold.[98]

The Third Mysore War (1790-2) caused a heavy drain of silver from Bengal and upset all these plans. The debt of Bengal had stood at CRs. 3,62,00,000 in 1786. The Third Mysore War increased it to CRs. 5,90,54,344 by 31 January 1792.[99] The regularity in the discharge of debt broke down and discount on government papers in the Calcutta money market increased from 10 to 12 per cent.[100] There was acute scarcity of species and the prosecution of the shroffs did not improve matters.

Cornwallis had thus no alternative to reopening the mints and gold was again resorted to as coin but he wanted that there should be free sale of gold and silver coins. A notification was issued on 18 November 1791 to the effect that in future the sale of gold and silver coins would be as free and unrestrained in every respect as the sale of gold and silver bullion and that the gold coin which would be offered for sale in exchange for silver or the silver coin which would be offered for sale in exchange for gold would be considered in effect as bullion and the exchangeable value or price of each would be determined by the course of trade in the same manner as the price of every other commodity that would come into the market.[101] The result was that the fiction of legal ratio was definitely abandoned but even then the *batta* continued though at much reduced rates. Moreover, different kinds of silver rupees were in circulation in the different districts and there was anything but uniformity in coining.

Cornwallis was anxious to establish one uniform currency all over the Presidency. But before taking any step, he wanted to be fully acquainted with the details of the currency situation of the different districts. The Board of Trade was accordingly instructed to ascertain the opinions of the Commercial Residents. They were expected to throw light mainly on two points: (i) whether the numerous artisans would be willing to accept Calcutta *sicca* rupees only in advances and (ii) supposing they were willing, whether the company would sustain any loss.[102]

## The Views of the Commercial Residents

Thomas Herbert Harris, the Resident of Chittagong, replied that many difficulties would arise if the Calcutta *sicca* rupees were circulated to the exclusion of others. The weaver's would be unwilling to accept any new coin.[103] E.E. Pote, from Patna informed that the Calcutta *sicca* rupees were in circulation all over Bihar and hence it would not be difficult to circulate the 19th sun *sicca* rupee in Bihar.[104] The experience of G. Udny, the Commercial Resident of Malda, was very different. He stated categorically that if it was a question of choice, the numerous manufacturers would profer to receive advances in sonaut and Patna rupees. There were eight *aurungs*[105] under the Malda Residency. In the three *aurungs* from where about ⅓ of the total of the Company's investment' was procured, the currency most acceptable was the *sicca* rupees. As the revenue was collected in this specie the weavers preferred to have payment in the *sicca* rupees of the 15 and 19 suns. The 11 and 12 sun *siccas* were also there but since there was a considerable difference between 15, 19, 11 and 12 suns, the weavers wanted advances in 15 and 19 suns. In the six *aurungs* wherefrom the remaining 2/3rds of the Company's 'investment' were procured, the weavers wanted advance's in sonauts and Patna rupees. They customarily paid their revenues in these species. On, the *sicca* rupees, they paid a *batta* of @ Re. 1-9 *annas* per cent. Consequently they suffered considerable loss on the *sicca* rupee. But Udny expressed the hope that if Calcutta *sicca* rupees were made the general currency and *revenue was collected in it,* the inconveniences and losses would gradually be done away with. The company would not lose in any way.[106]

Mr. Fletcher from Santipur was of the opinion that the establishment of one uniform silver coinage of Calcutta throughout the country would be most beneficial to the inhabitants in general provided that the particular species were received in the *revenue collection* without any *batta*. In such circumstances the company would not sustain any loss.[107]

Robert Gosling, Resident of Khirpai, estimated that the Company would incur a loss of one rupee and nine *annas* per cent because this was the difference between the Calcutta *sicca* rupee and the Murshidabad 12 sun *sicca*, the currency acceptable at Khirpai. In the Revenue Department this difference was always charged and unless this difference was allowed, the weavers would suffer.[108]

John Cheap, the Resident of Sonamukhi, expected, that the Calcutta *sicca* rupee would be acceptable to the manufacturers and he saw no reason why the manufacturers would suffer because when the prices were settled in sonauts with a *batta*, an equal reduction to that *batta* would take place in fixing the rates in *siccas*. He thought that a general currency was highly desirable and that it would do away with the system of *batta*. It would be advantageous to the ryots, whose ignorance in regard to the relative value of different types of coins was fully exploited by the Poddars.[109]

Collins, the Resident of Haripal, confirmed that the manufacturers in his residency would be encouraged to accept advances in Calcutta *sicca* rupee. He did not see any reason why the Company would suffer since the revenue of the place was accepted in *sicca* rupees.[110]

Phillip Coales, the Resident of Midnapore, pointed out that there would be no difficulty in making the Calcutta *sicca* rupee the only currency in his district provided the prices of the goods were fixed in the same valuation and no *batta* was charged.[111]

C.R. Crommelin, the Resident of Cossimbazar, informed that in Murshidabad and its dependencies, the *sicca* rupees of 11, 12, 15 and 19 suns were in general circulation. But the case with silk ryots was different. The mulberry leaves were purchased with sonauts and the company's advances were, made in *siccas* but the accounts of the silk investments were maintained in sonauts. As a result, the manufactures suffered @ 2 per cent for *batta*. The rate of *batta* varied very often at the arbitrary will of shroffs and one uniform currency would tend greatly to relieve the poor people in general from the exactions of the shroffs.[112]

J. Lumsden, Resident of Jangipur, thought that the want of uniformity in the coinage had been the chief cause of the fluctuation of exchange between *sicca* and sonaut rupees. The *batta* had become 'a burdensome tax' upon the poorer section of the people. The Shroffs and bankers combined to regulate the exchange in such a way as to promote their own interest at the expense of the community as a whole. He wrote 'were an uniform coinage established, I am inclined to think that it would tend greatly to check this lucrative traffic'. He hoped to persuade the people to accept the Calcutta *sicca* rupees in advances. He was afraid that the principal shroffs would do their utmost to undo any measure that was likely to injure their gains and all possible safeguards ought to be taken to prevent any temporary inconvenience which might result from a combination amongst them. The 11, 12, 15 and 19 sun *siccas* were the most common rupees and *batta* on the first three was very considerable.[113] James Taylor, Resident of Kumarkhali stated that the manufacturers received advances mostly in *sicca* rupees though the sonaut and Arcot rupees were also in demand in certain places. He believed that it would be possible to circulate one specie all over the Residency. The establishment of a uniform currency would simplify accounts, facilitate trade and commerce and do away with all the impositions of the shroffs and money dealers.[114]

Charles Collison, the Resident of Baulea, replied that the *pykars* would readily accept the Calcutta *sicca* rupees and hence the company would not lose.[115]

Richard Brecher, the Resident.of Rumour, informed that the manufacturers would receive the *sicca* rupees in advances. But the Company would have to sustain loss. The Collections were made mostly in the *sicca* rupees and the zamindars did not allow any *batta* on the *sicca* rupees when paid as revenue. The French Arcot rupees were the general currency and advances were made in that specie. The manufacturers could receive *sicca* rupees from the Resident as equivalent to the French Arcot rupees and consequently the *batta* would be the Company's loss.[116]

P. Touchet, Resident of Radhanagar, thought that great benefit would result form the introduction of a uniform currency. The manufacturers received advances in Calcutta *sicca* rupees only. The 12 sun *siccas* were the most acceptable coins and the Farmers and Collectors of revenue took *batta* of half *anna* in the rupee but on the 11, 15 and 19 suns, they demanded a *batta* of 5/4ths of an *anna* in the rupee. Hence, the manufacturers would certainly be glad to receive their advances in rupees not liable to *batta* and there would be no loss on the part of the Company.[115]

Henry Scott, Resident of Lakhipur, stated that if the new circulation was strictly enforced, the whole country would benefit by it and the company's 'investment' would be procured equally cheap and with greater ease. The company would sustain no loss.[118]

John Bebb, the resident of Dacca, welcomed the proposed measure. The currency of Dacca had, over these years, been in a very debased state and as many as 52 varieties of coins of different weights and fineness circulated and the shroffs and Poddars had fully exploited the situation to their advantage. Bebb thought that the shroffs and Poddars were very powerful and they in conjunction with the renters and inferior native officers of the Revenue

Department derived so much benefit from the confused state of the coinage that even the 'Talents of Sir Issac Newton and Mr. Locke' would not be able to counteract their manoeuvres. The establishment of one uniform currency would not succeed unless just and wise regulations were enacted and strictly enforced.[119]

## The 19th Sun Sicca Rupee Made the Only Currency

It appears that all the residents were in favour of establishing one currency for the whole of the Presidency. Though the residents of Chittagong and Malda had spoken of difficulties in the way of the enforcement of a single currency, they too had assured that they would do their utmost to make it a success. On the basis of these recommendations. Cornwallis declared that the 19th sun *sicca* rupee would be the only rupee in the province. To facilitate the recoinage of the different types of rupees he ordered the reopening of the mints of Dacca, Patna and Murshidabad. The Mint of Calcutta was accommodated in a new house with godowns for conducting the business in all its branches.[120] It was also ordered that individuals delivering bullion into the mint would be immediately given the amount of its assay value from the treasury.[121]

The declartion was received with enthusiasm. People brought out their debased currency to be exchanged for the new coins but it was not long before the collectors realized that it was beyond their capacity to supply new coins (19th sun *sicca*) in exchange for the old ones. The mints could not turn out new coins in large quantities. The work was taken up in right earnest and initially a certain quantity of new coins were produced. It was expected that the old coins would be melted and recoined and hence the supply of new coins would remain uninterrupted. But the whole process involved some time. Inefficient management was partly responsible for the failure of the mint to cope with the spurt in the demand for new coins. The collectors had either to refuse to receive local currency or to take it on credit. The treasuries could not supply new coins in exchange for the old ones for lack of adequate supply from the mints. A new difficulty cropped up unexpectedly. The

Commercial Residents had expressed the hope that they would be able to implement the circulation of one currency but in reality they came up against a lot of difficulties. These arose mainly from the stubborn opposition of the shroffs and zamindars. They combined and at least for some time, in certain districts of Bengal, to foil the bid to circulate the new currency in full value. The Residents found themselves helpless in the face of this resistance. In 1791 the entire allotment for 'investment' for Chittagong was sent in *sicca* rupees. It was sent out as late as the month of July of the same year. The Resident was apprehensive that it would be difficult to get the weavers to accept the new rupees. The season was already much advanced and to procure the full quota of 'investment' within the next six months, it would have been better, if the supplies had been sent in Arcot rupees.[122] At Puttahaut the orders of the government that advances would be made in *sicca* rupees produced instant reaction. The Arcot and Duss Massa rupees became dearer. The standard rate of exchange fixed by the government was altogether ignored and a loss of nearly 8 per cent was incurred in exchanging *sicca* rupees for Arcot and Duss Massa rupees. The *sicca* rupees were thus considerably depreciated in value. The Resident thought that it would need time and patience to popularize the new rupee. Yet since 'investment' had to be procured in time and Duss Massa rupees were purchased from the shroffs the loss was unavoidable. In his opinion, circulation of the new rupee could best be effected by inducing the zamindars to accept *sicca* rupees for payment of land revenue.[123] That was a way of reducing difficulties. In Dacca the Poddars and shroffs combined to depreciate the *sicca* rupees considerably. On 1 January 1792, 110½ Hal Challan and 109½ Sabek Challan Arcot rupees could be obtained for 100 *sicca* rupees. On 1 February 1792, the Hal Challan had dropped to 108 and the Sabek to 106½. It fell further in the succeeding months.[124] At Colinda (under Puttahaut factory) there was a sharp fluctuation in *batta* and the government rate could not be enforced. The *sicca* rupees were better than the Duss Massa rupee by 1½ *annas* (each rupee) but the latter became so scarce and dear that the rate of *batta* was upset and the Resident had to advance the *sicca* rupees only at ½ *anna* better than the Duss Massa.[125] The Resident held the view that unless the Arcot and Duss Massa rupees were withdrawn, the *sicca* rupee would not obtain its true value at least in the moffussil areas. The Poddars and zamindars were playing a crucial role in trying to keep these rupees in circulation for their own advantage.[126] The shroffs sometimes stood as security for the zamindars for the payment of revenue. They also used to advance money to them and entered into collusion with the zamindars against the English. In Rangpur, the *sicca* rupees were greatly debased and the value of the French Arcots increased considerably. The circumstances of Rangpur were of a special kind. Rice, oil, sugar and tobacco were exported to other parts of the country in large quantities and a huge amount of *sicca* rupees were imported in exchange. The money market thus became over-stocked with *siccas*. The merchants had not been able to exchange them for French Arcots and because of a glut the *siccas* became less valuable than French arcots.[127] The Resident of Malda informed the Board of Trade that prices of cloths and the rates of cocoons were all settled in sonaut rupees. And when the weavers and *pykars* were paid in the *sicca* rupees, they would exchange them for sonauts at a *batta*. The rate of *batta* at Kaliganj, Singhia, Jaganathpur Swarupganj, Malda and Buddaul was Re 1-9 *anna* per cent and at the Nirchandpur, Jellalpur and Gopinathpur, silk *aurungs*, the rate was Rs. 3-2 *anna* per cent. At the Tanur *aurung*, the rate was Rs. 2-8 *annas* per cent. But the factory rate of *batta* was only Re 1-8 *anna* percent.[128]

But Cornwallis would not retrace his steps. He was determined to go ahead with the measure and he wanted to flood the districts with the new rupees. To look into the delay of the mints in striking new coins Cornwallis appointed Committee in May 1792.

On the basis of the recommendations of this Committee, Cornwallis issued the 13 Regulations for the mints on 24 October 1792.[129] It was ordered that after 10th April 1794, only the 19th Sun *sicca* rupees would be received at the treasuries and issued therefrom. It was provided that for all bullion or old coin of *sicca* standard delivered into the mint, an equal weight of *sicca* rupees be returned to the proprietor without any charge whatsoever. It also provided that the rupees coined at Dacca, Patna and

Murshidabad should be made precisely of the same weight, shape and standard and should bear the same impression as the 19th sun *sicca* rupees coined at Calcutta in order that the rupees struck at the said mints may not be distinguishable from each other and that they may be received and paid indiscriminately in all public and private transactions. The insertion of the Hijra year on the coins was also discontinued.

Another important measure to prevent discount on gold *mohurs* adopted by Cornwallis on the recommendation of the Mint Committee was the imposition of a duty of 2½ per cent on the coinage of gold *mohur*. In fixing the relative value of gold and silver in Bengal in all the previous bimetallic experiments gold was always overvalued and its value in coin was much higher in Bengal than in Fort St. George (Madras) and other parts of India with which Bengal had extensive trade relations. The consequence of this overvaluation was that gold was imported very generally in preference to silver in the payment of balance of trade. It was hoped that the regulation would discourage the importation of gold and encourage that of silver and the scarcity of silver in Bengal would to a certain extent be removed.[130]

The wholesale demonetization of all the silver currencies except that of the 19th sun *sicca* envisaged by the Regulation of 1792 was an important step and had the government taken prompt action, it would have succeeded in establishing the 19th sun *sicca* rupee as the only circulating medium in the whole of the Presidency. But it turned out to be a difficult task. At that time, as many as twenty-seven varieties of coins were in circulation and it was extremely difficult to counteract the manoeuvres of the money-changers who did their best to obstruct these measures. The withdrawal of all the rupees except the 19th sun *siccas* caused a tremendous scarcity of rupees in circulation. Since the government was unable to quickly replace the old rupees with new ones particularly in the distant parts the hardship of the people was very great indeed for the time being. The scarcity was also due to the large exports of silver to the south. The scarcity became so acute and the mints were so slow in turning out new coins in place of the old ones that the final date of demonetization had to be deferred by one year, that is, from 10 April 1794 to 10 April 1795.[131]

## Third Bimetallic Experiment of 1792

To relieve the temporary scarcity of silver rupees, bimetallism was re-introduced in 1792 and it was ordered that gold *mohurs* coined in the Calcutta mint since 20 March 1769 would be a legal tender in all public and private transactions throughout, the country at the rate of sixteen *sicca* rupees for each *mohur* and proportionately for its sub-divisions. The collectors were instructed to notify the proclamation in country language in the cutcherry of every village within the limits of their respective districts.[132] This measure instead of solving the problem tended to create fresh difficulties.

## Difficulties in Popularizing Gold *Mohurs*

It was soon realized that it was difficult to make advances in gold *mohurs* to the numerous artisans engaged in the Company's investment. The weavers of Golagar complained that at the time of purchasing cotton or thread in the local hauts (markets) the gold coins would not be accepted. The Resident could see that the shroffs, *izaradars*, landholders and the monied men had formed a group and controlled the operation of the market and gold could be exchanged for silver rupees only at a *batta*.[133] The Sonamukhi Resident felt that as the *mohurs* were of too great a value to circulate in the villages among the manufacturers, the sub-division's of gold *mohurs* must be sent in adequate numbers.[134] At Malda, the Resident promised to circulate gold *mohurs* but only of the value of rupees four, two and one. He found that *mohurs* worth more than rupees four would not circulate under the circumstances.[135] Mr. Fletcher, the Resident of Santipur, confirmed that since gold would be received in revenue payments, it would equally be acceptable in commercial transactions. Yet he thought that gold coins could not function by themselves. It needed to rely on adequate supply of silver coins. As an example he stated that when the advance would be given for only one piece of cloth or any other article whose price was less than the lowest denomination of the gold coin, it could only be made in silver. And when it exceeded the price but did not exactly correspond with any sub-divisions of the *mohur*, a part was to be advanced in silver. He insisted that at Burron, it would not be possible to make the advances in gold. The price of a considerable portion of the cloths manufactured at Burron was less than four rupees per piece and only few pieces would cost more than seven and none of one gold *mohur* value. He further came to know that silver could in no case be procured in exchange for gold in villages they visited. They had to go to Jessore to procure silver from the Poddars at a considerable *batta*. The loss of time also hampered the progress of their work.[136]

The Radhanagar Agent (Mr. Touchet) also thought that gold *mohur* would not circulate without the assistance of smaller coin in silver.[137]

W. Wilton, the Resident of Khirpai stated that gold *mohurs* were not circulating for want of exchange for silver rupees. There had been acute scarcity of silver all over the area. The cause of this scarcity, he was informed, was that the zamindars were sending silver to Calcutta and making a profit of 2 per cent.[138] Further, the zamindars of his area instead of depositing their collections in the coins actually collected were paying the land revenue wholly in gold. They were exporting silver to Calcutta and a regular trade had developed. The net result was a. serious scarcity of silver rupees.[139]

Dwelling on the scarcity of silver coins at Radhanagar, Mr. Touchet concluded that the Poddars, shroffs were the only people obstructing the free and large scale circulation of the gold currency. If they accepted the gold coins freely he was sure that every person including the Revenue farmers and *gomastas* would receive it without any *batta*. But the actual situation was very different. The Resident thought that it was time the government could make it clear to the money-changers that to make a profit by creating distinctions in the coins was an offence punishable by law. Unless at least some of them were penalized, it would not be possible to remove the distinctions and abolish *batta*.[140] But the Board of Trade replied that they could neither compel the shroffs to exchange silver for gold or any other commodity nor penalize them for not doing it. Such a move would be opposed by them and the faith of the people as a whole in Government would be shaken. The weakness of the government would stand clearly revealed.[141]

As a result of the advances made in gold the weavers of Khirpai suffered to the extent of ten to twelve *annas* on every *mohur*.[142] Besides it resulted in the inordinate delay in the procurement of the company's investment. There was confusion all around.[143]

The Resident of Santipur went a step further and specified the periods when he needed the silver rupees most. It seemed that incertain months of the year it would be well nigh impossible to do transactions in gold coins. Specifically these months were March, April, May and June. He pointed out that because during these months the collection of revenue remained totally suspended in the district and gold coins would not circulate.[144]

It is clear that the bimetallic experiment of 1792 could claim only a limited success. Under this scheme one gold *mohur* was held equivalent to sixteen *sicca* rupees. This was exactly in keeping with the market value of gold and silver as bullion. Harrison argued that here the government erred on the other side and slightly undervalued gold in terms of silver.[145] It is difficult to determine if this was actually so. But the *batta* was going up and in April, 1794 it became as high as 3.35 per cent.[146] At the same time, there was a rise in prices of different commodities.[147] The measures of Cornwallis evidently proved abortive. The real cause this debacle however, was not so much the scarcity of silver as the failure of the administration to bring in new coins in large quantities. The government had ordered the wholesale demonetization of all the silver currencies except the 19th sun *siccas*. This could have been achieved only if the administration had been prompt enough to convert the existing silver coins into standard silver currency. Having failed to do so the administration had no way of avoiding the dislocation in the economic life which was bound to follow. Total demonetization created a void which could not be filled by gold coins. Cornwallis tried to fill this temporary void by his experiment with gold currency but met with little success. The combined opposition of the shroffs and bankers proved to be crucial. They were determined to undo the measure and Cornwallis could not do anything effective to counter the influence of these groups.

## The Nature of the Problem during Shore's Administration

Shore had to face up the legacy of failed experiments with gold coins. It could not be definitely ascertained whether gold in Bengal was overvalued in terms of silver but the disturbing fact was that *batta* on gold coins continued as before. The annual loss of the company on account of *batta* on gold *mohurs* was not less than 5 lakh of rupees per annum.[148] Hence its abolition demanded the urgent attention of Shore. He thought of establishing a single currency for the whole of the province. Of the two metals, gold and silver, it seemed to him that silver would be most convenient currency for a poor province like Bengal. Introduction of silver currency would mean demonetization of all the gold coins in circulation, the total amount of which, according to one modest calculation, would be more than 2 crores and 45 lakh. It was beyond the capacity of treasuries to give in exchange silver rupees for all these gold coins. The immediate adoption of a silver standard was thus out of question. Shore next thought of altering the value of gold and silver in such a proportion that gold would be undervalued in terms of silver. This, he hoped, would discourage the importation of silver into Bengal. He contemplated many other measures without being able to give effect to any of them. The *batta* rose most generally in the months of April, May and June. During these months the payment of land revenue remained nearly suspended and most of the rupees sent out to the interior did not immediately flow back to Calcutta. As a result of its temporary scarcity the silver rupees continued to command a *batta*.

## The Regulation of July 1795

The obviate the difficulty the Governor-General passed regulations with a view to eliminate the distinction between the payments in silver and payments in gold. It was provided that (i) in the Salt and Commercial departments all payments under four rupees and such fractional parts of larger payments as were too small to be made in silver, be made in silver; (ii) That all other payments be made in gold and silver indifferently except in the months of April, May and June when the payments were to be made half in silver and half in gold until the currency of the gold coin was more generally established; (iii) The collectors of revenue were directed to discharge in silver such part of each commercial or salt assignment as the Residents or Agents might state to be requisite for disbursement under four rupees; (iv) That until the currency of gold became more generally established the remaining part of such assignments as were payable in the months of April, May and June be issued half in silver and half in gold; (v) That the remaining parts of all the other assignments were to be issued in silver according to its availability; (vi) All issues of gold in discharge of commercial assignments were to be made in the smallest coins in the collector's treasury.[149]

The Board of Trade was not optimistic about the success of these regulations. Their argument was that in a poor country like Bengal where the necessaries of life were cheap, gold and silver would never pass at the mint rates of the two coins gold and silver. Under the circumstances the same commodity would have one price in gold *mohur* and another price ia silver *sicca* – thus a double price system is likely to emerge.[150]

The fears of the Board of Trade were to a large extent confirmed. For even after the promulgation of the regulations, the *batta* on gold *mohurs* was demanded as before and the measure largely failed. The Commercial Residents kept complaining about the difficulties created by the system of advances in gold by the collectors. The collectors reported that they were not receiving payments of revenue in silver. The scarcity became acute in some places.

The weavers of Golagar complained that as they were not getting silver at all in advances they had to purchase thread in exchange for silver rupees and on each gold *mohur* they lost 8 *annas* as *batta*.[151] They were unwilling to work for the company unless advanced were made in silver rupees.[152]

Michael Atkinson, the Resident of Jangipur informed that *batta* on gold *mohur* was 10 *annas* and 6 pie at Murshidabad on each *mohur* and as high as one rupee at the other place's. The *pykars* were refusing to accept *mohurs*. When only *mohurs* were offered they demanded a higher price for silk to compensate for the loss sustained on the *batta*.[153] The collectors of many districts were not in a position to send silver rupees in sufficient quantity. In 1796 the Haripal Resident did not receive any silver from the collector of Burdwan. Consequently there was a stalemate.[154] The weavers of Haripal refused to receive advances in gold.[155]

The weavers of Midnapore complained that despite the provision of the regulation that advances would be given half in gold and half in silver, they were given more gold. As *batta* was as high as 10 *annas* on each *mohur*, they were losing heavily by doing the Company's work.[156] The Resident of Haripal finding no alternative tried to purchase silver in the open market but to his utter surprise found that silver had nearly disappeared from circulation.[157] The weaver's of Radhanagar in April 1796 declared their intention not to receive advances in gold coins.[158]

The general refusal of the manufacturers to receive gold *mohurs* created a crisis in Company's investment and the Board of Trade was apprehensive that the private merchants would take advantage of this situation. They suggested that the Commercial Residents might be authorized to purchase silver in the open market irrespective of the *batta* charged on it.[159]

The Resident of Sonamukhi in 1796 received the entire amount of the advances to be made to the manufacturers in gold. He was placed in a difficult situation. The weavers had made it clear that they would accept advance only in silver rupees. The Resident was left with no alternative but to purchase silver in exchange for gold *mohurs* at considerable *batta* ranging from Rs. 3-6 as per cent to Rs. 5 per cent.[160] He was afraid that as *batta* on gold *mohur* was going up it was unlikely that silver rupees would be paid to the collector's treasury in sufficient quantity. As a way out he suggested that gold pieces of one and two rupees should be circulated, otherwise the *batta* could not be entirely done away with.[161]

The Radhanagar Resident, too, received the entire amount of

advances of SRs, 58,082-9-2 in 1798 in gold. The Resident reported that it was difficult to get silver rupees in exchange and that the *batta* was 3½ per cent.[162]

At the root of everything was a great scarcity of money. Even by paying the maximum *batta* the Commercial Residents could not get full exchange value of the money they had at their disposal for investment. The private traders also felt the shortage of money. It had become a general complaint.[163] Money could not be borrowed by the public at a rate of 12 per cent interest even with the deposit of Government paper.[164] This state of affairs was aggravated by the drain of specie from Bengal to other parts of India by way of financial assistance and by the increasing remittance of wealth out of the country in investments. The government itself could not borrow at a lower rate than 12 per cent.[165] Government borrowing at this critical moment only served to enhance the complications of public and mercantile credit.

Thus we find that till the close of the eighteenth century, scarcity of silver rupee was acute and *batta* on gold *mohurs* became a regular feature of the entire system and the Residents were asked to enter the charges incurred on the head of *batta* in the regular accounts in conformity with the circular orders dated 8 November 1796.[166] This situation continued well upto 1798 and did not improve at all. The depreciation of public securities took place on an average to the extent of 20 per cent on the 6 per cent papers and 13 per cent on the 8 per cent papers.[167] Hence, a sinking fund was established in Bengal. But still things did not improve appreciably. From 1799, however, there was improvement. In 1799-1800 silver bullion worth SRs. 62,24,718 and SRs. 29,65,797 were imported into Bengal from Europe and America respectively.[168] In the same year, the total imports of gold coin and bullion amounted to about SRs. 117 lakh.[169] But the average annual imports into Bengal during 1795-6 to 1798-9 was valued at only a little over 19 lakh of rupees.[170] Moreover, the imports of bullion on account of private trade between London and Bengal was also considerablc during this period. The total imports in 1797-8 were worth SRs. 3,46,176. In 1798-9 it was SRs. 7,30,209 but in 1799-1800, it went up to SRs. 16,36,405.[171] If we take the perspective of the whole of

India, we find that there was serious fluctuation in the imports of bullion during the period under review. In 1798, the total import of bullion to India on account of the Company amounted to £ 7,19,235 ; in 1799 it was as low as £ 1,21,135 but in 1800, it was as high as £ 6,01,976.[172] It is very difficult to assign any definite reason for fluctuation in the import of bullion at a time when trade was not free. It is also more difficult to make any definite statement as to the impact of bullion import on a money market like that of India where there was no free flow of capital. But this much could be said that the huge imports of bullion had definitely eased the market to a great extent and the *batta* on gold *mohurs* was definitely checked.[173] Though this did not altogether disappear, it no longer weighed so heavily on the merchants and the vexed *batta* which had plagued the economic life for quite a considerable time was greatly reduced, if not absolutely eliminated. The Mint Committee noted with satisfaction that since 1799, the amount of silver rupees in circulation had been increasing and the charging of *batta* on gold had nearly ceased. It was also found that in the payment of the revenues of Bengal, Bihar and Orissa, the quantity of silver money was gradually increasing and the principal part of the currency in circulation in Calcutta and in the lower provinces consisted of silver money.[174] The receipt of increasing quantity of silver money is not difficult to explain. In the fir'st place, stability in the currency had to a great extent been achieved by the close of the eighteenth century. The gold *mohurs* passed equally current with the silver rupees and hence there was no question of its hoarding. Second, from 1800 on the East India Company imported bullion in considerable quantities. The picture was as follows:

| *Year* | *Imports of bullion by the Company* |
|---|---|
| 1800 | £ 2,31,666 |
| 1801 | £ 3,12,736 |
| 1802 | £ 10,05,549 |
| 1803 | £ 5,86,634 |
| 1804 | £ 11,31,219 |
| 1805 | £ 4,99,483[175] |

The import of bullion on account of private trade was also considerable. It has been estimated that between 1802-3 and 1810-11 the total amount of bullion imported on private account was SRs. 52,19,768.[176]

The figures for increasing receipt of silver rupees in revenues were as follows:

Revenue of Bengal, Bihar and Orissa

| *Year* | *Gold* mohurs | *Value in SRs.* | *Silver Rs.* | *Total* |
|---|---|---|---|---|
| 1796-7 | 12,58,211.11 | 2,01,31,387 | 67,73,005 | 2,69,04,392 |
| 1797-8 | 12,22,604.12 | 1,96,61,676 | 70,63,417 | 2,86,25,693 |
| 1798-9 | 11,57,009.3 | 1,85,12,157 | 78,84,345 | 2,63,96,502 |
| 1799-1800 | 11,02,831.6 | 1,76,45,302 | 99,54,440 | 2,75,99,742 |
| 1800-1 | 11,40,763.1 | 1,82,52.209 | 94,07,494 | 2,76,59,703 |
| 1801-2 | 12,09,006.15 | 1,93,44,111 | 89,87,037 | 2,83,31,148 |
| 1802-3 | 10,20,303 | 1,63,24,863 | 1,20,15,873 | 2,83,40,736 |
| 1803-4 | 8,29,290 | 1,32,67,048 | 1,47,66,661 | 2,80,33,709 |
| 1804-5 | 6,34,550 | 1,01,52,808 | 1,76,53,641 | 2,78,06,449 |
| 1805-6 | 4,80,846 | 76,93,546 | 2,08,99,964 | 2,85,93,510 |
| 1806-7 | 2,63,559 | 42,16,944 | 2,41,98,712 | 2,84,15,656 |
| 1807-8 | 1,48,028 | 23,69,667 | 2,52,46,730 | 2,76,15,187 |
| 1808-9 | 1,09,881.8 | 17,58,104 | 2,69,73,589 | 2,87,28,693 |

*Source: Mint Committee Proceedings*, 1807-11, Letters Sent, no. 66.

An analysis of the table reveals that the receipt of gold *mohurs* in land revenue payments distinctly increased in 1799-1800, It increased slightly in 1800-1 but became as high as SRs. 1,93,44,111 in 1801-2 as against SRs. 1,76,45,302 in 1799-1800. But it steadily declined from 1802-3 onwards. It fell as low as SRs. 17,58,104 in 1808-9 as against SRs. 2,31,387 in 1796-7. On the other hand, the receipt of land revenue in 'silver rupees slowly increased in 1797-8, 1798-9, and 1799-1800. It slightly declined in the two following years, viz., 1800-1 and 1801-2 but started increasing again from 1802-3 onwards, and the rate of increase was quite considerable. The maximum was reached in 1808-9 when the total amount was SRs. 2,69,589 against SRs. 67,73,005 in 1796-7.

We have seen that from the days of Clive till the close of the eighteenth century very many attempts on the part of the company to establish a single currency for the whole of the province had failed and varieties of currency existed and were in use. This was particularly true of the outlying districts where one or two types of coins were current and without the'se coins transactions could not be carried on. The Company's government tried hard to eliminate local currencies but failed to do so and at least for the time being had to accept the existing state of affairs as given.

It is interesting to note that in almost every district, a distinct type of currency was required in the markets though all other types of coins were also in demand to a limited extent. The Export Warehouse keeper in reply to the Board of Trade's enquiry in 1775 intimated that the following varieties of rupees were required for providing the company's investment. Sonaut rupees were required for Patna, Sonamukhi and Malda.[177] *Sicca* rupees alone were needed at Cossimbazar, Khirpai, Santipur, Golagar, Cuttara, Chandernagar and Burron. Arcot rupees were required for Dacca, Lakhipur, Chittagong, Baranagar, Calcutta and Haripal while French Arcot rupees were needed for Rungpur. At Midnapore, arcot or *sicca* rupees were the circulating medium.[178] The predominance of one or two types of rupees within a narrow sphere of influence implied the existence of a vast multidue of individual market's with minimum relation between one another. The currency remained immobile and this was partly the result of lack of communication. The currency picture bore near resemblance to that of Europe in the tenth and eleventh centuries. In Europe also there were different types of rupees in almost all the countries and since commerce had declined sharply the diversity of currencies was not an obstacle to the circulation of money. Pirenne remarked: 'In a society in which almost all transactions took place in local markets, men were perfectly content with money which was current only within the frontiers of this or that territory.[179]

## Notes

1. P. Datta, 'Rise of the Calcutta Money Market in Relation to Public Borrowing and Public Credit', in *Calcutta Review,* 1933, p. 172.
2. K.N. Chaudhuri, *The Trading World of Asia etc.,* p. 183.
3. J.C. Sinha, *Economic Annals of Bengal* (London, 1927), p. 54.
4. Letter to Court, 25 September 1769, para 33.
5. Abdul Majed Khan, *The Transition in Bengal,* p. 174.
6. Ibid.
7. K.N. Chaudhuri, *The Cambridge Economic History of India,* vol. II, p. 819.
8. Ibid.
9. Letter to Court, 26 September 1967 and 5 April 1768.
10. Letter to Court 5 April 1769 para 8, *Fort William-India House Correspondence,* vol. V.
11. Michael Greenberg, *British Trade and the Opening of China,* p. 11.
12. Verelst, *A View of the Rise, Progress and the Present Position of the English in Bengal* (London, 1772), p. 85.
13. P.J. Mirshall, *East India Fortunes,* p. 98.
14. Quoted in ibid., p. 98.
15. Ibid., p. 250.
16. Letter from Court, 11 November 1768, para 30, *Fort William-India House Correspondence,* vol. V.
17. Letter to Court, *26* September 1768, para 11.
18. *Fort William-India House Correspondence,* vol. VI, Introduction.
19. Ibid.
20. Letter to Court, 24 March 1768, para 9.
21. Letter from Court, 11 November 1768, para 34.
22. Verelst, op. cit., p. 86.
23. Letter to Court, 5 April 1760, para 7.
24. Letter to Court, 26 September 1768, para 11.
25. Sir James Steuart, *The Principles of Money Applied to the Present State of Coin in Bengal.*
26. P.J. Marshall, *East Indian Fortunes,* pp. 262-3.
27. Letter from Court, 16 March 1768, *Fort William-India House Correspondence,* vol. V, pp. 85-6, paras 58-60.
28. Ibid.
29. Quoted in J.C. Sinha, op. cit., p. 58.
30. Steuart, op. cit., p. 13.
31. Hunter, *Annals of Bengal* (Calcutta, 1865), p. 157.
32. Letter from Court, 11 November 1768, para 57, *Port William-India House Correspondence,* vol. V, pp. 143-4.
33. Ibid.
34. Hunter, op. cit., p. 159.

35. Ibid.
36. Quoted in Hunter, op. cit., p. 159.
37. Lipson, *The Economic History of England,* vol. III, p. 75.
38. Hunter, op. cit., p. 158.
39. Letter to Court, 13 September 1768, para 81, p. 440.
40. Ibid.
41. Lane (ed.), *Enterprise and Secular Change,* p. 238.
42. Ibid.
43. Ibid., pp. 238-9.
44. Letter to Court, 13 September 1768, para 80, p. 440.
45. Letter to Court, 25 September 1768, para 17, p. 472.
46. Letter to Court, 25 September 1768, para 84, pp. 440-1.
47. Letter to Court, 21 November 1768.
48. N.L. Chatterjee, *Verelst's Rule in Bengal,* p. 205.
49. Ibid.
50. Letter to Court, 5 April 1769.
51. Quoted in N.L. Chatterjee, op. cit., p. 207.
52. Quoted in Hunter, op. cit., p. 160.
53. Lane, op. cit., p. 239.
54. Ibid.
55. Ibid.
56. Ibid., p. 241.
57. *The Cambridge Economic History of Europe,* vol. V, p. 291.
58. Ibid.
59. Ibid., pp. 291-2.
60. Ibid., p. 292.
61. Chatterjee, op. cit., p. 209.
62. Ibid.
63. Letter from Court, 20 November 1767, para 125, 11 November 1768.
64. Public Letter to Court, 30 August 1771, para 28, pp. 306-7.
65. Ibid., para 29, p. 307.
66. Letter from Court, 30 March 1774, para 47, p. 68, *Fort William-India House Correspondence,* vol. VII.
67. Letter from Court, 30 March 1774, para 48, p. *69,*
68. Steuart, op. cit., p. 35.
69. Ibid.
70. Letter from Court, 30 March 1774, para 46, p. 68. *Fort William-India House Correspondence,* vol. VII.
71. Steuart, op. cit., p. 10.
72. Ibid. p. 11.
73. Verelst, op. cit., pp. 87-8.
74. Ibid., p. 89.
75. Quoted in J.C. Sinha, op. cit., p. 131.
76. *Proceeding Board of Trade,* 12 May 1775, vol. 3, pt. II.

77. Ibid.
78. Letter from Court, 3 March, 1775, paras 125-32, pp. 113-14. *Port William-India House Correspondence,* vol. VII.
79. *Proceedings Board of Trade,* 24 June 1777, Prog no. 43, vol. II, pt. II.
80. Hicky's *Bengal Gazette,* 13 to 20 May 1780, no. XVII.
81. *Proceedings Board of Trade,* 11 July 1777, Prog no. 47, vol. 12.
82. Ibid., 14 April 1778, Prog no. 27, vol. 15.
83. Ibid., 16 May 1780, Prog no. 29, vol. 23, the letter was dated 6 May 1780.
84. Ibid., 21 January 1783, Prog no. 4, vol. 35.
85. Ibid., 13 May 1783, Prog no. 26, vol. 26.
86. *Dinajpur District Records,* vol. 1, p. 38.
87. *Board of Trade's Minute,* 29 July 1784, Prog no. 35, vol. 44.
88. Referred in P. Datta, 'Rise of the Calcutta Money Market', in *Calcutta Review,* 1933, p. 182.
89. In 1785, a plan was promulgated to transfer India debt to England.
90. *Calcutta Gazette,* 6 September and 20 September, 1787.
91. *Proceedings Board of Trade,* 10 July 1787, Prog no. 66, vol. 58.
92. Ibid., 24 July 1787, Prog no. 70, vol. 58.
93. Ibid., 1 August 1788, Prog no. 80, vol. 70.
94. A. Tripathi, *Trade and Finance in the Bengal Presidency,* p. 5.
95. Seton Karr, *Selections from Calcutta Gazette,* vol. I, p. 252.
96. Ibid., p. 252.
97. Sinha, op. cit., pp. 213-14.
98. Seton Karr, op. cit., vol. II, p. 57.
99. Tripathi, op. cit., p. 5.
100. Referred in P. Datta, op. cit., p. 183.
101. Seton Karr, op. cit., vol. II, p. 57.
102. *Proceedings Board of Trade,* 13 January 1789, Prog no. 4, vol. 75.
103. Ibid., 1 May 1789, Prog no. 10, vol. 79, pt. I.
104. Ibid., Letter dated 4 January 1789.
105. D.B. Mitra, *The Cotton Weavers of Bengal,* p. 155.
106. *Proceedings Board of Trade,* 1 May 1789, Prog no. 10, vol. 79, pt. I.
107. Ibid., Letter dated 2 February 1789.
108. Ibid., 1 May 1789, Prog no. 10, vol. 79, pt. I.
109. Ibid., Letter dated 12 April 1789.
110. Ibid., 1 May 1789, Prog no. 10, vol. 74, pt. I.
111. Ibid., Letter dated 31 January, 1789.
112. Ibid.. Letter dated 3 February 1789.
113. Ibid., 1 May 1789, Prog. no. 10, vol. 79, pt. I.
114. Ibid.
115. Ibid., Letter dated 26 February 1789.
116. Ibid., Letter dated 5 February 1789; *Ananda Ranga Pillai's Dairy,* vol. I contains data of big supply of French Arcot rupees.
117. *Proceedings Board of Trade,* 1 May 1789, Prog no. 10, vol. 79, pt. 1.

118. Ibid., Letters dated 26 January 1789.
119. *Proceedings Board of Trade,* 15 May 1789, Prog no. 43.
120. Letter to Court, 10 August 1791, para 132: *Fort William-India House Correspondence*, vol. XI, p. 417.
121. Ibid., para 135.
122. Ibid., 22 July 1791, Prog no. 49, vol. 93.
123. Ibid., 9 March 1792, Prog no. 18, vol. 97.
124. Ibid., 8 June 1792, Prog no. 20, vol. 98.
125. Ibid., 29 June 1792, Prog no. 45, vol. 98.
126. Ibid., 10 August 1792, Prog no. 56, vol. 99.
127. Ibid., 24 July 1792, Prog no. 5, vol. 99.
128. Ibid., 11th August 1792, Prog no. 56, vol. 99.
129. Details see Seton Karr, op. cit., vol. II, pp. 70-4.
130. *Mini Committee Proceedings,* 31 March 1803 letters sent.
131. Seton Karr, op. cit., vol. II, pp. 156-7.
132. Ibid., 15 August 1793, Prog no. 59, vol. 105
133. Ibid., 15 August 1793, Prog no. 59, vol. 105.
134. Ibid., 7 October 1793, Prog no. 71, vol. 105.
135. Ibid., 12 December 1793, Prog no. 89, vol. 107.
136. Ibid., 2 January 1794, Prog no. 1, vol. 108.
137. Ibid., 20 February 1794, Prog no. 13, vol. 108.
138. Ibid., 27 February 1794, Prog no. 15, vol. 108.
139. Ibid., 21 May 1794, Prog no. 31, vol. 110.
140. Ibid., 27 March 1794, Prog no. 21, vol. 109, para 1.
141. Ibid.
142. Ibid., 8 July 1794, Prog no. 40, vol. 111, pt. 1.
143. Ibid., 12 September 1791, Prog no. 60, vol. 112.
144. Ibid., 13 January 1795, Prog no. 3, vol. 114.
145. Quoted in J.C. Sinha, op. cit.. p. 228.
146. Seton Karr, op. cit., vol. II, p. 381.
147. D.B. Mitra, *Monetary Systems in the Bengal Presidency, 1757-1835*, (Calcutta, 1991), Chapter VII, pp. 220-1.
148. J.C. Sinha, op. cit., p. 234.
149. *Proceedings Board of Trade,* 21 July 1795, Prog no. 44, vol. 117.
150. Ibid., 21 August 1795, Prog no. 53, vol. 117.
151. Ibid., 15 January 1796, Prog no. 4, vol. 120.
152. Ibid., 1 April 1796, Prog no. 15, vol. 121
153. Ibid., 5 April 1796, Prog no. 26, vol. 121
154. Ibid., 8 April 1796, Prog no. 27, vol. 121
155. Ibid., 3 May 1796, Prog no. 34, vol. 122.
156. Ibid., 19 April 1796, Prog no. 30, vol. 121
157. Ibid., 13 May 1796, Prog no. 37, vol. 122.
158. Ibid.
159. *Proceedings Board of Trade,* 10 June 1796, Prog no. 45, vol. 123.

160. Ibid., 17 June 1796, Prog no. 47, vol. 123.

| | | | | | | | | | |
|---|---|---|---|---|---|---|---|---|---|
| SRs. | 7,372 @ | SRs. | 3-6 % | and | the | *batta* | was | SRs. | 248-13-0 |
| " | 2,000 @ | " | 3-9 % | " | " | " | | " | 71-4-0 |
| " | 600 @ | " | 3-8 % | " | " | " | | " | 28-0-0 |
| " | 500 @ | " | 4 % | " | " | " | | " | 20-0-0 |
| " | 7,328 @ | " | 4-8 % | " | " | " | | " | 320-9-6 |
| " | 2,000 @ | " | 5 % | " | " | " | | " | 100-0-0 |
| | | | | | | | | | 788-10-0 |

161. *Proceedings Board of Trade,* 18 October 1796, Prog no. 81, vol. 125.
162. Ibid., 10 April 1798, Prog no. 26 vol. 134, part II.
163. Ibid., 20 December 1796, Prog no. 99, vol. 126, part II.
164. *Minute of Wellesley* (*Financial*), 12 June 1798, quoted in Datta, op. cit., p. 184.
165. Ibid.
166. Ibid., 17 July 1798, Prog no. 55, vol. 137.
167. *Minute of Wellesley* (*Financial*), 12 June 1798.
168. *Parliamentary Papers, House of Commons,* 1833, vol. 23.
169. Ibid.
170. Ibid., no. 390 of 1833.
171. Ibid., 1813, Paper no. 78.
172. Ibid., 181, Paper no. 152.
173. S. Karr, op. cit., vol. III, p. 254.
174. *Mint Committee Proceedings 1807-11*; Letters sent no. 66, Letter from Crisp, Egerton, Davidson dated 28 April 1810.
175. *Parliamentary Papers, House of Commons,* 1813, Paper no. 152.
176. Ibid., 1813, Paper no. 78.
177. *Proceedings Board of Trade,* 12 May 1775, vol. 3, pt. II.
178. Ibid., 12 May 1775, vol. III, pt. II.
179. Henri Pirenne, *Social and Economic History of Medieval Europe* (London, 1936), p. 111.

*SOUTH ASIA*

# 8

# Observations on the Copper Coinage Wanted for the Circars

A. Dalrymple

To
The Honourable The Court of Directors
of the East India Company,
William Devaynes, Esq. Chairman,
Thomas Cheap, Esq. Deputy-Chairman;
Directors,

William Bensley } Esqrs.
Jacob Bosanquet }
Sir John Smith Burges, Bart,
Lionel Darell, Esq,
Hon. William Elphinstone
Walter Ewer }
Thomas Fitzhugh } Esqrs.
Simon Fraser }
John Hunter
Sir Stephen Luinington, Bart
Charles Mills }
Thomas Parry }
Thomas Pattle }
Abram Robarts }
John Roberts }
David Scott }
Nathaniel Smith } Esqrs.
George Tatem }
Robert Thornton }
John Townson }
John Travers }
Stephen Williams }

These observations on the copper-coinage, printed at their desire, are presented by the Company's old and faithful servant,

No. 52, High Street, Mary-le-bone. A. DALRYMPLE
28 March 1794.

## Mem[orandum]

For the conveniency of examining the Calculations, which is necessary to be done, it may be expedient to take notice, that the *ton* being 2240 lb and the *candy* 500 lb.

Copper at £96 per *ton*, will, per Candy, be £21. 8.6¾ or 20,571 farthings

| | | farthings |
|---|---|---|
| *Candy* of Copper | £21.8.6¾ | or 20,571 |
| Coinage of Copper | 12.10.0 | 12,000 |
| *Candy* of Copper coined | 33.18.6¾ | or 32,571 |
| | farthings | |
| The lb of Copper uncoined | 41,142 | |
| The lb of Copper coined | 65, 142 | |

The present *dub* being 1/34 of a lb

| | farthings |
|---|---|
| Copper of 1 *dub* uncoined | 1,2200882352941176170588 |
| Price of 1 *dub* coined | 1, 91594117547058823529411 |

A *Candy* of Copper will be 17,000 *dubs.*

The Madrass *pagoda* at 8s. 4d ¼ lb. or 401 farthings
will be worth of copper coined 6,155782751527432 or
209,29661355193270086876570 *dubs*
1000 to Madrass *pagoda*, each will be worth 0,401. farthings
and weight 1,9009 dwt avoird
2000 to Do. [Madrass *pagoda*] will be worth 0,2005 farthings

## ADVERTISEMENT

Dr. Roxburgh in a letter dated 30 June 1791 observes 'that I might introduce into the *Oriental Repertory* a paper on the current coin in circulation over The Company's Territories, which might be productive of the most solid and lading advantage to the governing and governed,' and after stating the calamities to which the poor were exposed, he says by a statement of the case, You may be able to correct the evil', and emphatically concludes 'by which you will certainly go to Heaven, if the prayers of the poor avail, and I may get a step nearer paradise'.

Whatever my inclination might have been to remove the calamities, to which the inhabitants of the *Circars* were exposed, I did not feel myself qualified to do justice to the subject; although in the Introduction to the 3d Number of the *Oriental Repertory,* I referred it to the consideration of those who had the management of the Company's affairs.

An accident brought the subject again under confederation; my observations being well received, by the Court of Directors of the East India Company, induced me to examine the matter more minutely, the result of that examination, and what occurred to me in the course of it, I laid before them, and recommended to them to get it printed, and distributed to those who were likely to give them further information, they accordingly desired me to print it.

In the following observations I have adopted Sir James Steuart's distinction of *money, coin* and *bullion; money* being that in *account,* whether *imaginary,* as £ sterling, Current Rupee, etc. or *real,* as *current pagoda,* etc. *coin* the *actual coin* in circulation, *bullion* the *metals* considered as a Commodity: though *bullion* is confined to *gold* and *silver; copper* is never so named.

## Copper Coinage for the Circars

In the *Circars,* at least those under *Masulapatam,* to which, chiefly, the following observations refer, the *current coins* are, the Madrass, or *three Swamy pagoda* of gold, and copper *dubs,* and half *dubs:* The value of the copper coin is always fluctuating; formerly the exchange was about 192 *dubs* for a Madrass *pagoda;* and this continues the rate in the Company's books; but it is stated to have been of late so much as 330 to 360 *dubs* for the Madrass *pagoda,* Dr. Roxburgh, 8 December 1791 says 'it fluctuates from 280 to 360 *dubs* for the Madrass *pagoda,* and frequently alters 24 *dubs* in the course of one day'.

It appears that, by a regulation in 1791, the currency was proposed to be 12 *fanams* to the *rupee,* of which 4 are reckoned to the Madrass *pagoda;* without regulating the number of *dubs* in the *fanam,* which, according to the exchange of that time, would have been 7 *dubs to* the *fanam,* the exchange then being 84 to the *rupee,* or 336 to the Madrass *pagoda.*

A *fanam* in those *Circars,* being only an *ideal* Money, not a *real coin* and the rupee not the proper, or necessary, currency; this Regulation seems to tend only to the introduction of greater perplexity than ever, by a multiplication of exchanges: Whereas the matter is perfectly clear, if no intermediate money or coin, real or imaginary, is introduced between the gold and the copper: and the only point to settle is, what number of the copper-coin, is to be reckoned equivalent to the gold. This must be determined by the price of copper, and expence of coinage.

'The Revenues are collected in Madrass *pagodas,* or rupees, at 4 to the Madrass *pagoda.*'[1]

The rupee cannot, however, be considered as an actual currency, since they make no difference what kind of *rupee* it is, notwithstanding their different values: under such circumstances, if it was considered really as a currency, none but the very worst would be introduced.[2]

The various sorts of grain, which yield the revenue, is sold by the farmer to the retailer at so many measures rupee or *pagoda;* The retailer fells it in small quantities to the labouring people, who are the great consumers, and it rarely happens, they can buy more than barely sufficient for one day's subsistence; this quantity is paid for in *dubs,* for he receives the hire of his day's labour in that coin, and whatever be the exchange the poor man's wages is never encreased; it may be the same at this day (5 to 6 *dubs*) as it was one thousand years ago, and what makes the matter worse for the labourer, is, that the price of provisions has been gradually on the rise for these 10 years past, exclusive of bad Seasons; in 1781 the common price of a *garce* of *rice,* which in this country [about Samul Cotah] is only half a Madrass-Garce,[3] was about 20 Madrass *pagodas,* or 80 *Rupees,* the same quantity of the same *rice* has gradually rose to 25 Madrass *pagodas,* or 100 *Rupees.*[4]

By the foregoing account of the copper coin, it is obvious that the weavers, and labourers of every kind, must receive the *dubs,* at a different and disadvantageous exchange, from that, at which they are obliged to purchase the necessaries of life: and the extraordinary fluctuation in the exchange, of 24 *dubs* in the course of a day, is equivalent to four days labour. To what a calamitous distress must such a fluctuation reduce the poor labourer, who earns his living from day-to-day: even at the most favourable Currency of there times, he does not receive much more than an equivalent, to one half of his former wages, although the price of rice has risen from 20 to 25. Besides 'their miseries are added to, by being only able to find labour for about six months of the twelve, for whenever the crop is cut, the labourer is dismissed to find an existence, as he can, for himfelf, his wife, and probably a numerous family of small children; for notwithstanding their poverty, they are prolific.'[5]

The necessity of some measure for the relief of the industrious inhabitants of the *Circars,* whom the late dreadful famine has spared, must be very obvious; but in matters where so much is at stake, there requires a serious attention to all possible consequences.

If the labourer's wages were doubled, the manufacture would be greatly increased in price; perhaps, to the total loss of the trade, by the manufacture becoming too dear for sale: and consequently the poor be thrown out of all work; and, if this did not happen to its worst extent, the manufacturer would scarcely be in a better condition than he formerly was, at the exchange of 192 *dubs* to the Madrass *pagoda,* comparatively with the present exchange of 360 *dubs* to the Madrass *pagoda.*

Affixing an excessive value on a current coin, above the intrinsic value, is attended with two evils; it debases the credit of the coin in currency, and encourages counterfeits: but by making the current and intrinsic values, nearly alike, those evils are avoided.

Not to mention the revenue, arising from an undue proportion between the current and intrinsic value, which originated in times, and under circumstances, when it was not known, that the prosperity of the people is the only inexhaustible source of revenue to the state. The only objection, to uniformity of current and intrinsic value, is, from the apprehention that the coin would be melted down for common use; but were this to happen in the present instance, it would promote the sale of one of our national staples.

But it is not likely to happen, because the expence of coinage being added to the price of the copper, there is no reason to suspect a destruction of the coin, so as to occasion any want for circulation, as that coin, unmelted down, would buy more copper from the Company's warehouse, than it would yield in the melting-pot.

Although these general positions are certain, they gain considerable additional weight, from local circumstances. The expense of coinage in England is stated to be five times greater than the expense of coinage in the Circars: At Vizagapatam, the expense of coinage according to the different kinds of copper, is from 16 to 25 rupees candy, which, taking the rupee at 2s. is £1.12.0 to £2.10.0 *candy*,[6] instead of £12.10.0 the expense of coinage in England.[7] This will operate against the currency, even if the coin is not rated at a high value: It is also stated that the Dutch copper, i.e. the Japan copper, brought by the Dutch, is so much finer than the English copper, that the *dubs* they coin at Bimlapatam, and Jaggernaikporam, to the amount of 10,000 *pagodas* worth annually,[8] are more in estimation, though lighter, than the English *dubs;* and consequently if a high rate is affixed to our new coinage, the Dutch *dub,* which has the same stamp as the English *dub* now in circulation, will totally supplant them, not only in circulation through the *Circars,* but in the Inland-trade.

It is stated that much of *our copper* is coined in the *Circars,* not for circulation there, but to be carried inland, on purpose to evade the duties, to which copper, as a commodity, would be liable, by passing it in the quality of coin, which pays no inland-duty. How far this evasion is warrantable, or politick, is not for me to say.

One very material circumstance to be considered is the necessity of a small copper-coin, because *cowries* not being in circulation, in any part of the *Circars* (except the Ganjam district) as they are in Bengal, unless there is a small copper-coinage the labourer cannot buy a single leaf of tobacco, of betle, a little salt, or other small comfort, but must purchase more than his immediate necessities require, or go without.

The advantage of a small copper coin in India is very great. In a country where the price of labour is 4d day, coins of one-third of a farthing are as necessary as half-pence are in England.

Of all countries, that I know, China seems to have brought the matter of currency to the greatest perfection, as there is no other coin than copper, or rather a base metal, unapplicable to any common use; these, called *cashes,* are, in count, 1,000 to a *tale,* or 3,000 to a £ sterling, whereas we have only 960 farthings in a £ sterling, so that our smallest copper-coin is more than three times greater than their common coin; but they had in the reign of *Kanghi,* even a smaller coin, than this viz., a half cash. It is alleged, and I have no doubt truely, that the *cashes* never in reality pass for 1,000 to the *tale,* but from 800 to 880: the general observation is not much affected, whether the Chinese *cashes* be a little more, or a little less, than three to four farthing; the exchange however is in favour of the Poor, as 800 to 880 would purchase a tale's worth of syzee, or pure, silver in which the emperor's duties are paid; whereas if 1,000 were current for a *tale,* be must give 1,000, for what he now purchases for 800 or 880, according to the fluctuation of exchange; which, I suspect, has arisen, from the great quantity of silver, that has been carried into China, by the European trade.

The great advantage of decimal numeration is well known to the Chinese, and it appears that making the copper-coin to be decimals of the gold, would tend very much to restrain the tricks of the money-changers, and facilitate the currency: which, however, will, at first, meet with obstruction, whatever be the form and value; but if ten of the smallest denomination be made one of the second, ten of the second one of the third, and ten of the third one Madrass *pagoda,* that is, 1,000 of the smallest denomination to a Madrass *pagoda,* a little time, by the facility of account, will overcome prejudice or artifice: The smallest denomination should not be reduced to a very diminutive size, but be thin, perhaps it would be most expedient or rather a little less.

The Chinese very sensibly make fine silver their ultimate standard: because fine Silver being a fixed thing, can never *intrinsically* alter; although the exchange may alter, by the influx of a great and unexpected quantity: it seems good policy in the Emperor to hoard the silver, which comes in from the duties the adoption of the dollar, as a voluntary Currency, in those parts of China connected with Europeans, seems an evil militating against their first principles of currency, and the trick of chopping the dollar, or plugging it with lead, or base metal, seems a happy counteraction to the abuse, as it restrains the circulation of the dollar and maintains the credit of syzee silver.

Gold being the natural produce of China, it must consequently fluctuate, according to the quantity dug out of the mines; and the demand for illicit exportation; for the Chinese, contrary to the maxims of other nations, prohibit the exportation of all metals, wrought or unwrought, that are produced in their own country, but allow the free egress of silver, which that country does not produce. Sometimes the exchange favours the importation of gold into China.

In India, there being no mines, either of gold or silver; there is no internal objection, or preference, to the one or the other: but gold is the most eligible standard, as the fluctuation on it is less, relatively to the whole, than upon silver, and it appears to me, that the greater the disproportion in value, between two metals in circulation, the less will be the fluctuation.

Whatever coinage be adopted, It will be expedient to have a stock of coin, more than the circulation could possible require; to prevent the effect of any attempt, by the money-changers, to stop the currency, by buying up what is at first distributed.

The Madrass *pagoda,* though coined in the East India Company's mint at Madrass, is not current there; the coin, current there, is the Star, or *current, pagoda,* coined also in the same mint.

Madrass, at least, is an exception to the position of those who have written on *coin,* 'that in every Country there is a nominal money without a correspondent coin'. It is true the £ sterling is ideal, as is the current *rupee* of *Bengal*; but at Madrass the accounts are kept in the actual coins, *pagodas* of gold, *fanams* of silver, 36 to the Star *pagoda*[10] and *Cash,* of copper, 80 to the *fanam.* By the papers lately sent from India it seems the *cash* is no longer an actual coin, and the *doodoo,* a *copper coin,* of 20 cash, the rate of which was 4 to the *fanam,* is now altered to 8 to the *fanam*, and 16 half *doodoos* to the *fanam,* when, or by what authority, this change was made, I am ignorant; but it, obviously, must affect the price of provisions to the poor; and perhaps the general disuse of *farthings* in this country, may have had an evil-influence on the necessaries of life.

Since it might be too great an innovation to make pure gold the standard; although, I think, that would be the best way in every country not meaning any imposition in their coin. A perfect knowledge of the subject, of copper coinage for India, requires an exact knowledge of the gold coin, to which it is to bear a relation; I shall therefore endeavour to explain the Madrass gold coins, both such as are for its own currency, and for that of the Circars.

In India the mode of reckoning the value of coin, or bullion, is more simple, and therefore better, than in England; where every thing is compared with the English standard, of 22 carats or 22/44 pure gold and 2/24 alloy in the lb weight troy[11] and the value of bullion, or other coins, is reckoned better or worse than standard, accordingly as there are more or less than 22 parts pure metal in 24; or the whole. In India the comparison is made with the pure metal, which is reckoned 100 *touch.*

The Star *pagoda* weigh $2^{\text{dwts}}$ $4^{\text{gr.}}$ 56/100 and is 80 *touch,* that is, contains 80/100 pure gold and 20/100 alloy; of which alloy ¾ ought to be pure silver, and ¼ copper; to effect this, the gold, delivered into the mint to be coined, should be refined; however this is not the usual custom, but so much pure gold, or, rather, gold finer than 80 *touch*, was added, to make it 80 *touch*, in case the Gold delivered in to be coined was less than 80 *touch;* and if more than 80 *touch,* the persons who sent bullion to be coined, used to reduce it to 80 touch, to send copper only; whereby instead of the alloy being ¾ pure silver, and ¼ copper, it might be all copper; and, consequently, the *pagoda* intrinsically worth less than it should be, by the different value of silver and copper in the alloy.

In 1758, at the time I was under the Assay Master, who had, in that capacity, the superintendance of the mint, very improperly, as the Assay Master ought to be a check on the Mint-Master, which station is always filled by the Governor, Mr. Pybus, then Assay-Master, thought of preventing this abuse; he required that when gold was delivered in, to be coined in the mint, the alloy added to reduce the gold to 80 *touch,* should be ¾ silver and ¼ copper: the consequence was, instead of delivering their *gold* to be coined, when of a higher *touch* than 80, they gave a bit to be ass*ayed:* when they had learnt the exact *touch* from the Assay Master's *Report,* they added, at their own house, the quantity of copper wanting to reduce the gold to 80 *touch,* and then delivered it in, to be coined in the mint: although refining the gold, is the direct way to preserve the exact standard of the coin, to $^{30}/_{100}$ pure gold $^{15}/_{100}$ pure silver and $^{5}/_{100}$ copper: yet refining the gold would be a great obstacle to the coinage in our mints, and encourage people to coin their bullion in other mints. If the Assay-Master was to refine the sample, he could, by finding what proportion of pure gold and of silver there was in it, consequently, know how much of each was requisite to add to the mass, to bring it to the true standard of $^{80}/_{100}$ pure gold $^{15}/_{100}$ pure silver and $^{5}/_{100}$ copper. The addition of pure silver is easily made in India, as the silver coin is there alloyed with lead, which is readily seperated from the silver.

The Madrass *pagoda* is 86¼ *touch* or 86$^{25}/_{100}$ and weighs $2^{dwt}\ 5^{gr}$.

There is an original simplicity in the operations of the Indians; when they have mixed the metals so as to bring the mass to the *touch* required, whilst it is in a state of fusion, in clay-pots (which they prefer, as they reduce them to dust, and by lavigation get the smallest grain of gold, that has been imbibed by, or has adhered to, the pot) they take out the melted gold in small pots, and whilst it is red-hot, just in transition from a fluid to a solid state, they empty the small pot of gold, into the hollow part of an old burst cannon, and then bruise it, by hand, with an iron hammer; this attrition reduces the gold to a powder: such parts, as have cooled in pieces larger than a *pagoda*-weight, are returned into the melting pot; those parts that are in fine powder, or in pieces smaller than a *pagoda*, are laid by, 'till the whole melting is over.

Having prepared cakes of clay, with a multitude of cells, which, according to the best of my recollection, are only made by the pressure of the thumb on the cake, they weigh the powdered gold, and put exactly a *pagoda*-weight into each cell; when the cells are filled, they put the cake into the furnace, 'till the powdered gold is melted into a round knob, or button, flatted on the under side, which buttons are again weighed, and if they are wanting in weight, or have met with any other accidental defect, they are again returned into the melting pot: Those buttons that are found of the true weight, are then coined; by a sledge hammer striking it on an anvil; one side of the coin being marked on the anvil, the other on the hammer; but as I have not seen the coining since 1758, and only speak from memory, I will not be positive how the impression is made: especially as some persons do not think it is given, in the manner I have mentioned, but by striking on a punch.

Both the Star *pagoda*, and the Madrass *pagoda*, appear to be *Hindoo* coins, for the reverse, or flat side, of the former is one *Swamy*, or *Hindoo divinity* of the latter *three swamys:* the arched side of both is *dotted*, but the Star *pagoda* has a *star* in the center of the dotts.

The rupee is a Mahometan [*sic*] coin, with Persian inscriptions notifying the year of the Mogul emperor, in which it was coined, and I believe, the place of coinage: but Arcot rupees were coined at Madrass, as well as Madrass *rupees*, the last weighed 7$^{\text{wds.}}$ 11$^{\text{gr}}$ and was 14½$^{\text{dwt}}$ better than English standard; the *Arcot* weighed 7$^{\text{dws.}}$ 8⅖$^{\text{gr.}}$ and was only 4½$^{\text{dwt.}}$ better than English Standard. These were meant for circulation *in* Mahometan countries, and, therefore, had Mahometan inscriptions; being, in fact, only imitations of Mahometan coins: but it would be very improper, a coin of ours, intended for the circulation of our own territories, should have any thing like a Mahometan inscription, as it might convey an idea, highly improper to be conveyed, of the Company's subjection, in India, to the Mahometan government.

It appears to me, that the Company's coins should have an engraving made on a copper plate, and a written explanation, in all the current languages of their value. If this explanation could be written in England, it might also be engraved on the plate, and the impressions should be affixed, in the manner that public advertisements now are, in the most conspicuous place.

The Company's coin should be received by them, whenever tendered, in payment; for nothing but a full confidence, that they can be changed for the nominal value, can ever give a free currency to coin.

Dr. Roxburgh, whose long residence in the *Circars,* assiduous attention to the distresses of the natives, and distinguished publick spirit, give great force to his opinions, recommends 'the new-coin to have simply the Company's mark on the one side, and the Year they are coined in, on the other'. I cannot however omit observing that the year, unless it be 'year first coined' may contribute to the trick of the money-changers, as it is usual to degrade the coin by every year that it has been coined, without attention to what it has really lost in weight by circulation, which is the only ground for making the old coin pass for less than the new, and which is scarcely deserving consideration in the copper coin, so long as it retains the impression, to prevent base counterfeits.

Although Mr. Boulton is a man of too much honour to take any unfair advantage of the Company, yet, as it is represented that no person could counterfeit the proposed coin, because the apparatus for such a purpose would cost several thousand pounds, it becomes a serious consideration how the coin is to be supplied, to keep up the circulation for the engine may go out of Mr. Boulton's hands into those of men who would make the most of it; and even Mr. Boulton must be paid an extra-price for the coinage, to indemnify him for the expence of the engine. May it not therefore be more expedient and economical for the Company to purchase the engine of Mr. Boulton; in case he should be willing to dispose of it, as it would, probably, in the end be a great saving in the expense of coinage.

The exorbitant rise in the price of copper to £ 114 ton, and the possibility of a still greater rise, as there is no limit, but the will of the copper-combination, or its agent, and the idea entertained of the necessity of the public to purchase: become objects of great consideration, since although Mr. Boulton is willing, at present, to supply the Company at £96 ton, that cannot be expected to extend beyond the present coinage: It occurred to me that there might be an advantage in substituting tin for copper, but this comprehends many points, such as what impression it would receive, the expence of coining it, etc. The fine medal Mr. Boulton made of the late king of France and his family, was a mixed metal, concerning which it may perhaps be worth making enquiry. Although tin is, equally with copper, a national-staple, yet as tin is also the produce of the East Indies. The Company cannot suffer from the inordinate demands of a combination. However, it is thought by some, that tin could not be introduced at all into the *Circars* by way of a current coin, as the natives would think it had no intrinsick value, since they could not convert it into pots, for common use as they can copper. The presjudices of mankind are so potent, that it is always difficult to conjecture to what extent they may go. A friend, on the suggestion concerning tin, proposed that there should be both a copper and a tin coinage: the smallest being tin, which I think a good idea: and the tin may be half the smallest copper.

The administration at Masulapatam, totally disapprove, of a new coinage of copper; their objections are, that the Company might be subject to a loss in calling in the present currency, and because the demand for copper might be lessened, as the merchants carrying on the inland trade, frequently have it coined into *dubs* to save the duties. They allege 'that it is impracticable to fix any standard value between copper coin and those of gold and silver, and that the attempt may exclude gold and silver from circulation altogether, or in a very great degree, either of which (they suppose) would be very detrimental to the Company as well as to the community. They apprehend if the present coin be called in; the Company will be overstocked; or if prohibited, that the individuals, in whose hands it might be, would be under the necessity of offering what they might have on hand, at a low price, which would tend equally to their ruin, and to the exclusion of all copper from the market,' they think it 'very problematical, if it were even practicable to introduce the circulation of the new-coin within the Company's own possessions, whether it could possibly be forced into the currency of the neighbouring countries, dependant on the *subah* particularly, where the present coin passes current; and if it were found to be practicable, this must be attended with disadvantage to the Company, as it would tend very much to prevent the inland demand for our coin, which at present passes duty free, as coming under the description of Money.' This (they say) explains by what means it has happened that so much more copper has been coined, than what is necessary, or could have even been admitted into circulation, within the Company's own possessions. They add 'the consumption of copper in coin cannot be very rapid, but it is much encreased by the great use made by the natives of brass and copper vessels and utensils, and for casting of guns. (They conclude) any circumstance impeding, or preventing, our copper-coin, which is much used for the above purposes, from finding its way inland, must prevent the Company's copper from being so easily disposed of, the greatest part of what is carried inland, being first: coined into *dubs*. And that it might not only be very difficult to introduce a new species of coin instead of the present one, but that it would be attended with disadvantages, and that it is better in all respects to adopt that coin for which there is a demand in the territories of the *subah* and other neighbouring countries.'

They impute 'the decrease of the demand for copper within these last few years, and the diminution of the value of the copper coin, when compared with gold and silver, principally to the large importations by the English, Dutch and Danes, which, if greater than the consumption, will of course overstock the market'; they add 'another circumstance which may have in some measure contributed, many individuals in the *subah's* country formerly had private mints, for the coinage of copper, and used to collect: the old *dubs*, that by long circulation had lost part of their value, to recoin them, by which they gained a profit to themselves, but about the year 1787 the *subah's* minister called all private coiners to a severe account, which is said to have put an end to the practice, and considerably to have lessened the demand of copper-coin to the westward.'

They say 'about 1779 *dubs* sold at the rate of 184 for one Madrass *pagoda*, and are now fallen (in 1789) to 250, notwithstanding which, Individuals still find it convenient to send the greatest part of the copper imported at Masulipatam, to the Company's mint, which is a proof that *dubs* have still an advantage in sale, over copper in any other form'. They further remark that the value of 'copper-coin has always stuctuated on that part of the coast', which they suppose the reason for its never having been received 'in in payment of the Company's revenues, and for government having forbid its being issued to the troops for pay'.

The administration at Masulipatam seem to me, to have misconceived the matter in question, which appears to be, 'The obvious necessity of some measure to establish a permanent currency in the company's territories, to prevent the ruin of the industrious inhabitants who are subject to our government', the sale of copper must be only a secondary consideration: the facts, of the great change in the value of the copper coin, and the great fluctuation in that value, are indisputable.

Admit that the *dubs*, at present in circulation in the *Circars*, are also in circulation, as a current coin, in the *subah's* dominions, which, however, is not mentioned with that detail of circumstances, as to establish it as a fact incontrovertible. This appears to be an argument in behalf of a new-coinage; for the current-coin of the *Circars*, being also current in so extensive and remote a country as the *subah's* dominions, would naturally tend to occasion a great fluctuation in the value, which is of all things the mod distressing to the industrious inhabitant, of the Company's territories; the protection and interest of whom is not only the Company's first duty, but most essential benefit.

If a new-coinage is issued in the *Circars*, for what reason should the Company call in the present coin? It is admitted great part was coined purposely for inland trade; great part coined by the Dutch: so that if a new-coinage supplants it in the *Circars*, the old would find its way inland. At present the Company do not receive it in payment of their revenues, nor issue it in payment of their troops, so that it can by no means be considered as a Company's coin, but by it being in present circulation, and left optional for the present, by that means, the new-coin may quietly be introduced, and when it is introduced, the circulation of the old may be prohibited. By seperating the circulating copper, from the copper wanted as a commodity. The Company will be better enabled uniformly to supply the market. That copper circulation 'would exclude gold and silver altogether, or in a very great degree', is an assertion without proof, but that 'either would be detrimental to the Company, or to the community' appears to me very doubtful. Gold and silver, by natural consequences, slow into those countries which have an extensive commerce, but whether the current-coin be all copper, as in China, or gold, silver and copper as in England, will make little difference in fact; as great commercial dealings will be made in money and not in coin. But where silver is a joint circulation with gold it will always produce a fluctuation, in England we cannot properly call silver a currency, for no sums are paid in silver, which is therefore only a convenient change for the smallest gold coin; or as a token for a large parcel of copper. The wants and interests of the lower class of people which comprehends the labourer and manufacturer, requires the utmost attention to the copper coinage, in which their disbursements must be made, and where a fluctuation in value, actually robs them of part of their labour.

There are no documents, that I have seen to indicate the quantity of copper, imported into the *Circars,* though it is said that it is not fold in any considerable quantity by the Company: nor does it appear what quantity of copper is carried inland annually, from the *Circars;* a few facts would be of more use than long declamatory opinions without facts.

The price of copper, and the value of the coin dependant thereon, come now to be considered.

If the price of copper in India be examined, it seems impossible from the great expence of coinage, in England, to make the coinage for the *Circars,* without very considerably diminishing the value of the copper in coin, below the price of copper uncoined, to bring the copper coined in England nearly to a level with the copper coined in India.

By the *Madrass Price Current,* January 1791, which is the latest to which I can have recourse, it appears Japan copper, and sheet copper were at 65 *star pagodas* per *candy* of 500 lb. Copper in sticks, in imitation of Japan, 60, and copper in slips 60 to 61, and copper in slabs 58 to 54.

| | | |
|---|---|---|
| At the highest rate of 65 Star *pagodas candy*, the price of a *candy* will be . . . | | £ 24. 18. 4 |
| Copper in England at £96 per ton is | £21. 8. 6¾ per *candy* | |
| Coinage . . . | 12. 10. 0 | |
| | | 33. 18. 6¾ |
| | | 9. 0. 2¾ |

Loss on the *candy* coined, or, on 600 *candy*, the quantity wanted for coin, £5406. 17. 6. If the coin in currency is made equivalent to the intrinsick value of the best copper at Madrass: however, as the price of copper, in the drears, is higher than at Madrass. The loss will not be quite fo great; and perhaps the Madrass price of copper may be lower than the average, from the market being glutted and overstocked, in consequence of the inclination of the East India Company, to export national produce to the utmost extent.

This conduct of the East India Company is ill-feconded by the copper-combination, who have, injudiciously, raised the price of copper; a conduct that will endanger the loss of that branch of commerce to this country, by throwing the copper-trade into the hands of the Swedes, Danes and Dutch.

If the currency of the new-coinage of copper be fixed at the old currency of 192 to the Madrass *pagoda*, without any reference to the present price of copper in India. The *dub* weighing 1/34 of a lb. avoirdupoiz, would at the price of £.96 per ton, or £21. 8.6¾ per *candy*

| | |
|---|---|
| Coinage . . . | 12. 10. 0 *each* cost |

1,91594117647058823529117, farthing &c. or for a

| | |
|---|---|
| Madrass *pagoda* | 367,86070588235294117646912 farthings |
| Actual value of a Madrass *pagoda* | 401 |
| | 33,13929611764705882353088 |

or more than 8d¼ per Madrass *pagoda*, nearly 8¼ per cent gain on the copper in currency.

Reckoning the *dub* at 360 to the Madrass *pagoda*, it would in *dubs* coined amount to

| | |
|---|---|
| | 689,7388235294117670587960 farthings |
| Actual value of the Madrass *pagoda* | 401 |
| | 288, 739/1000, or 6 shillings loss, on the |

Madrass *pagoda* of 8^s. 4^d¼, which the industrious poor, now suffer on their small pittance,

At 209 *dubs* to the Madrass *pagoda* there will be only fractional difference of a farthing between the value in currency and cost of copper and coinage, viz.

| | |
|---|---|
| | 400,3210662 farthings |
| Actual value of Madrass *pagoda* | 401 |
| | 0,6789338 farthings |

1000 to the Madrass *pagoda* will be each, farthings 0,401
and weigh 1,9009 dwt. avoirdupoise
2000 Do. 0,2005

## Notes

1. Dr. N.B. Roxburgh. There is no rupee of so little value as the ¼ of a Madrass *pagoda*, Query, is the difference of exchange of the rupee made a perquisite?
2. Mr. Russell says, that in the Circar under Vizagapatam, the rupee and not the *pagoda* is the currency, but that there is no difference made in the kind of rupee, the exchange of all kinds being 370 to 100 Madrass *pagodas*.
3. A *Madrass Garce* contains 300,000 cubic inches and when grain is fold by weight 9256½ are allowed to a garce Madrass *almanac.*
4. Dr. N.B. Roxburgh, Although their daily hire be only 6 *dubs*, which at the exchange of 192 to the Madrass *pagoda*, is about 3d, rice at 35 Madrass *pagodas* grace will be under ¾ lb.
5. Assay Master's Report of copper coins, 16 January 1789.
6. The Charges of Coinage is stated to be lb, the whole *pieces* 4¾, the *half pieces* 5 .... medium 4.62 carriage, casks, etc. estimated at 43/4 lb ... 0.75/5.37 but, as the *pieces* proposed are smaller, taking the expence at 6d lb will not be over-rated.
7. Dr. Roxburgh.
8. Although 56 *fanams* were reckoned to the Star *pagoda* an account, there actually has been above 40 to the Star *pagoda,* for many years past: Credit was given, for the difference in exchange, under the head of *Batta:* A Spirit

of Innovation, without any authority from the East India Company, in May 1791 altered the number of *fanams* in account, from 36 to 45 to the Star *pagoda:* since the relative value is always fluctuating. This alteration was very absurd.

9. The English standard for silver is 11 oz. 2 dwt. silver and 18 dwt. copper alloy.

# 9

# The Substitution of Silver for Gold in the Currency of South India

H. Dodwell

The fact that a gold currency was formerly in use in south India has often been alleged as an argument in favour of the possibility of maintaining a gold currency in India today. However, those, who have quoted this example have in reality had very few facts regarding it at their disposal. I believe it to be the case that the more closely this early gold currency is examined, the less evident will become its value as an argument for establishing a gold currency today. One will find it distinguished by the same characteristics in the eighteenth century as distinguished it before the war. Then, as now, it demanded a relatively large import in order to maintain a relatively small volume in circulation.

On the Coromandel Coast, the precious metals were, in the eighteenth century, obtained entirely, or almost entirely, by foreign trade. The principal share was derived from Europe in payment for the piece-goods which formed the staple export to the West, The remainder came from the various regions with which the coast was connected by the country trade. Both silver and gold came from Manilla, which obtained the first from America and the second from China. A certain quantity of gold dust was brought from the islands of the Indian Archipelago. The European trade to China produced occasional exports of gold from Canton to Madras, Pondicherry, and Nagapatam, when the price of tea and silk was too high to permit returns being made to Europe in those commodities. And finally silver, which had found its way overland from Europe, was imported from Jeddah and the

Red Sea. But it is not possible, until the close of the century, to form any estimate of either the volume of these imports or the ratio of imported gold to silver.

One fact, however, stands out from this mass of uncertainty. Silver was tending to replace gold as the principal export from Europe to the Coast. In the seventeenth century gold had been the more regular and constant export from the West. Thus in 1647 dollars gave a loss of 7 per cent, while gold yielded a profit of 13½ per cent.[1] Ten years later we read that *reals* and all kinds of silver were in low esteem.[2] Another ten years and we are told that in Governor Langhoene's time dollars had exchanged at so low a rate as 20 for 10 *pagodas*.[3] However, in the last quarter of that century silver rose considerably in value. In 1681 dollars sold at 16½, and in 1682 at 15⅝ for 10 *pagodas*.[4] And although heavy imports of dollars by the English temporarily reduced the rate, in 1690 rupees were quoted at a price which was equivalent to 12¾ dollars per 10 *pagodas*. This last value was not maintained for long; but in 1700 Lockyer reckoned the dollar at 15,[5] and this rate continued approximately constant for the next forty years. Silver was imported steadily by the French and English; and it is interesting to note that the former had to sell almost all their imports at Madras, as in those days that place was an important financial centre, where all the bankers of note kept representatives. I do not find that the French ever realized less than a rate of about 16½, or more than 14⅓. They certainly averaged 15 dollars per 10 *pagodas*.[6]

This stability of rates was, however, illusive. Silver was really depreciating, but the fact was concealed by a progressive debasement of the *pagoda*. In the Carnatic about this time there are said to have been 22 mints under the Nawab. Besides these, the English had mints at Madras and St. David's; the French at Pondicherry; and the Dutch at Nagapatam and Pulicat. In the seventeenth century these issued a great variety of coins, indeed in more than one case numismatists have been unable to determine what exactly constituted the coins the names of which have survived. But in spite of this, there is reason for supposing that all the *pagodas* circulating in the south of the peninsula differed but little amongst themselves. At all events, there were two principal types coined: the one for circulation in the Carnatic, and the other for use in the countries to the Northward, later known to us as the Northern Circars. For a century or so after our arrival on the. Coromandel Coast, the standard of these coins seems to have been well-maintained; at all events we find no complaints of the variation of the standard. However, from about the year 1720, the Nawab's mints began to issue coins of a lower touch than had been customary. Their fineness had been 86¼ per cent. In 1722 this fell to 85; and in 1724 to 84 11⁄16 per cent. By 1731 it had been reduced to 83¾; in 1736 it had fallen to barely 80, and before 1740 to 77 and in some cases still lower. Roughly speaking, we may say that in the twenty years 1720-39 the Carnatic *pagoda* was diminished in value by over 12 per cent.[7]

This greatly inconvenienced the European nations established on the Coast. Their chief bullion import was silver, which was really falling in value, so that it realized no more of the debased *pagodas* than it had done of the standard *pagodas* of an earlier date, while the cloth which they wished to buy had risen in proportion to the fall in value of the circulating coin. Each nation therefore endeavoured to prohibit the currency of these country *pagodas* within their limits, and attempted to maintain the standard by continuing to issue coins of the old fineness. But each found, very naturally, that their coinage simply disappeared as fast as it was issued. As the French Council wrote a little later,

> On receiving gold, the Malabars (i.e. the Tamils) always carry it to the mint that will give them most *pagodas*. Many have been re-coined at Alam-barai, Villupuram and Wandiwash; and both at Pondicherry and Madras, people collect old *pagodas* in order to re-coin them.[8]

We do not know the precise action taken by the Dutch, except that they prohibited for a time the currency of *pagodas* of less than a certain degree of fineness.[9] But regarding the French we have more information. In 1737, on representations of the merchants that, unless the Pondicherry standard was lowered, they would be obliged to carry their gold elsewhere, the fineness of the Pondicherry or Crescent *pagoda* was substantially reduce.[10] In the next year, when the standard of the country mints had fallen below 80 per cent, all merchants were forbidden to receive or pay out *pagodas* worse than 80⅝ per cent fine, and all *pagodas* below that were to be re-coined. At the same time a quantity of poor coin received in payment for silver was ordered to be reminted.[11] In 1739 the English plan was imitated, the standard was fixed at 80 per cent tine, but coins not worse than 77½ per cent might circulate at 1 per cent discount.[12] However, these regulations must have been very ineffective. In the two years previous, the French had coined only 170,000 *pagodas*, while these had been received at only the same rate as the debased country *pagodas*, and had immediately disappeared from circulation.[13]

Meanwhile the English had succeeded in establishing a standard coin. Their first effort was a failure, probably owing to their having tried, like the French and Dutch, to prevent the baser coins from passing from hand to hand. But the second attempt was better judged. The great shroffs, who were bankers rather than mere moneychangers, supported the scheme. A coin, 80 per cent fine, was established as the standard, called the Star *pagoda* from the large five-pointed star stamped on its rounded side; but other species were to circulate at their bullion value. The only special mint-regulation seems to have been the suspension of the ½ per cent charged as mintage-duty.[14] The now coin at once rose to a premium over the country *pagoda*. As early as 1742 the English Council was able to report the complete success of the scheme. The Star *pagoda* was eagerly demanded even in so distant a cloth-weaving centre as Salem, and the Nawab was rumoured to be about to raise his coin to the same standard as that of the English.[15] Two or three attempts were actually made to do so; but the Nawab's mints did not command great confidence and the efforts were not maintained. Meanwhile the Star *pagoda* established itself as the principal variety of *pagoda* in circulation. In 1746 we find it preferred to the Crescent *pagoda*;[1] and when Godehsu reached the Coast in 1754, he had to deplore the popularity of the English coin, even in the French settlement itself.[17]

However, with that perversity which seems especially attached to currency history, the appearance of the Star *pagoda* coincided with the first premonitory symptom of that conversion of the currency from gold to silver which is our principal subject. About 1740 there were three types of coin in use in the Carnatic and the southern countries dependent on it. The best-known of these, and that in which all large wholesale transactions were conducted, was the *pagoda*, the history of which we have been tracing. These were often sealed up in bags of 1,000, which are said to have sometimes passed from merchant to merchant for years without being opened. Nevertheless this was not the common coin of the people. That was a small gold piece of heavily alloyed metal, called emphatically in the language of the country the *fanam*, i.e. money. These varied much from place to place. At Golconda they went 12 to the *pagoda*, at Porto Novo and in the extreme South 18, at Pulicat and Pondicherry 24, at Madras 36. Everywhere these formed the coin of retail transactions. When the merchants made advances to the weavers in *pagodas*, the latter made haste to exchange these inconveniently large coins – they may roughly be reckoned at 8s. sterling – for the *fanams* with which they bought their yarn and daily supplies of food.[18] Beside these, there was yet another coin in circulation. This was the rupee, which had only been introduced in the Carnatic when the Mughals established themselves there at the end of the seventeenth and the beginning of the eighteenth century. As we shall see, this was not in extensive use; but it must have been found in considerable numbers in the principal Muhammadan centres, such as Arcot, and, a little later, Trichinopoly. It was used, I conjecture, chiefly in the payment of the troops maintained by the Nawab. Part of the 'country' revenues seem to have been received in it; thus in 1750 the revenues of Trichinopoly were reckoned partly in grain and partly in rupees; the revenue of the temple at Tirupati was paid partly in rupees and partly in *pagodas*; and, when the English rented out the revenues of Madura and Tinnevelly, a little later, the rent was calculated in lakhs of rupees. But in the middle of the eighteenth century the rupee certainly was not in general use, and there were many districts where it did not pass current.

However, about this time both the French and English made attempts to establish it as the standard coin for their trade. Ever since the seventeenth century the English had minted a special coin called the Madras rupee, for export to Bengal. By 1740 the three European nations, English, French, and Dutch, had secured the privilege of coining the Arcot rupee; and had actually produced this specie in considerable quantities. But this was less for local use than with the object of avoiding the delays and disputes incident to using the Nawab's mints in Bengal, to which province all alike sent great quantities of silver. Thus it was natural that when they were involved in difficulties by the debasement of the gold circulation, they should try to avoid their difficulties by substituting the silver coin.

Accordingly in 1739 the French Council resolved that rupees should be current at the rate of 320 per 100 *pagodas.*[19] But this at once involved them in worse difficulties than ever. The market rate on the Coast was at this time seldom under 350; and while the measure must have been very acceptable to all debtors, creditors were exceedingly averse to it. Besides, the cloth-merchants were never willing to accept advances for cloth in any money but *pagodas*; so the Company's business was impeded. When these obstacles were reported in France, the Company recommended that silver should be sent to China, to be exchanged for gold;[20] but the Pondicherry government never seems to have had enough funds at its disposal to do so on any effective scale. Ten years later Dupleix was still reporting the great difficulty of getting the merchants to accept rupees – at Karikal they were demanding 370 or 380 per 100 *pagodas*[21] and desiring an annual, supply of at least 200,000 *pagodas* a year in gold, which he does not seem to have obtained.[22]

In spite of all difficulties, the English had been able to maintain their gold payments till a much later date. In 1744 there had been a heavy drain of gold to Bengal, where the Maratha raids had set a premium on the more precious and easily concealed metal.[23] But it was not until the War of the Austrian Succession and the capture of Madras in 1746, that their supplies of gold began to fail. After the latter event the English at Fort St. David could hardly find enough gold to pay their garrison; and after the heavy expenditure in which they were involved by the siege of Pondicherry in

1748, they too succumbed to silver. In 1749 it was announced that rupees were to be current in the English settlement at 350 per 100 *pagodas*.[24] This was an undervaluation of gold, similar to that of the French in 1739. It was accentuated by the coming of Nasir Jang from the north in the following year, for his army was paid in rupees, so that this specie became commoner and cheaper than ever.[25] When it became evident that the maintenance of the rupee currency would involve a great rise in prices, it was determined to restore the *pagoda*.[26] In December 1750, the English Council wrote home for a supply of gold from China and resolved that all the receipts and payments of the Company's Treasury should be made in *pagodas*.[27] However, the receipts did not equal the outgoings, and in the following March, there was not enough gold in the Treasury to pay the troops, so that the Council ws reduced to the expensive necessity of selling rupees for what they would fetch.[28] After this luckily the situation eased down. Gold was imported, and rupees, which in 1750 had been as low as 400, had risen by 1756 to 364 per 100 *pagodas*.[29]

Thus the attempts of both French and English to establish the rupee in general circulation both failed. The chief reason probably was that their commerce was not extensive enough by itself to support a new standard of value, which was unpopular with the mass of the inhabitants, owing to its large fluctuations both in *pagodas* and in *fanams*. But in spite of their failure, it is likely that the circulation of rupees increased appreciably about this time. I have already mentioned the flood of rupees which Nasir Jang's army let loose. But from this time until the fall of Pondicherry in 1761 the French and English kept large forces in the field, and, although soldiers' pay in garrison at this time was discharged in gold, their *batta*, or additional allowances in the field, was reckoned and paid in silver. A considerable quantity of rupees must therefore have been absorbed between 1750 and 1761 in exchange for provisions, forage, and cattle-hire.

These same years included another event which was to exercise a great influence on the currency position of the south. This was the establishment of the English as the predominant power in Bengal in 1757. It was as important financially as politically. From this event dates the reduction of the Company's bullion exports to India, and the commencement of the movement of gold and silver from Bengal to Madras. Till then the movement had been the other way. The commerce of Bengal with the Coast was conducted by sea. It consisted in the export from Bengal of silk, opium, sugar, and rice; and the returns had been made principally in the silver which came from Europe for the purchase of the Coast piece-goods. This was the circumstance which enabled south India to take large quantities of silver and yet refrain from using it as currency. But for this re-export of silver to Bengal, the value of silver on the Coast must have declined much more than it had actually done.

In consequence of the prolonged struggle with the French, the Company's finances at Madras became straitened, and the Nawab's debt rose high by the advances made on his account. These conditions were exaggerated by the cessation of the Company's bullion exports, owing to the glowing accounts which Clive sent home of the great revenues of Bengal. In 1759 and again in 1760 the conduct of the campaign was dependent on the supplies of treasure received from Fort William. This was sent principally in silver, and was employed to meet the current expenses of the army, which in 1760 were reckoned at two lakhs of rupees a month. More silver was sent into circulation by coining the bullion which had been intended to provide the Company's investment in China.

The financial situation was similar in the next war – the First Mysore War. Financial help was again needed from the wealthy presidency of Bengal; but this time the assistance was afforded in gold. Clive's unfortunate scheme to establish a gold currency in Bengal had just failed, and the gold *mohurs* which he had coined were sent down to Madras to be re-issued as *pagodas*. In the years 1767 and 1768 7,80,000 *pagodas* were thus provided. The result well illustrates the sensitive nature of the Madras bullion market. In 1767 when there were no *pagodas* in the Treasury, the price of rupees was so low that the Council preferred borrowing *pagodas* at interest to issuing rupees at such unfavourable rates. But with the importation of gold from Bengal, the price dropped from 370 per 100 *pagodas* in 1768 to 320 in 1771; and even in the latter year silver continued very dear, in spite of considerable payments made to the Company by the Nawab in rupees.[30]

In 1774-5 a certain amount of specie, principally gold, was exported to England on private account. This was due, not to the rapacious greed of individuals, but to the shortage of the normal forms of remittance to England. Ever since the time of the famous Governor Pitt, these remittances had usually been made in diamonds. But about the year 1770 the supply seems suddenly to have dried up. The Company too had cut down the amount of money that might be remitted through its Treasury at Madras. A third method, the export of merchandise to Canton, where the proceeds were paid into the Company's cash for bills on England, had been completely stopped. At this time we find the whole circulation of the Carnatic estimated at below 20 lakh of *pagodas*. The Nawab, possibly basing his opinion on the authority of the *sowcars*, put it at 15 lakh; while a member of the Madras Council suggested 17 lakh. But even when we remember the restricted area within which the active circulation was confined, this seems much too low. At the close of the century it was reckoned at 80 lakh, and there had probably been small change in the volume.[31]

I have not hitherto found evidence in support of the commonly accepted view, that such exports were regular and considerable.[32] But there were certainly other ways by which the currency of the Carnatic was constantly exposed to loss. This was by way of the inland trade into Mysore, the dominions of the Nizam, and the northern Circars. The last two of these is capable of clearer definition than is the case with most currency phenomena of the period which we are discussing. We have already seen that two kinds of *pagodas* were coined in the south – at Madras these were the Star *pagoda*, which circulated in the Carnatic and the adjacent districts; and the Madras *pagoda*, which circulated in the northern Circars and Hyderabad.[33] From 1767 onwards, with one trivial exception, none of the latter were coined on the Company's account, presumably because the cloth investments in those regions were paid for out of the territorial revenues collected on the Company's account. Nevertheless these coins continued to be minted in surprising quantities for private merchants. For the ten years 1770-9) the coinage of Madras *pagodas* averaged 2,24,000; in the ten years 1780-9 it averaged 3,46,000. Altogether in these twenty years the total coinage of Madras *pagodas* by the English alone amounted to 60,71,000,[34] while that of Star *pagodas* was 90,80,000.[35] The proportion was moreover higher oven than these figures would suggest, for the Madras *pagoda* was worth 10 per cent more than the Star. If this is taken into account, it appears that of all the gold coined in these years at Madras, no less than 42 per cent was designed for export to the Circars and Hyderabad. Nor was there any return of coin or metal from those districts. While Madras imported from the northward in considerable quantity cotton-cloth and grain, the first for re-export, the second for consumption, its returns in merchandise were small. The drain from Madras to Mysore, though not so distinguishable as that to the northward, is well avouched by contemporaries.[36] It probably was less considerable, perhaps a half. Altogether this internal drain at the lowest computation must be set at 4½ lakh of Star *pagodas* a year, of which five-sixths was gold. But besides this, deductions also have to be made for gold converted into ornaments. In 1799 this was estimated at a lakh of Star *pagodas* a year. If we set it at a half of this, we have an annual average subtraction from the currency of the Carnatic of 5 lakh of Star *pagodas*, of which 4,50,000 was in gold.

This might very well continue so long as the normal imports sufficed to make the loss good. In the years we are considering, 1770-90, this was certainly the case. The Carnatic obtained gold from two chief sources. The Dutch imported gold, derived from their Eastern trade, to the extent of 4 lakh of *pagodas* a year.[37] Native merchants were believed to import about one lakh a year in gold dust from Achin and other places in the Archipelago. Portuguese vessels brought a small but uncertain quantity, perhaps half a lakh, from Macao. The imports thus sufficed to maintain the stock of gold in the Carnatic; but if anything should happen to interfere with them, evidently that stock would waste rapidly.

But although the stock of gold was being maintained for the moment, another change was going forward. Once gold had recovered from the effects of the import from Bengal in 1768-9, the price of silver remained pretty constantly in the neighbourhood of 350 rupees per 100 *pagodas* until the year 1780. But then the outbreak of the Second Mysore War involved great expenditure. Considerable issues of rupees were made for current expenditure; and the price fell. In order to prevent any increase in the loss thus caused, at the close of the year, the Council gave orders that Arcot rupees should pass at 375 per 100 *pagodas* in payment of all sums under 300 *pagodas*. Within these limits rupees would be received at the Company's Treasury.[38] This regulation might perhaps have succeeded, had it not been accompanied by heavy imports of silver; but it was as usual necessary for Bengal to supply the financial needs of Madras, This was done in silver; and before the end of the war rupees were down to 400 per 100 *pagodas*.[39] After a time this was somewhat corrected by imports of gold from Bengal.[40] By May 1790, 6 lakh of *pagodas* had been imported, and the rupee had risen; but in the following year 31 lakh of rupees arrived, and the rupee relapsed to 383.[41] On this the Council resolved to fix the exchange at 365, and to receive rupees into the Treasury at that rate. This resolve was only taken after consulting the principal merchants and shroffs, who unanimously approved of the measure and promised their full concurrence and support.[42]

This was on the face of it an over-valuation of the rupee. Within the immediate region of its influence, that is, in Madras itself, it can only have caused a withdrawal of *pagodas* from circulation and the substitution of rupees in their place. Thin tendency must have been strengthened too by the outbreak of the war with France in 1793, and the subsequent extension of hostilities to the Dutch. For this latter cut off the principal source of regular gold supply. While the drain inland continued unaffected, silver passed in Madras at more than its local gold rate, and at the same time the normal import of gold was materially reduced. The consequence necessarily was that the stock of gold in Madras and its immediate neighbourhood was rapidly reduced, and the circulating coin came to consist more and more largely of silver. This tendency was temporarily checked by the heavy exports of bullion and specie which political events imposed upon Mysore in 1792 and 1799; but as two-thirds of this seems to have been sent almost at once to answer private mercantile obligations in Bengal and China,[43] the effects can only have been transitory. Nor was the balance made good by the government import of treasure from Bengal. In the ten years 1790-9 that only averaged 1,60,000 *pagodas* a year in gold, while the silver similarly imported averaged 5½ lakh of rupees. Yet in spite of the shortage of gold and the considerable imports of silver, government was able in 1797 further to enhance the value of the rupee by fixing the exchange at 350.[44] Some opposition was made to this; but as it was entirely ineffectual, I suppose that the money in circulation at Madras was principally silver. Indeed in the five years 1795-9 more than half the coin minted at Madras was in rupees; and in the five years which followed more than three-quarters of it was silver; while the gold that was issued must have disappeared from circulation as rapidly as it would today. In 1806 we are told that while gold constituted the nominal standard at Madras, silver formed the currency.[45]

However the extreme looseness of the financial organization, coupled with the economic conservatism of the people, seems to have permitted what would today be impossible. Silver was certainly overvalued at Madras; but it was at the same time undervalued in the districts. For example, we are told in 1796 that in the Baramahal the tahsildars insisted on the revenue collections being made in rupees, which they kept themselves, paying *pagodas* into the Treasury instead. They are said to have gained 7 per cent on such transactions. The bazaar rate of exchange at Salem must therefore have been about 340.[46] About the same time we learn that, although rupees had a considerable currency in the Masulipatam district, yet the revenue was paid almost wholly in Madras *pagodas*.[47] Evidently the latter coin was undervalued at the official rate of exchange and was worth more locally. Even so late as 1818, the Madras *pagoda* was overvalued in the Circars, although by then rupees formed the main part of the currency elsewhere.[48]

We may take it, I think, that the local value of silver varied considerably from place to place. It was low in the Coast towns, and the immediately surrounding districts, on the southern half of the Madras Coast, because these were in immediate touch with foreign traffic and directly received the bullion, mostly silver, in which the exports were paid for. It was low, though somewhat higher, in the weaving centres, from which the Coast exports were drawn, and where some fifty years of pressure had induced the weavers to accept their advances in silver rupees, instead of insisting, as formerly, on *pagodas* or gold *fanams*. It was rarer and dearer in the other inland districts of the Carnatic (with probable exceptions at Arcot and Trichinopoly) where it only filtered through in driblets, in payment for their exports of surplus grain, either to weaving centres or to the Coast towns.

Nor was the system of collecting the revenues such as to tend with any force to a general levelling of conditions. At the close of the eighteenth century, the Company still only collected the revenues in the districts immediately around Madras, in the northern Circars, and in certain districts ceded by Mysore in 1792, together with what was called the Poligar Peshkash in the extreme south. In all these, except in the neighbourhood of Madras itself, the fixed rate of exchange tended to keep gold, not silver, in circulation. At first this led to remittances of *pagodas* to Madras; and at the same time it was advantageous to send rupees out of Madras to districts where a profit could he made on the local difference between the bazaar and the Treasury rates of exchange. The Assumption of the Carnatic in 1802, which established English Treasuries all over the country, and thus multiplied the number of places where the Madras rate was obtainable, must have tended strongly to the general assimilation of conditions and the disappearance of these anomalies.

The Assumption of the Carnatic not only levelled down the price of silver in south India, but also led to a reform of the currency itself. One of the evils from which the country had suffered was a multiplicity of mints, issuing many different kinds of coin; and the first English collectors had to receive on account of the revenue at least 72 varieties of gold and 60 varieties of silver coin. Now that the only mints were English, there was no reason why so evident an inconvenience should be any longer tolerated. Accordingly it was resolved in 1806 that all these different varieties should be reduced to two – the Star *pagoda* and the Arcot rupee. This great and important reform was gradually carried out by a steady re-coinage spread over a period of nine or ten years.

Meanwhile the Company at home was exercised over the wider problem of Indian currency. In a circular letter to the three presidencies in 1806 it dwelt on the inconvenience arising both to private persons and to the Company itself from the variety of coins in circulation, and discussed the possibility of establishing a uniform currency for all three presidencies. For this purpose it considered the rupee the most suitable coin, on account of the prevalence of that specie at Calcutta and Bombay; but at the same time it explicitly declared that it did not wish to discourage the circulation of gold, although, in accordance with the strict mono-metallism at that time becoming prevalent in England, it declared against establishing a legal rate of exchange between the two metals, as it could not be maintained and led only to loss. Gold coin might, however, be received at its bullion value.[49] The discussion was prolonged for ten years, and then in 1816 the Company announced its resolution to establish the rupee as the standard of value and the coin of account.[50]

In this, so far as Madras was concerned, it was doing little but recognize an accomplished fact. In 1812 the Mint Committee had observed that silver had already become the standard of value in the countries dependent on Madras;[51] and the only region which was mentioned as still possessing any considerable gold currency in 1818 was the northern Circars. Even the troops stationed in the numerous district garrisons, whose payment in the latter part of the eighteenth century had caused endless troubles owing to fluctuations of the exchange of the various coins, had in 1816 long been paid in rupees;[52] while the *pagoda* had become only a coin of account. In the years 1812-17 the total gold coinage at Madras only amounted to 2,50,000 *pagodas* a year,[53] and this was the only source of gold supply for the Carnatic and the dependent districts. Fifty years earlier, the Madras mint alone had coined 6,00,000 or 7,00,000 *pagodas* a year; the Dutch had coined 4,00,000; and the divers mints of the Nawab had issued a large though indeterminate quantity. Thus the gold coinage had shrunk certainly to less than a quarter, probably to less than a fifth, of its former volume; and it had long since fallen to the point at which the issues failed to make good the losses. When, then, in 1818 the rupee replaced the Star *pagoda* as the money of account, the change was but nominal.

Looking at the whole process broadly, we find it an interesting example of the operation of large causes, in which regulation counted for very little. In the seventeenth century the relative value of silver was much higher in India than in Europe; silver also formed the currency of northern India, which then as now produced the bulk of the exports to the West. The European nations had thus every motive for buying those exports with silver rather than gold. However, the Coromandel Coast formed an exception to these conditions. The existence of gold deposits in the south, though neither very rich nor very extensive, had in the first instance permitted the establishment of a gold currency. The trade with the Archipelago and China brought in enough gold to permit its maintenance, in spite of a steady drain northwards and inland. Then came the development of a considerable trade with Europe. At first the Coromandel cloth was bought mainly with gold imported from the west. But, as the volume of silver was accumulating in Europe much more rapidly than that of gold, and as the value of silver was tending to fall, the latter metal began to be sent in large regular quantities to the south as well as to the north. At first this involved considerable difficulties, partly obscured by the debasement of the normal currency of the country. Meanwhile the establishment of a Mughal *subahdar* at Arcot had led to the introduction of the rupee. This tendency was strengthened by the wars between the French and the English and between the English and Mysore. Up to 1793, however, the stock of gold in circulation in all probability had not absolutely declined, although it had fallen relatively to the volume of trade. After 1793, when the principal imports were cut off by the exclusion of Dutch commerce, and only replaced by spasmodic imports from Bengal, the stock began to waste by the drain inland. At this time the silver in circulation seems to have been distributed with great irregularity, and its value varied much from district to district. But this inequality was rapidly reduced by the influence of the district treasuries as soon as British administration was extended over the Carnatic in 1802. In these years the coinage of rupees, both on public and private account, was abnormally large. Thus the value of gold in silver gradually rose in the districts until it exceeded the rating which had been established at Madras. Once this overvaluation of gold had disappeared, the currency of gold was doomed. All the influences of convenience, the love of jewellery, the passion for hiding one's wealth, contributed to bring the southern part of the peninsula into line with the richer northern provinces. The gold which was sent into circulation thereafter – and certain quantities were coined and issued long after 1818 – was liable to constant subtraction. It was, in fact, in much the same position as the sovereigns which circulated in India in 1913. In the east, as elsewhere, when both metals are unlimited legal tender gold can only be maintained in circulation by being overvalued as currency. The currency of gold at Madras vanished with the disappearance of that overrating.

TABLE 1: COINAGE IN THE MADRAS MINT, 1767-1804

*(000's omitted)*

| *Year* | | *Gold* | | | | *Silver* | | | *Total* |
|---|---|---|---|---|---|---|---|---|---|
| | | *Star* pagodas | | | | *Rupees* | | | |
| | *Madras pagodas*[54] | *Private* | *Coy.* | *Total* | *Total Gold in Star pagodas*[55] | *Private* | *Coy.* | *Total* | *Coinage in Star pagodas*[56] |
| 1767 | 171 | 268 | 43 | 312 | 500 | 609 | 251 | 863 | 750 |
| 1768 | 236 | 141 | 510 | 682 | 931 | 54 | 181 | 236 | 998 |
| 1769 | 307 | 20 | 413 | 433 | 750 | 116 | 31 | 351 | 793 |
| 1770 | 359 | 122 | .. | 122 | 516 | 358 | .. | 358 | 616 |
| 1771 | 240 | .. | 179 | 179 | 430 | 840 | .. | 840 | 670 |
| 1772 | 346 | 62 | 2 | 64 | 444 | 545 | .. | 545 | 597 |
| 1773 | 217 | 526 | .. | 526 | 763 | 445 | .. | 445 | 890 |
| 1774 | 260 | 250 | .. | 250 | 536 | 404 | 6 | 410 | 653 |

*contd.*

TABLE 1 *contd.*

| | | | | | | | | | |
|---|---|---|---|---|---|---|---|---|---|
| 1775 | 358 | 249 | .. | 249 | 642 | 253 | .. | 253 | 714 |
| 1776 | 42 | 803 | .. | 803 | 849 | 131 | .. | 131 | 886 |
| 1777 | 38 | 653 | .. | 653 | 704 | 220 | 55 | 275 | 783 |
| 1778 | 169 | 399 | 230 | 629 | 814 | 415 | 46 | 461 | 946 |
| 1779 | 217 | 254 | 228 | 482 | 720 | 160 | .. | 160 | 769 |
| 1780 | 101 | 1152 | 53 | 1205 | 1316 | 256 | 265 | 521 | 1465 |
| 1781 | 259 | 254 | 295 | 549 | 823 | 172 | 1005 | 1177 | 1159 |
| 1782 | 489 | .. | 726 | 726 | 1263 | 194 | 779 | 973 | 1544 |
| 1783 | 555 | 16 | 114 | 130 | 740 | 80 | 266 | 346 | 839 |
| 1784 | 484 | 21 | 189 | 210 | 742 | 285 | 273 | 558 | 899 |
| 1785[57] | .. | .. | .. | .. | .. | .. | .. | .. | .. |
| 1786[58] | 185 | 270 | .. | 270 | 473 | 123 | 29 | 152 | 516 |
| 1787 | 312 | 232 | .. | 232 | 573 | 90 | .. | 90 | 599 |
| 1788 | 310 | 191 | .. | 191 | 522 | 95 | .. | 95 | 549 |
| 1789 | 429 | 181 | .. | 181 | 652 | 90 | .. | 90 | 878 |
| 1790 | 93 | 242 | 408 | 651 | 753 | 266 | 1455 | 1721 | 1245 |
| 1791 | 144 | 215 | 516 | 731 | 889 | 323 | 8036 | 8359 | 3249 |
| 1792 | 368 | 124 | 781 | 905 | 1309 | .. | 84 | 84 | 1333 |
| 1793 | 198 | 434 | 545 | 980 | 1197 | 270 | .. | 270 | 1274 |
| 1794 | 117 | 148 | 107 | 256 | 381 | 418 | .. | 418 | 503 |
| 1795 | 186 | 4 | 10 | 15 | 219 | 339 | .. | 339 | 316 |
| 1796 | 143 | 2 | 224 | 227 | 384 | 282 | .. | 282 | 464 |
| 1797 | 70 | 8 | 587 | 595 | 672 | 179 | 535 | 715 | 876 |
| 1798 | 78 | 17 | 228 | 245 | 330 | 869 | 2149 | 3019 | 1191 |
| 1799 | 301 | 6 | 217 | 223 | 554 | 63 | 4102 | 4165 | 1744 |
| 1800 | 416 | .. | .. | .. | 447 | 530 | 1296 | 1827 | 950 |
| 1801 | 320 | .. | .. | .. | 352 | 496 | 3435 | 3931 | 1475 |
| 1802 | ... | 240 | 96 | 337 | 337 | 2394 | 1147 | 3542 | 1349 |
| 1803 | ... | 253 | 281 | 534 | 534 | 3436 | 4784 | 8220 | 2880 |
| 1804 | ... | 111 | 370 | 481 | 481 | 1796 | 4931 | 6727 | 2403 |

## Notes

1. Foster's *English Factories in India*, vol. VIII, p. 165.
2. Love's *Vestiges of Old Madras*, vol. I, p. 194.
3. *Records of Fort St. George—Despatches from England*, 1681-6, pp. 78-9.
4. Loc. cit.
5. Lockyer, *The Trade to India*.
6. See the valuable volumes of the proceedings of the *Conseil Supérieur* of Pondicherry, published by the *Société de l'Histoire de l'Inde Française*.
7. Letter from the French Company to Pondicherry, dated 21 August 1789, with the answer *en apostille* of 18 October 1740 (Pondicherry Records, no. 28).
8. Pondicherry to Madras, 25 May 1788 (Pondicherry Records, no. 13).
9. Pondicherry to Karikal, 13 September 1740 (ibid).
10. *Conseil Supérieur*, 20 March 1737 (vol. III, p. 78).
11. Ibid., 6 May 1738 (vol. III, p. 139).
12. Ibid., 11 May 1789 (vol. III, p. 203).
13. Ibid., 28 August 1789 (vol. III, p. 238).
14. Despatch from Madras to the Company, February 1742.
15. Ibid., and Madras to the Company, 15 February 1745.
16. *Diary of Ananda Banga Pillai*, vol. III, p. 224.
17. *Mémoire sour le sieur Godehsu*, Piece no. 2.
18. They seem frequently to have received their advances in *fanams*, e.g. at Salem (Fort St. David to Madras, 26 October 1741).
19. *Conseil Supérieur*, 15 July 1739 (vol. III, p. 224).
20. French Company to Pondicherry, 25 November 1741.
21. Pondicherry to the Company, 20 September 1750.
22. Dupleix to the Company, 3 October 1750.
23. Madras Consultations, 9 July1744.
24. Fort St. David Consultations, 25 April 1749.
25. Madras despatch to the Company, 24 October 1750.
26. Fort St. David Consultations, 3 December 1750.
27. Ibid.
28. Fort St. David Consultations, 11 March 1751.
29. Madras Mayor's Court Pleadings, 1767, f. 560.
30. Madras Public Consultation, 5 October 1767, f. 582; Jourdan to Dracot and Craufurd, 26 March 1768; Verelst, p. 96. Rupees had dropped to 345 by August 1768.
31. Madras Public Consultation, 16 and 19 January 1775; Public despatch to the Company, 25 January 1775; Military Country Correspondence, 1775, ff. 25-6.
32. Mr. Hamilton in his *Trade Relations between England and India* discusses this point.

33. In 1767 it was determined to attempt to circulate Star *pagodas* in the northern Circars. The Masulipatam merchants then said that it depended on the bankers at Hyderabad. Madras Public Consultations, 27 January 1767, f. 32. The experiment came to nothing.
34. Identical coins were minted by the French and Dutch as well. The French coinage in the latter part of the century was inconsiderable; but the Dutch at this period were the largest importers of gold to the Carnatic.
35. See the figures in the appendix.
36. E.g., Petrie, who produced a valuable minute for the Committee of Reform, 1799.
37. Petrie's minute *ut supra*. Cf. Milburn's *Oriental Commerce,* vol. I, p. 365.
38. Madras G.O.G., 31 December 1780.
39. Military Consultations, 20 September 1788, letter from Bengal.
40. A statement of the imports of treasure from Bengal between 1785-6 and 1798-9 occurs in the proceedings of the Committee of Reform, 1799.
41. Public Consultation, 1 March 1791.
42. Loc. cit.
43. Petrie's minute *ut supra.*
44. Public Consultations, 6 October 1797, f. 3312.
45. Report of the Committee of Finance, app. Public Consultations, 1806, ff. 425, etc.
46. Munro to Read, 20 January 1796 (Baramahal Records).
47. Pro. Board of Revenue, 23 March 1793.
48. Public Consultations, 24 April 1818, no. 419.
49. Public Despatch from England, 25 April 1806.
50. Ibid., 12 June 1316.
51. Mint Committee's Report, 12 April 1812.
52. Public Consultations, 7 January 1818.
53. Parliamentary Return of 1864.
54. All the Madras *pagodas* coined in these years, with one exception too trivial to be shown, were on private account.
55. Madras *pagodas* valued at 10 per cent more than Stars.
56. The rupee is converted at 350 per 100 *pagodas.*
57. Accounts are missing for this year.
58. Accounts are available for eight months only of this year.

# 10

# Madras Currency under the Early British Rule

## *The History of Coinage of India is as Old as the Recorded History of the Country*

C. Ramachandran

## The Early Media of Exchange

The history of coinage of India is as old as the recorded history of the country. Right from the age of later Vedic civilization, units of value either of copper or silver like the *nishka*, the *satamana* and *krishnala*, though not regular coins, had been in vogue. By the beginning of the early Magadhan epoch, even though the system of barter continued to be widely prevalent, regular coins had come into general circulation. Foreign commerce during the Maurya-Scythian era brought in a large quantity of specie to India, for Pliny complained about the drain of Roman coins to this country. It is believed that the institution of a gold coinage by the Kushans from the time of Kadphises II was much due to the influx of gold from the Roman Empire. The period that followed was marked by the use of improved coins. Imperial Guptas and their successors put gold and silver coins into circulation. Besides, other precious things like cowries and small pearls, were also used as media of exchange. More changes came about during the Muslim rule. Mohammad bin Tughluq, who was called the 'Prince of moneyers', experimented with the currency systems.

Sher Shah in a bid to promote the general economic condition of his empire reformed the mint and took steps aimed at checking any debasement of the currency. Akbar, as indicated in the *Ain-i-Akbari*, appointed Khwaja Abdus Samad of Shiraz as Master of Imperial Mint at Delhi and one officer each in charge of the chief Provincial mints of Bengal, Lahore, Jaipur, Ahmedabad and Patna. The Mughal coins especially of Akbar, seemed perfect in respect of purity of metal, fullness of weight and artistry.

The rise of numerous independent kingdoms on the ruins of Mughal empire led to the introduction of a multiplicity of currency, as the issue of coins was regarded as one of the insignias of sovereignty. It has been estimated that as many as 994 different types of coins of both gold and silver were current in India during this period. However, according to Mr. Rapson,

> Numismatics which forms an interesting and important branch of archaeology in relation to the history of the rest of India has so far not yielded except in a few instances any striking data on the general history of South India. This is because South Indian coinages have as yet not received so scientific a treatment as the coins of the North did.[1]

The south Indian coins were mostly of gold and copper and seldom of silver.[2] The foreign visitors noted the extensive use of gold for minting coins and making ornaments in the south. 'It is remarkable,' says Ferishta 'that (in the plunder of Malik Kafur) silver is not mentioned as having been taken during the expedition to the Carnatic. . . . No person wore bracelets, chains, or rings of any other metal than gold; while all the plates in the houses of the great and in the temples were of beaten gold.'[3] It is stated that Malik Kafur presented Sultan Ala-ud-din Khalji with 96,000 maunds of gold.[4]

Thus we can conclude that gold continued to be the standard currency till about the fourteenth century. Ferishta says: 'there is reason to conclude that silver was not used in that Country at all in those days'.[5] But this does not seem correct, for we have specimens of Chola silver coins of the Raja Raja type in the eleventh century weighting from 30 to 62.6 grains.[6] The Vijayanagar Emperors improved the currency system of the south. The *matrix* was replaced by the *punch*; and the standard coins were made uniform in weight. The shape and metallic value of the different coins were fixed and several denominations were introduced.[7] Harhara II issued an order that taxes must be paid in money instead of in kind. This necessitated the minting of more coins of different denomination.[8] According to Abdur Razak the units of currency that were in circulation in the Vijayanagar Empire during his visit were:[9]

| *Gold* | *Silver* |
|---|---|
| 1. *Varaha* | *Tar* (1/6 of a *fanam*). |
| 2. *Pratab* (half *varaha*) | *Copper* |
| 3. *Fanam* (1/10 *pratab*) | 1/3 *tar* |

The currency of south India even at the ruling of the eighteenth century was based essentially upon gold which was the chief circulating medium. The standard coin was known variously as *varahu* or as *hun.*[10] But in European writing it was usually referred to as *pagoda* and its average value in northern India was equal to three and half of Akbar's Rupees.[11] It was worth about eight shillings and eight and five-eight *mattu* in fineness (ten *mattu* being characteristic of pure gold and corresponding to twenty-four crafts) and weighed about fifty-three grains.

## Beginning of British Currency

In the Carnatic about the beginning of the eighteenth century there were about twenty-two mints under the Nawab at important commercial centres like Arcot, St. Thome and Covelong.[12] These mints issued coins of various types but inferior in standard because of defective organization, supervision and control.

The English had mints at Madras and Fort Saint David, the French at Pondicherry and the Dutch at Pulicat.[13] During this time these issued a great variety of coins; the principal being the *pagoda*. All the *pagodas* circulating in the South of the Peninsula differed but little among themselves. Two principal types were coined; one for the use in the Carnatic and the other for use in the countries to the north, later known as the northern Circars.[14]

Wholesale transactions were settled by bags of *pagodas*. All the European nations settled on the Coromandel coast enjoyed the privilege of minting.[15] *Pagodas* were commonly circulated in bags of 1,000 sealed by the shroffs (moneychangers). For nearly a hundred years, the standard of these European coins was maintained without variation. However, by the year 1720 the Nawab's mints began to issue coins of lower touch. The high rate of profit gained by the Company's mint at Madras was a matter of jealousy for the Nawab's officials. In order to attract more people to their mints and divert the flow of bullion from the Company's mint, they contrived to make more rupees or *pagodas* out of the same quantity of silver or gold, than were made by the Company. For instance out of every hundred ounces of silver the mints at Arcot and St. Thome turned out to the merchants rupees 266 and *annas* 14, while the Company's mint turned out rupees 257 and *annas* 7. Thus the merchants obtained nine rupees and seven *annas* more for their hundred ounces of silver at St. Thome and Arcot mints than he could obtain at the Company's mint. The same case was with gold also.[16] The result was that the merchants preferred coining their bullion in the Nawab's mints. In consequence the currency of the Coast suffered a progressive debasement between 1720 and 1740.[17] In 1720, the *pagoda* circulating in the Carnatic had been eight and five-eighth *mattu,* i.e. of ten parts, eight and five eighth parts were fine gold. In 1731 they had fallen to eight and three eighth, in 1736 to eight and one sixteenth. After this, the decline accelerated and *pagodas* of seven *mattu* were common and those of even five were circulated. In fact, all regulations had been ignored; the mints coined *pagodas* of whatever touch the proprietor of the bullion desired.[18] In 1730 Governor George Morton Pitt had introduced a new *pagoda* called the 'MM' *pagoda* from its having those letters stamped upon it.[19] They proved to be a conspicuous failure, because they were not accepted at the Nawab's treasury.[20] When the Council made payments they had to purchase current *pagodas* and mint them into 'MM' *pagodas* which carried a premium. In course of time the shroffs had them reminted into standard coins. Thus the 'MM' *pagodas* were repeatedly sent to the fire. After a trial of five years, the government resolved to give them up. In order to counter the progressive debasement of the coin, the Madras shroffs were ordered not to seal up any *pagoda* of a lower touch than eight and one-fortieth.[21] The shroffs, however, never observed this regulation and took to sealing up *pagodas* of inferior value.[22] This rendered it essential to introduce a new coin exactly eight *mattus* fineness distinguished by a star on the granulated surface of the reverse.[23] This was the famous Star *pagoda*, which quickly became the standard coin of south India and remained until the early part of the nineteenth century. The coin bore a star on the reverse in place of simple granulation. They were first mentioned under the name in June 1741, when a quantity of *pagodas* in the Company's account was recoined into 'new star money'.[24]

But this was not the standard coin of the country. That was a small gold piece of heavily alloyed metal called emphatically in the language *fanam*, i.e. money. It varied in value from place to place.[25] At Golconda twelve *fanams* were equal to the *pagoda*, at Portonovo and in the extreme south eighteen, at Pulicat and Pondicherry twenty-four and at Madras thirty-six.[26] Everywhere the *fanams* formed the medium of exchange in retail transaction. The merchants made advance to the weaver often in *pagodas*, but the latter hastened to exchange these inconveniently large coins (they roughly reckoned at eight shillings) for the *fanams*. The copper money was denominated as Cash (*kasu*) and the *fanam* was exchanged for eighty Cash. The single Cash was merely a coin of account, for the smallest piece struck being four 'Cash'.

Besides these there was yet another coin in circulation. This was the Rupee, which had only been introduced in the Carnatic by the Mughals at the end of the seventeenth century. This was not in extensive use; but found in considerable circulation in the principal Mohammadan centres like Arcot and subsequently at Trichinopoly. It was used chiefly for paying the troops, maintained by the Nawab. A portion of the 'country' revenue of the temple in Tirupathi was paid partly in rupees and partly in *pagodas*; and when the English rented out the revenue of Madura and Tirunelvelly in the second half of the eighteenth century the rent was calculated in terms of Rupees. But in the middle of the eighteenth century the Rupee was certainly not in general use and was not in circulation in many districts.[27]

## Need for Currency Reform

Hence what engaged the serious attention of the early Governors of Madras was the rectification of the confused currency. However, frequent wars and political disorders, that came in the wake of the disintegration of the Mughal Empire. Anglo-French rivalry and incursions by Mysore and Maratha powers added to the uncertainties. During this period the English East India Company extended its sphere of influence in south India progressively. In 1765 the Nizam at the request of Lord Clive granted northern Circars. The Nawab of Arcot gave away the country around Madras known as the Jaghir to the Company partly in 1750 and partly in 1763 in return for the services rendered to him. In 1792 by the treaty Srirangapatnam, the British acquired from Mysore the Baramahal (Salem), Dindigal and Malabar. In consequence of the Fourth Mysore war in 1799 the Company annexed Canara and Soondah from Mysore. In 1801 the English took possession of the Carnatic from the Nawab of Arcot. These developments gave the right to the English to enact the needed legislation including the reform of the currency for the acquired provinces.

## Report of the Committee of Finance

In the year 1798 the Government of Fort St. George appointed a committee of finance to go into the details of the currency of Madras and suggest suitable remedies wherever necessary. The report of the Committee of Finance, submitted in 1800, was one of the important documents on the history of Madras Currency. The committee took into consideration the then existing state of the Madras coinage and pointed out the evils. The subjects, dealt with by the committee ranged from the management of the Lottery fund and the establishment of a government bank, to the condition of the Company's junior servants and the reorganization of the post office. The financial anomalies of this period were ascribed chiefly to the dearth of specie because of export to Manilla and China, Hyderabad and Mysore. The Committee also found that the Company incurred a heavy loss of a sum of *pagodas* 1,50,611 owing to recoinage of various gold and silver coins not current in Madras territories received into the treasuries on their intrinsic worth between 1786 and 1800. They suggested that the shortage of specie and loss due to recoinage could be overcome by the establishment of a general bank and issue of bank notes. But owing to some reason or other no action seems to have been taken until 1805 in this regard.[28] The Committee concluded its report by suggesting the introduction of a uniform currency throughout the Carnatic with uniform weight and standard to overcome the evils of the day. The report of the Committee which was sent to the Court of Directors received their special attention.

As pointed out by Dr. Ambedkar 'diseased money is worse than want of money. The latter at least saves the cost. But society must have money and it must be good money'.[29] The task therefore, of evolving good money out of bad money fell upon the shoulders of the English East India Company.

The lines were first laid down in the despatch of the Court of Directors to India on 25 April 1806.[30]

In this despatch the Court of Directors laid down the principles on which they considered the general currency of India should be established. Their subsequent letters of 6 April 1808 and 6 March 1810 in the public department reaffirmed their view. These despatches seem to be the outcome of a systematic and a thorough probe into the affairs of the Company. The Court of Directors considered the inadequacy of the then existing system of mints and coinage, the losses the Company had constantly suffered and the inconvenience caused to the public services in consequence of the circulation of a large variety of gold and silver coins of different values in different districts. To rectify these difficulties they suggested the introduction of a uniform coinage of one metal, one weight and fineness, so that it could be made the standard for the entire British India.

In the prosecution of their inquiries the Court of Directors referred to a treatise from the Earl of Liverpool to the King on the *Coins of Realm* which suggested that the 'money or coin which is to be principal measure of property ought to be of one metal only'.[31] According to J.C. Coyajee this treatise which appeared in

1806 directly influenced the currency policy. In England it was the precursor of the Act which established gold standard in 1806 while in India it contributed to the abolition of bimetallism as suggested by the Court of Directors in 1806.[32] They observed

> it is the opinion supported by the best authorities and proved by experience that coins of gold and silver cannot circulate as legal tender of payment at fixed relative values as in England, in India without great loss; this loss is occasioned by the fluctuating value of the metals of which the coins are formed.[33]

The Court of Directors therefore declared themselves in favour of monometalism in principle as the ideal for the Indian[1] currency of the future.

## Establishment of Silver Standard

The Court of Directors felt that the standard coins should be of silver. Several factors led them to make this decision. Gold had been considered from time immemorial the standard of value by which the pay of troops, the price of investment and collection of revenue was rated. But the extent of public receipts and disbursements and general trade rendered gold altogether inadequate for general circulation. On the other hand, the supply of silver was considered adequate. With a view to probably prevent the depreciation of the metal likely to become the principal currency, the rate was fixed at 350 Arcot Rupees per 100 *pagodas*. But this was found disproportionate because of the constant importation and increase of silver and its consequent depreciation in relation to gold. Therefore public investment continued to be rated in gold coin, even after the exchange rate for silver was fixed. The gold coin was always preferred in payment or else its equivalent in silver demanded, not as fixed by the authority but at the fluctuating market rate, which was somewhere between 400 and 420 Arcot Rupees for 100 *pagodas*. Hence it was found that in those districts where the silver circulation had most rapidly increased the difference was so manifest as to induce the necessity of making it up.

If, then, the coin for general use in India as the principal measure of property was to be silver, the next problem was to determine the weight of the coin. The standard weight of the silver coins issued from the Mints of India were as follows:

| | | |
|---|---|---|
| Calcutta Sicca Rupee | Troy grains | 178⅔ |
| Madras Arcot Rupee | Troy grains | 176⅖ |
| Bombay Rupee | Troy grains | 179 |

The weight of the coin originally issued from the Mughal mints was uniformly one Sicca or ten massa, by troy grains 179⅔ or 179.5511 dwts. The Court of Directors recommended 180 Troy grains as the nearest to the Sicca weight, as it was thought that the measure would provide for the simplicity.[34] The third question that engaged the attention of the Company was the standard of fineness. The Court of Directors suggested that 11/12 silver and 1/12 alloy of copper would be proper for silver coin. In their opinion it had certainly had the advantage in the standard of valuation of the coin; as such they proposed the adoption of this proportion in which case the new Rupee ought to be the gross weight of

| | |
|---|---|
| Troy grains | 180 |
| Deduct 1/12 alloy | 15 |
| Containing pure silver Troy grains | 165 |

(The fine silver in the Calcutta Sicca Rupee was Troy grains 175.927, Madras Arcot Rupee 166.447 and Bombay Rupee 164.14.)

## Introduction of Silver Rupee

In 1808 the Governor in Council appointed a committee of three members, known as the Madras Mint Committee to supervise the affairs of the Madras Mint and to suggest the needed steps for the implementation of the reforms in currency as suggested by the Court of Directors.[35]

The Mint Committee, after considering the reports from the provinces, concluded that evils in currency could be removed by replacing bimetallism with monometallism, as suggested by the Court of Directors and by fixing a standard of value for the new money and maintaining its proportionate predominance in their circulation.[36] The Mint Committee concluded that silver should be the standard of value and money of account in the Presidency of Madras. It fixed the exchange rate as three-and-half rupees for one Star *pagoda*. The coin which appeared to be of advantage was the Arcot Rupee. It was a silver coin already known in the territories, subjected to the Presidency of Madras. This weighted 176-2/5 grains and contained pure silver 166-191/400. The rupee proposed by the Court of Directors for general circulation contained therefore 1-191/400 grains less silver than the Arcot Rupee.[37]

The Mint Committee recommended commencement of the coinage of Rupees, halves and quarters of a standard and weight recommended by the Court of Directors leaving such old coins as the *fanam* pieces to remain in circulation until the fractions of the rupee were fully established.[38] But the Mint Committee deviated here from the original orders of the Court of Directors by slightly altering the ratio of alloy to be mixed with silver coins. Instead of 165 grains pure silver and fifteen grains of alloy as proposed by the Court of Directors the Mint Committee modified it by having 166.5 grains of pure silver and 13.5 grains of alloy. This was done to evercome any inconvenience likely to occur consequent on the introduction of the silver Rupee of eleven-twelfth fineness. As it helped the government to retain the full quantity of silver maintained in the old Arcot Rupee the Mint Committee felt that it would pass into circulation along with Arcot Rupee without any loss of volume.[39]

By the Proclamation dated 21 April 1812[40] the coinage of *pagodas* and their fractions and *fanams* and their fractions ceased: yet the old coins were allowed in circulation and issued and received at all public treasuries at the same rate and value before. The coinage of Rupees, Half Rupees and Quarter Rupees of English standard fineness was commenced at the Madras Mint. The Rupee weighed 180 grains of English Troy weight and contained 166½ grains of pure silver and 13½ grains alloy. The Half Rupee weighed 90 grains English Troy weight and contained 83¼ grains of pure silver and 6¾ grains of alloy. The Quarter Rupee weighed 45 grains English troy weight and contained 41⅝ grains pure silver and 3⅜ grains of alloy.[41] But the Court of Directors in their letter dated 12 June 1816[42] disapproved of the modification of their orders (in fixing the standard of the new silver Rupee with 166½ grains of pure silver and 13½ grains of alloy instead of their suggestion of 165 grains of pure silver and 15 grains of alloy) and desired that the government should take early action to carry into effect so much of their proposition of 1806 as regards the standard weight and fineness of coin that at least one complete step might be made towards the adoption of that general system which the Court had so long contemplated.

On this point the Mint Committee reluctantly agreed and readjusted the ratio as directed by the Court.[43] The Court also proposed that the Rupee should become the money of account and that the accounts or government should be converted from gold into silver at the ratio of one *pagoda* for three Rupees and a half.[44] Thus the task of reducing the existing units of currency to that proposed by the Court of Directors was first accomplished in Madras.[45]

The proclamation dated 7 January 1818[46] issued by the Governor in Council in obedience to the orders of the Court of Directors, declared the silver Rupee as the Standard coin of the Presidency of Madras. The public accounts were accordingly to be converted from the Star *pagoda* into the Madras Rupee at the exchange rate of 350 Rupees per 100 Star *pagodas* and all engagements of the government were in future to be concluded in Rupees and the pay and allowances of all their servants to be fixed in the same coin.[47]

The new coinage of silver was to consist of the following, viz., *Rupee* containing 165 grains of pure silver 15 grains of alloy and weighing 180 grains.[48]

*Half Rupee* containing 82½ grains of pure silver and 7½ grains of alloy and weighing 90 grains.

*Quarter Rupee* containing 41¼ grains of pure silver and 3¾ grains of alloy and weighing 45 grains.

*Double Anna* containing 20⅝ grains of pure silver and 1⅞ grains of alloy and weighing 22½ grains.

*Anna* containing 10⁵⁄₁₆ grains of silver and ¹⁵⁄₁₆ grains of alloy and weighing 11¼ grains.

A pure copper coin at the rate of twelve pice for one *anna* was to be issued. In spite of this change the *pagodas*, *fanams* and Cash remained in circulation.

Thus the Madras government took steps towards the enforcement of the ideal unit, proposed by the Court of Directors.[49] This important reform was effected by a gradual withdrawal of all the debased coins from circulation and by a steady recoinage over a period of nine years.

At the end of 1833, therefore, the position was that the Court of Directors desired to have a uniform currency with a single standard silver, while the authorities in India insisted upon a common currency with a bimetallic standard. The Charter Act of 1833 envisaged an Imperial system of administration with a centralization of all legislative and executive authority over the whole of India. This change in the administrative system *perforce* called forth further changes in the prevailing monetary system.[50]

## The Imperial Currency

It required the local coinage to be replaced by Imperial coinage; in other words, it favoured a common currency as against uniform currency. The Imperial government set up by the English parliament was not content to act the part of the Dewan or agent of the Mughals, and did not like to issue the coins in the name of the defunct Mughal Emperors. Determined to throw off the false garb, the Company issued an Imperial coinage in its own name which, being common to the whole of India, would convey its sway to the masses. Accordingly, an Act of Imperial Government (XVII of 1835) introduced a common currency for the whole of India as the sole legal tender.[51]

Thus India in 1835 gave up its crude bimetallism and adopted the silver standard. To Madras fell the honour of giving its Rupee as the standard coin for the entire India, envisaged by the Act XVII of 1835, because Madras was the first Presidency to effect the decision of the Court of Directors. The Act also laid down that gold should not thenceforth be legal tender of payment to British India and demonetized all the gold coins, which till then remained in circulation in the country. As a result of the acceptance of the Madras Rupee as the standard coin for the country, government did away with the prevailing confusion over the currency and laid the foundation for a stable system.

## Conclusion

One of the evils that affected the economy was a multiplicity of mints issuing many different varieties if coins. The first English collectors had to receive on account of revenue at least seventy varieties of gold and sixty varieties of silver coins.[52] is needless to say that this multiplicity of coins – most of them in different stages of debasement – caused extreme hardship to the people. Thus the transformation of the currency of Madras from multiplicity to uniformity helped the government to a great deal in its day-to-day administration.

However, the immediate result was not quite favourable, for, the demonetizing and discarding of the numerous varieties of rupees led to a shortage of legal tender money in the country and aggravated the fail of prices.[53] As Sir J.C. Coyajee rightly observes 'the progress of uniformity of currency though ultimately beneficial brought much immediate and wide hardship on the people, for, the withdrawal of debased currency led to a reduction of the circulating medium for a time and led to a great fluctuation of prices'.[54]

While the government took this wise measure of transformation of currency from multiplicity to uniformity, it took a very unwise step in the year 1836 by closing the Madras Mint on grounds of economy. This resulted in the gross dislocation of the entire monetary administration of Madras. The recoinage of obsolete and demonetized coins into coins of legal tender was greatly delayed because it had to be done by the Calcutta Mint. It resulted in the dearth of specie and thereby land revenue could not be collected properly, leading to a chaotic administration. But fortunately the Madras Mint was re-established a 1841; and slowly matters were set right.

But in a country where trade was not very much developed, money economy had not progressed much, and banking system had rot developed yet, large quantities of coins were reuired to furnish a currency; It was, therefore, a right step to bring down the confused bimetallism so silver monometallism which went a long way, after the initial set-backs, to stabilize the economy of the country.

Several objections were raised against the introduction of the Rupee in many of the southern districts right from the beginning. It was contended that in those districts gold had always been the measure of value and that the introduction of the silver rupee would upset the whole system of local accounts. But these objections were of local nature. Yielding to such objections would have defeated the object of a general reform, for, under the great variety of currency prevailing throughout the Presidency of Madras it would have been impossible to establish any general system, without altering in a certain degree the prevailing customs of particular districts. But such alterations were made, by and large without any apparent inconvenience and with positive advantages.

It cannot be disputed, of course, that the original currency of all the southern districts was gold and copper. But silver coinage, though of later origin, had by the beginning of the nineteenth century already become the predominant currency, and the Company's system had to be adapted to the existing circumstances.

Thus the provisions of the Act XVII of 1835 was a grim surprise. However, the *volte face* displayed there, will ever remain memorable in the annals of Indian monetary system. 'It marked the culminating point of a long and arduous process of monetary reform and placed India on a silver monometallic basis with a Rupee weighing 180 grains and containing 165 grains of fine silver as the common currency and sole legal tender throughout the country.'[55]

## Notes

1. E.J. Rapson, *Sources of Indian History* (*Coins*), 1897, p. 128.
2. A. Appadorai, *Economic Conditions in Southern India, 1000-1500* AD, 2 vols., University of Madras, vol. II, 1936, p, 706.
3. Ferishta's *History of the Rise of Mehemedan Power in India, till the year* AD *1612*. Translated from original Persian by John Briggs in four volumes. Calcutta, 1908, vol. I, p. 374.
4. Appadorai, op. cit., p. 706.
5. Farishta's *History*, vol. I, p. 374.
6. Walter Elliot (Sir), 'Coins of Southern India', *The International Numismata Orientalia*, London, 1885, p. 152.
7. *Vijayanagar Six Centenary Volume*, Dharwar, 1936, p. 107.
8. Ibid.
9. H.M. Elliot (Sir) and J. Dawson, *History of India as Told by Its Own Historians*, 4 vols., vol. IV, Allahabad: Kitab Mahal, 1964, p. 109.
10. G. Bidie, 'The Pagoda or Varaha coins of Southern India', *The Journal of Asiatic Society of Bengal*, vol. I, part I, 1883.
11. W.H. Moreland, *India at the Death of Akbar: An Economic Study*, London, 1920, p. 54.
12. Henry H. Dodwell, 'Substitution of Silver for Gold in South India', *Indian Journal of Economics*, January 1921.
13. Ibid.
14. Ibid.
15. Prof. J.C. Sinha in his *Economic Annals of Bengal*, London, 1927, p. 111, says that the English East India Company at Fort Saint George obtained the privilege of minting even before the close of the seventeenth century. So the Company had its own mints at Fort St. George and Fort St. David. But in Bengal there was no mint for the Company until 1757, because Mughal Emperor refused to grant the request of the Company or the establishment of a mint. At last in 1757 the Company in Bengal succeeded in establishing its own mint in Calcutta and the first Rupee struck there on 29 August of that year,
16. *Diary and Consultation Book* for the year 1725, p. 39.
17. Henry H. Dodwell, *Calender of Madras Records: 1740-1744*, Madras, 1917, p. x.
18. Ibid.
19. *Madras Diary and Consultation Book*, vol. LX, p. 126.
20. Madras State Archives, Madras, 'Public Consultation M.S.', vol. LXXI, p. 112.
21. Ibid., p. 362.
22. Ibid.
23. Ibid.

24. Ibid., vol. LXX, consultation dated 7 June 1741.
25. Dodwell, 'Substitution of Silver for Gold in South India', op. cit.
26. Ibid.
27. Ibid.
28. Madras State Archives, Report of the Committee of Finance, 26 March 1800 (Public Sundries) MS, p. 692.
29. B.R. Ambedkar, *The Problems of the Indian Rupee: Its Origin and Solutions*, London, 1923, p. 8.
30. Madras State Archives, Public Despatches from England for the year 1806, MS.
31. Quoted in Public letter, dated 25 April 1806.
32. J.C. Coyajee (Sir), *Indian Currency System 1835-36*, William Mayer Lectures, Madras University, 1930, p. 10.
33. Madras State Archives, Public Despatches from England, 1806, MS.
34. Ibid.
35. Madras State Archives, Mint Master's Government Letter Book for 1806-8. Letter dated 20 August 1808 from the Chief Secretary to Government to the newly-constituted Mint Committee Members, MS.
36. Madras State Archives, Proceedings of the Madras Mint Committee from 13 March to 9 October 1812 (Proceedings dated 13 March 1812), MS.
37. Ibid., Letter dated 8 April 1812.
38. Ibid.
39. Ibid.
40. Madras State Archives, Public Consultation dated 21 April 1812, MS.
41. Ibid.
42. Madras State Archives, Public Despatches from England for the year 1816, MS.
43. Proceedings of the Mint Committee from 30 May to 30 December 1817. Proceedings dated 3 October 1817, MS.
44. Madras State Archives, Public Despatches from England, 1816, MS.
45. Ambedkar, op. cit., p. 18.
46. Extracts from the Proclamation of the Governor in Council in the Proceedings of the Mint Committee from 6 January to 30 June 1818 under the date 27 January 1818, MS.
47. Ibid.
48. Ibid.
49. Ambedkar, op. cit., p. 18.
50. Ibid., p. 21.
51. Ibid., p. 22.
52. Report of the Committee of Finance, 1800, MS, p. 692.
53. P.J. Thomas and B.N. Pillai, *Economic Depression in Madras Presidency from 1820 to 1854*, Madras University, 1933, p. 11.
54. Coyajee, op. cit., p. 6.
55. Ambedkar, op. cit., p. 23.

*WESTERN INDIA*

# 11

# The Coinages of the East India Company at Bombay, under the Charters of Charles II, with a Note on the Indian Exchanges of the Period

EDWARD THOMAS

We derive much indirect information on this subject from the contemporary testimony of Tavernier, that adventurous traveller and experienced trader in 'precious stones', who was in India during part of the reigns of Shah Jahan and Aurangzeb. He is said to have been born in AD 1605 and to have died, at Moscow, in 1689. He tells us in his preface, 'si la première education est comme une seconde naissance, je puis dire que je suis venn au monde avec le désir de voyager' – and further, 'ainsi j'ai vû avec loisir dans mes six voyages et par differens chemins toute la Turquie, toute la Perse, et toutes les Indes'.[1] His memoirs were only written out from his notes, by others, after his return to Europe,[2] so that it is often difficult, to fix the precise date to which he refers for any special incident. He was in England in the time of James the 1st, and we find him, after many wanderings, at Agra in AD 1641 and again in AD 1665.

The following passages contain his leading remarks on the English coinages in India:

Figure 1 and 2 is the money which the English coin in their Fort St. George or else at Madraspatan, upon the coast of Coromandel. They call them *Pagods*, as those of the Kings and *Rajas* of the country are called. They are of the same weight, the same goodness and pass for the same value. Formerly the English never coined any silver or copper money. . . .

But since the present King of England married the Princess of Portugal, who had in part of her portion the famous port of Bombeye where the English are very hard at work to build a strong Fort, they coin both silver, copper and tin ['estain' pewter?] But that money will not go at Surat, nor in any part of the Great Mogul's dominions, or in any of the territories of the Indian Kings; only it passes among the English in their Fort, and some 2 or 3 leagues up in the country, and in the villages along the coast.

As regards the first part of this quotation, it would seem that the Portuguese and Dutch had already introduced a system of imitating the native currencies to meet the facilities of commerce,[3] in which practice we naturally followed them. As a general rule, the nations of the Peninsula were more inclined to accept the adjudication of the moneychanger, than to give credence to any royal stamp: in short, they preferred the tests of *scales* and the *cupel* to the impressed authentication of the officers of the king's Mint. Ferishtah[4] has preserved a curious record of how, on the conquest of the Dekhan, the Muhammadans were much put out by the pertinacious local habit of passing their new money through the crucible and its immediate conversion into *pagodas*, etc. The motive for this was supposed to have been due to the religious zeal of the Hindus, who desired to perpetuate the sacred emblems of their creed in supersession of the pious legends of Islam, but it seems more reasonable to suppose that these measures were simply prompted by a desire to secure certainty of value in the form usually accepted by the masses and sanctioned by the ancient guilds of the crafts of goldsmiths and sarrafs.

'The Portugals,' in the time of Tavernier, had got beyond mere local issues, and coined fine gold, with European devices,[5] for the dependencies of Goa, but they also had 'Silver Pardos' [Patacas] and 'a great quantity of small copper and tin money, not much unlike that of the kings already mentioned'.[6]

We can complete the details of the latter portion of the passage contributed by Tavernier from our home annals, and can produce specimens from our own Mints, which will probably explain why the money we first coined at Bombay did not find acceptance outside of our own domains.

Charles II came to the throne in AD 1660. His marriage contract with Catherine, the sister of Alphonso VI of Portugal, was arranged late in 1661, and completed in about May 1662. Under its terms he obtained the cession of the Island of Bombay, which was made over to the East India Company on 27 March 1668,[7] and finally passed into their possession on the 23 September of that year, with its then revenue of £2,833 per annum, and the king's garrison of two companies of foot, and who volunteered into the 'Company's Service, and thus formed its first military establishment at Bombay.'[8] In 1671, Bombay, rising in importance, 'a Mint was ordered, and the building of 2 ships and 2 brigantines commenced upon.'[9] 'In 1676 (28th Charles II) by the King's letters patent dated 5th October, a Mint was authorised at Bombay to coin Rupees, Pice and Bud-grooks,' which should be current not only 'in the Island, but in all the dependencies of the Company in the East Indies.'

Of course, it is somewhat venturesome to speculate on international trade exchanges upon such limited materials as the available coins afford. But it would seem that they essentially confirm and explain Tavernier's statement of the non-currency of the earlier Bombay issues outside the Island, a fact, indeed, which is virtually admitted by the king's letters patent of 1676. They, moreover, appear to support the inference of the 2s.-3d. rate of exchange per rupee, which our own countrymen clearly looked upon as a *quasi* normal tariff. I shall have occasion to revert to the question of English money as estimated against Indian metallic values, but this much may be stated here, that the old Company, in the first instance, clearly underrated the value of the local rupee, as may be seen by comparing the weight of no. 1, or the Company's Coin of the 7th year of their Charter of 1668 = AD 1675, with the increased weights given to the subsequent issues nos. 3, 4, bearing the Royal Arms.[10]

I have selected the eight subjoined examples of Anglo-Indian money issued during the reign of Charles II, and added a single specimen of the Bombay Rupees of James II of 1687, which reverts to the arms of the East India Company.

## Charles II

No. 1. Silver, weight 1778 grains. Date *Anno-septino* 7th year[11] – British Museum.

Obverse.

*Centre.*

MON:
BOMBAY
ANGLIC
REGIMS
A° 7°

*Margin.* – A: DEO: PAX: ETINCREMENTVM:

Reverse.

*Centre.* – Shield, with the arms of the East India Company. *Above,* two rosettes at the sides, in the middle two lions and two *fleur de lis* quartered. *Below,* two ships and a brig.

*Margin.* – IND: OKI: HON: SOC: ANG:

No. 2. Silver, Weight 1678 grains. Date AD 1677. B.M.

Obverse.

*Centre.*

THE
RUPEE
OF BOMBAIM

above one, below two, rosettes.

*Margin.* – 1677. BY ATHORITY OF CHARLES THE SECOND.

Reverse.

*Centre.* – The Royal Arms of England, in a shield; viz. three lions, the Scottish lion, the Irish harp, and the three *fleur de lis* of France. Above the shield a crown.

*Margin.* – KING OF GREAT BRITAIN, FRANCE AND IRELAND.

No. 3. Silver, weight 183-2 grains, date AD 1678. Edge *milled*[12] B.M.

Similar types and legends to No. 2.

No. 4. Silver, weight 1982 grains, dated AD 1678. Edge plain, BM.

Similar types and legends to No. 2.

No. 5. Copper (pice) weight? AD (16) 99 ? 1599.[13]

OBVERSE.

*Centre.* MOET
BOMBAY
ANGLIC
REGIME
A° D 99

*Margin.* – As in the Silver coins ? Traces of INCREME ?

REVERSE.

*Centre.* – Shield, with the arms of the E.I.C. *Above,* dotted stars, in place of rosettes at the sides; in the middle, two *fleurs de lis,* and two compartments filled in with dots. *Below* – three ships.

*Margin.* – Illegible traces of the letters SOC: ANG:

No. 6. A farthing of Charles II. date AD 1674 B.M.

OBVERSE. CAROLVSA
CAROLO

REVERSE. REN
BRITANNIA.

Re-struck with the die for the silver Rupees, No. 2 above.

No. 7. – *Lead.* AD 1768 ? B.M.

Types and legends as in the *Silver* Rupees.

No. 8. – Fanam[14]

OBVERSE.

*Centre.* – Two linked C's, the monogram of Charles the second), with 2 or 3 dots, at the sides.

REVERSE.

*Centre.* – The ordinary standing figure of the Indian god *(Vishnu* ?)

## JAMES II

No. 9. – Silver, Weight ? Date AD 1687.[15]

OBVERSE.

*Centre.* PAX
DEO

*Margin.* – BOMBAIEXSIS MONETA: 1687.

REVERSE.

*Centre.* – Shield, with the arms of the East India Company. *Above,* two rosettes and two dots at the sides, in the middle two lions and two *fleur de lis* quartered. *Below* three ships and three small stars.

## *Note on the Indian Exchanges*

A controversy has lately been raised as to the exchange value of the Rupees of the Delhi Mughals, as compared with the English money of the period – and, perhaps these quasi-English coins may aid in determining the question. One of the arguments advanced for the reduction of the par value of the Rupee, to less than two shillings, has been based upon the returns given by Foreign writers, *in French livres.* The selection of this test, however, does not appear to have been fortunate, inasmuch as the English translator of Tavernier in 1677,[16] in his Table of Values gives the Rupee of Gold as £1-11-6, and the Rupee of Silver as two shillings and three pence. In the same way, the English Editor of Bernier's Work[17] estimates the Rupee at 29 pence, and so converts the sum of six *crures* of Rupees into 7½ millions of English pounds.[18] Harris, in 1701, in recapitulating the authorities collected by Ramusio goes beyond this and fixes the Rupee at 2s 6*d.* Thus, in giving the totals of Aurangzeb's Revenues at 1207,18,76,840 *dams,* or Rupees 30,17,96.864, he estimates these sums in English money at £37,724,615.[19]

The next series of definitions of exchange rates consist, for the most part, of the contemporary testimony of Englishmen, who probably carried British shillings to India, and there practically ascertained what they would go for. The first on the list is the eccentric Thomas Coryate, who defines the Mughal Revenues in 1615, as '40 millions of crowns of six shillings each'. We need not here attempt to reconcile these totals, as in another place he allows us to infer that he places the rupee at 2s. in defining a *lack* at £10,000 sterling.[20]

Terry in 1616 speaks of the rupees as 'of divers values, the meanest being worth 2 shillings, and the best about 2 shillings and *nine* pence',[21] an estimate which is accepted by De Laet in ' Rupias . . . quae communiter valent duos solidos et *novem* denarios Angl. interdum etiam tantum duos.'[22] Finally Sir Thomas Herbert, in his 'Some yeares of Travaile, begunne in 1626,'[23] tells us 'a Mahrnudi is 12 pence, a rupee 2 shillings and three pence'.

But with all this, we must remember that our King's shilling was only a *token,* not a measure of value. Twelve pence in silver instead of being equal to *one-twentieth* (1⁄20) of the standard pound, had been very extensively reduced at this date, as will be seen from the accompanying Tables of English Silver Coins. But this difficulty of relative values may possibly be disposed of by the parallel definitions, *in gold*, which are so often to be met with.[24]

On the other hand, the true measure of value in India was dependent upon, so to say, three different standards: (1) the copper, which had not vet lost its early *status* as an arbiter of values – seeing that the revenues of the State were still estimated in *dams;* (2) the silver, which was fast taking the place of the lower metal; and (3) the gold, which in the increase of the material riches of the land, was beginning to have a fixed and recognised ratio as against silver.

And here it will be necessary to advert, briefly, to the English Monetary System. William the Norman brought over with him the method of dividing the *Saxon* pound of 5,400 grains into 20 shillings, and the shillings into 12 pence. This pound was called the *moneyer's pound,*[25] and constituted the Mint standard, 'until the reign of Henry VIII, in AD 1528, when the Troy pound was made the Mint weight in room of the *moneyer's* pound or the *Tower* pound, which was 1⁄10 less, or 5,400 grains'.[26]

In process of time the 240 pennies of the old standard came to be 792 pence of 7.2727 grains each, in lieu of William the Conqueror's full 22.5 grains, and the 20 *nominal* shillings (or 21⅓ of the pound Troy), expanded into 62 in 18th Charles II, 1665, and into 66 in 1816 with parallel reductions in value in each case.

The subjoined Tables exhibit – No. I the absolute variations; No. II the working results. No. III the relative values of Gold and Silver in the English system. It has not been attempted to reconcile minor discrepancies: but the authority for No. I is distinctly avowed, and the materials for No. II are grounded on the actual weights of extant coins, which Mr. E. Hawkins, as head of the Medal Room in the British Museum had so many opportunities of verifying, while the data for No. III are sufficiently defined in the standard work of Ruding.

## Preliminary Note

Whatever the division of money may have been in England in the Anglo-Saxon times, there is no doubt that it has been the same ever since the reign of William the Conqueror as at present [1805], viz. 12 pennies in a shilling, which never was a real coin till the year 1504, and 20 shillings in a pound, which though not a real coin, was a real pound, containing 12 ounces of standard silver, till the reign of Edward I, from which period the weight of the nominal pound has gradually been diminished, till it is now about one-third of what it originally was. The depreciation which money has suffered in respect to the value of necessary food and other useful commodities, is the effect of the increase of bullion in Europe, by the importation from America, and the increase of taxes, which in very many articles now constitute the greatest part of the price.

Table I: Showing at one view how many pounds, shillings, and pennies, have been coined out of a pound of silver at different times in England

| *Before* AD *1300, a pound of Standard Silver contained** | | | *Fine Silver* | | *Alloy* | | *£.* | *s.* | *d.* |
|---|---|---|---|---|---|---|---|---|---|
| | | | *oz.* | *dwt.* | *oz.* | *dwt.* | | | |
| | | | 11 | 2 | 0 | 18 | 1 | 0 | 0 |
| AD 1300 | 28 | Edward I | 11 | 2 | 0 | 18 | 1 | 0 | 3 |
| AD 1344 | 18 | Edward III | 11 | 2 | 0 | I8 | 1 | 2 | 2 |
| AD 1346 | 20 | Edward III | 11 | 2 | 0 | 18 | 1 | 2 | 6 |
| AD 1353 | 27 | Edward III | 11 | 2 | 0 | 18 | 1 | 5 | 0 |
| AD 1412 | 13 | Henry IV | 11 | 2 | 0 | 18 | 1 | 10 | 0 |
| AD 1464 | 4 | Edward IV | 11 | 2 | 0 | 18 | 1 | 17 | 6 |
| AD 1527 | 18 | Henry VIII | 11 | 2 | 0 | 18 | 2 | 5 | 0 |

*Note:* All these numerals denote the regnal years of the respective rulers. [Ed.]

| | | | | | | | | | |
|---|---|---|---|---|---|---|---|---|---|
| AD 1543 | 34 | Henry VIII | 10 | 0 | 2 | 0 | 2 | 8 | 0 |
| AD 1545 | 36 | Henry VIII | 6 | 0 | 6 | 0 | 2 | 8 | 0 |
| AD 1546 | 37 | Henry VIII | 4 | 0 | 8 | 0 | 2 | 8 | 0 |
| AD 1549 | 3 | Edward VI | 6 | 0 | 6 | 0 | 3 | 12 | 0 |
| AD 1551[27] | 5 | Edward VI | 3 | 0 | 9 | 0 | 3 | 12 | 0 |
| AD 1551 end of 1552 | 6 | Edward VI | 11 | 1 | 0 | 19 | 3 | 0 | 0 |
| AD 1553 | 1 | Mary | 11 | 0 | 1 | 0 | 3 | 0 | 0 |
| AD 1560 | 2 | Elizabeth | 11 | 2 | 0 | 18 | 3 | 0 | 0 |
| AD 1601 | 43 | Elizabeth | 11 | 2 | 0 | 18 | 3 | 2 | 0 |

*Note:* These rates of English money are taken by Mr. Folkes from the indentures made with the Masters of the Mint, and consequently may be depended on as authentic. – MacPherson's *Annals of Commerce*, vol. IV, Appendix II, London, 1805.

TABLE II: OF THE WEIGHTS OF THE DIFFERENT DENOMINATIONS OF SILVER COINS (INCLUDING ALLOY)

| | AD | *Silver penny* | *Shilling* |
|---|---|---|---|
| William I | 1066 | 22½ grams. | |
| Edward I | 1300 | 22 | |
| Edward III | 1344 | 20¼ | |
| Edward III | 1346 | 20 | |
| Edward III | 1351 | 18 | |
| Henry IV | 1412 | 15 | |
| Edward IV | 1464 | 12 | |
| Henry VII | 1504 | | 141 grains |
| Henry VIII | 1543 | 10 | 120 |
| Edward VI | 1549 | | 80 |
| Edward VI | 1552 | 8 | 96 |
| Mary | 1553 | | 96 |
| Elizabeth | 1601 | 7½ | 92¼ |

Such continued to be the weight of the several coins until the 56th George III (1816), when at the great recoinage the following weights were established.

| *6d.* | *Shilling½* | *Crown* | *Crown* |
|---|---|---|---|
| 40⅓ | 80⅔ | 201⅗ | 403½[27] |

## *English Gold*

The first gold coin struck, after the Norman conquest, was the '*gold pennie*' of the 41st year of Henry III, it weighed two *startings* or silver-penee. and passed for 20 pence.[28] 'In the 40th year of the reign it was raised from its original value to 2-4 pence.'[29] We may disregard the intermediate changes and come to the *sovereigns* of 20 shillings each, first minted by Henry VII, and subsequently fixed under the name of *unites* by James I. at 22 *carats* fine (i.e. 11/13 fine gold, 1/13 alloy) and 33½ pieces to the pound troy. Under Charles II (1660), a new coinage of guineas at 44½ to the pound troy, was issued. This coin varied in its current price from 20 shillings up to 39, until the year 1717, when it was fixed authoritatively at 21 shillings Sovereigns of 20 shillings were finally introduced in 1816,[30] 46 23/40 pieces going to the troy pound; thus each coin contained 4 dwt. 17.001 grains, or 113.001 grains of *pure* gold.

For the purposes of comparison of exchange computations and exhibiting the persistent fall in the value of silver, I quote the subjoined abstract of a Table prepared by Ruding[31] of the relative values of the higher metals.

The *fractions* which are, at times of considerable importance, have been omitted in this summary.

TABLE III: OF THE RELATIVE VALUE OF GOLD AND SILVER

| | *Gold* | *Silver*[32] | *Proportion* |
|---|---|---|---|
| Henry I. 5 | fine | 11.2-18 | 1 to 9 |
| Henry III. 14 | „ | „ | 1 to 10 |
| Henry III. 41 | „ | .. | 1 to 9 |
| Edward I. 6 | .. | „ | 1 to 10 |
| | Car gr. alloy | „ | |
| Edward III. 18 | 233½ 0½ | 11.2-18 | 1 to 12 |
| Edward III. 20 | .. | „ | 1 to 11 |
| Henry IV. 13 | .. | | 1 to 10 |
| Edward IV. 4 | .. | | 1 to 11 |
| Henry VIII. 18 | .. | | 1 to 11 old standard |

| | | | | | |
|---|---|---|---|---|---|
| Henry VIII. 18 | 22 | 2 | | | 1 to 11 new standard[33] |
| Henry VIII. 34 | Debasement | | | | 1 to 10 |
| Henry VIII. 36 | ,, | | .. | | 1 to 6 |
| Henry VIII. 37 | ,, | | .. | | 1 to 5 |
| Edward VI. 3 | ,, | | .. | | 1 to 5, |
| Edward VI. 4 | ,, | | | | 1 to 4 |
| Edward VI. 5 | ,, | | .. | | 1 to 2 |
| Edward VI. 6 | 233½ | 0½ | | | 1 to 11 old standard |
| Edward VI. | 22.0 | 2 | .. | | 1 to 11 new standard |
| * | | * | | * | * |
| Elizabeth. *2* | ,, | | .. | | 1 to 11 |
| James 1, *2*, 3 | ,, | | .. | | 1 to 12 old standard |
| James 1, *2*, 3 | | | | | 1 to 12 new standard |
| James 9 | | | | | 1 to 13 |
| * | | * | | * | * |
| Charles II. 15 | 22 | 2 | .. | | 1 to 14 |
| William & Mary | ,, | | .. | | 1 to 15 |
| George I. 3 | ,, | | .. | | 1 to 15 |
| George I. 18 | | | | | 1 to 15 [34] |

## *Indian Silver*

The origin of the Indian rupee may be traced up to very early times, in the Aryan *sataraktika,* or *satakrisnala,* the *even* one hundred *rati* weight, which formed the basis of the standard gold and silver pieces of the early Pathan kings of Delhi (AD 1228), each of which weighed 100 *ratis* or 175 grains, and were conventionally termed *tankas.*[35] Muhammad bin Tughlak, in AD 1324, reverted to the local weight of Manu,[36] the *karsha* or *suvarna* of 80 *ratis* or 140 grains for his silver standard, and raised the weight of his gold pieces to 200 grains, which seems to imply some readjustment of the relative values of the two metals. Some uncertainty in the Mint arrangements continued until Sher Shah reformed the Indian coinages and introduced a new silver piece, now definitively called a rupee, of 178 grains.[37] Akbar followed the same standard, in weight, but claims to have improved the fineness of the metal.[38] And we have extant rupees of Shah Jahan weighing 178 grains, and numerous specimens of 177.5 grains.[39] To judge by the assay of his gold coinage, these rupees must have ranged at a better average than those of his predecessors.[40] Tavernier has a curious notice of the copper money current in India, in his day, which is worth preserving:

> The Indians have also a sort of small copper money, which they call *Pecha,* which is worth about 2½ of our *liards,* a *liard* being the 4th part of a *sous.* There is also ½ *pecha,* 2 *pechas,* and 4 *pechas.*
>
> According to the custom of the province where you travel, you have for a *Roupy* of silver more or less of these *peclias.*
>
> In my last travels, a Roupy went at Surat for 49 *pechas.* But the time was, when it was worth 50, and another time when it went but for 46. At Agra and Gehanabat, the *roupy* is valued at 55 and 56 *pechas,* and the reason is because the nearer you go to the copper mines, the more *pechas* you have for the *roupy.* (p. 22.)

Cowries, too, were subject to similar laws of distance from the Maldives. Near the sea, they were rated at 80 to the pice, at Agra, they went for 50 to 55 per pice (pp. 2, 8, 22). So with the bitter almonds, which made up the small change of the western coast, whose tariff was regulated by the productiveness of the trees in the deserts of Laristan.

## Indian Gold

The value of gold, in Asia, seems to have been largely affected by geographical surroundings, proximity to sites of production, facilities of transport, and other casual laws of supply and demand.[41] The Southern Peninsula of India had, as it appears, gold mines of its own, and Ocean commerce brought it bountiful supplies. In the North, the Bactrian Greeks were satisfied with currencies of silver and copper, whereas the Indo-Skythians coined gold in large quantities, and not only obtained directly extensive supplies of Roman gold coin, but imitated and possibly re-struck many of the Imperial *dinarii.*[42] The kingdom of Kanauj continued, in modified types, an extensive issue of that metal, which lasted till the Muhammadan conquest by Muhammad bin Sam, who indeed reproduced, in altered terms, the local devices. Mahmud of Ghazni's mints very early utilized Central Asian gold, and the plunder of India, from time to time, contributed fresh stores of precious metal for the moneyer's purpose.

The Pathan kings of Dehli, as we have seen, coined both gold and silver in equal weights, both being as pure as they could make them, but relative values had clearly to be readjusted as altered circumstances demanded. At first the scale appears to have been 1 to 8. In Akbar's time it was 1 to 9.4,[43] in Aurangzeb's reign 1 to 14.[44] And at this rate of 1 to 14 oar own East India Company, in 1766, coined gold as 149.72 fine, to the rupee, containing 175.92 of pure silver.[45] The proportion was not, however, found sufficient to secure the currency of the experimental gold *mohur,* and in consequence, in 1769, a new Regulation was passed raising the gold *mohur* up to 1,90,086 fine, as against 16 rupees of the old standard of AD 1766.[46]

It may be mentioned in connection with these later details of the East India Company's mintages and exchange rates, that Stewart, in his *History of Bengal,* p. 8, estimates the rupee at 8 to the £ sterling (i.e. 2s. 6d. per rupee), and practically illustrates its effect, in citing the sale, in October 1811, of 40 lakh of rupees to the Bank of England for £495,527 sterling.

In conclusion, I may say that I have had no motive in collecting these statistics beyond the aim of placing the question of exchanges in its true light, and a desire to extend these new data to those who, past or present, seek to amend my first inferences by unsound arguments.

But, on the other hand, as regards the future, it is as well that political or other associations seeking to restore silver to its *old mission,* in India or elsewhere, should recognize the fact that, in the former case, things are changed from the compensating all-round trade in goods and metals of the old East India Company to the leech-like heavy charges of the present Home Government, which draws indiscriminately, for its own wants bills in *Rupees,* on its hapless dependency, in season and out of season, whether the balance of trade or metallic exchange is for or against them.

## Notes

1. The earliest edition of his works appeared in Paris in 1676, with reprints in 1677, and 1679, Amsterdam 1678, and 'Made English by J.P.' in London, 1678. Harris's *Voyages,* 1764, vol. I, p. 810, reproduces most of the text, and Pinkerton, 1811, vol. VIII, gives the chapter on Diamonds, &c.
2. Les *Voyages de Tavernier,* ont ete rediges d'apres see propres notes, en partie par Chapuzean, son ami, et en partie par Daulier des Landes, qui l'a accompagnc dans l'un de ses voyages.—*Nouveau Dictionnaire Bibliographique,* S.V.
3. Tavernier, pp. 6, 141. The *pagodas* of the Hollanders were 'better gold by 1 or 2 per cent' than those of the English.
4. *Ferishtah,* Bombay Persian text, Lithographed Edition, vol. I, p. 537; *Chronicles of the Pathan Kings of Dehli,* by Edward Thomas, p. 343.
5. These were known by the name of St. Thomas. Tavernier gives an engraving of a specimen—*Obverse,* the arms of the King in a shield, with G.A. at the sides, and REX PORTUGALLE; in the margin. *Reverse,* Figure of a man, with date 1660. Margin ST. THOME.
6. Tavernier, p. 13.
7. The grant bears date in 1668. 'Bombay was to be held [by the Company] of the king in free and common soccage, as of the manor of East Greenwich, on the payment of the annual rent of £10 in gold, on the 30th of September in each year.' Mill's *History,* vol. I, p. 97. See also, Hume, *Hist. England,* vol. VII, pp. 349, 378, etc.; MacPherson's *Annals of Commerce,* 1805, vol. II, p. 502; Harris's *Voyages,* vol. I, p. 898.
8. *Chronological Table of European and British Connection with India,* compiled by Capt. H.B. Henderson. This admirable resume was first published in Prinsep's *Useful Tables,* as an appendix to the *Journal of the Asiatic Society of Bengal,* vol. IV, for 1835, p. 153.
9. Bruce's *Annals,* pp. 280, 392.
10. Jahangir's Rupees of *Ahmedabad* weigh 176 and 1754 grains; Marsden, p. 167. Shah Jahan's *Surat* Rupee is also 176 grains; Marsden, p. 639.
11. Ruding, London, edn. 1819, Pl. IV, fig. 11, Suppl. ii, vol. V, p. 396.
12. The system of milling was first introduced into the English Mint by Blondean, in April 1662, and the first *milled* shilling was struck in 1663. Ruding, XXXIV, 12; Hawkins, pp. 213-18.
13. Ruding, Pl. XV, no. 13, vol. V, p. 369.
14. Ruding. vol. V, p. 296; Pl. VI, Suppt., figs. 16, 17; Pembroke, Pl. IV, T. 14; Leake, p. 376.
15. Ruding, Pl. XV, fig. 12.
16. *The Persian Travel,* London, 1677.
17. Second edition, London, 1676, vol. II, p. 164.
18. In the Appendix to vol. IV of this edition, p. 175, Bernier adds some particulars forgotten to be inserted in my first Book, and therein define the

Rupee as 'equivalent to 29 or 30 pence'. Bernier *himself* seems to have said at p. 53, vol. III, 'I have said elsewhere that a Roupie is almost equivalent to half a crown'.

19. Harris's *Voyages*, vol. I, p. 652; *The Revenue Resources of the Mughal Empire*, by Edward Thomas, London, 1371, pp. 32, 49, and *n.* p. 50.
20. Coryate's *Crudities* edition of 1776, 3 vols., 8vo, and *Purchas*, vol. I, p. 591, Kerr, vol. IX, pp. 422, 428.
21. *Purchas*, London, 1625, vol. II, p. 1464; Kerr, vol. IX. p. 292.
22. *De Imperto Magm Mogolis,* sive India Vera. Lugd. Bat. 1631; *Calcutta Review,* October 1870, *Revenue Resources,* pp. 19-22.
23. London, 1631, p. 41.
24. *Persian Travels,* London, 1676; Sir T. Herbert, p. 41.
25. Ruding, vol. I, p. 18. The Tower pound consisted of 12 oz , each ounce of 20 dwts., each dwt. of 24 grains, the whole was lighter than the Troy pound by ¼ of an ounce.
26. Kelly's *Universal Cambist,* p. xxi.
27. In this lowest depreciation of the English money the value of the nominal pound sterling was only 4 shillings and $7\frac{3}{4}$*d.* of modern money.
28. Edward Hawkins, *The Silver Coins of England,* London, 1841, p. 7.
29. Kuding, vol. II, pp. 70-1.
30. *Measures, Weights and Moneys* by W.S.B. Woolhouse (Weale's series), 3rd edn., 1867.
31. Ruding, 1819, vol. I, p. 28.
32. Ounces and dwt.
33. Excluding fractions.
34. A rise of 5 per cent. The whole rise from James I, 1, that is, a space of 115 years was = $39\frac{22}{67}$ per cent.
35. *Pathan Kings of Dehli,* pp. 3, 134, etc.; *Numismata Orientalia,* 'Ancient Indian Weights', London, 1874, pp. 12, 36, 70.
36. Manu, vol. VIII, p. 136.
37. *Pathon Kings of Dehli,* p. 405
38. Prinsep's *Essays,* London, 1858, p. 43. Akbar's Gold *mohur* of 186.60 grains is *pure* gold; so is the average return at p. 56.
39. Marsden's *Numismata Orientalia,* London, 1823, pp. 644, 649, etc.
40. Prinsep's *Essays, U.T.,* pp. 43, 50.
41. Marco Polo gives the varying rates, in different localities, as gold to silver, 1 : 5 : 1 : 6; and 1 : 8.
42. *Jainism or, the early faith of Asoka,* Trubner, London, 1877, p. 63; *Journal R.A.S.,* N.S., vol. IX, p. 220; *Proceedings,* Asiatic Society of Bengal, 1879, Plate III.
43. *Pathan Kings of Dehli,* pp. 232, 424.
44. Tavernier, pp. 20, 101; *Journal, R.A.S.,* vol. II, N.S., 1866, pp. 160, 163.
45. I omit the alloy in both cases.
46. Prinsep's *Essays, Useful Tables,* pp. 72, 73.

# 12

# The Monetary System of British India

ANONYMOUS

The currency of a country may, to use a homely illustration, be aptly compared to the blood in the human body. If it circulate too rapidly, a state of feverish excitement is betrayed; if too slowly, a falling-off in social health or prosperity becomes quickly apparent. There may be too much or too little iron in the blood; so likewise there may be too much or too little paper in a currency. A sudden accession or diminution of wealth from extraordinary causes has, moreover, an injurious effect on a country, somewhat similar to that which a sudden change from high to low living, or *vice versa,* produces on the human constitution. The circulation of the blood is, comparatively speaking, but a recent discovery. We are of opinion that the problem of the monetary system, best adapted to the wants of mankind, still remains to be solved. The question has lately received much of that attention which its importance demands; and as many thoughtful men are apparently devoting their best energies to its solution, we may reasonably conclude that, ere long, they will throw light upon this obscure subject.

It must be admitted that the problem is an exceedingly complicated one. Without undertaking its solution, we may here address ourselves to the humbler, but, we trust, not unserviceable task of reviewing briefly the various alterations which it has been, from time to time, proposed to make in the monetary system of British India.

It will be proper to advert, in the first instance, to the older monetary schemes, which had been adopted within the Peninsula.

Prior to the advent of the British two systems had existed, the Hindoo and the Mussulman. The unit of the former was of gold, the *pagoda* of about 60 grains weight – and that of the latter of silver, the Rupee weighing from 170 to 175 grains. The Hindoo system has become nearly extinct, having been almost entirely superseded by the Mussulman.

The *pagoda* is a Portuguese appellation, derived from the pyramidal temple depicted on one side of the gold pieces issued in the most recent Hindoo coinage. Its proper name is Varaya, signifying wild boar, and originating in the device of the boar incarnation of Vishnoo, which is found on the ancient coinage of the Carnatic. It is supposed that the name of this coin in ancient times varied according to the image or idol stamped upon it. The *pagoda* is also known by the term Hun, a word signifying gold in the old Carnatic language.

The *Pagoda* was subdivided into *fanams* and Cash: thus 80 Cash = 1 *fanam.*

3,360 Cash = 42 *fanams* = 1 *pagoda.*

There is reason to believe that the Rupee (properly Rupya silver piece) was introduced by Sher Shah, Emperor of Delhi, about the year 1542. Prior to that time the Arab coins, the *dirhem* (silver drachma) and the gold *dinar* (*denarius auri*) and the copper *fuloos* formed the currency of the Moghul dominions.

The period when the gold *mohur* was first coined appears to be uncertain. It is supposed to have had a common origin with the rupee, and to have been struck about the same time. The old *mohurs* vary in weight from 159 to 207 grains.

There is little known respecting the ancient copper coinage of India. Almost every town and village had, until very lately, a separate copper currency, and a fluctuating rate of exchange for the rupee, which occasioned great inconvenience to travellers, and frequent loss to the poorer classes. The native copper coins vary in weight from 34 to 280 grains. At Fairs, and in the neighbourhood of old towns in Upper India, not only ancient Hindoo coins but Bactrian and Roman copper coins may be met with.[1]

The following table exhibits the scheme of the British Indian monetary system as at present existing:

| *Gold Mohur* | *Silver Rupee* | *Copper Anna* | *Pysa* | *Pie* |
|---|---|---|---|---|
| 1 | 15 | 240 | 960 | 2880 |
| | 1 | 16 | 64 | 192 |
| | | 1 | 4 | 12 |
| | | | 1 | 8 |
| | | | | 1 |

The subdivisions used in the public and other accounts are rupees, annas, and pies. Many mercantile houses and traders in Bombay still retain, however, the old subdivision of rupees, quarters, and reas; one hundred reas, an imaginary coin, being counted as equivalent to a quarter of a rupee.

Small shells called couries are also made use of in the districts for fractional payments, and are reckoned as follows:

4 Cowries = 1 Gunda; 20 Gundas = 1 Pun; 5 Puns = 1 Anna.

Although the gold mohur and copper anna form subdivisions in the scheme of the British Indian currency, those coins are *not* current. The former because it is not a legal tender, and the latter because it has never been coined. Silver halves, quarters, and eighths should perhaps have been included in the scheme, as they *are* current; likewise the copper half anna, and half pysa, the former being in extensive circulation, and the latter having been recently ordered to be struck.

Preliminary to the adoption of the existing monetary system, the subject was fully discussed between the years 1812 and 1827 in all its bearings, both at home and in India. The arithmetical convenience of a decimal division of the currency was at the same time considered. It was, however, rejected, almost without discussion, as being not only inferior for every practical purpose to the sex-decimal arrangement, but as unsuitable to British India.

The decimal scheme then proposed, which emanated from Major Hawkins, the first Mint Master of the present Bombay

Mint, involved the subdivision of the rupee into real and imaginary parts, the latter being supposed to consist of 1,000, as will be seen from the following table:

| | |
|---|---|
| 10 Reas or Milreas | = 1 Pice |
| 10 Pice | = 1 Anna |
| 10 Annas | = 1 Rupee |

The decimal subdivision advocated in the *Bombay Times* in May last is, we are of opinion, preferable to the scheme suggested in 1827. It is as follows:

| | | | | | |
|---|---|---|---|---|---|
| Gold 10 Rupees | expressed decimally | = 10.0 | = 1000 | Doganees | = 2000 Pies. |
| Silver 1 Rupees | do. | = 1.0 | = 100 | do. | = 200 do. |
| Copper 1 Decime | do. | = .10 | = 10 | do. | = 20 do. |
| Ditto 1 Doganee | do. | = .01 | = 1 | do. | = 2 do. |

The coin denominated Pie had no place in the monetary system of India prior to 1827. If the pie had existed previously, and a decimal currency based on that coin instead of an imaginary one, the milrea, had been then suggested, it is, we think, probable that the adoption of a decimal, instead of a sexdecimal currency, would have been the result. It will be perceived from these remarks, that we concur with those who consider that the least valuable coin current is the unit, on which any modification or reform of a currency should be based. It is the standard coin of the poorest and most ignorant class, and, being hence the one most extensively known, it must surely be also the most suitable one upon which to construct a new monetary system.

There being only 192 pies in the rupee instead of 200, presents a difficulty, certainly, to the carrying out of the proposed new decimal scheme; but we are sanguine that this difficulty alone is not an insurmountable obstacle. In the first place, the proposed increase in the number of pies for a rupee is only 1/25th. Secondly, copper coin possesses little intrinsic value, it is a mere token; and its current value may therefore be modified, to a limited extent, with little or no inconvenience to the Government and the public generally; and lastly, the change would be of advantage to the poorer classes, since it would lessen the value of the pie. They would receive in exchange for a rupee 200 pies instead of only 192 as at present, and it is therefore probable that they might obtain more goods in the bazars for their money than they do at present.

The most serious objection to the scheme, to our apprehension, is, that it involves a new copper coinage. If the pie were the only copper coin current, there would be little difficulty in adapting that coin to the decimal system at once. There are, however, also current the half-anna and pysa, which would both have to be withdrawn from circulation in order to effect the desired change; and as the pie cannot at the same time bear two values, that coin would also necessarily have to be withdrawn.

It may perhaps be suggested, why not alter the value of those coins in the same manner as you propose altering the value of the pie? It may be asked in reply, what value would our querist himself assign to those coins? Their value relative to the pie, according to the decimal scheme, is respectively 6¼ and 3⅛ pies, both awkward fractions, and such as would be utterly unintelligible to the poorer classes. And as the quarter and eighth of a pie would, to their apprehensions, be imaginary, so would likewise be the extra hazar supplies, that the poor would receive on their account from the Marwarrees, who would thus entirely reap the benefit which, it has already been assumed, the poorer classes of our fellow-subjects might derive from the proposed change in the existing system of the currency.

Suppose, however, for the sake of argument, that it is determined the half-anna shall be considered as equivalent to 7 instead of 6 pies, and that the quarter-anna or pysa shall continue current at its present value. What would be the result of this arrangement?

The shroffs in exchanging half and quarter-annas for rupees would gain on the former 20 pies, and on the latter lose only 6 pies on each rupee. It may readily be imagined that, under these circumstances, the half annas would change hands very rapidly, for there is no class more alive to their pecuniary interests than the money changers of India. But the objections that might be urged to such a plan of carrying out the scheme are so numerous, that it could not be seriously entertained for a moment.

The only means that we can perceive of surmounting the difficulty is to coin a considerable number of half cent., one cent., and two-and-a-half cent. copper pieces, and to forward them to the several treasuries ready for circulation; then to prohibit the reissue of pies, and halt and quarter-annas, from the Government treasuries until a new value had been stamped upon them; that is on the pie the words half cent., on the pysa or quarter-anna one cent., and on the half-anna two-and-a-half cents.; and to issue simultaneously the new and the re-stamped coins. The restamped coins might be withdrawn from circulation at pleasure. In regard to the size of the copper coins, we have to observe that we see no greater necessity for a copper coin of the value of 6 cents. than there has been for the issue of an anna piece.

We should prefer seeing the accounts kept in rupees and cents., or doganees, and the value of each of the silver coins in cents. or doganees stamped upon them.

Assuming that a new copper coinage would be indispensably necessary, the next point to consider is, whether the advantages anticipated from the alteration would be adequate to the expense it would entail, and the temporary inconvenience and confusion which would inevitably result from even the most perfect arrangements that could be adopted, in carrying out so important a change.

When the reform of the copper currency of British India was under consideration, previous to 1827, it was estimated that upwards of 25 lakhs of rupees worth of new coin would have to be struck to replace the old or native coinage then in circulation in the Bombay Presidency. There is reason to suppose that this was an under-estimate, for, according to our calculations, nearly 36 lakhs of rupees worth of new copper coins have been coined at the Bombay mint since the year 1830, the period when the new coinage was begun; and although a considerable amount of the old coin is still extant, especially in the Deccan and Candeish districts, it is an undoubted fact that there has, for some time past, been a great demand on all sides for more copper coin.

Now as 36 lakhs of rupees worth of copper would weigh about 1,790 tons, – and it would occupy at least six years to coin that quantity of copper money in the prescribed proportions, i.e. 3/5ths of quarter-annas, 1/5th of half-annas, and 1/5th of pies, and the charges of the mint are about 2 lakhs per annum – it follows that the expense of replacing the coins now in circulation, within the Bombay Presidency alone, would amount to about 12 lakhs of rupees; and this is exclusive of loss from the difference between the invoice cost of the copper (about 50 per cwt.) and the price (about Rs. 47) that would probably be realized for the withdrawn coin, after it had either been melted down or broken up. The total expense of changing the copper currency of the whole of India, as proposed, would not, we estimate, fall short of 50 lakhs of rupees.

It may be urged that, whenever the copper coins now in circulation are withdrawn, the heavy expense above alluded to would have to be incurred; and that to call in the whole of the coin, and replace it as suggested, would be merely to anticipate the charge by a few years; but it should be remembered that, in the one case, the measure would be effected so very gradually that the expense would be scarcely felt; whereas, in the other, it would be impossible to carry it out without previous financial arrangement and great immediate cost.

We have also to observe on this point that, although some of the new or Company's copper currency has now been in circulation about twenty-seven years, we cannot perceive any necessity for withdrawing any portion of it at present; that it is probable such a measure need not be resorted to during the next thirty years; and that the profit which will ultimately have been derived from the copper coin having been issued at a value so much below its intrinsic worth would probably cover the cost of its recoinage. We do not here allude, it may be necessary to state, to the gain derived from the difference between the invoice value of the copper coin and its nominal value, but to compound interest – say at 5 per cent on that difference; and as the interest might safely be calculated on half the total coinage, the nominal value of the copper coin being about double its intrinsic value, it is evident that the gain from this source would amount to a very considerable sum; according to our calculations it would fall little short of 60 lakhs of rupees.

Preferring to employ decimal fractions in all ordinary calculations, we are little disposed to under-estimate the value of a decimal currency. It would undoubtedly save much time and labour. At the same time it must be admitted that the gain which would be derived from a decimal currency would be simply arithmetical. The loss on the other hand which the change of system would entail would be real. It would, in fact, be so serious, and the confusion and inconvenience it would occasion, for some time at least, would be so great and extensive, that we feel reluctantly compelled to side with those who deprecate the change. Such an important reform might have been successfully carried out in 1827, when it was determined that the currency of India should be made uniform. It is now, we believe, almost impracticable.

We now approach, but with considerable hesitation, the consideration of the very intricate and abstruse question, whether the common measure of commodities and principal instrument of commerce in British India should continue to be of one metal, and whether, in that case, the favoured metal should be silver?

The ablest writers on the subject have decided that only *one* metal can be the principal standard measure of property and medium of commerce. It is, however, a controverted point whether gold or silver is best adapted for that purpose. The Earl of Liverpool in his able treatise, addressed to King George III. In 1805, on the coins of Great Britain, argued that gold coin was the most suitable standard for Great Britain, and his recommendation was attended to; and we believe that subsequent experience has not shaken the confidence which was at the time reposed in that nobleman's judgement. The chief argument brought forward by the Earl of Liverpool in favour of gold was, that a gold currency was consonant with the practice and feelings of the people, and had become a necessity in consequence of the increased commerce of the country. These grounds appear to be as really, if not in the same degree, applicable to British India.

But before entering on the proposed discussion, it may be

well to give some account of the nature and properties of money, and to show why the standard of property should be of only one metal; and this we cannot do better, perhaps, than in the Earl of Liverpool's own words:

The money or coin of a country is the standard measure by which the value of all things bought and sold is regulated and ascertained; and it is itself, at the same time, the value, or equivalent, for which goods are exchanged, and in which contracts are generally made payable. In this last respect, money, as a measure, differs from all others; and to the combination of the two qualities before defined, which constitute the essence of money, the principal difficulties that attend it, in speculation and practice, both as a measure and an equivalent, are to be ascribed. These two qualities can never be brought perfectly to unite and agree; for if money were a measure alone, and made like all other measures of a material of little or no value, it would not answer the purpose of an equivalent. And if it is made, in order to answer the purpose of an equivalent, of a material of value, subject to frequent variations, according to the price at which such material sells at the market, it fails on that account in the quality of a standard or measure, and will not continue to be perfectly uniform and at all times the same.

Certain portions of gold, silver, and copper, with an impression struck upon them, by order of the sovereign, as a guarantee of their purity and weight, serve as coin.

Coins made of gold or silver, or of any other metal, whether considered as a measure or equivalent, are, however, subject to the following imperfections:

As each of these metals varies in its value with respect to the commodities for which it is exchanged, so it will vary for the same reason also in its value, in successive periods, even with respect to itself; and this variation is occasioned by the greater or less quantity that may happen to be, at different times, in the market or in circulation. Any given quantity or weight of gold or silver is at present of much less value than the same quantity or weight before the discovery of the mines in America. And if any commodity is either manufactured or produced at present, in exactly the same quantity as it was in the reign of Henry VII, when these mines were first discovered, and the demand for this commodity should be equal, a pound of gold or silver will not purchase as much of it now, as it would have purchased in the former period. Coins are on that account an imperfect measure, though they are made of one metal only.

But if coins are made of two of these metals, a second imperfection is then introduced; for any two of these metals, in successive periods, vary in value with respect to each other. The value of fine gold, compared with that of fine silver, was rated, in the 43rd of Elizabeth, at less than 11 to 1 at the English mint. But when guineas were first coined in 1663 the value of tine gold, compared with that of fine silver, was rated in the English mint at $14\ {}^{331}/_{682}$ to 1. Guineas were then coined as 20 shilling pieces, and declared by the mint indenture to be current as such. They have since been made current by proclamation as 21 shilling pieces. The relative value therefore of tine gold to fine silver, in the coins of this kingdom, is now as $15\ {}^{2859}/_{13640}$ to 1. And in the mints of several foreign countries the value of gold, compared with that of silver, is rated still higher. These metals will also occasionally vary in their value, even at the same time, in different countries; and exchange brokers and many bankers are induced on this account to carry on a traffic in these metals and in the coins made of them, to their own profit, and to the loss of others.

If the sovereign takes upon himself to determine the rate or value at which coins made of different metals shall at the same time pass in currency, *a.* third imperfection is introduced into the system; for it is not possible that he should be able to pursue, with sufficient accuracy, the various fluctuations and changes that may in a short time happen in the relative values of those different metals. Their prices at the market will therefore frequently differ from the rate at which he has valued them in his coins; and when coins made of different metals are equally legal tender, there will of course be two measures of property differing occasionally from each other. A profit will always in such case be made by those who traffic in coins, by exchanging that coin which has the least intrinsic value for that which has the greatest. The debtor will find it his interest to make his payments in the coin made of that metal which is overvalued at the mint; and such coins as are made of the metal undervalued at the mint, will always be melted down and exported.

Another imperfection arises from the gradual wear of the coins made of either of these metals; for though the materials of which they are made are less subject to diminution by daily and common use than almost any other commodity, they are still subject to it in a certain degree, from friction, and sometimes from other causes. If this diminution is considerable, the money jobber will avail himself of the inequality to which pieces of coin of the same denomination are, in this respect, subject; he will collect and convert into bullion the most weighty of them, and make a profit thereby; and those coins only which are less perfect will be left in general circulation.

Of the four imperfections before stated, the first, which arises from the variation in the price or value of any one metal, in successive periods, with respect to itself, is so inherent in the very subject, that it does not admit of a remedy. It produces, however, less inconvenience than either of the other three. It chiefly affects leases, contracts, and grants of long continuance. The three other imperfections may in some degree be remedied.

In how striking a manner have the truths or principles above set forth been recently illustrated! The discovery of gold in South America could not, we imagine, have disturbed the metallic currencies of the civilised world in the sixteenth century to a greater extent than the recent discoveries of auriferous deposits in California and Australia have deranged those of the present time. The standard of property in France being of both gold and silver, combined with the facts that the standard of property in India is of silver, and the balance of trade in its favour, is causing France to be denuded of its silver currency. Gold is in reality displacing silver as a standard of property throughout Europe and America, in precisely the same manner that silver has supplanted the old gold currencies of this country.

But is it advisable that the standard coin of India should continue of a different metal from that of the rest of the world? Or is silver preferable to gold as the chief circulating medium, and are the practice and feelings of the people of India in favor of silver as their standard of property?

It has been observed, that because the bulk of the people of India are poor and semi-barbarous, and their condition so rude that their exchanges are frequently made by barter, without the accommodation of coin, any other standard of property than silver would be unsuitable to them. That they prefer silver to gold is not, however, asserted (the very general desire which prevails for gold ornaments would be a sufficient refutation of any such statement); but simply that a silver currency is better adapted to their very moderate daily expenditure. It might be argued, we believe, with equal justice, that copper coin would be a still more suitable standard; since there can be no doubt that it circulates more freely, or, in other words, is more generally employed than silver coin, notwithstanding that so small a silver coin as a two-anna piece has been struck; but we do not think it likely that any one will attempt on this reasoning, or on any other, to recommend the substitution of copper coin for the existing silver currency. It may be proper here to observe that the authorities in India are understood to be averse to an excessive issue of copper coin, as having a tendency to impoverish the country. We have, indeed, heard that the Court of Directors has, on more than one occasion, sent out less copper for coinage than had been indented for, and expressly stated that it was highly desirable that the coinage of copper should be limited to the absolute demand for such money according to the terms on which it is issued; that is, that there should only be sufficient in circulation to enable the public to exchange copper for silver to the extent of one rupee's worth and no more. Nevertheless, the demand for copper coin continues. It has, however, been lately unnaturally stimulated in consequence of the several railways and other public works in course of construction. The prescribed proportion for the smaller silver coins, viz., 12 per cent – 2 per cent of eighths, 4 of quarters, and 6 of halves, ought to be an effectual preventive to an excessive circulation of copper coin, but it is doubtful if it be so. This proportion has not, however, we learn, been lately attended to, owing to its having been found necessary to devote the whole power of the mint to the coinage of rupees.

The people of India are not of one class any more than they are of one caste: their dealings are not, moreover, all on the very moderate scale above described. Independent of the Europeans in India, who are daily growing more numerous, there is likewise springing up on all sides a wealthy class whose commercial dealings are extending to all parts of the world. If for the poor a silver and copper currency is indispensable, a gold currency is not less necessary, we contend, for the civilized and the wealthy inhabitants of British India. A silver currency is too slow, too cumbrous, for extensive mercantile dealings, and is utterly unsuitable for government purposes, especially in periods of emergency or difficulty; and although it has been attempted to fill the void by a paper currency, yet its range is too limited and its value too indefinite and precarious to justify its extended use, or its ever being adopted authoritatively into the currency of the country.

The *Calcutta Quarterly Review*, in an article published in September 1856, recommended that bank notes should be issued solely by Government; that they should be made a legal tender; be payable on demand; and that an amount equivalent in value to the notes in circulation should, at all times, be retained in the coffers of Government. The sole object aimed at in this suggestion was to enable Government to reduce the balances in the Mofussil treasuries, and thus have at command in the general treasuries of the several presidencies large amounts of available funds, irrespective of the deposits on account of bank notes, which were to be reserved solely to exchange for the notes in circulation when coin was demanded. A somewhat similar scheme has recently been proposed for adoption in England, a Mr. Duncan having recommended that bank notes should be used for *internal* trade, and gold for *external* commerce. The suggestions of these writers appear to proceed too much from mere theory; and we believe that they argue contrary to the conviction and common sense of mankind in treating the precious metals, especially when in the form of coin, otherwise than as real property, and bank notes duly stamped and issued as representing value equally with gold and silver.

The general opinion of *practical* men on this subject we understand to be, that paper currency should only be employed where payment in specie is inconvenient; or, in other words, when the circulating medium is insufficient; and that a *forced* circulation of notes, whether arising from the measures of Government or the speculation of private companies, operates injuriously, by driving out of circulation the precious metals, and thus destroying that reserve which all countries should possess in order to be in a condition to meet, with more facility, extraordinary demands for coin; such, for instance, as occur in war-time. England at present possesses this reserve in a super-eminent degree, as was experienced in the last war; but would she long continue to do so were her internal currency restricted chiefly to bank notes? Neither can we perceive how the writer in the *Calcutta Review* intended to reduce the balances in the Mofussil treasuries by legalizing the issue of bank notes, if those notes were to be made payable on demand;

for the very fact of their being thus payable would necessitate the keeping of large balances in those treasuries to enable the collectors to give coin for the notes when required, and to prevent local bankruptcy in the event of a panic – a contingency to which the people of this country would seem excessively liable.

Bank notes, in our opinion, have hitherto been only tolerated by, and will never be a favourite currency with, the people of India. Were gold coin declared a legal tender, we are thoroughly satisfied that bank notes would soon be driven out of circulation. The traditions of this country have made its people too timorous to use bank notes as they are used in England. India has been governed by foreign nations for centuries, and its inhabitants have consequently been liable to, and still live in the apprehension of, war and intestine commotions. Under these circumstances it is natural that they should desire to possess real property, or rather valuables, such as precious stones and coins, which can be hidden in the earth, and be readily carried about the person. We admit that the amount which the inhabitants of India have sunk in Government promissory notes is in some degree opposed to the above conclusions. The circumstances of the case are, however, very different; but as a discussion on this subject would be foreign to the purpose of this paper, and unduly lengthen it, we shall restrict ourselves to a quotation of the following passage from the Earl of Liverpool's Treatise, before alluded to, in reference to this question:

It has been a common artifice, practised by those who have written on paper currency, to confound paper credit with paper currency, and even the higher sorts of paper currency with the inferior sorts, such as immediately interfere with the use of the coins of the realm. Paper credit is not only highly convenient and beneficial, but is even absolutely necessary in carrying on the trade of a great commercial kingdom. Paper currency is a very undefined term as used by speculative writers. To find arguments in its support, at least to the extent to which it is at present carried, they have been obliged to connect it with paper credit; so that the principles on which the use of paper credit is truly founded may be brought in support of a great emission of paper currency. I do not mean to say that even the higher orders of paper currency may not be very convenient in carrying on many branches of the trade of a country so wealthy as Great Britain: the sort of paper currency to which I principally object is that which interferes with the use of the coins of the realm, more especially in the payment of labourers and artificers, of the sailor and soldier, and in the smaller branches of the retail trade of the kingdom.

As we have suggested that gold coin should be made the standard of property in British India, it is, we conceive, our duty to state what description of gold coin should, in our opinion, be adopted, and how we would propose to introduce it into circulation.

We do not think that it would be wise suddenly to substitute gold for silver as the standard of property, or that the importation of silver should, be abruptly stopped, since there can be no doubt that a large amount of coin in that metal is necessary for the retail trade of India. We consider it very desirable, however, for several reasons, that the importation of silver should be reduced to and kept within more moderate bounds. With this view we would suggest that the sovereign be declared a legal tender, in the first instance, at the seats of Government; that is, in the cities of Calcutta, Madras, and Bombay, and that it be not coined in India until the people have become acquainted with it, and the necessity for its coinage is unquestionable.

If there be really a demand for a gold currency, as is generally supposed, the circulation of sovereigns being restricted to the seats of Government would not prevent their circulation extending to the districts in the manner that the Bank of Bombay notes have done. And in such case it would doubtless be deemed expedient to authorize their receipt into the Government treasuries on account of revenue and otherwise. This would place Government in possession of a coin much more convenient for remittance than the rupee, and, we contend, be a much more feasible and satisfactory arrangement than legalizing the issue of bank notes, as advised by the writer in the *Calcutta Review*. India has not yet, we conceive, arrived at the bank note era. Even a coin, much less only a paper representative of coin, should not, we are of opinion, be *forced* into circulation. When a paper currency is necessary, the very necessity for it will originate it; and to anticipate that period would, we are satisfied, prove either a dangerous or a useless experiment, according to the manner in which the issue of the notes might be conducted.

We do not imagine that the British Government would object to the sovereign being adopted into the currency of our Eastern Empire, although it might possibly demur to its being coined in this country. Yet we nevertheless do not perceive that the latter measure labours under any other difficulties than such as might have been equally urged against the coinage of sovereigns in Australia; where nevertheless the step has been already authorized. All that would probably be requisite would be to show that the coinage of sovereigns is highly advisable; and if they were once admitted into circulation, we feel assured that arguments would not be wanting to prove the absolute necessity for their coinage also in India.

The sovereign would, we are of opinion, be a highly useful, indeed invaluable, coin to adopt into the currency of India. Its intrinsic value being within a fraction of ten rupees, and the facility with which it might in consequence be admitted into the scheme of the Indian currency, are among its least important advantages.

Every country trading with Great Britain – and to what country or people has British trade not extended? – is acquainted with the sovereign. It is, like the English language, becoming universal. The advantages that would be derived from the adoption into the Indian currency of a coin so universally circulated, and which is held in such general estimation for its integrity, are as important as they are numerous. The increased facilities it would afford for the prosecution of either trade or war in the East can scarcely be over-estimated. All that is requisite to ensure the complete supercession of the Venetian and Spanish dollar, which have hitherto held sway on the coasts of Asia, is the adoption into the Indian currency of the British sovereign. The English have succeeded in Asia to the power and wealth which the nations that those coins represent once possessed; and it is but fitting that English coins should take their place in the currencies of the East. The rupee would never effect this, nor is it desirable that it should, since it does not represent, as the sovereign does, the wealth and power of Great Britain.

No apprehensions need, we think, be entertained lest, were the sovereign declared a legal tender in India generally, the silver coin now in circulation should diminish to an inconvenient extent.

The balance of trade being in favour of this country would alone prevent such a result. At least one half of the existing currency might, we are of opinion, be displaced by a gold currency with advantage; but we deem it probable that any diminution in the former currency is unlikely, unless a great demand for silver on account of increased trade with China should arise.

We estimate that not less than twenty-five crores of silver bullion have been tendered to the Bombay mint for coinage by merchants during the last twenty-eight years. Within the same period there have probably been re-coined of the old native currencies (which have been nearly all re-coined), including the old Bombay and Surat rupees, about seven crores. The silver coin now in circulation within the Bombay Presidency and Scinde may hence, we conclude, be estimated to amount to about thirty crores of rupees. Assuming that the silver coin in circulation in the Madras Presidency is at least double that of Bombay, and that of Bengal, the North-West Provinces, and the Punjaub, in threefold proportion, the total silver currency of British India would not fall short, at this computation, of 180 crores of rupees.

While India possesses such a circulation, and the balance of trade continues in its favour – and, judging from present circumstances, there seems little probability of its being otherwise for some time to come – there appears no reason whatever, we contend, to anticipate any injurious consequences from the proposed alteration in the standard of property in this country – but, on the contrary, great benefit. And if that change be promoted, even in the slightest degree, by the arguments herein brought forward, the object of our present remarks will have been fully attained.

## Note

1. For the forgoing account of the ancient coins of India, we are indebted to Prinsep's Useful Tables, a work now out of print, and difficult to be met with.

# *A 'UNIVERSAL CURRENCY' FOR INDIA*

# 13

# James Prinsep and the Currency Reform

Sanjay Garg

Coins have always played a significant role in the history of mankind. During the era of metallic currency, an effective and efficient coinage meant an effective and efficient currency system, which in turn meant an effective and efficient government, and this was also true in the reverse order.

Like many great dynasties of the past, the Mughals too, greatly cherished their right to issue coins. This is evident by the coins issued during the time when the Mughal rule in India was at its zenith. These coins are of standard weight and purity.[1]

However, with the decline of the Mughal authority, there was a corresponding decline in the standard of the coinage too. The minting rights were gradually appropriated by a large number of Indian revivalist powers as well as by the European trading companies, who were slowly assuming political character.

The minting activities of the East India Company are divisible into three phases:

1. The Period of Prohibition
2. The Period of Concession
3. The Period of Administration

In Bengal, the trading activities of the East India Company required a large amount of coined money for investment. At first the Company was not allowed by the Mughal Governor of Bengal to mint its coins. Later some concessions were granted by allowing it to get its bullion coined at the Mughal mints at Rajmahal,

Murshidabad and Patna. Finally in 1757 the English were able to establish their own mint at Calcutta.[2] However, it was not until 1765, when the East India Company acquired the Diwani rights of Bengal, Behar and Orissa, that the Calcutta Mint commenced its minting activities in a right earnest.

The money market during the mid-eighteenth century presented a totally confusing state of affairs. Not only were there a large variety of coins in the market, but one also had to pay different species of coins for purchasing different commodities.[3]

The East India Company, from very early days was keen to introduce reforms in the ailing currency system. As early as in 1772, an English political economist James Stuert was asked by the Court of Directors to study the currency problems of the Bengal Presidency.[4] Then in 1787, a Currency Committee was formed.[5] This was the first-ever official inquiry into the currency problems and was to suggest corrective measures. Again in 1792, a Mint Committee was created to monitor and superintend the affairs of the minting activities of the East India Company.[6] From 1793 onwards a series of currency regulations were passed, but without the desired success.

The man on whose shoulders the responsibility of evolving good money out of bad money fell, was James Prinsep.

James Prinsep had the genes of a coiner in his blood. His father John Prinsep, who was a famous contractor of the East India Company, had the privilege of setting up his private mint at Falta, where, from 1780 to 1784, he produced a large number of copper coins for the Bengal Presidency. John Prinsep's mint was far more advanced in its mechanical equipment than the government mint at Calcutta – a fact well borne out by the surviving specimens of its mintage.[7]

When James was compelled to abandon his plans for career in architecture, a career in the mint was offered to him as an alternative.[8]

## The Coins Brought James Prinsep to India

James Prinsep arrived at Calcutta on 18 September 1819.[9] Immediately he joined the Calcutta Mint in a double role as an Assistant

Assay Master to the then Assay Master, H.H. Wilson, and as Assistant Mint Master 'whenever his services may be required in that capacity'.[10]

The mints of the East India Company were placed under the twin charge of the Mint Master and the Assay Master. The Mint Master served as the production manager while the Assay Master was responsible for determining the purity contents of the metal, which was brought to the mint for coinage and thus had to act as the quality control manager. The mints were opened to all. Anyone could bring gold or silver bullion for coinage. On receipt of the bullion, the Mint Master examined the bullion by cutting and burning a portion of the metal so as to ascertain that there was no fraudulent admixture. He then issued a mint receipt to the proprietor of the bullion. A specimen of the bullion was then sent to the assay office. The Assay Master performed the assay by chemical analysis and determined the contents of pure metal and the alloy. After the assay was over, the proprietor of the bullion exchanged the mint receipt at the assay office for a certificate of the standard value of the bullion in gold or silver money. This certificate was convertible into coins at the treasury, as soon as the new coin was transmitted there by the mint. A deduction was, however, made from the assay produce of the bullion as seignorage or the minting charge which varied from two to four percent.[11]

Besides assaying private and the Company's own bullion for coinage, the assay office also assayed a large number of coin specimens sent to Calcutta by different English officials that were current in their respective jurisdiction. An assay of these spurious, debased, light weight coins of differing values was conducted at the Calcutta mint, so as to fix an official rate of exchange of these species of coins for the purpose of revenue collections as well as payments.[12]

Thus the task of the Assay Master was crucial. Prinsep, a young boy of 20 years, had the opportunity to work under the supervision of H.H. Wilson only for couple of months. By the same Resolution that appointed James Prinsep as Assistant Assay Master at Calcutta, H.H. Wilson was appointed as the Assay Master of the Benares mint. However Wilson's deputation was postponed 'until Mr. Prinsep shall had the advantage of acting under him tor some time, and of benefiting by his experience'.[13] Prinsep proved to be a fast learner. Within two months he mastered the fine art of assay, and from November 1819, he single-handedly performed all assays in the Calcutta mint. On 8 September 1820, he was nominated to succeed H.H. Wilson as the Assay Master of the Benaras mint.[14]

About Prinsep's decade long sojourn at Benaras mint (1820-1830) nothing much is known except that he improved the design of the building of the mint and later of an incident of embezzle ment of funds of the Benaras mint, where his name was also arraigned.[15]

Few know that the future currency reformer in Prinsep's personality was shaped at Benaras.

During his stay at Benaras, Prinsep was instrumental in introducing three very important currency regulations:

1. Regulation V of 1821
2. Regulation II of 1824
3. Regulation VII of 1826

First of these regulations, Regulation V of 1821, prescribed the rates at which Benaras and Farrukhabad rupees were to be received in payment of revenue of *malguzars* or the revenue collectors. The second Regulation, viz., Regulation II of 1824 gives us an insight into the mind of James Prinsep, who was visualising a uniform coinage for the whole of British India. By this Regulation, the Farrukhabad mint was abolished. Lesser the mints, greater the control. At the same time, the Farrukhabad Rupee was declared legal currency of the recently acquired Saguar and Nerbuddah territories. A uniform coinage was introduced into the entire northern and central India – a no mean achievement for a 25 year old.

By the third Regulation, viz., Regulation VII of 1826, the government, which was by now more than assured of the remarkable capabilities of the young Assay Master, transferred the control of the Benaras mint from the Board of Revenue in Central Provinces, to a Local Committee, and appointed James Prinsep as its Secretary. This was just the beginning; Prinsep – the currency reformer was yet to reveal himself.

By the end of 1829, the Benaras mint was abolished. It was finally wound up in January 1830. Consequently, Prinsep came to Calcutta with all his apparatuses, office records and other material.[16]

In March 1830, Prinsep was appointed as the Deputy Assay Master at the Calcutta mint.[17] Once again he had the opportunity to work under the able supervision of Dr. H.H. Wilson. But again, not for long. In 1832 Wilson was appointed as the Boden Professor of Sanskrit at the Oxford University. He proceeded to Oxford on 5 January 1833,[18] and on 15 January Prinsep was appointed as the Assay Master of the Calcutta mint.[19] He also stepped into Wilson's shoes as the Officiating Secretary to the Calcutta Mint Committee, pending a formal order of the Government.[20]

Within an incredible short span of two years, between 1833 and 1835, Prinsep was able to achieve what the East India Company had been contriving for over half a century – a uniform coinage for its domains.

Prinsep studied the coinage system of India through the ages and concluded that to affect any change in the existing monetary system, the first step had to be a change in its metrology. He felt the necessity of examining carefully the coinage of successive years before suggesting any measure for its reform.

During this time the weights throughout the country were expressed in terms of the principal coin and thus *ser* and *man* were simply the multiples of the principal coin current in that area. In Bengal two systems of weights were prevalent. First was the 'Factory weight', based on the English avoirdupois pound system, while the second, called the '*Bazar* or the *Sikka* weight', was based on the Murshidabad rupee. Prinsep was aware that any change in the weight system was not an easy task. He writes:

> However desirable it may be, in theory, to reduce the system of weights throughout the vast continent of India to order and uniformity; in practice, it is well known that insuperable difficulties oppose the execution of such a project.[21]

To start with, such a change required a corresponding adjustment in all the weights in use at the Mint, the Custom House, the

Treasury, the banks, the Collector's offices, besides a number of other Government offices.

Undeterred by the apparent difficulties, Prinsep, on 11 April 1833, prepared and submitted to the government, a project for reforming weights and measures.[22] By his mathematical calculations and statistical analysis, he successfully demonstrated that only by a slight modification in the *sicca* weight, it could be adopted as the standard unit for the weights as well as for the new rupee coins.

Prinsep's plan was approved by William Bentinck, who conveyed his deep appreciation for Prinsep's work. The Secretary to the government wrote to the Mint Committee:

> The Governor-General in Council desires that you will convey to Mr. Prinsep the acknowledgement of the Government for the very satisfactory examination which he has given to the above subject, and inform him that his report is considered highly interesting and instructive.[23]

The Regulation VII of 1833, passed on 13 July 1833, converted Prinsep's proposals into legislation. By this Regulation, the weight of the Farrukhabad rupee – one of the principal coins of northern India, was fixed at 180 grains troy, corresponding to the traditional Indian weight for the silver rupee, i.e. one *tola* of 12 *mashas.*[24] This coin was then adopted as the unit of a general system of weights for government transactions throughout India.

According to the new system, the traditional Indian weight was harmonised with the English pound system.[25] Thus:

| | | | | | |
|---|---|---|---|---|---|
| 8 *ruttees* | = | 1 *masha* | = | 15 | grains troy |
| 12 *mashas* | = | 1 *tola* | = | 180 | grains troy |
| 80 *tolas* | = | 1 *ser* | = | 2½ | grains troy |
| 40 *sers* | = | 1 *man* or bazar maund | = | 100 | lbs troy |

At the same time, by this alteration in the weight, the Farrukhabad rupee was also assimilated in the weights of the Surat rupee and the Arcot rupee – the principal coins of the Bombay and the Madras Presidencies respectively. Now all the three presidencies of the East India Company had their principal coins of uniform weight. A uniform coinage was a *fait accompli.*

Prinsep at the same time was also convinced that such a wide ranging change touching almost every aspect of public life, could not be affected by force. Thus we find that the said Regulation expressly avoided any penal provision for default. He was sure that: 'the sense of public convenience would quickly ensure its substitution for the irregular system now prevalent'.[26]

The uniformity of coinage thus achieved, the next target for Prinsep was the introduction of a Universal Coinage. Having made the Mughal Emperor its pensioner, the East India Company had been, for a long time, contemplating to alter the device of the coins issued from its mints. It was felt that a mint much larger in capacity than the existing one at Calcutta would be required to issue coins conforming to the uniform system. Therefore, as early as in 1819 the Calcutta Mint Committee had recommended the erection of a new mint at Calcutta equipped with modern machinery and that a change in the coin device should be adopted at the time of the opening of the new mint. Later, in the same year when Lieut. Forbes was deputed to England to commission the machinery for the new mint, he was also instructed to bring this proposal to the notice of the Court of Directors. The foundation of the new mint at Calcutta was subsequently laid on 31 March 1824, and the matter then required an immediate attention. In their dispatch dated 23 April 1824, the Court of Directors directed the Government of Bengal 'to consider and report what will be the best device for the rupee to be coined on the opening of the new mint'.[27] This communication from the Court of Directors produced 'valuable Minutes from the then Members [of the Mint Committee] Mr. Holt Mackenzie, Mr. H. Wood, Mr. W. Money and the fullest information on the subject was obtained from the reports of Mr. H.H. Wilson and Captain Forbes'.[28] All the members were in favour of a pictorial design in the first instance; and the majority, in favour of the king's head for the obverse and the Company's arms, or an emblematical device for the reverse. The Mint Committee, vide their letter dated 2 November 1825, forwarded all these reports to the government, 'suggesting further in connection with the question of the uniform currency for the whole of India that the same impression should extend to Bombay and Madras coinage'.[29] There was again an unexpected delay in taking the decision on the proposed device for the new coinage. Meanwhile the building of the new mint was completed on 1 August 1829. The whole matter was once again referred to the Court of Directors in November 1829 for a final decision, but no reply was received from them till 1833, when Prinsep revived the question in his Note dated 1 October 1833.

Prinsep wrote:

> I think it much to be regretted that the device of our coin was not reformed on the opening of the new mint, but it is needless to expatiate on what cannot now be remedied....[30]

The new mint at Calcutta was fully commissioned by the end of 1833. There were now five hydraulic presses, costing 11 lakh rupees. Of these machines, two were of 40 horsepower each, and three were of 24, 20 and 14 horsepower respectively. Their total capacity was one crore thirty-thousand pieces per annum.

For the production of a large coinage, a large number of dies were also required, not only for the Calcutta mint but also for Bombay as well as other *mofussil* mints. Regarding this almost everybody in the government was in favour of obtaining the services of a competent die-engraver from England.

Prinsep's views, however, were in sharp contrast to those of many of his compatriots. He had full faith in the capabilities of his Indian co-workers. Finally, when the hunt for the chief die-engraver for the proposed new device for the coins was made, three names were short listed:

1. Dela Combe, the engraver of the map of Calcutta;
2. Kashi Nath, the engraver of the device for the Government Promissory Notes; and
3. Hari Mohun Roy, a seal engraver.

Being himself an accomplished artist, Prinsep was able to choose the best. His choice fell on Kashi Nath. He wrote:

> There can be no hesitation however, in pronouncing Kashi Nath's engraving to be superior to the other two, and indeed his skill as the engraver, for copy work is without an equal in Calcutta.[31]

A little later, on 8 November 1833, Prinsep submitted a detailed Note 'On the Device of the Indian Coin,' wherein he reiterated his recommendation for 'the appointment of a competent Native Engraver.' Apart from the excellent workmanship of Kashi Nath, Prinsep advocated the appointment of an Indian die-cutter, on the principles of economy and manageability. He adds that, 'Justice to our Indian subjects ought to be an additional motive to the encouragement of Native talent and skill'.[32]

Prinsep was now a man in a hurry. In the same Note he urged the government for 'the immediate reform of the device here without waiting longer for the reply of the Hon'ble Court of Directors to the reference made in 1829, which has doubtless been lost sight of . . .'.[33]

In order to demonstrate the skill of Kashi Nath, Prinsep obtained the permission of the Calcutta Mint Committee to engage him for executing a matrix die bearing the head of King William IV.[34] The result of the experiment – the pair of the matrix die and five specimen coins struck from it – was placed before the Mint Committee on 6 April 1834.[35] The Mint Committee was fully satisfied with the execution of the die by Kashi Nath. In their letter dated 15 April 1834 to the Government of Bengal, they recorded their sentiments in the following words:

> We think that the present experiment has fully established the competency of a native die engraver to execute the reform of the dies whereas hitherto it has been assumed to be indispensable to defer any attempt to effect this object until an European artist should be obtained from England.[36]

Meanwhile, there was a significant change in the administrative set-up of the East India Company. The Charter Act of 1833, which came into effect from 22 April 1834, gave the Government of India wide-ranging powers. The Governor-General of Bengal now became the Governor-General of India. He was now empowered to legislate without seeking the prior approval of the British parliament. The change in the administrative system, perforce, called forth an immediate change in the prevailing monetary systems.

The matter was now referred to the Governor-General, William Bentinck.[37] The Governor-General approved of the device of the coin but expressed some reservations about the Latin inscription that it bore.[38]

As the engraving of the new dies was to take quite some time, Prinsep, on 2 January 1835, submitted sketches of various designs bearing different inscriptions, as a prototype for the new coinage. These included 'three designs in pencil by Mr. James Atkinson prepared some years ago' and eight designs delineated by him:

1. Britannia from the English penny;
2. A Lion from an antique Greek coin;
3. An Elephant (this device is adopted on the Coins of Ceylon);
4. A Ship, emblematical of British commerce;
5. A British Senator, between a Hindu and a Musalman, presenting the Charter;
6. An emblematical figure of Justice and Plenty;
7. Typical figures of Britannia and India;
8. The Banyan tree, taken from the seal of the Royal Asiatic Society of London.

Besides, 'the finely sculptured Lion of Flaxman large medalic die reduced to the dimension of the new rupee' was also submitted.[39]

Along with these designs, Prinsep submitted to the government a lengthy note entitled, 'Reasons for Reforming Currency'.[40] In this note, Prinsep put up a strong case for the immediate change in the device of the Company's rupee. As for the expediency for such a change, he wrote:

> The sovereignty of the King of England over India has now been broadly declared and promulgated over the world, after which to continue striking coins with the unmeaning distich of Shah Alum is ridiculous, if it be not lese [*sic.* less].[41]

The argument put forth by Prinsep in the above Note and the various designs submitted by him were forwarded to the Governor-General on 5 January.[42] In the reply dated 12 January from the Secretary to Government, the Mint Committee was informed that while the reverse design was satisfactory, the Governor-General was disposed to give preference to Flaxman's lion device for the obverse of the new coin. He desired that the dies be prepared accordingly.[43]

However, by the time the new dies were prepared, William Bentinck retired from the office in March 1835, and was succeeded by Sir Charles Metcalfe. The specimen from the new die were now forwarded to Metcalfe for approval.[44]

The change of device for the Company's new Rupee was approved by the Governor-General on 27 May 1835 and a legislation for the establishment of a One Uniform Rupee for the whole of British India was framed.[45] The draft of the proposed Act was sent to the Court of Directors on 24 June 1835.[46] However, without waiting for the consent of the Court of Directors, the bill was introduced in the Governor-General's Council on 29 June 1835[47] and was finally passed by it on 17 August 1835 as Act XVII of 1835.[48]

Prinsep's job was, however, not yet completed. The integration of the copper currency of India into the uniform monetary system posed far more serious problems. The main reason for this was the heavy expense involved in withdrawing the existing copper coins and substituting them with the new coins.[49] At the same time for the successful implementation of the Universal Coinage for the British India, the extension of these measures to the copper coins as well was crucial. The universal copper coinage was seen as an aid to lessen the difficulties in the circulation of the Company's new rupee by providing a fractional medium circulating at par with the rupee.

As early as 1 October 1833 Prinsep had proposed a modification of the Bombay copper coin as a suitable device for the Bengal copper currency.[50] Later he got a design for the device for the quarter *anna* or *pysa* of 100 grains executed by Kashi Nath, and submitted it to the Mint Committee on 6 April 1834.[51] The matter of the copper currency was once again raised by Prinsep in his note dated 2 January 1835.[52] With no immediate reply forthcoming, the matter was once again submitted to the government on 23 April 1835.[53] Finally on 1 July 1835 the government resolved that no new copper coin be struck at Calcutta Mint in the name of Shah Alam, and that an English device be adopted for the copper coins.[54] Specimens of an English device for the proposed copper coinage were now solicited from the Calcutta Mint Committee.[55] These devices, along with a detailed Note suggesting measures for adopting the copper currency of Bengal to the uniform rupee established by the Act XVII of 1835, were submitted for the approval of the Governor-General on 10 October 1835.[56] In his reply dated 11 November, the Secretary to the Government directed the Mint Committee to take steps to prepare the necessary Dies for commencing a coinage of copper with the device of the Company's arms.[57] Accordingly, another legislation for the introduction of a uniform copper coinage was framed and was presented in the Council of the Governor-General on 2 December 1835.[58] This legislation, passed by the Governor-General in Council on 7 December 1835 as Act XXI of 1835, completed Prinsep's task of monetary integration of British India.[59]

The noted numismatist F. Pridmore records:

> The principal individual involved in the scheme for a uniform or Company's rupee was James Prinsep, then Assay Master of the Calcutta Mint and Secretary to the Mint Committee. The success of the measures to carry out this major change, especially those for adapting the existing copper currency to the new rupee, rests with him.[60]

What Europe has done today by introducing a single Euro currency for the whole of Europe, Prinsep achieved for India more than 150 years ago.[61]

## Notes

1. Tapan Raychaudhuri and Irfan Habib (eds), *The Cambridge Economic History of India,* vol. I: *c. 1200-c. 1750*, Cambridge, 1982, p. 360. See also, Irfan Habib, 'The Currency System of the Mughal Empire', *Medieval India Quarterly,* vol. IV, nos. 1-2, 1961, pp. 1-21; and Om Prakash, 'On Coinage in Mughal India', *Indian Economic and Social History Review,* vol. 25, no. 4, 1998, pp. 476-91.
2. Sanjay Garg, 'Establishment of Calcutta Mint, 1757', *Proceedings of Indian History Congress,* 51st Session, Calcutta (December 1990), pp. 383-92.

3. J.C. Sinha, 'Currency in Early British Days', *Indian Journal of Economics,* vol. VII, pt. 3, January 1927, pp. 168-70.
4. James Stuert, *The Principles of Money applied to the Present State of the Coin of Bengal Being an inquiry into the Methods for correcting the defects for stopping the drains which carry off the coin: and for extending circulation by means of paper currency,* London, 1772.
5. J.C. Sinha, 'Earliest Currency Committee in India, 1787', *Proceedings of the Indian Historical Records Commission* (hereafter *PIHRC),* VII, Lahore Session, 1925, p. 183.
6. National Archives of India (hereafter NAI), Finance Department, Original Consultations (hereafter O.C.), 2 May 1792.
7. F. Pridmore, *The Coins of the British Commonwealth of Nations to the end of the Reign of George VI, 1952*: Part 4: *India*: vol. I: *East India Company Presidency Series c.1642-1835,* London, 1975, pp. 204-5, 262-3.
8. For early life of James Prinsep, see P.T. Nair, *James Prinsep: Life and Works,* vol. I, Calcutta, 1999.
9. This is the correct date of James Prinsep's arrival in Calcutta, as recorded by him in a letter bearing the date 'Saturday, 18 September, 1819', and addressed to B. Bayley, Chief Secretary to the Government. He writes, 'Sir, I have the honour to report for the information of His Excellency the Most Noble the Governor-General-in-Council that I this morning arrived in Calcutta from on board the *Hooghly* in which ship I took my passage for this country under the orders of the Hon. the Court of Directors.' This letter, in James Prinsep's own handwriting, is incidentally also his first official letter in the holdings of the National Archives of India. See NAI, Finance Department, O.C., 24 September 1819, no. 4.
10. The Resolution of Prinsep's appointment was already passed by the Government on 10 September 1819, see NAI, Finance Department, O.C., 24 September 1819, no. 5.
11. James Prinsep, *Useful Tables, Illustrative of the Coins, Weights and Measures of the British India,* ed. Edward Thomas, London, 1858 (rpt. New Delhi), p. 8.
12. NAI, Financial (India) Department, Mint Branch, O.C., 6 February 1835, no. 4.
13. NAI, Finance Department, O.C., 24 September 1819, no. 4.
14. Ibid., 8 September 1820, no. 4.
15. O.P. Kejariwal, 'James Prinsep: A Little Known Incident of His Life', *Indian Museum Bulletin,* vol. XXXII, 1997, pp. 157-63.
16. NAI, Finance Department, O.C., 2 March 1830, no. 11 (Enclosure): James Prinsep to H.H. Wilson, dated 'Benaras Mint, 27 January 1830'.
17. Ibid., O.C., 2 March 1830, no. 17.
18. NAI, Financial (India) Department, Mint Branch, 8 January 1833, nos. 20-1.
19. Ibid., 22 February 1833, Body Sheet.

20. Ibid., Mint Committee Proceedings, February, 1833, no. 13: James Prinsep to the Mint Committee, dated 'Calcutta, 7 February, 1833'.
21. Prinsep, *Useful Tables*, p. 109.
22. Ibid., 1 July 1833, no. 2.
23. NAI, Financial (India) Department, Mint Branch, July 1833, no. 15: G.A. Bushby, Officiating Secretary to the Government, to the Mint Committee, dated 1 July 1833.
24. Regulation VII of 1833: A Regulation for altering the weight of the new Farruckabad Rupee and for assimilating it to the legal currency of the Madras and Bombay Presidencies; for adjusting the weight of the Calcutta Sicca Rupee, and for fixing a standard unit of weight for India.
25. Ibid., Section 4.
26. Prinsep, *Useful Tables*, p. 103.
27. NAI, Finance Department, Mint Committee Proceedings, November 1833, no. 19: Note by James Prinsep 'On the Device of the Indian Coin', dated 8 November 1833.
28. Ibid.
29. Quoted in ibid.
30. NAI, Finance Department, Mint Committee Proceedings, November 1833, no. 18.
31. Ibid.
32. Ibid., no. 19.
33. Ibid.
34. Ibid., December 1833, no. 15.
35. Ibid., April 1834, no. 3.
36. Ibid.
37. Ibid., 25 November 1834, no. 1.
38. Ibid., no. 3.
39. Ibid., 12 January 1835, no. 2 (Enclosure to no. 1).
40. Ibid., no. 3.
41. Ibid.
42. Ibid., no. 1.
43. Ibid., no. 4.
44. Ibid., 8 April 1835, no. 1.
45. Ibid., 27 May 1835, no. 1.
46. NAI, Finance Department, Mint Branch, Letters to Court, no. 17 of 1835, dated 24 June 1835.
47. NAI, Home Department, Judicial (Civil) Branch, Proceedings, 29 June 1835, no. 3.
48. Dayal Das, 'First Uniform Currency for India', *PIHRC,* Bhubaneswar Session, XXXII, pt. II, 1958, pp. 65-76. For full text of the Act, see Part II: Records, pp. 415-17.
49. NAI, Finance Department. Mint Committee, O.C., 20 May 1835, nos. 1-6.

50. Ibid., Financial (India) Department, Mint Branch, Proceedings, November 1833, no. 18.
51. Ibid., 15 April 1834, no. 3.
52. Ibid., 12 January 1835, no. 2 (Enclosure to no. 1).
53. Ibid.. 20 May 1835, no. 1.
54. Ibid., 1 July 1835, no. 1.
55. Ibid.
56. Ibid., 11 November 1835, no. 1.
57. Ibid., no. 4.
58. Ibid., 2 December 1835, no. 1.
59. For full text of this Act please see Part II: Records, pp. 417-18.
60. F. Pridmore, *The Coins of the British Commonwealth of Nations to the End of the Reign of George VI, 1952:* Part 4: *India*: vol. 2: *Uniform Coinage East India Company 1835-58, Imperial Period 1858-1947,* London, 1980, p. 3.
61. I am grateful to O.P. Kejariwal for going through the draft of this paper and making some valuable suggestions (not all of which I have followed).

# 14

# First Uniform Currency for India

DAYAL DAS

Till the first quarter of the nineteenth century there existed in India various currencies which were simultaneously in circulation in different parts of the country, each having a different standard and value, and bearing a different device. Thus there were *sicca* rupees, Sonat rupees, Farruckabad rupees, Arcot rupees, Madras rupees and Bombay repees, and the computation of their respective values involved considerable difficulty. It also resulted in great inconvenience in business transactions, both Government as well as private, and was thus a great stumbling block in the way of the commercial prosperity of India.

The imperative need for some reform of the Indian currency which might put an end to the existing confusion and facilitate the transaction of business was greatly felt. As early as 1773, Warren Hastings had tried to tackle this knotty problem, but he 'bungled in his attempts to solve it'. It was not till the time of Lord William Bentinck that some concrete stops were taken in this direction, and Bentinck ordered the immediate introduction of a uniform currency through out the British territory in India.[1] But his sudden and premature departure from India left this important and arduous task to his successor, Sir Charles Metcalfe.

The Calcutta Mint Committee submitted[2] for the consideration of the Governor-General in Council various devices for the proposed new coin including one bearing the replica of the head of the King of England, and recommended its adoption as they considered the facial image to be much more difficult of imitation than lion or any other similar device. The Governor-General in Council, therefore, resolved to give preference to this device for the general coin, and decided to take immediate measures for establishing the new coin as the general currency of all the presidencies.[3] It was also thought that by giving the coin an impression of the likeness of the reigning sovereign of the British empire it might be possible to aid its circulation as a general colonial currency in the East, and asserting by the same act the British supremacy in India itself.[4] The reverse of the coin was to bear the words 'East India Company' together with the nominal value of the coin in English, Persian and Nagari, and the ornamental devices of a lotus flower and myrtle wreath. The engraving of the specimen was executed by an Indian workman employed at the Calcutta Mint, but the Court of Directors were requested kindly to furnish matrix dies of the same device by English engravers, which might serve as a model to the Indian workmen employed in preparing dies for the new coinage.[5]

It had also been decided by the Governor-General in Council that the change in the silver coinage was to be followed up by a corresponding change in the gold and copper currency of British India, as soon as the reports and suggestions of the Calcutta Mint Committee in this respect were rcceived.[6]

In pursuance of the above decisions for the introduction of a uniform currency for the whole of British India, the Governor-General in Council in their letter[7] dated 24 June 1835, forwarded to the Court of Directors the draft of an Act proposed to be passed by them on the subject of the new silver and gold coinage of British India. The proposed Act was considered necessary to legalize the issue of the new coins and to regulate their weight, standard and device, and in respect to the new rupee to fix the rate at which it was to be paid and received in discharge of sums calculated in any of the then existing legal currencies. It was deemed essential to provide for all these matters by a legislative enactment; but in regard to all other questions relating to the coining of money and the establishment or removal of mints, it was considered desirable that their direction be vested in the Governor-General of India in Council in his executive capacity, and a separate section to this effect was, therefore, introduced in the draft of the proposed Act.[8]

The main provisions of the Act were as follows:

[The text of the Act is omitted here. Please see pp. 265-7 supra for full text. Ed.]

The draft of the Act was read in the Council of India for the first time on 29 June 1835[9] and was finally passed by the Governor-General of India in Council on 17 August 1835, as Act XVII of 1835.[10]

As regards the copper currency, some difficulty was anticipated in the beginning in introducing an entirely now copper coin for the whole of British India, due to the heavy expense involved in withdrawing the existing copper coins and substituting them by the new coin.[11] The two main copper coins then in circulation were the 'Trisooli pice and the 'Calcutta pice'. It was, therefore, necessary to protect the new coin by a device the skill of which would have precluded its imitation at the Indian mints as well as by clandestine fabricators in the British territory itself. Hence the Governor-General in Council decided[12] to adopt an English device for the new copper coin. However, the general introduction of the new copper currency was not immediately contemplated. It was intended that the 'Calcutta pice' should be supplied to treasuries in the provinces so long as stores of that coin were available, and in the meantime the Mint Committee was requested to furnish specimens of an English device for the new copper currency'.[13]

Subsequently, however, the Governor-General in Council thought[14] that the temporary inconveniences attendant in Bengal on the transition from the general circulation of the *sicca* and other rupees to that of the new or Company's Rupee would be lessened by providing as quickly as possible a copper currency to circulate at par with the latter, that is at the rate of 64 pice to the Company's Rupee. It was also felt that such a measure was much desired by the mercantile community in British India, and was necessary for the protection of the people, especially those belonging to the lower classes, against loss in their transactions in copper coins.

In order to legalize the circulation of the new copper coin, a legislative enactment (Act XXI of 1835) was passed by the

Government of India. The draft of this Act was orginally prepared in the Financial Department, and was taken into consideration by the Governor-General in Council at their meeting in the Legislative Department, dated 7 December 1835.[15] It was decided in that meeting that with effect from 20 December 1835. the following copper coins only were to be issued from any Mint within the Presidency of Bengal:[16]

I. A Pice weighing 100 grains Troy.
II. A Double Pice weighing 200 grains Troy.
III. A Pie or one-twelfth of an Anna weighing 33⅓ grains Troy.

The above coins were to have such devices as were fixed by Governor-General in Council, in accordance with the provisions of Section 10 of Act XVII of 1835 (Act regarding the uniform Silver and Gold currency for the whole of British India). The new pice was declared to be a legal tender for 1/64 of the Company's Rupee, the double pice for 1/32 of the Company's Rupee and the pie for 1/192 or the Company's Rupee. It was at the same time provided that after 20 December 1835, no copper coin, in any part of the territories of the East India Company was to be legal tender, except for fractions of a rupee.[17]

Thus Sir Charles Metcalfe succeeded in introducing a uniform currency in the whole of British India a measure calculated to increase the commercial prosperity of the country by facilitating transactions, and removed once for all the existing confusion due to the use of multiple currencies or the circulation of coins having different standards, denominations and values. It also helped in making government disbursements, and Metcalfe even directed that all salaries, allowances and pensions payable to the servants of the East India Company, were to be audited in the new currency established under Act XVII of 1835.[18] For this purpose he fixed the rate of exchange from the *sicca* rupee to the Company's rupee at 4½ per cent, i. e. 100 *sicca* rupees were to be considered as equivalent to 104½ Company's rupees.[19] As the Company's rupee became more popular and the other rupees were gradually withdrawn from circulation, Metcalfe ordered that all government accounts at the different presidencies were to be kept in the Company's rupees,[20] and thus completed the change-over to the new uniform currency.

But strangely enough this measure, full of wisdom and farsightedness as it was, did not find favour with the Court of Directors.[21] They apprehended that the prevailing confusion due to the existence of different currencies in India would become worse still by the addition of one more and an entirely new currency. But their anger was mainly directed against 'a change so extensive and important having been determined upon' merely in anticipation of their approval and without waiting for their formal orders. However, the Court of Directors intimated to the Governor-General of India in Council that

> We are aware of the inconvenience and confusion which would now result from the abandonment or suspension of the plan which you have thus prematurely and unadvisedly determined to adopt. We shall not therefore at present direct any departure from it though we cannot but entertain the apprehension that the course you have pursued . . . may yet involve your Government in very serious embarrassment, while the alteration of the currency in which your Accounts are slated will unquestionably occasion great inconvenience and confusion.[22]

Whether the fears expressed by the Court of Directors were well founded or not will be best illustrated by the results of this important reform introduced by Sir Charles Metcalfe, and this alone should be the criterion for judging Metcalfe's wisdom, farsightedness and administrative ability in taking this important step. It may be pointed out that the system of uniform currency, and even the denominations of most of the coins introduced by Sir Charles Metcalfe in India about one hundred and twenty years back, are in vogue even today. A reform which has stood the test of a century and a quarter should not only be above all condemnation, but deserves our hearty praise and appreciation.

## Notes

1. Fin. Mint Cons., 25 November 1834, nos. 1-3; and 12 January 1835, nos. 1-4.
2. Fin. Mint Cons., 8 April 1835, nos. 1-4.

3. Ibid.
4. Fin. Mint Letters to Court, no. 10 of 1835, dated 8 April 1835.
5. Ibid., paras 10-11.
6. Ibid., para 8.
7. Fin. Mint Letters to Court, no. 17 of 1835, dated 24 June 1835.
8. Ibid., para 3.
9. Home, Judl. (Civil) Progs., 29 June 1835, no. 3.
10. *The Acts of the Supreme Government of India,* from 1834-99, vol. I, W. Thacker & Co., Calcutta, 1842.
11. Fin. Mint Cons., 20 May 1835, nos. 1-6.
12. Fin. Mint Cons., 1 July 1835, no. 1.
13. Fin. Mint Letter to Court, no. 2 of 1836, dated 27 January 1836, para 6.
14. Fin. Mint Cons., 2 December 1835, nos. 1-2.
15. Leg. Letters to Court, no. 4 of 1836 dated 29 February 1836, para 14.
16. Leg. Cons., 7 December 1835, nos. 17-20.
17. Ibid.
18. Fin. Gen. Letters to Court, no. 76 B of 835, dated, 9 September 1835.
19. Ibid.
20. Fin. Cons., 10 February 1836, no 1.
21. Fin Genl. Letters from Court, no. 9 of 1836, dated 27 July 1836 and no. 13 of 1836 dated 12 October 1836.
22. Fin Genl. Letters from Court, no. 9 of 1836, dated 27 July 1936, para 5.

# *THE ERA OF IMPERIAL CURRENCY*

# 15

# Imperial and Colonial Coinages

Paul Stevens*

## Introduction

In attempting to review the contribution of the [British Numismatic] Society to the numismatic knowledge of Britain's overseas territories, it is first necessary to determine the scope of such an undertaking. The British Empire was a dynamic concept that developed from the desire of the English to expand economically, and was created by a variety of techniques such as: colonization in North America, direct conquest in South-East Asia, convict colonies in Australia, and direct occupation of other colonial powers' territories such as the islands of the Mediterranean or Egypt. The control of these differently-acquired territories started at different times, and ended at different times and in different ways. How then to determine the scope? I have chosen here to include coins and tokens that were issued under the direct control of institutions that were British, but to exclude coins that were issued by those authorities only nominally controlled by the British. So, for instance, coins issued from Maratha mints in India following their capture by the British would be included, but coins issued by the princes of the Indian Native States would be excluded. Once countries achieved dominion status, even if they still owed nominal allegiance to the British crown, their coins fall outside of the scope of this paper. This decision could be the subject of many debates. Just to chose one example, should

* I would like to thank John Roberts-Lewis for his helpful suggestions during the production of this paper.

Australian coins be excluded from the date of Australia achieving dominion status (1900); or after the Statute of Westminster ended the control of Britain over the affairs of Australia (1931); or when this measure was actually ratified by the Australian parliament (1942); or should present-day Australian coins be included on the grounds that Queen Elizabeth continues as Queen of Australia even today? A similar discussion could be had for each of the dominions, but this matter is better left for debate elsewhere.[1] I have excluded coins of England, Scotland and Ireland because they are better covered elsewhere.

It must be admitted that other authors have chosen a much broader scope than that presented here,[2] but since this differs between authors it is not possible to find one agreed definition. This scope is fairly arbitrary, therefore, but seems to allow an examination of the numismatic contribution of Britain to the world. What's more, it is largely similar to, though not exactly the same as, that adopted by previous authors such as Atkins[3] and Pridmore[4] and is therefore familiar, and this familiarity has been extended to grouping of the various territories by continent. Obviously, this scope is so large that I have had to be selective in the details that have been included in this paper, and here I have tried to choose areas that relate to the contributions of the Society to this subject.

## America

The coins of the British in the Americas fall into three parts: North America up until the mid-1770s. Canada up until 1867 when it achieved dominion status, and the West Indies until each island achieved independence. The Falkland Islands also fall into this sphere, but will not be further discussed here.

The first attempts by England to create an overseas empire were driven by envy of the great wealth that Spain derived from her control of the South American gold and silver mines. During the 1580s attempts were made to start colonies in Newfoundland and Roanoke Island in North America. However, these came to nothing, and it was not until the early seventeenth century that successful colonies were established in places such as Virginia

(1607). This soon expanded to extend down most of the eastern seaboard of North America from Newfoundland in the north down to South Carolina, and these colonies continued under British rule until the American war of independence in the mid 1770s. The United States then split away from Britain, leaving the provinces of Canada as the only mainland colonies.

P. Nelson was the first of our members to contribute a paper on the coinage of North America.[5] In volume 1 of the [British Numismatic] Journal he discussed the coinage of William Wood, who obtained the right to issue coins for 'the plantations' (i.e. North American colonies) for fourteen years starting in 1722. These coins have become known as 'Rosa Americanas' and were issued in three denominations – two pence, penny and half penny – showing the bust of George I on the obverse and a device with a rose of different styles on the reverse. The same author also read a paper to the Society on the pre-revolutionary coinage of America in 1912.[6] These early coins, apart from Wood's coins, were made current in the different colonies such as: Massachusetts where the willow, oak and pine tree coins were struck; Maryland where coins were issued by Lord Baltimore; and New Jersey, which used St Patrick half pennies and farthings. The latest coin in the British American colonial series was the half penny of George III dated 1773 for use in Virginia. Both of the papers published by Nelson essentially built on the work done in the 1870s by Sylvester Crosby,[7] who brought together the early coins of America into a single work for the first time. Nelson's paper on the Rosa Americana series not only describes the coins and ascribes the source of the rose design to a pattern penny of Elizabeth I, but is remarkable for its beautiful illustrations of the coins.

The British formally took control of Canada in 1763, and in 1791 the country was divided into two provinces of Upper and Lower Canada. These were re-united in 1840 and then amalgamated into the Dominion of Canada with New Brunswick and Nova Scotia in 1867. Manitoba was added in 1870, British Columbia in 1871. Prince Edward Island in 1873 and other territories in 1876 and 1880.[8] Most of the early numismatic history of Canada is related to the tokens that were issued by local tradesmen in the absence of available small change, and no papers have appeared in *BNJ* on this subject. However, Doty, in his book sponsored by the Society about the Soho Mint, does discuss tokens produced for four Canadian banks and the Province of New Brunswick by the Soho Mint between 1837 and 1844.[9]

The different provinces issued the early coins of Canada. Thus there are coins for the province of Canada itself, but also Nova Scotia, New Brunswick, Prince Edward Island and Newfoundland.[10] J.B. Caldecott was responsible for the first paper from our Society discussing the coins of Canada when he wrote a short note on a countermarked Spanish dollar, dated 1765, that he believed was for use in Canada.[11]

T.V. Buttrey wrote about cut coins in Canada in a paper that explored the relationship between coins and archaeology.[12] Buttrey discussed the fact that it is very difficult to assign cut money as being used in a particular place (rather than imported later for collectors) unless the fragments bear some kind of identifying countermark. Dated archaeological evidence would be the only way to be certain about such pieces, and Buttrey reported just such evidence being found at Fairfax in Ontario. A quarter part of a Spanish 8 reales was discovered in the debris in the cellar of a building that had been destroyed following the burning of the settlement in October 1813, thereby establishing with certainty that such pieces circulated in Canada early in the nineteenth century.

In the islands of the West Indies, Barbados was the first to host a British colony, and by 1660 St Kitts, Antigua, Nevis, Montserrat and Jamaica had been occupied. Further gains and losses occurred during wars with other colonial powers. The islands are usually considered together with the territories on the mainland such as British Guiana, British Honduras and the Mosquito Coast. Most of these territories became independent states during the late twentieth century.

The coins generally fall into two major types: the cut and countermarked coins (very often Spanish Dollars) and, once the West Indian colonies had become more established in the eighteenth and nineteenth centuries, those coins specially struck for use in some of the islands. Examples are the 'pineapple' pennies of Barbados, nickel pennies from Victoria onwards for Jamaica and coins struck for use in British Guiana (formerly Essequibo and Demarary). British Honduras also had its own machine-struck coinage.

J.B. Caldecott was the first to discuss the coins of the West Indies, in a paper reviewing the use of cut and countermarked Spanish Dollars as urrency.[13] He presented a basic numismatic study of the subject without adding much supporting documentary background. H.A. Parsons discussed a Massachusetts shilling cut into four parts to form three penny-pieces for use in the Leeward Islands.[14] This short paper established three important points: first, that the islands of the Leeward group used Massachusetts money – a nice example of one colony using the coins of another; second, that coins were cut to meet smaller denominational requirements: and third that, at least in the early days, cut money was not countermarked with a local stamp.

Thompson examined the transfer of counterfeit currency to the West Indies in a paper giving extracts from contemporary (1797) documents describing the importation of forged stampees or 'black dogs' to Martinique.[15] In addition it would seem that the culprit, a Mr. Dick, was also in the habit of importing forged gold Johannes into the West Indies. The fact that Dick was found to be doing no more than was accepted practice illustrates that the problem of forgery of these early West Indian coins was widely accepted and understood even by contemporary authorities. However, as will be seen time and again, a much more complete analysis of West Indian colonial coinage was not available until Major F. Pridmore, the doyen of the British Commonwealth coinage and an honorary member of the Society, examined this fascinating series in great detail.[16] His treatise still remains the major work on the subject, although some new information has been added since the time of his publication in 1965. (For instance, a paper on these early coins was read to the Society in 1996 by R. Lyall,[17] who has also produced a major work on the tokens of the West Indies.[18])

Doty drew attention to the coins struck at the Soho Mint for use in the West Indies. In 1792/3 Boulton produced a copper penny coinage for Bermuda. In this instance he re-used for the obverse a die that had been prepared in 1788 by Jean-Pierre Droz for a proposed British coinage that never came to fruition. This obverse was combined with a reverse showing a sailing ship, a traditional design found on the rare early 'hog money' coinage of Bermuda. The same re-use of dies was seen in the coinage of the Bahamas penny in 1806, when Boulton used the obverse die of the British half penny for the obverse of the Bahamas penny, only having to produce a new reverse die.

In short, the Society has made some significant contributions to understanding the British Colonial coins of America. However, whilst there are disparate sources of information on these coins, there is no single source of reference for the whole group other than standard listings available from catalogues such as Krause.

## Asia

### *India*

India was, of course, the 'jewel in the crown' of the British Empire, and the complexity of coinage associated with the British makes it the largest single numismatic subject covered by this review. In addition, it is this area of Imperial and Colonial coinage that has received most attention from members and publications of the Society. It therefore deserves to be given more space and treated separately from other territories.

The sixteenth century saw the beginnings of the formation of companies holding monopolies of trade between England and certain other markets, and it was a company of this type, formed on 31 December 1600, that was granted a charter for the exclusive right to trade with the East Indies. The first two voyages did not go to India but to the islands of the East Indies, but the third expedition, in 1607 was sent to explore the opportunities for trade in the Arabian Sea and specifically to call, inter alia, at Surat in Gujarat on the west coast of India. One of the ships of the small fleet of this third voyage, commanded by a Captain Hawkins, eventually reached Surat on 28 August 1608. Initially the English could only base themselves near to Surat at a place named Swalley Hole, but the twelfth voyage, commanded by Thomas Best, arrived at Surat in 1612 and finally succeeded in obtaining the necessary permission to establish a factory, possibly because the Moghuls were beginning to realize that the English were seriously capable of challenging Portuguese naval power. In 1635 the Portuguese and the English signed, in Goa, a treaty that gave the English access to Portuguese trading posts all around the Arabian Sea, including the posts along the west coast of India. One of the islands controlled by the Portuguese was Bombay, and this island was ceded to Charles II as part of the dowry for his marriage to the Portuguese princess, Catherine of Braganza, in 1661. Charles then let Bombay to the East India Company in 1668 for a rent of £10 p.a.

Meanwhile, two Dutchmen with experience of trading in the East had arrived in London in 1609 and offered to lead a voyage to the east or Coromandel coast and to explore trade between there and Siam and Bantam. Floris and Antheuniss, the two Dutchmen, sailed from England in January 1611 and by August they had arrived on the east coast of India at the ports of Masulipatam and Petapoli in Golconda. Whilst the local trade with Siam did not live up to expectations in the longer term, Masulipatam became established as a factory of the EIC on and off for many years. In the 1630s the headquarters of the English was moved from Masulipatam to Armagon and then back again, as the English tried to deal with the various vicissitudes facing them, such as famine, the animosity of the Dutch, and local wars between Golconda and its neighbours. In 1639 the English agent at Armagon, Francis Day, sailed down the coast, visiting the Portuguese fort of San Thome and then on to a small fishing village called Madraspatam. Here he negotiated with the local *naik* the right to build a fort on a piece of land measuring about one square mile, whither he determined to remove the Armagon agency.

Further up the east coast, in the Bay of Bengal, Antheuniss had made contact with Bengal in the 1620s, but it was not until the 1640s and 1650s that serious trade began. Factories were established in various places including Hoogli, Patna and Dakka, and by 1681 the area was afforded the status of a separate presidency. However, Calcutta was not then the major factory. This did not happen until after the farcical affair of the attempted invasion of

Mogul India (with a standing army of perhaps 100,000 men) by a British army of 308 men. After various skirmishes, and the effective annihilation of the British infantry, the arrival of a British fleet allowed a truce agreeable to both sides to be reached. Part of the agreement allowed Job Charnock, the leader of the British forces, to select a site for a factory, and he eventually chose a place near a village called Kalighat, later modified to Kalikata and then Calcutta.[19]

Each of these small trading posts at Bombay, Madras and Calcutta gradually expanded its influence to surrounding areas until they controlled very large parts of India. Initially, the East India Company ran these territories, but increasing political pressure forced the British government to take more responsibility until it assumed complete control in 1858. India, Pakistan and (eventually) Bangladesh gained independence in 1947.

The coins of the British in India fall into two main series, both recorded by Pridmore[20] – the Presidency series issued by Madras, Bombay and Bengal, and the Uniform Coinage of British India issued from 1835 up to independence in 1947.

The early coins of Madras are either based on the south Indian system of gold *pagodas* and silver fanams with copper cash coins, or on the Moghul system of gold *mohurs* and silver rupees. In 1807 machinery was introduced into the mint at Madras and a more standard coinage was produced, although initially there was still a mixture of *pagodas* and rupees. However in 1812, following the intervention of the authorities in London, a silver rupee-based coinage was selected, essentially as a step towards the unification of the coinage across the whole of British India.

In Bombay, at the end of the seventeenth century, a series of European designs were tried but did not generally gain wide circulation, and throughout the eighteenth century Moghul style rupees were issued from the Mint in Bombay. At the beginning of the nineteenth-century Bombay, like Madras, settled on the rupee standard.

In Bengal, the silver rupee was the standard coin from the beginning of British rule although, as more territory was acquired towards the North-West Frontier rupees of different weight standards came to be used within the presidency (e.g. Farrukhabad rupee compared to Banaras rupee) and so even here standardization proved difficult.

Eventually, in 1835, the whole of British India moved to a single standard based on the silver rupee and this continued with slight modifications until independence in 1947.

The attention of members of the BNS has been drawn to the coins of the British in India throughout the life of the society. In 1906, J.B. Caldecott exhibited coins of the Patna mint struck by the EIC,[21] and there are some nice illustrations published with the proceedings. In 1908 R.P. Jackson published a paper describing copper coins of the EIC.[22] Whilst the paper is merely a description of small copper coins that he ascribes to Madras, there are some interesting points to be noted that are worth further discussion. Firstly, his coin no. 15 shows on the obverse the balemark of the EIC and on the reverse the date 1710. Pridmore actually assigns this coin to the Malabar Coast under the Bombay Presidency (no. 313), presumably on the basis of style, although he does note that his listings are provisional. Second, Jackson's coins nos. 22, 23 & 24, with the balemark on the obverse and the date 1803 on the reverse, again assigned to Madras, are assigned to Bombay by Pridmore (nos. 319 & 321). More recently, arguments have been made that these coins are more likely to belong to Madras rather than Bombay, thus supporting the original attribution of Jackson.[23] In 1912 Major Jackson published another paper on the coins of southern India, where he recorded some interesting coins of Madras including coins with the mintname Chinapatan (Madras).[24]

In 1929/30, H.A. Parsons published a paper on the early coins of the Bombay Presidency and particularly examined the dating of the copperoons.[25] The early forms of these coins show the date as A°7° or A°9° and had been supposed by earlier authors to represent the seventh and ninth regnal years of Charles II (i.e. 1667 and 1669 respectively). However, William Foster[26] had already established that the first of these coins was struck at Bombay in 1672 and that the coins were dated from 1665 when the English formally received the island of Bombay from the Portuguese. Thus,

7 represented 1672 and 9 represented 1674. Parsons was able to confirm this date by the publication of a coin showing the A°9° date together with the numerals 74 (for 1674) in the outer legend on the reverse.

More recently, Major Pridmore published his paper on the coins designed by Spencer for the Indian coinage of George VI.[27] This is a complete account of the work of the artist/engraver responsible for the design of the Indian coinage of George VI and is based on coins from the Spencer collection.

Despite all these contributions, it was not until the publication of the final two volumes of Pridmore's works that British Indian numismatics really received the detailed analysis that such a complex series requires. However, several lacunae still existed to be filled by new research. For instance, coins issued from mints that were captured by the British and continued to issue coins in the native styles have been published by Wiggins[28] but still require further analysis, and Pridmore's assessment of the coinage of the Malabar Coast left some unanswered questions, although these have recently been addressed.[29]

Doty has presented an excellent account of the events surrounding the building of a steam driven mint, supplied by Boulton. Watt & Co. during the 1820s for the Calcutta Mint.[30] This story is worth recounting as an example of the trials and tribulations faced by the people involved in producing the Indian coinage. Matthew Boulton was first approached about the possibility of building a mint for the East India Company as early as 1808. The initial discussion revolved around the possibility of building two mints, one at Calcutta and one at Madras, but this changed to building just one at Madras and then again to building just one at Calcutta, but smaller than previously planned, having five coining presses instead of the original eight. Sometime during 1809, this project was dropped for reasons that are not entirely clear. By 1819, it was obvious that the Calcutta mint was incapable of meeting the requirements placed upon it, and agreement was reached that someone should be sent to England to explore the possibility of obtaining a steam driven mint to be shipped out to India. A Lieutenant of the Bengal Engineers named William Nairn Forbes was selected for this task, and he was to become the major player in the construction and operation of the new mint at Calcutta for more than thirty years, ending as Calcutta Mint Master.

Forbes arrived in England in 1820, and by the end of that year agreement had been reached that Boulton. Watt & Co. would act as the main contractors for the construction of the mint and would provide not only the steam engines but also the coining and cutting-out presses. John and George Rennie would act as sub-contractors, supplying the rolling mill, while Henry Maudsley would provide other parts such as the draw bench, lathes and melting furnaces. Plans for the new mint were drawn up early in 1821 and approved on 2 April, and during that year Forbes learned more about the science of coining when he helped to produce a copper coinage for St Helena at the Soho mint.

By March of 1823 the equipment was ready for shipping to India. It was sent out on three separate ships, and had arrived by 21 October 1823, when Forbes himself arrived back in Calcutta. No time was lost in selecting a suitable site for the new mint on the banks of the Hoogli, and work began on draining the site and establishing the foundations.

As well as providing the machinery, it was necessary for Boulton & Watt to recruit a number of trained mechanics to go to India to help build the mint. The names of the men recruited for the project, and their fates, are shown in Table 1.

TABLE I: THE FATE OF PEOPLE INVOLVED IN CONSTRUCTING THE MINT AT CALCUTTA

| *Name* | *Date started in India* | *Fate* |
|---|---|---|
| Thomas Hughes | 1823 | Died in India 1824 |
| Edward Gozzard | 1823 | Survived |
| Joseph Mears | 1823 | Died in India 1824 |
| Gregory Wilkinson | 1823 | Died in India 1826 |
| Josiah Stratford | 1823 | Took to drink. Sent home 1825 |
| William Lewellyn | 1823 | Died in India 1825 |
| Thomas Pigg | 1823? | ? |
| Richard Burley | 1823 | Died in India 1824 |

| | | |
|---|---|---|
| John Rose | 1823? | ? |
| William Dunn | 1823? | ? |
| Thomas O'Brien | 1825 | Fell ill and was sent home in 1826 |
| Henry Daniels | 1825 | Fell ill and was sent home in 1826. Returned in 1827. |
| George Hudson | 1827 | ? |
| Charles Cashmore | 1827 | ? |
| Taylor | 1827 | ? |

It is immediately apparent that many of the men sent out to provide the necessary mechanical expertise did not survive very long in the pestilential climate of Calcutta. Forbes did his best 10 get new recruits trained and sent out from England, and to redeploy those who survived, but the mint was not completed until 1829 or 1830. However, once complete it is clear that it met all expectations, and Forbes was clearly delighted with the first output during the summer of 1830. Doty suggests that the coins struck in 1830 would have been the one-pie coins authorized for circulation in 1831. He argues that the coins could have been prepared in advance of being put into circulation. This seems to open an unnecessary complication. Pridmore has recorded that the mint-master proposed making changes to the copper pice in 1829, and that specimens were submitted to the Mint Committee on 26 August 1830. It is therefore much more likely that any coins struck in advance of the necessary legal bureaucracy authorizing their issue would have been these pice and not the one-pie coins, the design of which was not agreed until 1831.

In his account, Doty notes interesting information about the huge numbers of blank dies that were shipped out to Calcutta from Soho. For instance in 1827, 2,000 blank dies for rupees were shipped out, and in 1830, 14,500 dies for rupees, half rupees and quarter rupees were ordered. Doty paints a similar picture for the installation of a new mint at Bombay, again during the 1820s, but this time the mint was not new, but a second-hand mint from Soho itself. In fact, this mint was the refurbished second Soho mint, built in 1798/9.

Doty also describes the coins produced at Soho for use in the different Indian presidencies, and a paper presented at the special summer meeting in 2001 on the copper coins of the Bombay Presidency struck at Soho in 1791-6 drew heavily on his work.[31] Up until very late in the eighteenth century the copper coins of the Bombay Presidency were poorly manufactured and very crude. In 1790 steps were initiated to correct this sorry state of affairs, and the Bombay authorities were informed that the copper coins then in circulation were to be replaced by a new coinage sent out from England. The initial idea was that this would be a gradual process, but by 1791 a decision had been taken to replace all circulating copper coins in one go with 100 tons of new coins. Accordingly, 35 tons of coins were sent from England to Bombay aboard the 'Essex', with instructions not to open the casks until the rest of the shipment arrived. A further 65 tons were duly received aboard the Rockingham with instructions on how to issue them. The total quantity shipped was 660 casks weighing 100 tons 14 cwts 2 qtrs 13½ lbs.[32]

These coins were to be issued at the rate of:

200s. @ 50 to a rupee
150s. @ 66½ to a rupee
100s. @ 100 to a rupee
50s. @ 200 to a rupee

The intention of this rate was to make one rupee worth 10,000 grains avoirdupois weight of copper, compared to the existing rate of 7,314 grains. This, combined with the greatly increased quality of the design, would reduce the amount of forgery that was obviously worrying the authorities at the time.

Major Pridmore makes a rather ambiguous comment about the fact that the Company had established a mint at French Ordinary Court in London, and that this may have played a part in the decision to manufacture the coins in England, rather than locally in Bombay. This might imply that the coins were struck at a mint in London. In fact, Matthew Boulton in his factory at Soho near Birmingham struck the first 100 tons. This can be seen from the minutes of the meetings of the Court of Directors,[33] who on 13 January 1791 agreed that Boulton would be employed to undertake the coinage. On 2 February Mr Williams was instructed to deliver 100 tons of copper to Mr Boulton at Soho, near Birmingham. Mr Williams didn't think that he could deliver the copper before the middle of March, and it presumably look some time to complete the coinage, because on 24 August the Court agreed to advance Boulton £6000 for the work that he was then carrying out. Doty has examined the records of the Soho mint in some detail, and his work confirms that these coins were indeed struck there.

Pridmore records that further deliveries occurred in 1792, 1793 and 1794. I have not been able to confirm the deliveries for 1792 and 1793, and am doubtful that they occurred. However, a second coinage was undertaken in 1793 and shipped to India in 1794 (Doty). The coinage consisted of double pice, pice and half pice. The coins were dated 1794. The 1½ pice denomination was discontinued, presumably because it caused confusion with the double pice. A further large coinage was undertaken in 1803 with the coins dated 1804.

In 1794, Boulton produced a dub and half-dub coinage for use in the Madras Presidency, and this was repeated in 1797. The coinage is interesting for the first use (on coinage as opposed to tokens) of a wide, raised rim bearing an incuse legend in an attempt to prevent forgery. Of course, this approach was later used on the British 'cartwheel' coins. Other coins produced by Boulton for Madras consisted of 20, 10, 5 and 1 cash coins dated 1804 and 1808. The one cash coin was so small that it required special production techniques, and these coins were produced last of all the denominations. Matthew Boulton had sent John Philip to London in 1802 to consult the EIC's experts on the designs, and he returned in October. Production of the three larger denominations began almost immediately, but production of the one-cash pieces caused problems until January 1803 when a new method was perfected.

The only coins that Doty records as being produced at the Soho mint for the Bengal Presidency were for a coinage of copper pice in 1809, but various problems caused this project to be abandoned and only the patterns remain. However, Vice has added to this with his research into the hexagonal patterns produced at Soho,[34] and has shown that Pridmore's view that these coins were to be used in the Bombay Presidency was wrong, and that they were planned for use in the Bengal Presidency to replace cowrie shells.

A paper has been presented to the Society on a pattern two annas of 1841,[35] confirming Pridmore's prediction that coins of this denomination should exist with plain edges, although at the time that he wrote no specimens were known and he had only archival sources for his prediction. The coinage of Madras at the beginning of the nineteenth century was discussed in another paper read to the Society.[36] In this instance new contemporary documents had revealed more details about the difficulties encountered in moving from a hammered to a machine-struck coinage. There are still many other gaps that need filling, and the British Indian field of numismatics offers a great opportunity for further study and research. However, Pridmore does leave later scholars with something of a challenge because, although he transcribes many quotes from 'the records' in his books, there is an annoying lack of reference back to the original documents, so that later researchers are left with the unenviable task of 'rediscovering' these records in order to advance the subject further.

### *Other Far Eastern Parts of the British Empire*

Close to India, the English East India Company acquired the island of Ceylon from the Dutch in 1795, although the interior was not conquered until 1815, and it became a British colony from 1802 until 1948. As with India, the early coins of the British period of occupation really have a local feel to them, although they were based on the earlier Dutch coins. They were replaced by coins struck at the Soho mint dated 1802 and denominated as sliver (l/48th rix dollar), half stiver (1/96th rix dollar) and quarter stiver {1/192nd rix dollar), with an elephant on the obverse and the value on the reverse.[37] Of course, all these coins circulated alongside each other for some considerable time.

These were then replaced by coins with a much more British

style, showing the British monarch's head on one side, and this style continued right up until independence. In addition to local denominations, tiny half and quarter farthings were struck in England for use in Ceylon during the nineteenth century, and these were locally valued at one-twelfth *fanam* and one twenty-fourth *fanam* respectively. A major part of the numismatic landscape of Ceylon comprises the tokens issued by the plantation (e.g. coffee) owners for their workers. These tokens provide a fascinating insight into the industrial history of the island, but have not been the subject of any publications of the Society. The Andaman Islands hosted a penal colony before becoming part of the independent India in 1947, and rupee tokens were issued during the early 1860s.

The Cocos-Keeling Islands were discovered in 1609 and became external territories of Australia in 1955. From a numismatic standpoint, these islands are interesting for the use of unusual materials (sheepskin, ivory and bone) in producing tokens.

In the Malay Archipelago, Penang was occupied in 1786 and Singapore established in 1819, Malacca was gained from the Dutch in 1824. Collectively these three territories became the Straits Settlements in 1826. Further states were added, and eventually they were all brought together as the Federation of Malaya, which gained independence as Malaysia in 1957, although Singapore later left the federation. Sarawak and British North Borneo also joined the federation of Malaysia but Brunei did not and was given independence in 1984. The coins of the different stales in the Malay archipelago form a very interesting series, simply because of their diversity of types and styles, varying from early locally-struck, European-type coins of Fort Marlborough, in Sumatra, to the merchant tokens of Singapore (mainly sLruck by Birmingham manufacturers, some at the Soho mint), with later coins tending to conform to the more standard imperial type showing the British monarch's bust on one face.

The British occupied Hong Kong Island in 1841 and the New Territories were added in 1898. It became part of China in 1997. The coins are generally of the standard colonial style, with a very interesting series of trials and patterns being prepared during the Victorian era.

Very little has been published in *BNJ* on any of the coins of Asia outside India. J.E. Cribb presented a paper on the coins of Hong Kong in 1988,[38] and he has published his research in his book discussing the collection of coins formed by the Hong Kong and Shanghai bank.[39] In this work he essentially rewrites the previous work undertaken by Pridmore concerning the Victorian patterns and reveals the different phases that these coins went through before the first currency coins were produced. Coins struck for more general use throughout South-East Asia include portcullis money produced at the end of the reign of Elizabeth, and these have been studied by P. Preston-Morley.[40]

In his book on the Soho Mint,[41] Doty presents a summary of the work undertaken by Boulton to produce coins for these areas of Asia. It is interesting to note that the first proper (as opposed to token) coinage undertaken by Boulton was for use at the Company's possession of Benculen in Sumatra. The coinage consisted of denominations of 3 and 2 kepings and 1 keping, weighing 150, 100 and 50 grains respectively. They were struck in 1786 and are dated accordingly, and were produced, not by machines driven by steam power, for which Boulton was to become so famous, but by water and man-powered machinery. Rolling and cutting of blanks was undertaken at the Soho factory in Birmingham but the actual coinage at a mint specially constructed in London. Many problems were encountered in producing these first coins but, despite this, a further order was received in 1787, with a total of over eighteen tons eventually being struck. By 1797, when Boulton received a further order for the same three denominations for Sumatra, he had perfected his coining techniques to such an extent that he was able to produced over fifteen tons of coins within two months of receiving the firm order. Boulton received the final order for copper coins for Sumatra in 1803 and these were dated 1804.

Once again coins of Asian areas outside India have been the subject of study by Pridmore, whose published work remains the only collected reference work on the series.[42] However, there do seem to be some gaps in this work, particularly surrounding the Hong Kong coins (see above), and these gaps may extend to other series, so it would seem that there is scope for further research in this whole area and perhaps an updating of Pridmore's work.

### *Asian Territories in the Near East*

Palestine became a British Mandated territory in 1917 and remained so until 1948. Aden was annexed to British India in 1839 and, after some territorial expansion, became a crown colony in 1937 before achieving independence in 1967,[43] and other Gulf and Middle Eastern states became British Protectorates at various times during the twentieth century. Coins of these territories have not been addressed by any publication of the Society, but Pridmore has covered those of Palestine.

## Australasia

The first settlers arrived from Britain in 1788 with the establishment of the penal colony at Botany Bay in what became New South Wales. Separate colonies were established in Van Diemen's Land (Tasmania), Western Australia. South Australia, Victoria and Queensland, before Australia achieved dominion status in 1900. followed by the union of the states into the Commonwealth of Australia in 1901. New Zealand began to attract European settlers from the 1840s and achieved dominion status in 1907.

The earliest coins used were imported from a variety of different sources, and in 1800 the Governor of New South Wales issued a proclamation establishing the rates at which these foreign coins should pass current. However, the numismatic history of nineteenth-century Australasia is really dominated by the tradesmen's tokens, of which over 600 have been recorded as issued between the late 1840s and the 1870s. Amongst the first of these tokens were those produced for Antiand Smith & Co. of Melbourne, and these, coincidentally. were the last tokens produced by Boulton & Watt in 1849, just before the company was shut down and the assets sold.[44] The earliest coins of Australia and New Zealand are the cut and countermarked Spanish dollars known as Holey Dollars and Dumps. Later, the discovery of gold in Australia led to the establishment of branches of the Royal Mint in Sydney. Melbourne and Perth, where sovereigns and half sovereigns were struck throughout the second half of the nineteenth century both for use at home and for export as bullion. With dominion status achieved for Australia in 1900, currency, coinage and legal tender became the concern of the new Federal Government of Australia, as it did for the Government of New Zealand in 1907.

Alfred Chitty, a corresponding member of the Society, published the first paper in *BNJ* dealing with the early coins of Australia.[45] After discussing the holey dollars and the fifteen pence bitts he went on to discuss a whole series of silver tokens, which eventually led to the resolution to strike a silver coinage for Australia following the creation of the Commonwealth of Australia. He then went on to discuss the gold coins produced following the discovery of gold deposits in 1851. Of particular interest are the so-called kangaroo pieces struck in weights of ¼, ½, 1 and 2 ounces. This paper was followed a few years later by a paper showing the mint accounts for the numbers of sovereigns and half sovereigns produced at Sydney, Melbourne and Perth.[46] In the mid-1930s Francis Gardner briefly reviewed the early coinage of Australia, although this paper contained little significant new information.[47] More recently, Freehill read a paper to the society on the subject of Australian coins.[48]

Australasia is one of the areas that was not covered by Pridmore's series on Commonwealth, coins, and the major work of reference remains Andrews's *Australasian Tokens & Coins.*[49] This is a superb book covering all the early coins and tokens of Australia and New Zealand but, since it was published in 1921, there have been a number of new discoveries that obviously are not included. A more recent work by Rennick is very difficult to obtain.[50]

Pacific Islands include New Guinea (1884-1904). Fiji (1874-1970), New Hebrides (1887-1980) and the Solomon Islands (1893-1978), Tongo (1900-70), Gilbert and Ellice Islands (1892-

1978/9) and various other islands of little numismatic importance. The coinage of these islands has not been addressed by the Society, nor was it the subject of Pridmore's work. However, since many of these islands became dependencies of Australia or New Zealand after those countries achieved dominion status, their coinages may be considered to fall outside the scope of this work.

In summary, the early coins and tokens of Australasia have received reasonable coverage by the Society, but there may be room for a reappraisal or updating of Andrews's work, with an extension to include the coinages of the Pacific Islands where appropriate.

## Europe

Territories considered as part of the British Empire in Europe outside the United Kingdom from a numismatic standpoint include: Channel Islands, Isle of Man, Lundy, Gibraltar, Ionian Islands, Cyprus and Malta. Major Pridmore covered this coinage as part of his work on Commonwealth coins,[51] and there have not been significant changes since that time, although there have been additional modern coins struck for use in various of these territories. Most of the territories have coins with their own distinctive features: the Isle of Man with the triune (three legs), Lundy with the puffin, Jersey and Guernsey with their shields of arms. Gibraltar with its castle and the Ionian Islands with the winged lion of St Mark.

Early contributions to knowledge of these coins came in 1907 with a paper on the Ionian coinage by N. Heywood.[52] During the Napoleonic wars, the British Look possession of six of the Mediterranean islands including Cephaionia and Corfu and formed them into the United States of the Ionian Islands under the Protectorate of Great Britain in 1815. They were ceded to Greece in 1863. The British coins consist of a copper penny (two oboli), half penny (obol) and farthing (half obol), dated 1819 or 1820. and a lepton or 1/5 obol bearing various dates from 1834 to 1862. In addition a curious coin was identified in 1904[53] as a mule between the obverse of an Irish penny of George IV and a reverse bearing the seated figure of Britannia as shown on the penny of the Ionian coins.

The Guernsey eight doubles of 1864 featured in a paper by D.L.F. Sealy written in 1965.[54] In this masterly work Sealy showed how six obverse dies and six reverse dies were chain-linked into a series to give ten die pairings. From this he was able to deduce that the firm of Henry Jay & Co., the manufacturers of the coins, probably only possessed one coining press. Furthermore, he was able to conclude that each die must have been engraved directly by hand and that the company did not possess any means of die multiplication. Guernsey coinage also features in Doty's book on the Soho mint, where he describes the minting of the 1830 four doubles and the 1834 eight doubles.

Doty also describes the first coins produced by Matthew Boulton for the Isle of Man. The duke of Atholl, who had sold the island to the Crown in 1765, suggested to the king in 1797 that Boulton should produce a copper coinage for the Isle of Man. This was agreed but the Royal Mint apparently caused delays, presumably because it considered that the coins should have been produced there. However, coinage eventually began in 1799 and consisted of pennies and half pennies dated 1798. A second order was placed in 1812 and filled with coins dated 1813.

Coins of the other colonies and dependencies within Europe have not received attention in the publications of the Society. However, as usual, Pridmore has comprehensively dealt with this series. Perhaps the major opportunity for future study lies in the more modern coins that were not addressed by him.

## Africa

Coins struck under the authority of the British in Africa can conveniently be divided into four sections based on the points of the compass. Initially contact was really confined to necessary watering holes on the route round the Cape to the markets of South-East Asia. However, in 1672 the Royal Africa Company was formed, and together with its successor companies it engaged in the triangular trade of goods exported from Britain to West

Africa, particularly the Gold Coast. Here they were exchanged for slaves, who were shipped to the American plantations, and exchanged for goods such as sugar and tobacco, which were taken back to Britain. By 1785, the British controlled the greater part of trade with the Gold Coast, although the slave trade was coming to an end and was abolished throughout the British Empire in 1807. In contrast to the Gold Coast, Sierra Leone was specifically founded in West Africa as a haven for freed slaves, particularly those who had fought with the British during the American War of Independence and who did not wish to stay in America as slaves after the war. From these beginnings the group of territories that formed British West Africa developed by 1901, consisting of the Gambia (independent 1965), Sierra Leone (independent 1961), the Gold Coast (independent 1957 as Ghana) and Nigeria (independent 1960).

In the south of the continent, Britain obtained control of Cape Colony from the Dutch following the Napoleonic wars in 1814, and expansion to the north into Southern and Northern Rhodesia (independent as Zimbabwe in 1965/80 and Zambia in 1964 respectively) was led by Cecil Rhodes in the drive for gold and Empire. To this southern group can be added Nyasaland (independent 1964 as Malawi). South Africa obtained dominion status in 1910.

In the Eastern sector of the continent, the British had an early interest in Zanzibar, and this expanded onto the mainland at the end of the nineteenth century to encompass Kenya and Uganda and following the First World War, Tanganyika (Tanzania).

To the north, the British took control of Egypt at the end of the nineteenth century, with Sudan to the south being part of this sphere of influence at various times. However, the country did not formally become a part of the Empire until 1914 when it was declared a protectorate, which it remained until 1922.

Coinage for all these different territories developed as British control grew. In the west, Sierra Leone had a coinage as early as 1791 (actually issued somewhat later than the date on the coins), and the Gold Coast in 1796, with a second issue in 1818. During most of the nineteenth-century cut and countermarked Spanish Dollars were used as currency, and it was not until the twentieth century that a uniform coinage was issued for all the territories in this region. The coinage of St. Helena can conveniently be included with the West African group. The British West African coinage has been studied by a number of eminent numismatists such as Pridmore[55] (though this did not form part of his series of books on Commonwealth coins), Parsons,[56] and Dolley.[57] The most comprehensive account of the coinage can be found in the work of Vice.[58] As far as the Society is concerned. Doty has included discussion of the coins, though much of this is based on the work of Vice.

In South Africa early coinage requirements were met through the use of tradesmen's tokens until after the Boer War. Nothing has heen written about these tokens in the Society's publications nor about the coins of Rhodesia and Nyasaland. Theron published the major work on the tokens of South Africa in 1978,[59] but this publication is very difficult to get hold of, as is an earlier work by Maynard.[60] Very little is published on the coins of Rhodesia and Nyasaland. Likewise the coins of Eastern Africa have not been published together in a collected work.

In Egypt the British instituted a gold, silver, nickel and bronze coinage with denominations ranging from 1 to 100 piastres, and Pridmore has described these.[61]

In short, the British imperial and colonial coins of West Africa have been well documented by Vice, but all other areas would benefit from similar treatment.

## Conclusion

In 1912 J.B. Caldecott read a paper to the Society in which he 'urged the necessity of a new and standard work' for the coinage of the British possessions and colonies.[62] Major Pridmore eventually filled this gap to some extent (excluding the coins of Africa, North America and Australasia), but it would seem that the time is now ripe for a new work of reference for the series. Work on the coinage of British India was started by the late Ken Wiggins, working with Bob Puddester, and is now being advanced by the current author in collaboration with others. I am not aware of work going on in other areas, but perhaps now is the time to reiterate Caldecott's call to arms and for the BNS and its members to take a lead in supporting a new, comprehensive work to address this fascinating part of British history.

## Notes

1. P.J. Marshall, *Cambridge Illustrated History of the British Empire* (Cambridge, 1996).
2. J. Remick et al., *The Guidebook and Catalogue of British Commonwealth Coins 1694-1971,* 3rd edn. (Winnipeg, 1971); A. De Claremont & J.D. Wheeler, *Spink's Catalogue of British Commonwealth Coins* (London, 1986).
3. J. Atkins, *Coins and Tokens of the British Possessions and Colonies of the British Empire 1960-79* (London, 1889).
4. F. Pridmore, *The Coins of the British Commonwealth of Nations,* pts. 1, 2, 3 & 4 (London, 1960-79).
5. P. Nelson, 'The Coinage of William Wood for the American Colonies, *BNJ* 1 (1904), 265-85.
6. P. Nelson, 'The Pre-Revolutionary Coinage of America', *BNJ* 9 (1912), 417.
7. S.S. Crosby, *The Early Coins of America* (1873-5). Reproduced in 1983 by Quarterman Publications Inc.
8. R. Chalmers, *History of Currencies in the British Colonies* (1893). Reprinted in 1972 by John Drury.
9. R. Doty, *The Soho Mint and the Industrialisation of Money,* BNS Special Publication No. 2 (London, 1998), p. 336.
10. L.V.W. Wright, *Colonial and Commonwealth Coins* (London, Toronto, Wellington, Sydney, 1959).
11. J.B. Caldecott, 'Countermarked Spanish Dollar for Old Canada', *BNJ* 1: (1904), 353-8.
12. T.V. Buttrey, 'Cut Coins in Canada', *BNJ* 36 (1967), 176-8.
13. J.B. Caldecott, 'The Spanish Dollar as Adapted for Currency in our West Indian Colonies', *BNJ* 1 (1904), 287-98.
14. H.A. Parsons, 'A Cut New England Threepence Attributed to the Leeward Islands', *BNJ* 15 (1919/20), 225-7.
15. J.D.A. Thompson, 'Documents Illustrating the Export of Counterfeit Currency to the West Indies', *BNJ* 27 (1952/4), 80-7.
16. F. Pridmore, *The Coins of the British Commonwealth of Nations,* pt. 3: *West Indies* (London, 1965).
17. R. Lyall, 'Black Doggs and Silver Bitts: Cuts Plugs and Countermarks of the Caribbean', *BNJ* 66 (1996), 187.
18. R. Lyall, *Tokens of the British Caribbean* (Token & Medal Society, 1988).
19. J. Keay, *The Honourable Company: A History of the English East India Company* (London, 1991).

20. F. Pridmore, *The Coins of the British Commonwealth of Nations,* Part 4: *India,* vol. I: *East India Company Presidency Series c. 1642-1835,* vol. 2: *Uniform Coinage East India Company, 1835-58, Imperial Period, 1858-1947* (1975-9).
21. J.B. Caldecott, 'Coins of the Patna Mint Struck by the East India Company', *BNJ* 3 (1906), 61.
22. R.P. Jackson, 'Some Copper Coins Issued by the English East India Company and Other European Powers in Southern India', *BNJ* 5 (1908), 341-7.
23. S. Bhandare & P.J.E. Stevens, 'Bombay Billys, the British Coinage of the Malabar Coast: A Reappraisal', *Supplement* 172 (2002) of the *Newsletter of the Oriental Numismatic Society.*
24. R.P. Jackson, 'The Dominions, Emblems and Coins of the South Indian Dynasties', *BNJ* 9 (1912), 296-396.
25. H.A. Parsons, 'The Bombay Pice Struck by the English East India Company during the Reign of Charles II', *BNJ* 20 (1929/30), 251-9.
26. W. Foster, 'A Note on the First English Coinage at Bombay', *NC,* 4th series 4 (1906), 351-7.
27. F. Pridmore, 'Mr A.P. Spencer, Artist/Engraver, His Majesty's Mint, Calcutta and the Re-designed Coinages of King George VI British India 1938-1947', *BNJ* 37 (1968), 158-74.
28. K.W. Wiggins, *Acquisition of Indian Mints by EICO* (New Delhi, 1996).
29. Bhandare & Stevens as in n. 23.
30. Doty, as in n. 9, pp. 190-205.
31. P.J.E. Stevens, Summer meeting of the BNS (2001).
32. India Office Collection, Dispatches to Bombay, E/4/1006, pp. 393-4.
33. India Office Collection, Minutes of the Meetings of the Board of Directors, B/112, p. 764.
34. D. Vice, 'A Pattern Cowrie Coinage for Bengal Presidency', Format 58 (1998), 2-5.
35. P.J.E. Stevens, 'An Indian Rarity of 1841', *BNJ* 54 (1984), 298.
36. P.J.E. Stevens, 'The Reformation of the Coinage of Madras at the Beginning of the Nineteenth Century', *BNJ* 67 (1997), 172.
37. Doty, as in n. 9, p. 324.
38. J.E. Cribb, 'Origins of the Hong Kong Coinage, 1841-1866' (1988).
39. J.B. Cribb, *Money in the Bank* (Spink & Son fur Hong Kong *&* Shanghai Banking Corp, 1987).
40. P.J. Preston-Morley, 'The East India Company Portcullis Money of 1600', *BNJ* 63 (1993), 167.
41. Doty, as in n. 9, pp. 299-300.
42. F. Pridmore, *The Coins of the British Commonwealth of Nations,* pt. 2: *Asian Territories* (London, 1965).
43. Ibid.
44. Doty, as in n. 9, p. 337.

45. A. Chitty, 'Early Australian Coins', *BNJ* 4 (1907), 179-87.
46. A. Chitty, 'The Australian Gold Coins Struck at the Sydney, Malbourne and Perth Mints', *BNJ* 8 (1911), 365-8.
47. F. Gardner, 'Some Notes Lin Australasian Currencies', *BNJ* 22 (1934/7), 17-27.
48. M. Freehill, 'On the Coinage of Australia'. *BNJ* 34 (1965), 188.
49. A. Andrews. *Australasian Tokens & Coins.* Issued by the trustees of the Mitchell Library, Sydney (1921).
50. Rennick, *Unofficial Coins of Colonial Australia and New Zealand* (1966).
51. F. Pridmore, *The Coins of the British Commonwealth of Nations,* pt. I: *European Territories* (London, 1560).
52. N. Heywood, 'The Coins of the Ionian State', *BNJ* 4 (1907), 189-92.
53. P. Nelson, 'The Coinage of Ireland in Copper, Tin and Pewter', *BNJ* 1 (1904), 221.
54. D.L.F. Sealy, 'The Guernsey Eight Doubles of 1864', *BNJ* 33 (1964), 164-7.
55. F. Pridmore, 'The Officially Mutilated Coinage of British West Africa circa 1813 (1825-?)-1839', *NCirc* LXII (1954), 60-41 'The Cut Quarters of Dollars Countermarked V.R.', *NCirc* LXIX (1961), 242-3; 'Notes on Colonial Coins, The Mint Letter G – A New Mint far the Coinage of British West Africa'. *NCirec* LXXI1I (1965), 259-60: 'The Coins of the Sierra Leone Company 1791-1807', *NCirc* LXXIV (1966), 206-8, 237-9, 277-9; St Helena, 'The East India Company's Coinages', *NCirc* LXX (1972), 410, 451-2.
56. H. A. Parsons, *The Colonial Coinage of British West Africa with the Adjacent Islands* (London, 1950).
57. M. Dolley, 'A Sesquicentennial Note on Some Official Restrikes of the British Colonial 1/50 and 1/100 Dollar Patterns Dated 1823', *NCirc* LXXXI (1973), 290-1.
58. D. Vice, *The Coinage of British West Africa & St Helena 1684-1958* (Peter Ireland [Format] Ltd., 1983).
59. G.P. Theron, *Token Coins of Sourthern Africa and their History* (1978).
60. E.J. Maynard, *Tokens of South Africa (*Africana Museum, Johannesburg, 1966).
61. F Pridmore, 'Notes on Colonial Coins: The British Protectorate of Egypt 18th December 1914-28th February 1922', *NCirc* LXXII (1964), 196-7.
62. J.B. Caldecott, 'Coins and Tokens of the British Possessions and Colonies'. *BNJ* 9 (1912), 419.

# PART II

# RECORDS

# 1

# Regulation XXXV of 1793

A Regulation for re-enacting with amendments, the Rules passed on the 20th October, and 31st November 1792, and subsequent dates, for the reform of the Gold and Silver Coin in Bengal, Behar, and Orissa; and for prohibiting the currency of any Gold or Silver Coin in those Provinces, but the Nineteenth Sun Sicca Rupee, and the Nineteenth Sun Gold Mohur, and their respective divisions and sub-divisions into Halves and Quarters; and for preventing the counterfeiting, defacing, or debasing of the Coin. - PASSED by the Governor-General in Council, on the 1st May 1793; corresponding with the 21st Bysaak 1200 Bengal Era; the 6th Bysaak 1200 Willaity; the 6th Bysaak 1850 Sumbut; and the 19th Ramzan 1207 Higeree.

---

[Preamble]

THE principal Districts in Bengal, Behar, and Orissa, have each a distinct Silver currency, consisting either of the Nineteenth Sun Sicca Rupee, or old or counterfeit Rupees of different Suns or Years, coined previous or subsequent to the Company's Administration, which are the standard measure of value in all transactions in the Districts in which they respectively circulate. The local circulation of these different sorts of Rupees, originated chiefly in the following circumstances. Under the native Government, it was customary to insert upon the Rupees, the year in which they were struck, and the Rupees coined at Patna, Dacca and Moorshedabad (at each of which cities there was art established Mint) bore different inscriptions, which in fact rendered the Rupees issued in each year from the respective Mints, a distinct species of Coin. Upon the Mints at Patna, Dacca, and Moorshedabad, being withdrawn soon after the commencement of the Company's administration, the Proprietors and Farmers of Land in the interior parts of the country, who were bound by their engagements to pay the Public Revenue in Sicca Rupees, experienced considerable difficulty in obtaining those Rupees, from the coinage of them being confined to Calcutta, at which place the only Mint that remained in the Provinces was established. They were in consequence compelled to collect the Rents from the Ryots, in the species of Sonaut, or other old Rupees, of which there happened to be the greatest number in their respective Districts, and which they were permitted to pay into the Public Treasuries at a fixed exchange. In consequence of the Ryots being required to pay their Rent in a particular sort of Rupee, they of course demanded it from the Manufacturers in payment for the grain, or raw materials, whilst the Manufacturers, actuated by similar principles with the Ryots, required the same species of Rupee from the traders who came to purchase their cloth, or other commodities. The various sorts of old Rupees accordingly soon became the established currency of particular Districts, and a necessary consequence, the value of each Rupee was enhanced in the District in which it was current, from being in demand of all transactions. As a further consequence, every other sort of Rupees brought into the District was rejected, from being a different measure of value from that by which the inhabitants had been accustomed to estimate their property, or, if it was received, discount was exacted upon it, equal to what the receiver would have been obliged to pay upon exchanging it at the house of a Shroff for the Rupee current in the District, or to allow upon passing it in payment to any other individual. Thus, if a Sicca Rupee of the Nineteenth Sun, which is intrinsically worth about seven per cent ore than an Arcot, was offered in payment in the Dacca Province, it was either reduced, or received nearly at the same value as an Arcot; whilst the holder of Arcots, or other sorts of Rupees, who carried them into Districts in which they were riot current, was subjected to similar loss. The Proprietors and Farmers of Land, or the persons concerned in making their payments to the Public Treasuries, derived a considerable advantage from this enhanced valuation of the particular species of Rupees current in their respective Districts, as they were enabled to obtain credit for them in exchange for Siccas, in which their Revenues were payable, at a rate considerably exceeding their intrinsic worth. The profits which the Shroffs or money changers derive from this disordered state of the coin is necessarily enormous. Their Agents in the different parts of the country, buy up all

Rupees which are brought into Districts in which they are not current, and consequently at a depreciated value, and send them for sale to Districts where they are the prevailing currency, and in which the dispose of them at an enhanced Value to persons who have payments or purchases to make in those Districts. The Merchants and Traders are under the necessity of submitting to the imposition, for no other Rupee but the Nineteenth Sun Sicca being coined at the Mints, the old Rupees are procurable only from the Shroffs, and consequently they must either pay the exchange demanded, or discontinue their purchases. From the rejection of the coin current in one Districts, when tendered in payment in another, the Merchants and Traders, and the Proprietors arid Cultivators of Land in the different parts of the country, are subjected in their commercial dealings with each other to the same losses by exchange, and all the other inconveniences that would necessarily result were the several Districts under separate and independent Governments, each having a different coin. The money changers are the only description of people who derive any benefit from this disordered state of the coin. The loss falls upon Government and the public at large, and must be perpetual, unless the various old and counterfeit Rupees now current in the different parts of the country, can be thrown out of circulation, and one species of Rupee made the general standard measure of value in all transactions between individuals, and between Government and its subjects. The Sicca Rupee of the Nineteenth Sun is the established Silver Coin of the country and the Rupee in which the public Revenues are payable. It was with a view to render it the general measure of value, that Government determined in the year 1773, that all Rupees coined in future should bear the impression of the Nineteenth Sun, or year, of the reign of Shah Alam, and no other species of Rupee (with the exception of some Arcots) has since been coined in the Calcutta Mint. The Rupees of the Eleventh, Twelfth, and Fifteenth Sun, were indeed directed to be considered current equally with the Nineteenth Sun Sicca Rupee. But this was a temporary measure, intended to be continued in force only until there should be a sufficiency of the Nineteenth Sun Sicca Rupee introduced into circulation. The number however of these three descriptions of Rupees, is of course inconsiderable compared with the number of the Nineteenth Sun Sicca Rupees that have been coined since the abovementioned year, and they are to much worn as to be no longer fit for circulation. The preceding remarks evince, that it is the interest of individuals of every description, excepting the money-changers, to cooperate with Government to render the Nineteenth Sun Sicca Rupee generally current, and the Standard of value throughout the country. Amongst the measures considered necessary to effect this important object, the following were the principal. First. To direct the officers employed in the provision of the investment, the manufacture of Salt, and all commercial transactions of the Company, to make their agreements with individuals for Sicca Rupees of the Nineteenth Sun; for if Government in their extensive commercial dealings, and in the provision of the Salt, make contrails with their subjects in other species of Rupees, they must necessarily continue the measure of value where those concerns are transacted, and it would be as ineffectual to declare the Nineteenth Sun Sicca Rupees the only legal currency, as it would be unjust to attempt to enforce the rule. Secondly. To oblige individuals to estimate their property by the Nineteenth Sun Sicca Rupee, by declaring the amount of Bonds and engagements entered into after a certain period (in fixing which a time was allowed that was presumed sufficient for the introduction of the necessary number of the Nineteenth Sun Sicca Rupees into circulation) whereby any sum of money might be stipulated to be paid in any species of Rupees excepting the Nineteenth Sun Siccas, not recoverable in any Court of Judicature. Thirdly. To prohibit the receipt of any Rupees excepting Siccas of the Nineteenth Sun, at the public treasuries after the date above alluded to. This last measure was calculated to oblige the Proprietors and Farmers of Land to require Nineteen Sun Sicca Rupees from their under Renters and Ryots, and consequently induce the latter to demand them from the Manufacturers, who for similar reasons, would necessarily require them from the Merchants, and Traders, and thus make it the interest of all descriptions of persons to receive the Nineteenth Sun Sicca Rupee, and to reject every other species of Rupee, upon the principles on which they before demanded the particular Rupee current in the respective districts. Fourthly. To establish Mints at the cities of Patna, Dacca, and Moorshedabad, to coin precisely the same Rupee as that struck at Calcutta. Without the adoption of this last arrangement, it would have been useless to declare the Nineteenth Sun Sicca Rupee the only legal tender of payment. For unless individuals had been afforded a ready means of procuring their old coin to be converted without loss into the new, they would have been obliged to have purchased the new money from the Shroffs, who would have demanded an exorbitant exchange upon it, as well with a view to reap the immediate advantage, as to prevent the establishment of the general currency of the Nineteenth Sun Sicca Rupee. Keeping open Mints in the interior parts of the country until the circulation may be filled up with that Coin, precludes the necessity of any person applying to Shroffs for it, and consequently deprives them of their influence (which is founded on the wants and necessities of individuals) by furnishing all persons with the new money at the cheapest rate, and with the least trouble. By the operation of these rules the various facts of old and light Rupee must in a course of time fall to their intrinsic worth compared with the Sicca of the Nineteenth Sun as they will produce no more in the Mint, and to which they will necessarily be brought to be converted into Siccas, as they will be no where passable or in demand as coin, from being no where a measure of value. The Rules by which the gold coin has been regulated, have been productive of evils similar to those which have prevailed with regard to the silver coin. Under the native administrations, and until the year 1766, the Gold Mohur was, not considered as a legal tender of payment in any public or private transaction, nor was the number of Rupees for which it was to pass current, ever fixed by the Government. It was struck for the convenience of individuals, and the value of it in the markets fluctuated like other commodities, silver being the metal which was the general measure of value throughout the country. In the year 1766 the value of the Gold coin with respect to the Silver, was first fixed, and the former coin declared a legal tender of payment. A Gold Mohur was struck, and ordered to pass for fourteen Sicca Rupees. But as this coin (calculating according to the relative value of the two metals) was much below the worth of the silver in the number of Rupees for which it was ordered to pass, it was found impossible to render it current, and it was accordingly called in, and a new Gold Mohur, being that now current, was issued in 1760, which was directed to pass as a legal tender of payment for Sixteen Sicca Rupees. The intrinsic worth of this coin, was estimated to be equal to the nominal value of it, or as nearly so as was deemed necessary to render it current at the prescribed rate. But whether owing to the effect of the orders for the introduction of the over rated Gold coin of 1766, the considerable value of the new Gold Mohur, and the want of divisions of it, so as to render the coin calculated for the dealings of the lower orders of the people in the interior parts of the country, or other causes, the currency of it has been confined almost entirely to Calcutta, where it has been received and paid in all public and private payments at the fixed value of Sixteen Sicca Rupees. But this partial currency of the Gold coin, has enabled the money changers to practice an abuse upon the public and individuals, of a nature similar to that which has prevailed regarding the Silver. Individuals are obliged to receive Gold Mohurs at the full value in all payments made to them from the Treasury at Calcutta. But as the coin will not pass in the interior parts of the country, the receivers are under the necessity, when they have occasion to make purchases or advances out of Calcutta, to fell heir Gold Mohurs to a Shroff for Silver of the currency of the District in which their purchases are to be made, or, what is the same for a bill on his house in the District payable in that currency, as the Shroff in the latter case exacts the discount in fixing the exchange. The Shroffs pay the Gold which they thus purchase at a discount, into the Treasury at Calcutta at par, whenever they have payments to make to Government. The Gold Mohurs are in this manner immediately thrown back upon the Treasury whenever an opportunity offers, and the Shroffs levy a discount on them as often as they are issued from it. The obstruction to the circulation of the Gold Coin out of Calcutta, necessarily affects its value in purchases in the markets within the town, where also discount is frequently exacted upon it. The means which appear best calculated to render the Gold Mohur generally current, are to declare it receivable at all the public Treasuries and in all public payments throughout the Provinces, at the rate of Sixteen Sicca Rupees; to make it a legal tender of payment in private transactions; to coin a great proportion of halves and quarters, and lastly, to impose a duty upon all Gold Bullion sent to the Mint to be coined, to as to prevent too large a proportion of Gold being introduced into circulation, by diminishing in tome degree the advantage at present derived from the importation of it in preference to Silver. Upon the above grounds, the Regulations of the 20th June, 24th October, and 21st November 1792 were adopted, and this detail of them, by apprizing individuals of the principles on which the coin of the country is regulated, will enable them to guard against the impositions of the money changers, who alone derive advantage from the want of a uniform Gold and Silver currency. The Regulations above mentioned, are hereby re-enacted with amendments.

II. Mints have been established at the Cities of Patna, Moorshedabad, and Dacca, in addition to the Mint at Calcutta, in which Sicca Rupees and Gold Mohurs of the Nineteenth Sun, of the following weight and standard, and half and quarter Rupees and Gold Mohurs, of the same standard, and proportionate weight, will be coined:

Mints established at Patna, Moorshedabad, and Dacca, in addition to the Calcutta Mint.

Coins to be struck in the Mints.

NINETEENTH SUN GOLD MOHUR

| | | | |
|---|---|---|---|
| Troy Weight, | Grains, | 190.894 | |
| | | Carat | Grs. |
| Assay compared with English standard | | | |
| Gold better, | | 1 | 3¼ |
| Bengal weight, | Annas, | | 17 |
| Touch, or parts of | | | |
| Bengal Assay fine Gold, in 100, | | | 99¼ |
| Alloy, | | | ¾ |

NINETENTH SUN SICCA RUPEE

| | | | |
|---|---|---|---|
| Troy Weight, | Grains, | 179 | 2/3 |
| Assay compared with English standard | | | |
| Silver better, | Dwts. | 13 | |
| Bengal weight, | Annas, | 16 | |
| Bengal Assay Touch or parts of fine | | | |
| Silver, in 100, | | | 97 11/12 |
| Alloy, | | | 2 1/12 |

III. All Gold Mohurs of the weight and standard specified in Section II, coined in the Calcutta Mint since the 20th March 1769, or which may be coined in that Mint, and in the Mints of Patna, Dacca, and Moorshedabad, after the date of this Regulation, and also their halves and quarters, are to be considered legal tender of payment in all public and private transactions throughout the Provinces of Bengal, Behar, and Orissa, at the rate of Sixteen Sicca Rupees of the Nineteenth Sun, for each Mohur and the half and quarter Mohur in

Gold Coin of full weight and standard coined since the 20th March 1769, to be a legal tender of payment at the rate of Sixteen Sicca Rupees.

proportion. If a Native Officer, of any public Treasury shall be convicted before the Court of Dewanny Adawlut of any Zillah or City, of refusing to receive in payment any such Gold Mohurs or the, halves or quarters of them, at the rates directed in this Section, the Court shall adjudge offender to be dismissed from his office, and further compel him pay to the complainant his cost of suit, and such damages as the Court may seem proper upon a consideration of the circumstances of the case.

Native Officers liable to dismission and to pay costs & damages upon being convicted of refusing to receive the gold coin.

IV. For all Silver Bullion, or old or light Silver coin, equal to, or above, Sicca standard, which may be delivered into the Mints, a number of the Nineteenth Sun Sicca Rupees, or halves or quarters of such Rupees, equal in weight to the Silver of Sicca Standard contained in such Bullion or old or light Coin, shall be returned to the Proprietor without any charge whatsoever.

For all Silver Bullion, or coin of, or above Sicca standard, Coin equal to the weight of the Standard Bullion to be returned without any charge.

V. All Silver Bullion, or old or light Silver Coin, under Sicca Standard, which may be delivered into the Mints, is to be refined to the Sicca Standard, and a number of the Nineteenth Sun Sicca Rupees, or halves or quarters of such Rupees, equal in weight to the refined Bullion, shall be returned to the proprietor after deducting twelve annas per cent for the expence of refining.

Twelve annas per cent to be charged for refining to Sicca Standard, Bullion or old or light Coin under that Standard.

VI. It shall be at the option of individuals to have their old or light Coin or Bullion if Gold, coined into Gold Mohurs, or half or quarter Gold Mohurs, and if Silver, into the Nineteenth Sun Sicca Rupees, or half or quarter Rupees, or into such proportions of each as they may think proper.

Option given to Individuals to have their old Gold or Silver Bullion or money, coined into Gold Mohurs or Rupees or halves or quarters in any proportion.

VII. To guard as far as possible against the counterfeiting, clipping, drilling, filing, defacing, or debasing the coin, the edges both of the Gold and Silver coin are to be milled, and the dies are to be made of the same size as the coin, so that

Coin to be milled and to be of the same size as the die, so as the whole of the impression may appear upon the surface of it.

to receive whole impression upon it.

VIII. The Nineteenth Sun Sicca Rupees, and the Nineteenth Sun Gold Mohurs, and the halves and quarters of each, which may be coined at the Mints established at Dacca, Patna and Moorshedabad, and at the Calcutta Mint, are to be precisely of the same shape, weight, and standard, and to bear the same impression both on the surface and the edges; and with a view to the effectual attainment of the last mentioned object, the dies for striking and milling the Gold and Silver Coin, are to be cut in the Calcutta Mint, and distributed by the Mint Master to the three subordinate Mints, and when there dies are broken, or no longer serviceable, they are to be returned to the Calcutta Mint.

Coins struck in several Mints to be precisely of the same shape, weight, and standard, and to have same impression. Precaution to be taken for preventing any difference in the impression or milling of the Coins struck in the three Mints.

IX. The Gold and Silver Coin struck at the different Mints, is to be received and paid indiscriminately at the prescribed value in all public and private Transactions.

Coin struck at the different Mints, to be received and paid indiscriminately.

X. The Mint Master is to cause, a private mark to be put upon all dies which may be prepared for the several Mints, but in such a manner as not to be distinguishable by the naked eye. These marks are to be varied as often as the Mint Mailer may judge proper upon new dies being made, and he is to keep a Register of them that in the event of any debased or defective coin being found in circulation, he may be able to ascertain from what Mint it may have been issued.

Mint Master to have private marks put up on the dies.

XI. The Magistrates of the Cities of Dacca, Patna, and Moorshedabad respectively, are required to proceed in person once every fortnight, or as often as they may judge it proper, to the Mints at Dacca, Patna, and Moorshedabad, without previously apprizing the Superintendent of the Mint, at the time when the Money is usually struck off, and with their own hand, to take indiscriminately out of the heaps at the foot of the striking presses three pieces of

Further precaution for preventing bad or defective Coin being issued from the Mints.

each description of Coin that may have been struck off, and transmit them to the Mint Master at Calcutta who is to cause the Coin to be examined and assayed, and it shall not be of the proper standard, or if it shall be defective in the workmanship, or in any other respect, he is to report the circumstances to the Governor General in Council.

XII. Persons charged with counterfeiting, clipping, filing, defacing, or debasing, the Gold or Silver Coin, are to be committed to the Criminal Courts, and punished according as the law may direct.

Persons charged with counterfeiting the Coinor other offences herein specified, to be committed to the Criminal Courts.

XIII. All Officers, Agents, Gomastahs, or others employed in the collection or payment of the Public Revenue, or the Rents of Individuals, or the provision of the Investment, the manufacture of Salt, or Opium, and all Proprietors and Farmers; of Land, Dependent Talookdars, under Farmers and Ryots, and all, persons whomsoever, are prohibited affixing any mark whatever to the Gold or Silver Coin, and all Rupees or Gold Mohurs, or half or quarter Rupees or Gold Mohurs; that may be so marked, are declared not to be legal tenders of payment in any public or private transaction, and the Officers of Government are directed to reject any Rupees or Gold Mohurs; or any half or quarter Rupees or Gold Mohurs, so marked, that may be tendered at the public Treasuries.

All persons prohibited affixing marks to the Coin. Coins so marked not to be legal tender of payment, and to be rejected at the Public Treasuries.

XIV. As the number of the Nineteenth Sun Sicca Rupees in circulation in some Districts, may not be sufficient to enable the Proprietors and Farmers of Land to pay such part of their Revenues as they may not pay in Gold, in Rupees of that description, the various sorts of Rupees current in the several Districts, will be received at the public Treasuries from the Proprietors and Farmers of Land in payment of their Revenue until the 10th April 1794, corresponding with the 30th Chyte 1200 Bengal Era, the 25th Chyte 1201 Fussily, the 30th Chyte 1201 Willaity, the 25th Chyte 1851 Sumbut, and the 9th Ramzaan 1208 Higeree, at the fixed rates specified in the following table, which are calculated agreeably to the difference, of the intrinsic value, that each

Rules and valuation according to which all Rupees not being Nineteenth Sun Sicca are to be received in discharge of the public Revenue until the 10th April 1794.

species of Rupee bears to the Nineteenth Sun Sicca Rupee, as ascertained by Assay in the Calcutta. Mint.

SORTS OF RUPEES

| | *Sicca Weight* | *19-sun*-siccas | | |
|---|---|---|---|---|
| Siccas of Moorshedabad, Patna and Dacca, per | 100 | 100 | 0 | 0 |
| Phooley Sonats, | do | 100 | 0 | 0 |
| Delhy Mahomet Shai, | do | 99 | 8 | 0 |
| Money Surat large, | do | 99 | 8 | 0 |
| Benares Sicca, | do | 99 | 8 | 0 |
| Bissun Arcot, | do | 97 | 14 | 6 |
| Sonats Sabic and Duckie, | do | 97 | 8 | 0 |
| Forshee Arcots, | do | 97 | 6 | 6 |
| French Arcots, | do | 97 | 0 | 0 |
| Patanca Arcots | do | 96 | 9 | 6 |
| Arungzebee Arcots, | do | 96 | 9 | 6 |
| Gursaul, | do | 96 | 9 | 6 |
| Madras Arcots new, | do | 96 | 4 | 9 |
| Masulipatam and Shardar Arcots, | do | 96 | 0 | 0 |
| Patna Sonats old | do | 96 | 0 | 0 |
| Benares Rupees old; | do | 95 | 14 | 6 |
| Madras Arcots old, | do | 95 | 14 | 6 |
| Farukabad Rupees, | do | 95 | 12 | 9 |
| Jehaujee Arcots, | do | 95 | 1 | 3 |
| Chaunta Arcots | do | 95 | 11 | 3 |
| Calcutta and Moorshedabad Arcots, | do | 95 | 6 | 6 |
| Old Arcots, | do | 95 | 3 | 3 |
| Dutch Arcots, | do | 95 | 0 | 0 |
| Surat Arcots, | do | 94 | 0 | 0 |
| Benares Trisolie, | do | 92 | 6 | 6 |
| Viziery Rupees, | do | 63 | 0 | 0 |
| Narrainy half Rupee new | do | 63 | 0 | 0 |

Explanation of the mode of receiving the Rupees agreeably to the above table.

XV. To prevent misconception of the mode of receiving Rupees of sorts under the above Table, it is to be understood, that one Hundred Sicca Weight of each of the sorts of Rupees specified in the first column (whatever number of the Rupees may go to that weight) is to be considered equal to the number of Nineteen Sun Sicca Rupees placed opposite to it in the second column.

XVI. If any other species of Rupees besides those specified in the Table, are tendered in payment at any of the Public Treasuries, One hundred Sicca weight of them, indiscriminately taken from the Sum paid in the presence of the payer or his agent, is to be sent to the nearest Mint to be assayed, and the payer shall receive credit for a number of the Nineteenth Sun Sicca Rupees equal in weight to the Silver of Sicca Standard that the Rupees so paid may be estimated to contain according to the Assay, after deducting twelve annas per cent. for the expence of refining, should the Rupees be under Sicca Standard.

Rules for the Rupees tendered at the Public Treasuries which are not specified in the table.

XVII. Rupees of sorts which may be received at the Public Treasuries agreeably to the table in Section XIV, or under Section XVI, are not on any account to be issued therefrom, but are to be sent to the Mints, and coined into Siccas of the Nineteenth Sun.

Rupees of sorts received at the Public Treasuries to be sent to the Mints.

XVIII. After the 10th April 1794, no other Rupee but the Nineteenth Sun Sicca, and no other Gold Mohur but the Nineteenth Sun Gold Mohur, or the halves and quarters of each, shall be received at any of the Public Treasuries or issued therefrom, on any account whatsoever; and no other Rupees or Gold Mohurs, excepting the Rupees and Gold Mohurs of the Nineteenth Sun, and the halves and quarters of each, shall be legal tenders of payment in any public or private transaction.

After the 10th April, 1794, no Silver or Gold Coin excepting Rupees or Gold Mohurs of the Nineteenth Sun or their respective divisions and subdivisions to be considered a legal tender for payment.

XIX. Bonds or writings or other agreements whether written verbal; entered into prior to the 10th April 1794, whereby a sum money is stipulated to be paid in any species of Rupee or Gold Mohur excepting the Nineteenth Sun Sicca or the Gold Mohur of the Nineteenth Sun, and which may not be discharged previous to the abovementioned date, may be liquidated at the option the debtor, either in the Rupee specified in the instrument, or the Nineteenth Sun Sicca Rupee at the valuation specified in the Table, in Section XIV, or in the Nineteenth Sun Gold Mohur.

Bonds or Agreements for money, executed prior to the 10th April, 1794, to be dischargeable prior to that date either in the Com stipulated in the deed, or in Nineteenth Sun Siccas at the rates in the table.

XX. After the 10th April 1794, no person shall recover in any Court of Judicature in the Provinces of Bengal, Behar, or Orissa, any sum of money under a Bond, or other writing, or any agreement, written or verbal, entered into after the abovementioned date, by which any sum of money shall be stipulated to be paid in any species of Rupees excepting Sicca Rupees, or Gold Mohurs, of the Nineteenth Sun, or the halves and quarters of each.

Agreements executed after the 10th April, 1794, stipulating for the payment of money in any other specie excepting Rupees or Gold Mohurs of the Nineteenth Sun, or the halves or quarters of them, not recoverable in any Court of Judicature.

XXI. All engagements hereafter entered into on the part of the Government for the provision of the investment, or the manufacture of Salt, are to be made in the Sicca Rupee, or the Gold Mohur of the Nineteenth Sun, and all Proprietors and Farmers Rupee, or the Gold Mohur of the Nineteenth Sun, and all Proprietors and Farmers of Land are prohibited from concluding engagements with their under Farmers, Ryots or Dependent Talookdars, after the 10th April 1794, in any species of Rupees or Gold Mohur excepting the Sicca Rupees and the Gold Mohurs of the Nineteen Sun, under the penalty of not being permitted to recover any arrears that may become due to them under such Engagements.

All engagements on the part of the Government for the provision of the Investment, or Salt, to be made in the Nineteenth Sun Sicca Rupee or Gold Mohur. Engagements for Rent and Revenue to be made in the same coin. Arrears on engagements stipulating the payment of any other Coin not recoverable.

XXII. If Sicca Rupees or the Nineteenth Sun of full weight, the halves or quarters of such Rupees, shall be tendered at any of the Public Treasuries, and any of the Native Officers shall refuse to receive them in payment of any public demand, and shall require any other species of Rupees, or if any of the species of Rupee mentioned in the Table in Section XIV, shall be tendered at the Public Treasuries prior to the date specified in Section XVIII, at the valuation specified in the Table, and any Native Officer shall refuse to receive them at such valuation, upon proof of such offence before the Dewanny Adawlut of the Zillah or City in which the complaint may be cognizable, the Court shall dismiss the Offender from his Office, and oblige him to pay costs of suit, and damages to the party complaining.

Punishment for Native Officers at any of the Treasuries refusing to receive the Nineteenth Sun Gold Muhur or Rupee in payment.

XXIII. After the date specified in Section XVIII, if any Native Officer at any of the Public Treasuries shall be convicted of receiving in payment of a public demand any Gold or Silver Coin, excepting the Gold Mohur or the Sicca Rupees of the Nineteenth Sun, or the halves and quarters of each, the Court shall dismiss him in his office, and adjudge him to pay such fine to Government as may appear to them adequate to the offence.

Native Officers at any of the Public Treasuries liable to fine and dismission for receiving any Coin but the Nineteenth Sun Rupee or Gold Mohur after the 10th April 1794.

XXIV. In consideration of the expence incurred in refining Gold, not of Gold Mohur standard, and with a view to discourage importation of Gold Bullion in preference to Silver Bullion, following duty is to be levied, on Gold Bullion sent to the Mints for Coinage.

Duty to be levied at the several Mints on Gold Bullion.

| | | | | |
|---|---|---|---|---|
| Bullion of, or above, Gold Mohur Standard; | | 2 | 8 | per cent |
| Do. ¾ to 5 per cent worse than that Standard; | | 2 | 12 | do |
| Do. from 5 to 10 per cent | do | 3 | 4 | do |
| Do. from 10 to 20 per cent | do | 3 | 12 | do |

XXV. No duty is to be charged on the re-coinage of old or light Gold Mohurs, or half or quarter Gold Mohurs, coined at the Calcutta Mint since the 20th March 1769, nor on the re-coinage of any Gold Mohurs, or half or quarter Gold Mohurs, which may coined in the Mints at Patna, Dacca, Moorshedabad, or Calcutta, after this date.

No duty to be levied on the recoinage of old Gold Mohurs, halves or quarters, coined in the

Calcutta Mint since the 20th March 1769, or which may hereafter coined in any of the Mints.

Order in which Bullion delivered into the Mints, is to be assayed, refined and coined.

XXVI. All Bullion delivered into the Mints, is to be assayed in the order in which it may be received; refined in the order in which may be assayed, and coined in the order in which it may be refined. Standard Bullion delivered into the Mints is to be registered as refined Bullion, on the date on which it may be assayed.

Registers to be kept for public inspection in the several Mints.

XXVII. *First.* The following Registers are to be kept open at the Mints of Calcutta, Patna, Dacca, and Moorshedabad, for public inspection.

*Second.* A Register of unassayed Bullion delivered into the Mint, specifying the quantity delivered, the date on which it was received, and the name of the Proprietor.

*Third.* A Register of Bullion assayed and refined, specifying the date on which it was assayed, and the date on which it was refined, the name of the Proprietor, and the produce in Sicca Rupees or Gold Mohurs, together with the date of the Certificate granted for the produce, and the date on which such Certificate was discharged.

European and Native Officers of Government herein specified liable to be sued for any breach of the Regulation respecting the coinage.

XXVIII. Collectors of the Revenue, Commercial Residents or Agents, Salt Agents, the Mint Master at Calcutta, the Superintendents of the subordinate Mints at the Cities of Patna, Dacca and Moorshedabad, and their respective Officers, are to be liable to be sued for damages in the Zillah or City Court to which they may be amenable, for any breach of this Regulation, or any other Regulation which may be enacted respecting the Coin.

# 2

# Despatch Addressed by the Court of Directors to the Governments of Bengal and Madras Dealing with the Coinage of India, 1806

Copy of a DESPATCH to BENGAL, MADRAS, and BOMBAY, in the PUBLIC DEPARTMENT, from the COURT of DIRECTORS, dated 25th April 1806

Sent per 'Marquis of Wellesley', 'Teignmouth' cruiser and extra ship 'Harriet'

1. The state of the coinage of India has been frequently brought before us in the correspondence of our several Governments; and we have been for some time fully impressed necessity of giving to this important subject a full consideration; but we have been more immediately stimulated to this, in consequence of a report made to us of a loss being suffered in the Calcutta Mint, in the recoining of dollars into Sicca rupees, to the amount of 2 per cent. This circumstance induced us at once to institute an inquiry into the situation of the mints and coinage under our several presidencies, with the intention of applying as effectual a remedy to the existing defects as may be in our power.

2. With the view of obtaining the fullest information, the Mint-Masters Accounts of Bengal and Madras from 1/99 to 1802 have been investigated, the Bengal Regulation of 1/93, No. 35, referred to, and, among the several papers and notices on the subject of coinage, &c, on the consultations of our different Governments, more particular attention has been given to the Minute of Sir John Shore (now Lord Teignmouth) on the Bengal Public Consultations

of 3rd October 1796, the Report of the Committee of Reform at Madras dated 26th March 1800, and to the Papers drawn up by Dr. Scott, under the inspection of Governor Duncan, as recorded on the Bombay Public Consultations of 31st January and 9th December 1801.

3. From the attention that has been given to the above-mentioned accounts and documents, we are fully convinced of the inefficiency of the present system of our mints and coinage, the losses we have constantly sustained, and the inconvenience the public service has suffered in consequence thereof, and from the circulation of so many denominations of gold and silver coins of different values, in different districts; these losses we find to be of a magnitude far beyond our expectation (*vide* Appendix No. 1).

4. We have noticed also the recommendation expressed in some of those Papers for the adoption of one general system for the formation of the coin for the currency of the whole of our possessions on the continent of Asia, which has our most entire approbation, as we are fully satisfied the various evils complained of can only be removed by the introduction of a gold and silver coinage of one weight and fineness, such coin to become the universal measure of value for British India.

5. It is our intention to enter into the consideration of the subject and to detail our views and opinions, that our several Governments may report their sentiments thereon, in order to supply us with the most perfect information upon this important subject, previous to our final decision upon a plan which shall embrace every practical advantage within our reach.

6. In the prosecution of our inquiries we have referred to a letter from the Earl of Liverpool to the King, on the coins of the realm (lately published), copies of which we transmit with the present Despatch. We think his Lordship has established the principle that 'the money or coin which is to be the principal measure of property ought to be of one metal only'. In applying this argument to a coin for general use in India, there cannot be a doubt, in our opinion, that such coin must be of silver.

7. Assuming that the coin for general use in India as the principal measure of property is to be of silver, we proceed to the inquiry of what weight this coin should be.

The standard weight of the silver coins issued from the mints of our several presidencies we find to be as follow:

| | Troy Grains |
|---|---|
| Calcutta Sicca Rupee | 179⅔ |
| Madras Arcot Rupee | 176⅔ |
| Bombay Rupee | 179 |

8. The weight of the coin originally issued from the Moghul mints, we understand, was uniformly one sicca, or 10 masha, being 179⅔ troy grains, or 179.5511. We should be inclined to propose this weight for the coin under consideration, did we not think it would answer a good purpose to fix the gross weight in whole numbers; we should therefore prefer the weight of 180 troy grains as the nearest to the sicca weight, and in so doing we are not aware of any inconvenience resulting therefrom at either of our presidencies; but we are rather inclined to think the measure will be found useful, inasmuch as it will produce a greater degree of simplicity in the valuation of the coin in respect to other money. But we are by no means desirous of effecting an alteration in the standard weight of the currency of Bengal, should our Government there be of opinion it would be likely to prove the foundation of a new batta, or of any other inconvenience sufficient to counterbalance the advantages we expect in the calculation of the relative value of Indian and other coins.

9. Assuming the standard weight of the new rupee to be 180 troy grains, the next point to be considered is the proper standard fineness. Upon the subject of the fittest alloy for coin, and its proportion to the quantity of fine metal, our attention has been directed to a 'Report made to the Right Honourable the Lords of the Committee of Privy Council, appointed to take into consideration the state of the coins of this country, and the present establishment and constitution of His Majesty's Mint, January 1803.' In this Report (copies of which are forwarded) the British standard for gold coin, one-twelfth alloy and eleven-twelfths fine,

is, by a variety of extensive experiments, proved to be the best proportion, or at least as good as any which could have been chosen, and that such alloy for gold coin may be of fine Swedish copper, so as to answer every purpose, of a mixed proportion of silver without occasioning any further waste of that metal. There is no reason to doubt that one-twelfth alloy of copper would be equally proper fur silver coin; it has certainly the advantage of greater facility in the valuation of the coin, therefore we are of opinion this proportion should *be* adopted for the coin proposed, in which case the new rupee would be of the gross weight of:

| | |
|---|---|
| Troy grains | 180 |
| Deduct one-twelfth alloy | 15 |
| And contain of fine silver, troy grains | 165 |

10. The fine silver in the Calcutta sicca rupee is troy grains 175.227 Madras Arcot rupee, 166.477, Bombay rupee, 164.740; the difference between the values of the Arcot and Bombay rupees, when compared with the recommended rupee, is $^{887}/_{1000}$ per cent. less fine silver in the now than in the Arcot rupee; and $^{357}/_{1000}$ per cent more fine silver in the new than in the Bombay rupee. These variations are certainly too small to present any difficulty to the completion of the object in the circulation of the new rupee at Madras and Bombay. The difference between the value of the new rupee and that of the Calcutta sicca is 10.927 troy grains fine silver, or 6.211 per cent. Though the Calcutta is so much more valuable than the new rupee, we do not apprehend any objection on the part of the people of Bengal, when they are made acquainted with the intention of Government, to receive the new rupee at the same value at which it is issued to them; at least, no objection but what a very short experience of the advantages of the general currency would remove. That the Shroffs

Troy Grains

| | | | |
|---|---|---|---|
| 166.477 | Arcot rupee | | |
| 165 | new rupee | | 165 |
| Difference 1.477 | | Bombay Rupee | 164.74 |
| | | Difference | .26 |

As 166.477 : 1.477 : : 100 : 857

As 165 : .26 : : 100 : 157

175.927 Calcutta Sicca

165

10.927 difference

As 75.927 : 10.927 : : 6.211

and other speculators in money and exchanges will endeavour to impede the circulation of the new rupee must be expected, as every change will be opposed by them that has in its consequences the prevention of their destructive interference anil the reduction of those profits they have hitherto obtained at the expense of the public and the Company.

11. But we trust the opposition of the description of persons above alluded to will not prevent the adoption of the recommended rupee for general currency, as it appears so extensively useful as a measure of value, by approaching so near the value of the Madras, Arcot, the Bombay, Benares, Lucknow, and Bareilly rupees, as also to the Sonaut rupee in which the pay of the Bengal Army is calculated.

| | |
|---|---|
| 109.251 | Banaras rupee |
| 165 | new rupee |
| 4.251 | difference |

As 169-251 : 4.251 : : 100 : 2.511

| | |
|---|---|
| 168.010 | Sonaut rupee |
| 165 | |
| 3.010 | difference |

As 168.010 : 3.010 : : 100 : 1.791

| | |
|---|---|
| 166.135 | Lucknow rupee |
| 165 | |
| 1.135 | difference |

As 166.135: 1.135 : : .683

| | |
|---|---|
| 165 | new rupee |
| 161.635 | |
| 3.365 | difference |

As 165 : 3.365 : : 100 : 2.039

| | | Troy grains. |
|---|---|---|
| *Fine silver in the Benares Rupee | | 169.251 |
| Do. | Lucknow | 166.135 |
| Do. | Bareilly | 161.635 |
| For every 100 sonauts, calculated pay, the Bengal Army have issued 95½ Sicca rupees, so that the Sonaut rupee is of the value of fine silver, troy grains | | 168.010 |

* *Vide* Lord Teignmouth's Minute.

| | |
|---|---|
| 12. The Benares rupee is per cent | 2.511 |
| The Sonaut rupee | 1.791 |
| The Madras Arcot | .887 |
| And the Lucknow rupee | .683 |

more valuable than the new rupee

| | |
|---|---|
| 13. The Bareilly rupee is per cent | 2.039 |
| And the Bombay rupee | .157 |

less valuable than the new rupee.

14. Should the new rupee he ultimately adopted, there may be coined also, for general convenience, the following denominations:

| | | |
|---|---|---|
| Half rupee weighing troy grains | | 90 |
| Quarter rupee | do | 45 |
| Anna | do | 11¼ |

the latter, being a larger coin than the English silver penny (which weighs less than eight troy grains), is not too small to strike. The anna, as a coin, would be found very useful in small payments, and, with a view to this consideration, we think a copper coinage should also be determined on for general circulation; and it is our opinion it should be struck in England, and to consist of pieces of the value of 6 pice or half-anna, 3 pice or quarter-anna, and 1 pice.

15. The value of the silver anna (one-sixteenth of the new rupee) is about one-fourth of the English sixpence, or one penny half penny, so that the value of the pice (one-twelfth of the anna) is about half a farthing English currency, the weight of this coin to be so adjusted, according to the price of copper and expenses of coining, as to leave a profit on its issue; which would have the good effect of preventing the melting of the coin, as its value in currency would be something more than the value of the metal, with all the export charges upon it.

16. Although we are fully satisfied of the propriety of the silver rupee being the principal measure of value and the money of account, yet we are by no means desirous of checking the circulation of gold, but of establishing a gold coin on a principle fitted for general use. This coin, in our opinion, should be called a gold rupee and be made of the same standard as the silver rupee, viz., 180 troy grains, gross weight, and 165 troy grains, fine gold, also divided into halves and quarters, that the coins of both gold and silver should be of the same denomination, weight, and fineness.

17. It is an opinion supported by the best authorities and proved by experience, that coins of gold and silver cannot circulate as legal tenders of payment at fixed relative-values, as in England and in India, without great loss; this loss is occasioned by the fluctuating value of the metals of which the coins are formed. A proportion

between the gold and silver coin is fixed by law, according to the value of the metals, and it may be on the jus test principles; hut owing to a change of circumstances gold may become of greater value in relation to stiver than at the time the proportion was fixed; it therefore becomes profitable to exchange silver for gold, so the coin of that metal is withdrawn from circulation; and, if silver should increase in its value in relation to gold, the same circumstances would tend to reduce the quantity of silver coin in circulation. As it is impossible to prevent the fluctuation in the value of the metals, so it is also equally impracticable to prevent the consequences thereof on the coins made from those metals. From these circumstances the coin of England bas been much disordered; and the papers referred to have plainly shown the losses and inconvenience experienced in India from similar causes. The loss in Bengal was certainly enhanced by giving to the gold coin, at the period of its issue, an improper value in relation to the silver coin. Loss and inconvenience have been occasioned at Madras by the contrary error, where the silver coin was rated at too high a value in relation to the gold coin. But there is a radical defect in the principle itself of giving a fixed value to metals (in coin) that are in their nature subject to continual change, because, the metals being articles of commerce, their value will fluctuate with the demand: Had the nicest proportion been fixed between the gold and silver coins of Bengal and Madras at the time of their issue, yet the first alteration in the price of the metals would have occasioned the batta so much complained of, though such batta had not existed before. The alteration in the value of the metals in Europe has been the principal cause of the present state of the English silver currency, a debused and counterfeit money having been introduced into circulation, which does not possess above one-third of the intrinsic value of the legal coin of the realm. To adjust the relative values of the gold and silver coin according to the fluctuations in the values of the metals would create continual difficulties, and the establishment of such a principle would of itself tend to perpetuate the inconvenience and loss.

18. It is from a consideration of these circumstances, we have been induced to conclude that our gold coin should not be forced

into circulation at a fixed value in regard to the silver coin, but left to find its own level according to the usefulness it may possess as a coin, being issued according to the market value of the metals, and received by our officers in the same manner. From this regulation no other loss could be suffered by the Company or the public than what might be occasioned by the varieties in the prices of the metals; and it is not to be apprehended these prices could be materially affected by any artifice or device, as there could not be a quantity of gold coin in circulation much beyond the wants of the community.

19. The contrary practice of forcing the gold coin into circulation, on the plea of a want of silver currency in Bengal, has had the effect of reducing: the value of the gold coin by its abundance beyond the difference in its real value, and increasing the batta accordingly. We do not imagine that any very considerable quantity of gold coin will obtain circulation in Bengal, and, although it has been alleged a gold coin is necessary to supply the place of the silver coin, which frequently disappears almost as soon as issued, yet it must be remembered no regulation or expedient can be devised to keep the coin in any country where the balance of trade is against it, and where to this principal cause of a deficiency in the circulation medium is added a prevailing disposition on the part of the people to hoard the silver coin; where these circumstances exist, all attempts to force a gold coin where silver only is the common medium will be attended with loss and disappointment.

20. We do not apprehend any difficulty can attend the introduction of a gold coin into Bengal on the principle that it should pass at its market value in relation to silver, without having any fixed relative value set upon it; neither are we aware of any impediment to the measure at Bombay. In respect to those countries under the Government of Madras where gold coins are the principal currency, money of account, and the measure by which the pay of the troops is generally calculated, some further consideration appears necessary.

21. We have before stated our opinion that silver should be the universal money of account, and that all our public accounts should be kept in the same denomination of rupees, annas, and

pice. The Committee of Reform recommended (para 54 of their Report) this plan for Madras, that their accounts might be assimilated as much as possible to the Government accounts of Bengal and Bombay.

22. It is not by any means our wish to introduce a silver currency to the exclusion of the gold, where the latter is the general measure of value, any more than to force a gold coin where silver is the general measure of value'; but, wherever the pagoda is the general currency, to substitute in its place the quarter gold rupee, which we are of opinion should be paid and received on all occasions as the pagoda, both in regard to the calculation and receipt of the revenue, as also in the issues of money for the. purchase of investment. The quarter gold rupee would contain of fine gold troy grains $41\frac{1}{4}$, the star pagoda contains ot one gold troy grains $42\frac{48}{1000}$. The difference between these coins is $1\frac{897}{1000}$ per cent, less fine gold in the former than in the latter. This difference does not appear so material as to induce us to entertain any doubt of the quarter gold rupee answering every purpose of the star pagoda in respect to the revenues and investment; neither does it appear to us inapplicable to the pay of the army; for, supposing the amount of pay as it stands at present in pagodas to be changed into quarter gold rupees, and this coin considered equal, to $3\frac{1}{2}$ new rupees, as the pagoda is to $3\frac{1}{2}$ Arcot rupees, the difference between the silver coins, being less than 1 per cent., cannot be expected, as before observed, to create any uneasiness.

| | Troy Grains |
|---|---|
| Gold Rupee | 105 fine |
| Half | 82.5 |
| Quarter | 41.25 |

| | |
|---|---|
| 42.048 | Star Pagoda |
| 41.250 | Quarter Gold Rupee |
| .798 | difference |

As 42.048 : .798 : : 100 : 1.897

23. Our recommendation of the gold coin passing generally at its market price, the silver coin only being the measure of value, may, we conceive, be carried into effect with great facility, in consequence of both coins possessing the same denomination, weight, and fineness; as also being alike divided into halves and quarters. For an example, we have supposed variations may take place in the values of the metals of from 14 to 1 to 15 to 1, and it will be seen in the margin that the value of any division of the gold rupee is found

| | |
|---|---|
| 14 of Silver to 1 of Gold makes the value of the | |
| Gold Rupee | 14 Silver Rupees |
| Half Rupee | 7 |
| Qtr. Rupee | 3.8 |
| 14¼ of Silver to 1 Gold | |
| Gold Rupee | 14.4 |
| Half Rupee | 7.2 |
| Qtr. Rupee | 3.0 |
| 14½ of Silver to 1 Gold | |
| Gold Rupee | 14.8 |
| Half Rupee | 7.4 |
| Qtr. Rupee | 3.10 |
| 14¾ of Silver to 1 Gold | |
| Gold Rupee | 14.12 |
| Half Rupee | 7.6 |
| Qtr. Rupee | 3.11 |
| 15 of Silver to 1 Gold | |
| Gold Rupee | 15 |
| Half Rupee | 7.8 |
| Qtr. Rupee | 3.12 |
| 15¼ of Silver to 1 Gold | |
| Gold Rupee | 15.4 |
| Half Rupee | 7.10 |
| Qtr. Rupee | 3.13 |

in rupees and annas only, on the presumption that the market values of the metals will not vary in proportions beyond or under one quarter.

24. We have thus stated our opinion in the view of its being unnecessary to continue a fixed relative value between the gold and silver coin. It appears to us no such necessity can exist in regard to Bengal and Bombay, and we hope no such measure will be found necessary at Madras; but, should our Governments, who are assuredly the most competent judges, be of opinion that local circumstances will render it proper to fix a relative value between the coins at Madras, the plan we have detailed seems capable of being carried into effect in this respect also with much ease. On the supposition of the quarter gold rupee supplying the place of the star pagoda at the value of 3½ new rupees, the proportion of gold to silver is as 1 to 14, which is very near the proportion recommended from Madras of 1 to .14¼. In the margin before referred to it will be seen this makes a difference, of one anna only on a quarter gold rupee, and the same difference is found for every advance in the proportions of one quarter.

25. We have, before observed the quarter gold rupee appears well fitted to supply the place of the star pagoda in the payment of the Madras Army; but we have thought it necessary to, direct our attention in a more particular manner to the mode of paying the troops there, in order to discover how far the recommended alteration will affect this important point.

Troy Grains.

| | |
|---|---|
| 160.477 | Arcot Rupee |
| 3½ | |
| 582.609 | |
| 12.764 | fine Silver Fanams |
| 45 | |
| 547.380 | |
| 12.764 | |
| 42 | |
| 536.088 | |
| 582.009 | |
| 573.380 | |
| 8.289 | |

As 582.009 : 8.289 : : 100 : 1.422

| | |
|---|---|
| 582.669 | |
| 530.088 | |
| 46.581 | |

As 582.009 : 46.581 : : 100 : 7.904

26. The pay is frequently issued in pagodas; the pagoda is ordered to pass for 3¼ Arcot rupees, by the authority of the Government, and the pagoda appears also to pass for 45 fanams. Three and a half Arcot rupees contain of fine silver troy grains $582\frac{669}{1000}$; 45 silver fanams contain fine silver troy grains $574\frac{380}{1000}$; 42 silver fanams, the usual number issued for 1 pagoda of calculated pay, when the Government pay the troops in fanams, contain of fine silver troy grains $536\frac{38}{1000}$ From which it appears 3½ Arcot rupees contain $1\frac{122}{1000}$ per cent more fine silver than 45 fanams, and $7\frac{994}{1000}$ per cent, more fine silver than 42 fanams; therefore it follows, from a comparison of the relative value of the pagoda to the Arcot rupee as fixed by the Madras Government, that if the soldier is paid in 45 fanams he receives nearly 1½ per cent, less fine silver than if he had been paid 3½ Arcot rupees: receives nearly 8 per cent, less line silver. This view of the subject clearly shows that on the present system much precision has not been observed in the mode of paying, the troops; how far they may suffer when paid in gold, by exchanging it for silver fanams (whether beyond the above difference of 8 per cent, or below it), we suppose, depends in a great measure on the circumstances of the moment; but, whether the exchanger exacts a larger or a smaller batta, it. appears evident the soldier is as much at the mercy of the exchanger as are persons carrying gold coin to market at Calcutta.

27. Should it be found necessary to continue the silver fanam for the accommodation of the places where the quarter gold rupee is to circulate in the room of the pagoda, the fanam should be calculated as at 45 to the pagoda (or quarter gold rupee); but,

Grains
180 New rupee
630 = 3½ New rupees
630
45 = 14 fanam

12)14
1.100 alloy
12.834 fine Silver fanam
45
577.530

Grains
105 New rupee
10.3125 anna
50
577.5000

instead of the present proportion of troy grains $14\frac{117}{1000}$ weight, and troy grains $12\frac{764}{1000}$ fine silver, to be made of the same proportions as the new rupee, the gross weight being troy grains 14, and the fine silver troy grains $12\frac{834}{1000}$ so that the quarter gold rupee or pagoda, when exchanged for 45 fanams at troy grains $12\frac{834}{1000}$ or, for 56 annas (3½ new rupees) at troy grains $10\frac{3125}{10000}$ fine silver. would be equivalent in value, the same quantity of fine silver being obtained either way. This would of certainly remove some of the inconveniences at present so justly complained of, but it does not appear to us the defect can be radically cured so long as the troops are paid in gold, because the money-changer would possess the power of exacting an arbitrary batta, although no real difference existed in the value of the coins. if it were practicable to pay the Madras Army entirely with silver (either 3½ new rupees, 56 annas, or 45 fanams for one pagoda), every difficulty would be removed, as the troops taking silver coin to the market would not be subject to any batta whatever. At the same time we are fully aware to alter the usual mode of paying the troops is a delicate matter, and that, should it be found advisable, the attempt must be carefully and gradually made.

28. The copper pice has been noticed as to its application to the rupee, and we find in the copper coin indented for from Madras it has been applied to the pagoda, a quantity being sent thereof:

5)3.600 cash
720 pice
Rupees Annas
3 8
56 annas
672 pice
672)3600(5.357

1 piece of 4 pice or 20 cash.
1 piece of 2 pice or 10 cash.
1 piece of 1 pice or 5 cash.
1 piece of $^{1}/_{5}$ pice or 1 cash.

calculated is 80 cash to 1 fanam, and 45 fanams or 3,600 cash to 1 pagoda; by this mode there may be obtained in exchange for 1 pagoda 720 pice, but in exchange for 3½ Arcot rupees there can be obtained only 672 pice, making a difference of 48 pice on each pagoda. One pice is equal to cash $5^{357}/_{1000}$, and 1 anna 3 pice is nearly equal to 1 fanam, but if this nearest proportion should be established there might be obtained for 45 fanams, or 1 pagoda, 6/5 copper pice, which is an increase of 3 pice beyond the quantity to be obtained in exchange for 3½ rupees. Therefore we are not inclined to recommend the cash as a coin on the new principle, and, although the coinage of fanams has been adverted to, yet it is our decided opinion to confine the denominations of the new coin, if possible, to gold rupees, halves, and quarters, silver rupees, halves, quarters, and annas; and copper pice to the exclusion of silver fanams and copper cash, the two latter appearing likely, in some measure, to continue the inconvenience it is the object of our plan entirely to remove.

29. Having stated our views concerning a general currency for British India, we deem it unnecessary to make any observations on the advantages attending such a measure, as our Governments abroad, by constant experience of the manifold evils of the present system, are fully competent to appreciate the benefits that would result from the adoption of a plan whereby a coin of one standard weight and fineness would become exclusively current as the general measure of value.

30. We shall now proceed to give some consideration to the state of the mints at our several presidencies. We are convinced they are defective not only in regard to a succession of officers properly qualified in the arts of assay and minting, but correct machinery is also wanting for the several operations, as well as an effectual check of control over the several establishments. To this may be added the difference in the manner of conducting the present mints, which alone is sufficient to counteract the benefits otherwise likely to accrue from the adoption of the general system we have before staled. From these considerations we are inclined to think, the evils of the present system cannot be so effectually removed as by the abolition of the existing mints, and the establishing one mint only, which should be at Calcutta. We are aware that this is a proposition of great magnitude, and might in practice

be attended with inconveniences greater than those intended to be removed by it; we therefore suggest it now only to draw your serious consideration to it. Such objections as we think are likely to be urged against it we shall here notice, with the answers that may be made to them, and we wish for your opinion upon the whole, and your final judgment upon this subject.

The advantages we expect to derive from the whole coinage of India passing through but one mint chiefly consist in the uniformity of the operation, the facility of instituting an effectual control over the coinage as to its standard, weight and fineness, and also in our increased ability to form an establishment on a scale sufficiently liberal and extensive to secure correctness in the coin, and every needful despatch in the various operations of the mint. In the formation of a mint establishment it is our intention to be guided, as far as circumstances will admit, by the constitution of His Majesty's Mint, of which Lord Liverpool speaks as follows (p. 201). 'The subsisting regulations for receiving bullion of any description into Your Majesty's Mint; for transferring it from one department to another; for preserving it in security while it continues in the custody of the different officers; and, lastly, for returning it in the shape of coins to those to whom it belongs; arc wise, and require no "alteration".' A description of this mint in all; its: branches of coinage and checks-will be forwarded.

32. In the contemplation of an effective future succession of officers for the principals of the several departments of the Mint, we consider it proper that a competent number of persons intended for civil stations in India shall be instructed in the various branches of the Assay and Mint Departments of His Majesty's Mint; and for this purpose a plan will be arranged to ensure to our new establishment every advantage that the knowledge of the most approved processes and machinery can effect, together with the experience resulting from a regular initiation under the most skilful artists. It is our intention to provide for the mint machinery similar to that about to be adopted in the King's Mint, for which purpose the necessary application will be made to Parliament.

33. We are aware it may be urged one mint will be unequal to the supply of British India with a sufficiency of circulating medium

for the constant demand; as also that mints will be necessary for the recoinage of old rupees, at least at Madras and Bombay, as the provinces under these Governments are so distant from Calcutta, and likewise for the coinage of bullion from Europe and America. To these objections we reply, first, that the machinery to be set up in His Majesty's Mint is stated to be equal to the coining of one hundred and twenty million (120,000,000) shillings annually. We do not suppose the wants of India can ever be carried to ass extent equal to this supply, after the new coin has been introduced into general use; therefore it appears to us unnecessary to incur the expense of three establishments, when one is more than equal to supply the whole demand; especially as the expense of those establishments would be incurred whether they were fully employed or not and, if one mint is fully sufficient, three could not be employed above four months in each year. Secondly, some of the benefits expected to be derived from the proportion of alloy recommended for the new rupee are, that it will lose less by wear: the impression will last much longer, and consequently render frequent recoinages unnecessary. One of the defects of the Bengal coin is its purity, which subjects it to loss in weight by friction, and the obliteration of the impression from the softness of the metal, thus becoming unfit as a measure of value, by being deprived of the principal requisites of a coin, the impression as the proof of its standard fineness, and the weight as the test of its value. Thirdly, in respect to the bullion from Europe and America. As far as regards the bullion sent by us from this country, it is our intention the whole should be coined into the new currency at His Majesty's Mint, as we do not apprehend any difficulty in the accomplishing of this object. And, to prevent all variation in the appearance of the coin struck in England and in India, the dies used in both mints must be sunk by the same artist. The private shipper of bullion cannot suffer any detriment by this arrangement, although it is our intention he should still have the choice of sending bullion in preference to coin, if more agreeable to his views, but would prefer, it is most likely, the coining of his bullion in this country, as it would be ready for immediate circulation at whatever place he may require it. The duty to be levied on the coinage of private bullion should be the same in England as in India, to place both upon the same footing, that the shipper should have no preference in this respect.

34. The charge of coinage to be the same on gold as on silver, and we think 2 per cent would be sufficient to cover our expenses, and not so much as to prevent the bringing of bullion to the mint, when that sum is to include every charge without any other deduction whatever. Our own supplies may be so arranged as to transmit the required proportion to each of our presidencies in coin instead of bullion. The only remaining difficulty applies to the importation of bullion into India from foreign Europe and America, and to the transmission of coin from one part of India to another. Dollars have been generally exchanged sit the several presidencies for the various currencies, and at different rates according to the plenty or scarcity of bullion at the time. This exchange may be improved by fixing a rate between dollars and the new rupees according to the fine silver in each, taking cure to deduct from the value of the dollars the charge for coinage, with such additional amount as the expense of transit and risk may demand; yet keeping such additional charge below the amount an individual would incur in forwarding his own bullion to the mint.

35. On this principle the Governments of Madras and Bombay to become the purchasers of all bullion tendered them, paying for the same in cash or in bills on Bengal at a rate to preserve the abovementioned advantages to this Company. The constant intercourse between Bengal, Madras, and Bombay, presents sufficient facilities for the accomplishment of this plan, and seems to leave no other impediment but the risk of transit; this risk is at present necessarily run in forwarding the supplies from one presidency to another; so that the only disadvantage to be expected would arise from the probability of more frequent recurrence of the risk. A table of rates of the intrinsic values of the several descriptions of Spanish dollars, and other coin usually imported into India, may be formed; and, when a new coin finds its way there from foreign Europe or America, it may be assayed at Calcutta, the real value ascertained, and a rate (at which it should be exchanged with the new rupee) established accordingly.

36. On the establishment of the new system it is our intention to institute a complete check on the mint at Calcutta; and to attain this important object we shall direct that, in addition to the ordinary checks, a member of the Bengal Council, do, from time to time during the operations of coinage, proceed to the mint, without giving any previous notice, and take from the fresh-struck coins samples of the several denominations of gold and silver, to the weight of one pound troy of each sort, to be packed on the spot, with a description of the pieces and the date of the selection, for despatch to Europe the first opportunity, to be assayed by His Majesty's Assay Master, that the state of the coin may be reported to the Court of Directors, for their satisfaction and approbation. The selection of the coin at the mint to be repeated at least once a month, if the business of the mint should render such frequent checks necessary. The quantity of a pound troy of each denomination has been fixed on, because it has been satisfactorily shown in Mr. Hachett's Report to the Lords of the Committee of Privy Council to be improper to estimate the value of a coin by insulated experiments on a few pieces.

| | | |
|---|---|---|
| Sicca rupees | 1800 | |
| Half rupee or ½ rupee | 1806 | 1806 |
| Quarter rupee or ¼ rupee | 1806 | 1806 |
| Anna | 1806 | |

37. We have thought the adoption of a new coinage for British India a fit opportunity for giving a new impression to our currency, and the most appropriate in our estimation is the Company's arms and motto, with an inscription 'English East India Company,' as also the denomination and value of the coin with the year of coinage; and tor the reverse, a Persian inscription, expressing the English one on the obverse, with the value and denomination of the coin, together with the date of coinage. If the smaller gold and silver coins (perhaps all below the half rupee) do not present surface sufficient for a clear impression, it would be proper to substitute for the arms the Company's crest, the inscriptions to remain alike in all.

38. The operation of the new machinery will render the conversion of the present currency into the new rupee easy and expeditious; and, to encourage the bringing in of the coin now in

circulation, it is our intention to receive it according to its relative value to the new rupee, making no charge or deduction for coinage for a period sufficiently extensive to allow the whole of the coin to be brought into the mint. The revenues and all imposts being calculated as at present, there would only remain to give notice how long the present coin is to be current, on the same principle as the change of 1793 in Bengal (vide Bengal Regulation of 1793, No. 35). After the period agreed on has elapsed, all coin (except the new) to be received only as bullion, deducting the charge for coinage from the quantity to be delivered; and that on no account, after the lapse of the limited period, shall any other coin be received in payments to Government except as bullion.

39. We have thus stated our conviction of the necessity of establishing one coin for the general currency of British India as the principal measure of property and medium of commerce; the standard weight and fineness of such coin; and also the metal of which we think it should be made. We have stated our views of a copper currency for the whole of our possessions, and have desired your opinion as to the propriety of establishing one mint only for the whole of the Indian coinage in future.

40. It will be necessary for our several Governments to furnish accounts of the estimated amount of circulating coin, showing also how far this supposed quantity falls short of what is necessary for the convenience of the several classes of the community, distinguishing gold, silver, and copper. From these accounts we shall be enabled to judge of the quantity of the different descriptions of coin necessary to be provided to carry our intended plan into execution. We expect the advantages to be offered to the possessors of the present currency, of receiving it without any charge for re-coinage, will bring all, or at least the far greater part, of the coin into our possession.

41. The extensive powers of the new machinery will return the present currency into circulation with great dispatch; and, as it is our intention to supply coin instead of bullion to the extent that may be required, we do not apprehend the provision of a sufficient quantity of coin on the new system will occupy more than one year, after the mint at Calcutta shall be put into complete

activity. In requiring the sentiments of our several Governments on the whole of this most important and interesting subject, we direct that our Governments of Madras and Bombay transmit their reports to Bengal with all convenient dispatch, and that our Government General lose no time in reporting to us on the plan herein detailed, as it applies to the several countries comprising British India; and also on such parts of the reports from Madras and Bombay as may appear to require their notice. By this procedure we shall possess all the requisite information for forming a complete arrangement, and for placing the coinage of British India on a footing equally respectable and correct; and to supply a coin far beyond the imitation of Asiatic artists inthe excellence of the workmanship, and of a regularity in appearance and value unknown to that part of the world.

We are, &c.
(signed) William Fullarton Elphinstone
Edward Parry & c.

# APPENDIX NO. 1

The estimated loss attending the present system of India is stated as under for Bengal and Madras. There is not any information in the Papers on the Bombay Consultations by which an estimate can be formed of the loss there, although the loss is stated as being very great. The expense of the three principal mints at the Presidencies of Bengal, Madras, and Bombay is also added to show the whole estimated loss and expense arising from the present system of the mints and coinage in the Company's possessions, as far as the same can be ascertained.

| | | | |
|---|---|---|---|
| Lord Teignmouth, in his Minute on the Bengal Public Consultations of 3rd October 1796, states the annual loss by Batta on the gold coin at five lacs. 'There is no allusion to the loss on any other description of coin Sicca rupees | — | — | 5,00,000 |
| The Committee of Reform at Madras state the annual loss by Batta re-coinage of gold and silver from Bengal, exchange, and payments to the troops to the southward, on an average of 13 years, at 57.000 pagodas per annum Sicca rupees | — | — | 1,88,000 |
| By an account drawn out from the Indian General Books for eight years of the bills drawn on Bengal from Madras, Bombay, Bcncoolen, Prince Wales' Island, and China, there appears an estimated annual loss of six lacs Sicca rupees, by taking the intrinsic value of the coin paid for the bills, and of the Sicca rupee in which the bills were paid. It is not intended to charge the whole of this annual loss to differences, supposed or real, in the values of the various coins, but it is supposed at least one-third of the amount of loss would not have been incurred, had there been but one coin universally current Sicca rupees | — | — | 2,00,000 |

| | | | |
|---|---|---|---|
| The gross annual expense of the Calcutta Mint, on an average of three years from 1799/1800 to 1801/2, appears by the Bengal General Books to be Sicca rupees | — | 1.66,000 | — |
| The gross annual expense of the Madras Mint adding the whole of the Mint Master and Sub Treasurer's salary to the charges of the Mint, appears by the Madras Books to be pagodas 12,616 or Sicca rupees | — | 41,000 | — |
| The gross animal expense of the Bombay Mint appears by Bombay Public Consultations of 5th April 1805, io be Bombay rupees 24,600, or Sicca rupees | — | 23,000 | — |
| On the quantity of dollars coined in the Calcutta Mint in 179/1800 on account of the Company the produce was less than it should be, according to the line silver in the dollar and the Sicca rupee, Sicca rupees | 2,38,624 | — | — |
| Not any dollars were re-coined on the Company's account in 1800/1. On the quantity re-coined in 1801/2 the produce was less by Sicca rupees | 66,291 | — | — |
| Two years Sicca rupees | 3,04,015 | — | — |
| Average | 1,52.457 | — | — |
| On the quantity of dollars re-coined in the Madras Mint for the Company in the years 1799/1800 to I801/2, the average annual produce was less by Arcot rupees 60.267 | 57,029 | 2,09,000 | — |
| Sicca rupees | — | 4,39,000 | — |
| No correct estimate can be formed of the loss on the coinage or re-coinage of any other description of coin but what is produced from dollars, the assay not being stated in the Mint Accounts; but, supposing there was a loss equal to that sustained on dollars, the amount would be | — | 97,000 | — |
| | | | 5,36,000 |
| Estimated annual loss and expense, Sicca rupees | | | 14,24,000 |

*Note*: The amount of duty charged in the coinage is not deducted from the gross expense of the Mints, as a duty will be charged on the system recommended. Tho amount of the average duty charged is added as under, as also what the amount of duty would be on the supposition of charging 2 per cent, also for gold and silver.

| | Sicca Rupees |
|---|---|
| Annual duty charged on an average of three years on the coinage of the Calcutta Mint | 66,000 |
| Annual duty charged on an average of three years on the coinage of the Madras Mint, Pagodas 7196 or | 24.000 |
| Annual duty charged on an average of three years on the coinage of the Bombay Mint, Bombay rupees 32,591, or | 30,000 |
| Sicca rupees | 1,20,000 |
| Annual average value of coinage of gold and silver for individuals in the Bengal, and Madras Mints Sicca rupees | 56,85,000 |
| Annual average value of coinage of gold and silver for individuals in the Bombay Mint Bombay rupees 10,86,000, or Sicca rupees 10,19,000 Sicca rupees 67,04,000 | |
| Two per cent, on which is | 1,34,000 |

By the above it is seen the Company would not sustain any loss by charging 2 per cent, on the coinage issued from their Mint, instead of the present charges.

*Source:* Parliamentary Papers, House of Commons, 1898 (127), East India (Currency). Copy of the Despatch addressed to the Court of Directors to the Government of Bengal and Madras on 25 April 1806, dealing with the coinage of India, dated 23 March 1898.

# 3

# Letter from H. Scott, Assay Master, Bombay Mint, to F. Warden, Secretary to Bombay Government, dated 7 December 1806

Honourable Sir,

1st. According to your desire, I now lay before you such observations as have occurred to me on the Honourable Company's letter No. 2 with its appendix. I shall proceed according to the order of the paragraphs that appear to me the most important. I am sure I need not intreat your intelligence on the subject so difficult and so extensive which besides the ordinary considerations of coins and money and commerce involves so many views of general policy.

2d. The court say in the commencement of their attention has been directed to the coinage chiefly from the loss sustained by the recoining of Dollars into sicca rupees in the Calcutta mint, which loss they state whether it be by a loss of Silver from the operation, or by a loss from the expenses exceeding the profits of the mint.

3d. Paragraph 8. It is perhaps impossible now to determining that the two coins issued from the Moghul mints were uniformly of one weight. Although in them all the rupee is now called a Tola or one sicca or Ten Alassa [Massa]; yet the weight of the sicca rupee differs in every mint derived from the Moghul government. That method of determining the smaller weights of which the Tola is composed is very far from accurate as a generally use the seeds of the Abrus for them. From these inaccuracies the deviation in time has been considerable every mint supposing that it alone keeps to the standard.

It would no doubt be simpler with regard to the English to adopt will 180 grains instead of the number of grains composing the Tola in different mints, but it must be remembered that this is not the case with regard to the natives missed their Tola is now an exact weight made generally of brass or Silver and no deviation from it can be authorized without some inconveniency. On this size rate the natives of every in the mint make their calculations and to it the importers of bullion or the traders from the Persian Gulph, the Red Sea, or other parts constantly refer.

The inconveniency of altering this Tola ever selected, is of some consideration, but I have no doubt that a little time would get over the slight suspicion and uneasiness that the change would in the first instance produce. Of these facts we are pretty sure from some recent circumstances and this place.

4th. Paragraph 9. The use of a copper alloy for gold would certainly produce some uneasiness here, but it proper explanations and by time it would wear off. Some attempts that purpose were lately made in this mint as a specimen. They succeeded very ill but it now appears (from Mr. Hatchett's very able report) that this was owing to the employment of improper copper.

5th. Paragraph 10. The rupee hear proposed is in all respects very near to the present coinage of this place and would not be objectable. The rupees of Guzarat, Broach, Baroda, Cambay &c. do not differ from it very much, and all might without disturbance be made equal the Shree sicca of the Mahratta states agrees with it nearly in the quantity of fine silver. These considerations are very much in favor of the proposed rupee for they show the facility of having them entirely equalized. Whatever may be the objection in Bengal where the Silver rupee differs so materially from the rupee of the rest of India, there ought to be none to the adoption here of the proposed silver coin (for comparison of the real value of rupees of many of the mints on this side of India see the Bombay calendar of this year).

It undoubtedly has occurred to the Honorable court that the depreciating the Bengal coinage by about 7 per cent is liable to all the objections that has been urged on a similar occasion by

Mr. Locke in his answer to Mr. Lowndes. Mr. Locke's assay [*sic* essay] is entitled to farther [*sic* further] considerations concerning raising the value of money in which he shews the consequences that must arise in all the contracts that subsist among individuals. Besides this, the Honourable Company seen in Bengal to have a further consideration of vast importance. I mean their bonded debt, such of the creditors as are paid in England, may have no reason but little to complain but I feel apprehensive that this might be far from the case with those were paid off in India. This is the case that no doubt the Honorable court has materially considered for the difference of seven per cent is very considerable. I need therefore enter into no explanation of my meaning; I should perhaps beg to be excused for taking any notice of a subject which can neither be overlooked or misconceived.

6th. Paragraph 15. The recommendations in this paragraph regarding a copper coin, seem very proper, like every other kind of coin, they are on ways can neither the from the circulation of this place and it is very fair that Government should have at all events some advantage from them.

7th. Paragraph 16. The people at this presidency and the southward are now much he used to coins of Gold, and in many respects prefer them. They answer better for large payments than silver, they are more easily transported or concealed and they form the material which generally compose their ornaments. Any check by Government on the circulation of Gold as a coin would certainly produce great inconvenience.

The Gold rupee proposed on this paragraph is (with a very insignificant difference) the Gold Mohur of our present coinage, and this arrangement of making the Silver and Gold rupee of the same weight and with the same alloy, has the advantage of great simplicity.

We formerly coined halves and thirds of a Gold Mohur, but we gave it up from finding that the people were apt to mistake the halves for the thirds and to be imposed on by the shroffs. The quarters besides being inconvenient for the accounts of the people were rather too small to be struck by our method. The no coined only old rupees and thirds or pieces worth 5 silver rupees. With better machinery it is no doubt that the proposed coinage would be very proper.

8. Paragraph 17. The reasonings in this paragraph are or together unexceptionable. We have known them long and the reflections to which they give rise have frequently occupied our minds. It is however very difficult to correct some evils although we feel the causes of them.

9. Paragraph 19. So far as it is possible for us to judge the gold coin has hitherto passed into the circulation here without any force on effort on the part of Government. It is most readily received by the community and whenever the amount in circulation has diminished to a certain degree the public feel the want of it and anxiously call for more. This has repeatedly happened of late years.

10. Paragraph 20 and 24. These are most important Paragraphs. The adoption of this proposal to requires in Bombay the utmost caution and consideration, but instead of the good that is intended, it may produce much inconvenience and very serious mischief. I many far from meaning to call in question the principle that it every country there can be but one metal which is the measure of property or as Lord Liverpool call it the principal measure of property. The question however is tilted Mr. Beatty cited whether the value of other coins is not to be determined by the public authority; let the other coins which are the representative of the coins which are the principal measure are to be regulated by the value of bullion in the market and the weight and a speculation of individuals. In this part of India I have no hesitation in saying that it is absolutely necessary to fix the value of every denomination of coin by the public authority. Should it be otherwise ordered, both the Government and the people would be a prey to the shroffs in a manner fortunately unknown to us in all time past.

11. No man without considerable experience in this country can form an opinion of the influence and the arts of shroffs. They hold in their hands almost the whole specie of the country; their houses are connected in every part of India; their whole life is spent in the trade of gaining money by exchange and by every

other means connected with this art. They form of the same trade from generation to generation, they are subtle and acute from long and early habit and are divided from the rest of the people, not more by their cast, then by their means of living in which they are allow none to participate. Their influence is great and extensive nor is it even in the power of Government on many occasions to protect itself against their combinations. If any denomination of the coin one left here to find its value in the market instead of being fixed by Government, it is certain that this would be done by the shroffs, as their own interest might dictate. No other part of his community would have any influence in fixing the rates for the shroffs hold in their hands almost all the specie and would-be the entire Masters of the exchange. In Europe and the people have many resources; the money of the country is there in many hands and if one class of men were disposed to be selfish and unreasonable others would be found off a different disposition who would correct or lessen the evil. If it has been thought that the leaving the value of some coins unfixed by Government would expose in Europe the people to frogs and impositions from Money Jobbers and others, how much more dreadful must the evil be in this country, where the people are more ignorant and where the Money Jobbers have been influence beyond all comparison more extensive.

The shroffs have the command of nearly all the specie or could soon secure command of it. They too would monopolize the bullion and it cannot be doubted that that whenever it was much for their interest, they would alter the values that the metals bear to each other in the market, the great loss of the Honorable Company and the ruin of individuals.

12. But this is not the whole of the objection that ought to be made to this proposal. It supposes that silver is the principal measure of property in Bombay, and that therefore the value of the gold coins may be left the discretion of individuals. Whatever may have been sometime ago the case in Bombay, it may be very much doubted I think the silver is now the principal measure of property. It is even very probable that the changes in the state of our trade have altered the relations in this disrespect of the precious

metals. The value of silver from the nature of this trade is subject to very great and very certain changes which would seem to render it a very unfit substance to repreresent the value of property in general. We are in this respect in a situation very peculiar and it is necessary to understand before any judgment can be formed of our monetary system.

13. The most important branch of our trade and this is a trade that has but of late attained so great a magnitude, is the cotton trade to Guzarat. The whole of this cotton is imported by the merchants of Bombay for the market of Canton, and it may annually amount to the sum of above 40 lacs prime cost (say there go annually but 80,000 bales or 40,000 candies of cotton to China, and the prime cost per candy of 100 rupees). This is under the truth. Besides this cotton that is also a date or a greater amount imported from Guzerat in grains and goods. In return for all this we have but very few articles to send them. I believe that the chief of them are metals or clothes from Europe, and silk and sugar from China, but the whole of the goods that weakens and is much inferior in value in comparison to what we receive. The Bombay merchants are therefore under the necessity of providing silver to pay for the purchase of their cotton, for gold in that country is not used as a coin, nor is it in demand to great extent. Silver therefore must be found or the much and must relinquish his trade in cotton altogether. It very often happens that the merchant has not found it possible to provide a sufficient quantity of bullion to pay for his purchases, and in that case he can do nothing better than to apply to the shroffs who give him Bills on Surat for the amount. When many of those Bills are wanted they are giving at a very unfavorable exchange, even as far as 12 per cent against the merchant - at such times he will avoid taking Bills as long as he is able and one of the first resources to which he flies is to pick up the whole of the silver money into circulation of his place. This is sent to Surat at a loss of about 1 or 1½ per cent for freight and insurance, but it affords a much more profitable remittance so far as it goes than Bills. Such at times has been the sudden and pressing demand for silver than dollars have sold here for 243 rupees per hundred page in the mint would have yielded the holder less than 220 rupees. Of

late the demand for money for the armies as greatly decreased in Guzerat, and Dollars to a great amount have been imported. The consequence has been as might have been foretold, and exchange has fallen to par or nearly so with Surat, and the merchants here have founded advantageous to carry their dollars to the mint.

This is state of things however will not remain long. Cotton and grain must annually be procured and it is highly probable that the importation of silver will not keep place at all times with the demand for it. Every Silver rupee will again be drawn from the circulation of displays and sent to Guzerat, and as usual, we shall have no coins but those of gold and copper.

14. For many years past the amount of silver coin in the circulation of this place, has from the causes already detailed been quite insignificant. The troops have been great by means of gold and copper and most of the ordinary business of the place has been carried on without the assistance of silver. When purchase of silver or gold are made in Europe, the theater is so extensive that it may be impossible for any man to determining which of the two metals has altered its value with regard to other goods. The matter is very different here. We see precisely the causes of the variation; and it is a demand for silver or a particular purpose, about what this place can for the time supply.

15. One of the immediate effects of this demand for silver is to the deprive us in Bombay of all other silver coin, nor does it appear to be possible to prevent it by any regulation of Government, or by any adjustment that it is possible to make between the coins of gold and silver. When the premium on Silver becomes 6.10 or even 12 per cent compared with gold or goods, it is evident that it does not depend on causes that we can connect by any system of coinage of any precaution of Government. It is necessary to repeat that we have little or no silver coin in circulation, and that until the state of our trade is altered we are not likely to have much. Gold therefore in Bombay seems to be the only steady stand the only true measure of property. It is the only valuable metal that we have in our circulation, and by which all payments are made. To leave our gold coin to be value with by the highly fluctuating the state of silver instead of its being done by Government, would

I am certain expose this society to a scene of fraud, mischief and confusion. Sorry indeed should I be to see such a proposal put in practice for evil, much evil, would arise from it.

Silver has really lost here one of the great qualities that usually attend the precious metals the straitness of their value at all times and by which they are so fitted to become the measure of value of every other kind of property.

16. Although gold as a coin has never been used in Surat or in any part of Guzerat, yet it has long been so in Bombay and its neighbourhood. Over all the coast of Malabar so connected by commerce with this place our gold coins have long circulated and every where readily received. Gold coin has been used in those countries from time immemorial, and its general circulation requires no kind of force force or assistance. The gold coin of Bombay has an extensive circulation, not only through Malabar and Canara but in the interior and more northern provinces. Like silver it is carried away from us and never again returns but it disappears gradually and insensibly from causes that appear at all times to operate, but the operation of those causes unlike to that which affects silver seems to be equable, without much increased or diminution. Of the quantity of gold that has been coined within these last 7 years, it is probable that 9/10 have already disappeared.

17. I am not convinced that any good can arise from fixing a value on one denomination of the coin only, but if they should be thought unnecessary measure I cannot have the least doubt for the reasons I have already given that the value of the coins of gold should be fixed, but those of silver are allowed to find their own value in the market. This is really what has in great measure happened without the interference of Government. When I consider the smallness of the amount of silver coin in our circulation, the extreme variation to which silver is subject in value and that gold alone is the metal or old consider the transactions in this place, I feel convinced that gold has become my general consent the measure of property and that it cannot be removed from that station without violence and inconveniency.

18. I have said already that coins of gold are received here without any interference or authority on the part of Government,

and without any appearance of the tens on the part of individuals. I know of no *batta* that has been exacted here injurious to individuals, not to I believe that I hazard too much in affirming that since that the formation of the coinage in 1799 the Honorable Company have in no way lost a single rupee by *batta* or any other cause arising from their own coins.

19. That the coinage of silver after it has circulated a certain number of years seems for same reason or other to be necessary in Bengal. He processed necessity has ever existed nor has any difference being made in the value of old and new coins. Our silver coins of the circulating a great many years even half a century, in whose but little of their weight. It is supposed that no more than a single grain is worn away in that time from a rupee and perhaps even less. This observation that done minters have made to me here confirms in a remarkable manner and observation of Mr. Hatchetts in his late valuable paper on the alloys &c. &c. of gold. 'But still it must be repeated' says Mr. Hatchetts, 'that the united effects of every species of friction to which the coins may be subjected fairly and unavoidably during circulation, cannot produce any other wear them that which is extremely casual and slow and such as will by no means a column for the great and rapid diminution which has been observed in the gold coin of this country.' In India the natives are acquainted with none of the acids received which dissolve gold or silver.

20. Paragraph 23. The gold coinage mentioned in this paragraph is simple and unexceptionable. The one there is stated of 11 to 1 is precisely the Gold Mohur of Bombay by the regulation of Government in 1799. If the proportion of 15 to 1 be chosen the proposed general coinage for India (within a small fraction) the very same with the present coinage of Bombay, not only with regard to silver but gold, so that when it is adopted there may be no change in the least material even in our silver or gold. The value picks Department to our gold rupee is 15 silver rupees which is estimating gold to Silver as 15 to one. This is certainly not far from the general price in the market of the metals, as may be proved from many considerations. The rate of 14¼ to one, as a set to prevail at Madras, is undoubtedly not that of Bombay. Not

an ounce of gold bullion would ever been brought to this mint for coinage at such a rate. In the year 1774 and alteration was made by Government in the Gold Mohur to make it represent 15 silver rupees as nearly as it was possible by the market prices of the two metals. In that coinage the rate of gold was to silver as 14.9 to one, and it is probable that such is extremely near to their present values in the market. The deviation from it by the subsisting regulation is but a small and so far as it goes it tends produce a greater revenue from the mint, for here we buy for coinage the gold but not silver bullion. District is arises from necessity and depends on causes, that it may be unnecessary to dwell on at present. We, however, see from our purchases of gold, that the dates of value in the metals as fixed for the coins does not differ much from their values in the market, for we seldom are able to gain more than a moderate mint duty, by the coinage of gold.

21. It certainly seems that the proposed coinage for India, would have great advantages over other present coinage of Bengal. The expenses of mint is would be diminished by the use of more annoyed and the pay of the coins would be less without taking into the account the great benefit that would arise from an uniform standard of fineness and weight.

22. As there are coins in different parts of India that can hardly be adjusted in even numbers to the rupee and gold Mohur, such as the gold or on the gold coins of Malabar, it would be of great use (should no farther alteration be thought advisable) to make those coins in future of exactly the same fineness as the general gold of silver coins of India cutting them afterwards according to the quantity of fine metal into the coins that have required. This would produce no inconveniencing [*sic*] as the shroffs would soon see that their value is not diminished. By being them, which is very generally in one large payments in India, their value in proportion to the general gold ore rupee would instantly appear and of any great source of fraud would be cut off even by this approximation to simplicity and uniformity.

23rd. Paragraph 30. This paragraph and goes which formulate proposed the establishment of a mint at Calcutta, and the suppression of all the mints now existing in the Company's territories.

Paragraph 31. It is the advantages to be derived from an establishment so extensive and so complete, and most readily do I subscribe to the truth in general of those statements. We have nothing in India that can be compared in point of perfection to what this must be. It would no doubt the most expeditious in its operations and the coins would be beautiful and uniform beyond all example in this country. This proposal, however, is of great magnitude. Before it is put in execution it should be well and long considered for it may produce in this country much uneasiness and discontent and its inconveniences may overbalance in the end its advantage.

24. Some of advantages that are expected to arise from it, I confess I do not entirely agree to. I allude chiefly to Appendix No. 1 which it is losses by exchange &c. Which no system of coinage will remove and perhaps hardly in any degree the correct. This appendix appears to merit an examination in this country; but as it chiefly relates to Bengal, it is there where it ought to be considered.

25th. One of the most material objections to the plan of a general mint is the inconveniency that will arise to many classes of men on the side of India, from the want of mints in their neighbourhood. The natives sometime immemorial have been accustomed with their princes of every cost to the conveniency of mint in which they could convert their silver gold into the ordinary coin of the country. We have at this moment several mints to the northward which were established in ancient times. Those are the mints of Surat, Cambay, Broach, and Baroda. In all of these mints declined rupees which it differ somewhat in value. This in the rich and populous country of Guzerat where many transactions are carried on daily to a vast amount must produce much loss and inconvenience to individuals and much gain to the shroffs. This in the quantity of value in the rupees off neighboring districts gives rise to a thousand speculations in a change in which neither individuals nor the government itself and at all times be protected from fraud, if the money of all could be equalized. The Surat rupee should be adopted for the whole or what is the same thing the general rupee as no proposed for India. The province of Guzerat would certainly afford a proof of the advantage to be expected from a general and uniform currency. In order to accomplish it, it would be necessary to suppress some of the mints, perhaps all of them but Surat. The distance between those parts is not very considerable, they are separated by civilized and highly cultivated countries not what the transport of money involve any very great risk or expense. The plan even to this extent could not be executed without opposition. The shroffs would instantly see the ill consequences of it themselves, they would alteration difficulties and excite murmurings. They would mislead the opinion of the people and although we should in the end carry the point, yet it would for a time they some suspicion and ill will.

26. I can have no doubt that a suppression of the greater parts of the mints in Guzerat would produce a temporary inconveniency in the weight I have mentioned, but if the people were farther gold that they were to have no mint at Surat, not even at Bombay, I cannot calculate to what length the general discontent might proceed. I daily think that such a measure in those rich and commercial countries would produce much ill will and suspicion towards this British Government. Interested individuals would blow the flame of discontent and the people at large accustomed to Government far from paternal would image to themselves 1000 evils while they would give no credit to our good intentions. The best, the most beneficent and the wisest schemes will here be received with distrust nor can it be removed but by long time and example.

27th. It must however be acknowledged that the holders of bullion on the side of India, would have very real cause of complaint from the suppression of all our mints. The fair trader and even the calculator would find his trade injured and his profits diminished. Suppose for instance (as is the case in a thousand situations) that they send or their crops for silver or gold brought from the interior of India, from China or the Red Sea or Persian Gulph. This silver and gold is in ingots or dollars or in the form off foreign coins. To render those metals as much as possible production to them they frequently turn them into the coin of the country. If they can no longer do this a part of their value is instantly lost. The metals can no longer answer the whole of the purposes on which their value depends. Loss and disappointment to a certain and even to a considerable extent must arise and a diminished degree of the general prosperity of the community must be the consequence.

28. In Paragraph 35. The Honourable court has foreseen the objection just stated to the plan of a general mint, and in order to obviate as far as they can't any loss on that account to the bullion holders on the side of India, they say 'on distance of the common to Madras and Bombay to become the purchasers of all bullion tendered [to] them, paying for the same in cash or in Bills on Bengal at a weight to preserve the above-mentioned advantages of the Company.'

This rate is determined in Paragraph 34 in the following words. 'By fixing a rate between dollars and the new rupees according to the fine silver in each taking care to deduct from the value of the dollars the charge for coinage with such additional amount as the expense off transit and risk may demand, yet keeping such additional charge below the amount, an individual would incur in forwarding his own bullion to the mint.' From this it appears that the bullion holder on the side of India is to pay for the expense off transit and of risk by the Honourable Company will be subjected to the loss of interest from the time of purchase in the bullion is converted into rupees. Such other dangers of the Bengal River that that is from it alone is probably more than equal to an ill Europe voyage. Freight and insurance to Calcutta from hands is never less in the time of peace than 3½ per cent but in the time of war it is 6 and frequently more. We shall suppose at the medium that it is but 4 so that by the time the bullion comes back to Bombay in the form of rupees a lost must arise on it to its proprietors of 8 per cent. It orders not the statement whether the property remains with the original holder on whether the Company have purchased it from him. The usual what premium from hence to Calcutta is 8 per cent on a Company's regular ship. The peace premium during the Southwest monsoon (the best season for sailing to Calcutta is 4-4½ and even 5 per cent on account of the then very great danger of the Hoogly.

From 1 to 1½ per cent is enough for freight and insurance to Surat. If the bullion holder, reside in Surat or any part of Guzerat, this loss therefore will be still greater by 2 or 3 per cent so that bullion received by merchants, manufacturers, or farmers, on the side of India would be less valuable than it is in Bengal by 8 per cent, or more, or it will be in future less valuable here it has hitherto been by 8 percent or more.

29. In Paragraph 35 The Honorable Court state that the constant intercourse between Bengal, Madras and Bombay, presents sufficient facilities for the accomplishment of this plan, and seems to leave no other impediment but that is of transit. This risk is at present necessarily seen in forwarding the supplies from one presidency to another, so that the only disadvantage to be expected, would arise from the probability of more frequent recurrence of this risk.

I believe it very seldom happens that bullion or money is sent from one presidency to another. There are better methods and without risk of managing those supplies. But if it were otherwise it seems to make nothing to the agreement. The purchase in the bullion as now proposed on the side of India will in no way assist our supplies. On the contrary it will rather diminished our means of supplying ourselves. The supplies must be made as usual to which this more can give no aid, nor to which (so far as I can understand the subject) it can have no relation. If we do run a risk with our supplies this new this would not lighten it nor alter it.

30. Then get is much intercourse with the presidencies by Sea is very true, but for many causes this intercourse is extremely regular. A ship at particular season may reach Calcutta from Bombay in three weeks, but in no different monsoon the passage is three times as long and advance as tedious as a voyage to Europe. The same thing is true with regard to Madras, which at a certain season of the year is inaccessible to ships altogether. Before bullion therefore could reach Bombay or Guzerat, after its conversion into rupees, in the Calcutta mint, there can be no doubt but that a period of 8 months would occasionally intervene, even if ships were sailing every week between those ports. The truth is that there may sail from Bengal annually to Bombay 15 or 20 vessels and those rate for a favourable time of the monsoon, but during the remainder of the year opportunities for transporting treasure

by Sea very very occur. The Honourable Company did for suffer a great loss by the loss of interest on this plan which could not be managed without much difficulty and delay.

It is supposed by some that the risk to the Honourable Company would in such a case be less than to the private merchant. This may be the case in a certain degree where they can employ their own ships but the nature of this scheme will make it necessary to take such as offer, or opportunities by their own ships very seldom occur. It is therefore very certain that the loss of interest of the Company would be an object of great consideration.

31st. I have hitherto spoken only of the natives of this country, and I have shewn what I think would be their sentiments on the suppression of the mints on the side of India. I am convinced they would look on it as an unprecedented grievance which would lessen the value of their bullion, and by that means diminish their means of living whether that may arise from agriculture or trade. So far as I know the use of their mints has never yet been denied to the inhabitants of this country by its various conquerors. I have had nothing of what I suppose the effect of it would be on the European merchants, or we can very well defend their own causes and I doubt not will be ready to complain. The measure to them too I believe would be very injurious and very odious.

32. If the British territory extended all the way from the side of India to Calcutta and if through the whole of it one general coinage one in circulation, I should see less objection to this plan than I do at present. Divided as the now are not only by an immense space but by countries over which we have no authority on which may be hostile to us, we are in a state so secluded that he must now depend at times on our own internal means. So situated, it will be perfectly easy for the shroffs who have nearly the whole of the money of the country in their hands to produce whenever it suited their purposes, the scarcity of it, or a good at pleasure by combination with each other in these the value of gold in proportion to Silver or Silver to gold. By such means that could easily expose the Honourable Company or the public through prodigious losses, and more especially in the coins of one of the precious metals were left unfixed by the public Authority, as I have before said.

33. I shall mention but to one bad effect more that would arise from the adoption of this measure. The natives would certainly as the last resource send their bullion to be coined in the Mahratta mints in their neighbourhood, and we should be overwhelmed by a base coinage. This constantly takes face to a certain degree even at present, when they have not the same motives for it. Much business is always done by this foreign coinage and great frauds are committed by means of it on individuals. The inscription on those rupees shews the mint in which they were struck, yet their value varies to a prodigious degree and individuals are often exposed to fraud. Although this foreign coin is not a legal tender of payment yet from custom it is received according to its probable value and a force a medium for many commercial transactions.

34. I have thus given, according to the best of my judgement, my opinion of the bed effects that would arise from stopping the coinage in all the mints on the side of India. I look on such a measure and great apprehension. The good that it could produce cannot be very material, the evil may be very great. It is the occasion loss and inconveniency to many individuals and most sincerely should I lament the adoption of so hazardous an experiment. What our change is made which they materially effect the natives of this country should be long and well considered for even those who know them best, cannot calculate the consequences in every case. If it is resolved, however, that this measure shall be finally adopted, I have only to recommend that it will be casually done. We shall thus see how it may be born before we do any mischief. For instance, it might certainly right to stop several of the mints of Guzerat. Let them all then be suppressed but that of Surat. That mint with the mint at the presidency may be sufficient for the conveniency of individuals in our territories on the western side of India. I can advise how nothing farther than this, for there ought to be one mint Guzerat. If, however, the experiment must be carried farther let in the next place the Surat mint be closed and finally that of the presidency. We shall thus gradually see the effects leave produce nor involve ourselves in evils which it may be difficult to remedy. The mint and this presidency and that of Surat should I think always remain and a system of check suffi-

cient for our purposes might be established for the two mints not much more expensive, that one of them only would demand.

35. It is needless for me to observe that conclusions drawn from Great Britain we in any cases but ill apply to this chose vast country. The transit of money from any part of Great Britain to another the assay, expeditious, and cheap. The distances are insignificant, and a need neither pass by see note to hostile nations. One of our sentiments in India is not more accessible to another than America is to England, and after all the facilities of communication that we have created or shall ever be able to create, they must have been the regard to each other many of the inconveniences that attend the connection of distant, and even, or foreign countries.

36. Before concluding this paper it may be proper to shew the Honourable court, the actual estate of our coinage and Bombay, since the establishment that was formed in the year 1799 and the material changes that were then adopted. Before this the state of the coinage was very faulty and the regulations for this mint far from sufficient to preserve the regularity in the coinage. The Surat mint was much worse managed so that government as well as the public were exposed to the losses and frauds that must always attend an uncertain state in the value of the coins. For these facts we made at present refer to them short history of the coins of Surat and Bombay drama sometime able by all of the Honourable the Governor. The Bombay mint was then an annual loss to Government.

37. By the abolition of 1799 the value between Silver in Gold was fixed in the coins at 15 to 1. The weight of the gold and Silver rupee was made equal (179 grains each) and the alloy in both to us altogether to be the same or 8 parts in hundred of the mass. Fifteen of these Silver rupees were ordered to pass for one of the gold rupees. This is a very simple estate of the coinage, and in every respect very convenient and it is within a mere fraction of what is now proposed by the Honourable Court, for the general currency of India.

38. The duty is collected on this coinage and the mint is 3 per cent from which it is expected that the whole of the mint charges

would-be defrayed and that besides some revenue would be derived to Government. It has always been the practice in this country in the native governments, to derive a certain revenue from the mint, and if this is done to a moderate extent, it appears to meet perfectly right that the Honorable Company should assume the same privilege. It will be felt by no individual, and it is as much sanctioned by practice and time and the opinion of men, as the duties at the custom House. The expectations that were formed on this head have not been disappointed for besides defraying the whole charges of the mint, a considerable gain has arisen from the duties to the Honorable Company.

39. In appendix No. 1 of the Honorable Court's letter, a loss is stated on the Bombay mint of rupees 24,000. This is the expense of the mint annually; but the game by the duties have on the whole considerably exceeded it, as will appear clearly to the court by a reference to the statement sent to them on that subject in the year 1805. It is probable that this statement had not arrived been Appendix No. 1 was prepared or again would have clearly appeared instead of a loss. The pleaded that has elapsed since 1799 has been one of the least favorable to the mint that can occur; from war and other causes. If with such disadvantages the expenses of the mintage have been wholly paid besides a considerable gain, we have reason to hope that it will be still better in more favorable times.

Some revenue has also arisen from the Surat mint besides paying its expenses which it would be freer to a to the account of the Bombay mint, another control of which it is placed to a certain degree by Government, and from which connected as they are in all respect's eight is impossible to separate it.

40. We are very far from thinking that the state of our coins on the regulation of our mint can be compared to that of his Majesty. We will know our inferiority but they still think we have attained a certain degree of perfection by which the chief ends of a coinage are accomplished in the wealthy community.

The principal European servants in the mint are a mint Master and Assay Master. The first of those officers receives and keeps the bullion &c. brought to the mint and issues it after a coinage.

The Assay Master inspects the coins that I struck and data mines in all doubtful cases the true value of bullion or coins brought by individuals. The more together make purchase of Gold guided by the market prices in conjunction with the quantity of fine Mandel contained in each bullion or coins as are offered them. Last of all there is a mint contractor whose station is very important. He exists the alloy from the foregoing estimates and fabricates the coin.

41. The rate and material imperfection of our coinage is undoubtedly its from [*sic* form]. The degree of fineness and the late and is really we regulated so as to answer every good purpose in this country. The native mint contractor and some of his people can assay gold with the nitrous and with great exactness and the assay of Silver with lead is universally practiced. Many of the native's are accustomed to work during their whole lives in the precious metals. The mint contractor should always be a man of character and he is authorized to find security in a large sum of money for the faithful discharge of his duty. Any coin from his mint being found off a better quality even after its abolition would subject him to see their penalties and this is a great source of security very weekend neither have that assistance not that extensive system of Jack that is so much to be admired in his Majesty's mint. If the hats of the mint's are to your there can be little desktop excessive fraud but much depends on their character we should be such as to satisfy the public mind. No scale of knowledge nor any Jack that began establish will ever make up for want of this kind.

There is no doubt but that the form of the coin is an important requisite although not the most essential. We have occasionally head falls coin is but not to a material amount from the facility off imitating cover simple operations. This nothing can correct what the mechanism of Europe, and with the assistance of eight we should at once attained a state of perfection in our coinage very sufficient for all of our purposes.

42. It is father but they have observed that says that abolition of 1799 neither the Company nor individuals have lost a rupee by our coins in any made what ever.

The loss of fine silver in our mint is moderate of the refining dollars to our standard, and making them into rupees a loss of Silver is sustained of no more than 44/100 or one per cent and is to taking dollars by tale and not by weight.

We have had no lost a *batta* nor recoinage nor do I know that loss has been incurred by any other means.

43. I have now given according to my conscience and do the best of my judgement is my opinion of this important, extensive, and very delicate subject. I may be long in some of my sentiments, but I have been influenced by no motive but the benefit of the public, and in this I cannot be mistaken.

Signed/H. Scott
[Assay Master]
7 December 1806

*Source:* NAI, Home Department, Public Branch, Proceedings Volume, 22-9 January 1807, no. 16, pp. 301-85.

# 4

# Notes by James Prinsep

## a. On the Device of the Indian Coin: Commencing with the Year 1824

In continuation of my note of the 1st October recommending the appointment of a native die engraver to the new mint, I now beg leave to submit an abstract of such of the records of the Mint Committee as bear upon the particular point of the device of our Indian coinage, commencing with the year 1821, prior to which, however, in 1819, upon the deputation of lieutenant (now captain) Forbes to England to commission out the machinery for the present mint, the subject had been taken up and had been included in the instructions to that officer, in order that he might bring it under consideration of the Honourable Court. It will be seen that it was fully contemplated by all parties that the change of device should be adopted on the opening of the new mint, and it is certainly much to be regretted that the delays of communication between the authorities at home and the local Government should have rendered this measure impracticable, and that the exquisite machinery, both of the Calcutta and the Bombay mints should have been employed (in the former for 3 years) in the continued promulgation of a system which every minute on record unites in condemning in the strongest terms.

In their general letter dated 23rd April 1824, announcing the dispatch of the last packages of the new machinery, the Honourable Court of Directors call upon the local Government of Bengal to consider and report what will be the best device for the rupee to be coined *on the opening of the new mint*. They advert to the proposition of adopting the Company's arms made by the Indian Government in 1819 and, without any direct recommendation of it, merely suggest a deliberate reconsideration of the whole matter as well as of the expediency of appointing a die engraver from England for the new mint.

The reference of the Court's letter to the Mint Committee produced valuable minutes from the then members, Mr Holt MacKenzie, Mr H. Wood and Mr W. Money, and the fullest information on the subject was obtained from the reports of Mr H.H. Wilson and Captain Forbes. The following is a brief abstract of the observations of the officers, bearing on the question of the device, the other question mixed up with it, namely the equalization of the weights and currency of the three Presidencies having been set at rest by the late regulations (Regulation VII, 1833) for the adoption of the rupee of 180 grains, although this regulation does not quite go the length recommended by Messrs. Wood and Mackenzie, viz the substitution of this 180 grain rupee for the sicca rupee of Bengal and the adoption of the same weight (of 180 grains) for the gold *mohurs* as has been already effected at Madras and Bombay.

Mr H.H. Wilson's report characterizes the present impression *as an absurdity and a falsehood* conveying no distinct idea to the majority of the people of India, and of very easy imitation.

He proposes to substitute the Company's arms for the reverse and an *emblematical device* for the obverse with a legend specifying the denomination, sphere of circulation and date of first issue: and on the edge, the weight and fineness. The latter would be a security against imitating the coin by casting in moulds, which gives a perfect copy of the face impression, however elaborate it may be, but cannot imitate the edge design because the two moulds there unite and leave a burr to be removed with the file. The inscriptions he would have in English alone as, if the multifarious languages of the people among whom it is to circulate ought to be consulted, the rupee must exhibit a polyglot association of Devanagari, Kythee, Maitali [Maithali], Telugu, Bengali, etc.

He thought an English artist of moderate skill would be sufficient to effect the desired reform.

Mr Wigram Money supported Mr Wilson's views and bore evidence that hardly a shroff in Bengal would be found capable of reading or translating even the present Persian inscription. Mr

Wood submitted designs for an impression in the four principal oriental characters, Devanagari, Persian, Bengallee and Telugu, arranged concentrically around and English legend, all five setting forth merely the name, weight and quality of the coin.

He objected to armorial bearings as wholly unintelligible to an Indian population.

Mr Holt Mackenzie thought the reasons for altering the impression fully sufficient to justify the measure and he defined the principles of a new device to be 'good taste, classical simplicity and difficult of imitation, – it concerns the credit of a government', he says, 'to have its coinage as beautiful as possible'. He objected to Company's arms as ugly and senseless and as liable to be altered with any change of government. He objected also to Mr Woods lettered device and thought that the matter would be better settled in England. For himself, he 'would adopt any inscription in lieu of one which declares the coin to be struck at Moorshidabad in the 19th year and under the happy auspicies of a dead defender of the religion of Mohammed'.

He recommended a call on Lieutenant Forbes, which is accordingly the next document on record.

Lieutenant Forbes uses equally strong terms in favour of a change of device 'the advantages of the new mint machinery will be altogether thrown away if the present inscription be retained or any mixture of native and English lettering be substituted.

In 1820 Captain Forbes had been instructed by the local government to consult the Court about the device. Little importance was here attached to its nature, and the opinion that the natives objected to animals was stated to be without foundation.

He had consulted the first engineers and artists at home who all agreed that the plain Company's arms were insufferably feeble and unmeaning, even with addition of the three lions rampant to ornament the field of the Penang copper coin, and in the hands of the best engravers in London the device turned out 'inelegant and barbarous. The crest lion was taken for a monkey and the supporters for ill designed cats'. When real lions were substituted for the heraldic animals 'the grotesque attitudes and splay footed positions made them look even more undesirably ludicrous'.

With the concurrence of the Court of Directors, Captain Forbes proposed himself 'the simple emblem of the Company, a solitary lion as an appropriate type of sovereignty and as an emblem known and respected wherever British rule has been extended. The ease and dignity and strength which he so nobly personified on some of the coins of ancient Greece would be still more consistent and characteristic when applied to India'. Moreover the lion might be completely localized by the ever flourishing palm, an Asiatic, although ancient, tasteful emblem of perpetuity.

The grouping of the tree and of the animal by giving full scope for the talent of an artist would admit of infinite beauty, and whist it left one table blank for a wreath circumscribing the weight or denomination of the coin, it would have the advantage of being admired even where it was not understood.

He submitted a very elegant design by Flaxman on the above principles and was confident that if approved by the Governor General in Council to whom the Court of Directors had expressly left the final consideration of the subject, it would be in every way acceptable to the Honourable Court.

Lieutenant (now Captain) Forbes also advocated the plain flat milling on the grounds first of its preserving the coin from abrasion incident to serrated and ornamental milling. 2nd because the simplicity of the plain milling best harmonises with the chasteness of such devices as are beautiful or appropriate in coins. 3rd because it is much less expensive in execution.

The members of the Committee highly approved Captain Forbes' design, Mr Money only suggesting the King's head for the reverse. They also adopted the plain edge or that with sunken letters proposed by Mr Wilson, and Mr Mackenzie urged that the legend should be solely in English as more intelligible than the 'barbarous doggerel that now disgraces our rupee'.

The letter of the Committee dated 2nd November 1825 incorporated their sentiments, suggesting further in connection with the question of an uniform currency for the whole of India that the same impression should extend to the Bombay and Madras coinage.

They concluded by recommending that the whole correspondence should be referred home for ultimate decision on the subject, and that an English die engraver should be applied for. The application from the local government to the Court for a die cutter and for their final orders respecting the device was dispatched in November 1829, but no reply has been yet received.

A letter from the Court of Directors dated 11th March 1829 generalized the system of copper for the three Presidencies and ordered half annas and pie to be coined, that the couree might be suspended gradually. The same dispatch suggested the preparation of all dies for Madras and Bombay at Calcutta.

In 1830 a reference came from the Bombay Mint as to the device to be adopted under the Courts orders for an assimilation of die. Major Hawkins of the Bombay Mint urgently recommended the King's head on one side and the Company's arms on the other, which was approved of by the mint officers here, but the Mint Committee in consideration of the reference home and the great advantage of having a uniform coinage for the three presidencies, advised that the present impression of the Bombay coins should continue until the final orders arrived, with the expected die cutter, from England.

The Bombay Mint accordingly confined its reform to the pice money.

The new mint at Calcutta was for the like reason compelled to commence work with no other alteration of the gold and silver than that of a plain edge on the rupee, which was adopted on the grounds of its greater facility of execution and saving of 25 per cent in dies.

The upright serrated milling was however afterwards successfully executed for the Madras rupee when a large remittance of that currency was recently ordered to be prepared in the Calcutta mint.

Upon a careful review of all that has been said and written on the subject, I am still in favour of the measure I ventured to propose on the 1st October: namely the appointment of a competent native engraver and the immediate reform of the device here without waiting longer for the reply of the Honourable Court of Directors to the reference made in 1829, which has doubtless been lost sight of in the numerous discussions of more weight and importance that have lately engaged the home Indian Government. The arguments are all before us: The nature of the device is in a measure pointed out by the concurrent testimony of all in favour of a pictorial design in the first instance, and the Company's arms or an emblematic device for the reverse. The question of executing such a device (considering it to be merely a copy from an English original) is set at rest by the labour of the artists whose specimens are before us. The employment of a native in preference to an European, I have already advocated on the principles of economy and manageability (and it must not be forgotten that the recent demand from Bombay for a matrix of the Bombay copper die has resulted in a strike of the English die cutter, to whose caprice the whole establishment was thus rendered subservient). I would add that justice to our Indian subjects ought to be an additional motive to the encouragement of native talent and skill. Should however the Committee and the Government consider it likely that an English artist will be sent out for the Calcutta mint, the appointment here may easily be made provisional, or the person selected may be retained to benefit by his instruction while he will be at all times ready to take his place should death or retirement occasion a vacancy.

*Source:* NAI, Financial Department, Mint Proceedings, November 1833, No. 19, pp. 570-9.

## b. On the Device of the British Indian Rupee

Upon the occasion of my last note on the device of the Indian coin submitted to your Committee on the 8th November wherein I advocated the appointment of Kasinath as Chief Die Engraver of the Calcutta Mint. In order that preparations might be at once made for a reform of the impression on our coin, it was agreed that although this native artist had proved himself competent to the engraving armorial bearings on steel, he might still fail in the much more difficult task of producing a creditable resemblance of the human face. To this I was unable to answer otherwise then by soliciting permission to engage his services for a fair remuneration, in preparing a pair of matrix dies for a specimen coin having on the obverse the head of His Majesty King William IV and on the reverse a suitable device expressing the name or value of the coin and its date in English. I hesitated not to propose this test of Kasinath's skill on the principle before argued, that the device of a King's head must necessarily be copied from some English model and as far as mere copying could go I had such experience of his ability in an engraving that I foresaw little chance of failure.

I have now the honor to submit the result of the experiment with equal confidence that the artist's labours will be found to merit the Committee's approbation.

The obverse of the model coin now presented is a facsimile of the King's head on the English Sovereign with the legend Gulielmus IIII D.G. Britanniarum Rex F.D. I could not procure a Double Sovereign nor a half Crown of his present Majesty, either of which would have been preferable in size for the die of the Rupee.[1]

The reverse consists of a wreath of laurel copied on the reduced scale from a very beautiful English model die in the possession of Capt. Forbes. It is perhaps rather too elaborate for the smaller size of our coin, but that can easily be remedied by the omission of some of the detail.[2] In the centre of the field are the name and the date *One Rupee 1834* and on the margin the same expressed in Nagaree, the Persian and the Bengali languages surmounted by the title of the Honourable Company as delegated Governors of the Country.

Although there may be difference of opinion as to the most appropriate legend to be inscribed on the British Indian Rupee, I believe the general form and character of the present coin will be found to embrace the chief objects prescribed in the Minutes and correspondence of the Mint Committee.

1. It is pictorial, tasteful and by no means easy of imitation.
2. It tacitly expresses the rule of the British monarch without any assumption of a title which might be obnoxious to political discussion.

3. The title of the Honourable Company as the organ of the Government is also introduced and if requisite the name of the Governor-General for the time being may be inserted on the rim where the introduction of letters will be a material safeguard against forgery. The practice of boring and plugging the Rupee is, from its great thickness, become so, common that unless some difficult device can be contrived on the edge, it will be absolutely necessary to increase the diameter considerably to prevent it.
4. The name and value of the coin are given prominently in English. But also in the three other principal characters of India. To these may be added the Telugu or that character may be substituted for the Bengali if thought advisable.

The term 'One Rupee' has been adopted in full expectation that the new Rupees is to be the sole currency of British India and for the same reason no place of coinage has been inserted. A private mark will be sufficient to distinguish the fabrication of each Mint. Another advantage of having the name in English is that the coin may with the permission of His Majesty's Government be allowed to circulate in other British colonies at its intrinsic value of two shillings, having now I trust shewn that the Native die engraver can be found competent to execute any improvement in the impression of our coin, without the necessity of renewing the application made to England in 1829. I beg leave to repeat a few of the advantages and facilities to which the appointment I have advocated will give rise.

The Honourable Court has recently ordered that nothing shall be indented for from home that can be prepared in this country. They will therefore I imagine be gratified to witness the capabilities of an Indian die engraver as saving the necessity of having a professional artist from England and as giving a fair promise of our being able eventually to substitute Native mechanics in other departments of the Mint, wherein English engineers have hitherto been found indispensable.

The perfect alteration in the device and character of the new Rupee would entirely obviate the difficulties of the introduction of the 180 grain coin throughout Bengal even while the Sicca Rupee should be still current in this Province whereas as long as the Sicca and the Farrukhabad Rupees bear nearly the same lettered inscriptions [which few can read] and are only distinguishable by the difference a dotted or a plain rim [of which few are aware] there may be real and serious objections to their being forced into general circulation together. The abolition of the Sicca Rupee can only be gradually effected by suspending its coinage altogether but even should its discontinuance not be determined upon at once, the reservation of the old impression on this species of coin would distinguish it in a manner that could not be mistaken, and the provisions of Regulations VII 1833 fixing the relative intrinsic values of the two would be quite sufficient to prevent any confusion in commercial dealing as long as it should remain a part of the currency.

The device proposed for the Rupee might by substitution of the word 'Mohur' for 'Rupee' be adopted to the gold coin of the Country but for my own part I am inclined to recommend a greater difference between the gold and silver moneys then a mere change of a few letters not read by the great majority of the community.

Firstly because it will prevent the fraudulent practice of gilding the Rupee, a practice more to be apprehended where the coins of the two metals [as in Madras and Bombay] are of the same weight, secondly, because the gold coin, partaking of the character of a medal from its not being the common currency of the country, may with propriety be made a chef d'oeuvre in workmanship and design in accordance with Mr. Holt Mackenzie's just remark that 'it concerns the credit of a Government to have its coinage as beautiful as possible.'

I would therefore recommend for the reverse of the gold coin of India, retaining always the King's head on the obverse, a figured emblematical device such as Captain Forbes has eloquently described in his report dated 27 June 1825 this or a similar design might be surmounted by an appropriate motto to convey the sentiment of India under British protection.

Flaxman's elegant device being already in possession of the

Honourable Court of Directors and an impression of it being with Captain Forbes it will be unnecessary to go to the expense of cutting a die for the purpose of striking off a pattern coin in that metal.

While on the subject of the gold coin I am desirous of impressing upon the Committee the great advantage of adopting the same weight for this coin as has being assumed for the standard of the silver coin namely 180 grains Troy. This has already been done both at Bombay and Madras and it has been frequently recommend here.

A recent examination of a collection of gold coins of the emperors of Delhi from Akbar downwards [which is printed in my paper on the monetary system page 40] shows that, the average value of the gold coins of the empire during the whole interval corresponds very closely with that of the Madras and Bombay Mohur as does that of the Gold Mohurs of the principal Native Princes at Lucknow, Hyderabad, Jypoore, Bhopal, Kota, Oojyn etc. on the other hand there is not one gold coin which assimilates with the Calcutta Mohur. The nearest to it is the Mohur of Surat and Boorhanpoor [from 2 to 3 per cent better than the Madras Mohur], but that has been long since superseded by the Bombay Mohur.

This subject was not brought forward when I addressed the committee on the equalization of the Farrukhabad and Madras Rupees because the adjustments then proposed and subsequently adopted were of a minute nature not affecting the current value of either as a coin while the change of the Gold Mohur will make a deterioration in its value of 13¾ per cent, which without some very conspicuous alteration in the impression at the same time, might prove a source of serious inconvenience to the public.

The adoption of the measure as a part of the present reform, however, can lead to no such embarrassment, on the contrary it will be rendered almost necessary, because when the gold coins of all the presidency bear the same pictorial device, it will be impossible otherwise to avoid the evil of pieces similar in appearance, but of different weights circulating together.

In my first note I proposed a modification of the Bombay copper coin impression as a suitable device for our own copper currency. Circumstances prevented the accomplishment of the object at the moment but that it may not be lost sight of I have had engraved by Kasinath a design for the Bengal quarter anna or pysa of 100 grains on that principle. I think the retention of the Honourable Company's armorial bearings on this piece will be essential advantage in preventing the copper coin from being whitened or gilded over and passed on the unwary as a silver or gold coin. The present gold mohur of Madras is objectionable in this respect, bearing on one side the same armorial device as the double pysa.

Having thus ventured to submit a general and simple series of designs for the equalized currency of British India, supported and indeed founded upon the valuable opinions of the officers of the home and of the local Government on record in the Proceedings of your Committee, I can not refrain from urging the palpable advantage of bringing the measure into operation upon the promulgation of the new charter. It must indeed require some time to make the requisite preparation of dies and other apparatus but it would answer every purpose were the public notification of the intentions of Government to be made coeval with that Epoch of British Indian rule.

It must not be supposed that the change of system would involve the necessity of a recoinage of the present extensive circulating medium of the country. It is, however, satisfactory to be able to shew that even such an extreme measure could be resorted to, without any loss to Government, by bringing into action the new process for the extraction of the small portion of gold which is known to exist in almost all the silver current in Eastern countries.

It is unnecessary at present to enter into a minute account of this process, but I may explain in general terms that the silver of the Indian coin contains about 1/5 per cent in weight or nearly three percent in value of pure gold. This can be separated by dissolving the silver in an acid incapable of acting on the more precious metal nitric acid is too expensive for the process, but concentrated sulphuric acid is made in Europe so cheap that it can be profitably employeed for the purpose and it is now invariably the practice on importing silver specie or bullion from India or China into England to separate the gold by this method, if upon assay it to be found to contain a sufficient proportion to pay the expense of the process.

The China merchants have more than once complained that the Calcutta Mint did not give them credit for the value of the gold in the Sycee silver but until provided with the means of separating the metals such could not be done.

The refineries at the new Mint are constructed on the old principal for the nitric acid process; now nitric acid costs 1 rupee per seer, whereas sulphuric acid in England costs but 2d a lb or a little more than an anna per seer. The former is therefore quite inapplicable to the present object. The nitric acid apparatus cannot be adapted to the sulphuric acid process because of the high heat requisite to boil the latter acid, which would endanger the thin glass vessels, and risk by their fracture a very serious loss.

In England and France platina vessels are known are used for boiling the sulphuric acid, their first cost is large but they are liable to no injury from fire or acid. It seems so desirable that this mint should possess a complete set of the platina apparatus[3] particularly with reference to the eventual reform and recoinage of the India currency, that I have requested Mr. Curnin, the Assistant Assay Master who has had opportunities of seeing the whole process at home, to draw out an estimate of the expense of setting it up, including a sulphuric acid chamber for the preparation of the acid in sufficient quantities for a daily refinage of 50,000 tolas of silver and I would recommend that this subject should be brought to the notice of the Honourable Court of Directors and the same time that the specimens of the proposed new coin are submitted for their approval.

In conclusion I beg to submit to the Committee a copy[4] of a printed essay on the system of Coins and Weights of India prepared by myself in conformity with the directions of Government on the promulgation of Regulation VII 1833.

I have condensed into it all the information which I could obtain on the subject of the Native Coins and as all weights and values are expressed in the newly adopted units 'the tola' and the '180 grain rupee'. The circulation of this document as an appendix to the scientific journal of which I am Editor will it is hoped materially assist in making known the advantages of the new system and in establishing the desired uniformity of weights and coins throughout the British territories in India.

One hundred fifty copies have been required by Government for circulation to its revenue officers.

Standard tolas of silver have also been adjusted with the greatest possible care for deposits in the Collector's office and the series brass weights of the standard seer and pusseree are under preparation in the Mint for a similar purpose.

*Source:* NAI, Financial Department, Mint Proceedings (India), January-December 1834, dated April 1834, No. 3, pp. 304-12.

## c. Note on the Name of the New Rupee

Babu Ramcomul Sen has brought to my notice that the Bank of Bengal is about to order out new plates for its notes with the words 'Company's Rupee' in English, Mehajani, Persian, Nagari and Bengali upon the field, in accordance with the Act VII, 1835

Now, the great object in equalizing the rupee of the three presidencies was to remove all distinction and make the term 'Rupee' in British India what the term 'Pound' or 'Shilling' is in England that it should have but one meaning; and that therefore nothing more than the single word 'Rupee' need be inserted in any account or document, as that one word alone (ONE RUPEE) and not 'one Company's rupee' is inserted on the coin itself. Where any distinction from other coin should be requisite the word Company's (or the native name already adopted of 'Badshahee', implying King's head) rupee would naturally be used as 'Sterling' is applied at home.

To affix this word [i.e. 'Company's' or 'Badshahee'], however, to the bank note, will, I conceive, have the bad effect of perpetuating an inconvenient and useless expression, besides, the notes so titled will not be payable in Farruckhabad rupees of late coinage nor in Madras, Bombay or Sagur rupees, all of which are now legally the same as declared by the proclamation.

The term 'Company' also in the native languages having already an adjectional termination can only be introduced substantively in the possessive case; thus *Kampanee ka do sou rupye* [also spelt out in native script] means rather 'the Company's two hundred rupees' rather than 'two hundred Company's rupees'; besides, the expression admits of another equivocal interpretation which, though founded on a pun, may be awkward at the moment of issuing a rupee worth only 15 annas; Kum-pana, 'to receive less', will be the obvious reading of the poor fellow who draws his tulub by tale.

I would earnestly suggest the propriety of addressing both the Government and public establishments recommending the use of the word 'Rupee' alone – at the headings of accounts, on notes etc. This will sufficiently distinguish them from the former varieties which have all had some cognomen or other – as Sa [Sicca], Fd [Farrukhabad], Sonat etc.

The universal British Indian rupee will require no such definition. If any term be used in conversation, I would rather 'New Rupee' be adopted, because 'new' will be dropped of itself when its use ceases.

*Source:* British Library, IOR P/162/86, dated September 1835, no. 9.

## d. Reasons for Reforming the Currency

*First: The expediency of establishing one uniform rupee for the British Dominions in India is evident. The disadvantage now felt and that would be removed thereby are the following:*

First. The trouble to public offices in the calculation of *batta* for the adjustment of receipts and payments. This may seem a trivial circumstance to be put first on the list, but in the management of debt it is very important the interest being payable in all parts and at all presidencies, and whenever a cash loan is opened subscriptions being received everywhere in the currency of the place. The pay of man and officers in the military service has likewise to be issued in all manner of various currencies according to the place where they are serving and that adjustment besides the trouble it gives produces not unfrequently much discontent so in the negotiation of Bills of Exchange etc. and most of all in the case of bullion remittances.

Second. The confusion in the bazaars from the number of Rupees current and the requries frauds and impoutions practiced by money changers and others in consequence on travellers more especially none of these abuses could exist if the currency throughout India were uniform nor if there were one rupee of the British Government distinguished from other miscellaneous coins and it were everywhere to be received and issued at its par without *batta.*

Third. The confusion at out colonies like Singapore, Mauritius etc. where the Persian legend of the different coins is not legible and the difference between each as for instance between the Moorshedabad and Farrukhabad is not distinguishable. This confusion prevents the Government coin of India being received generally at such colonies for local circulation, and has a tendency to produce a disparagement and depreciation of all coin of the same denomination though known to be of true weight and touch each separately after its kind.

Fourth. The coin of one part of India is not at present promptly available to relieve the wants of other parts, for if sent in kind it has generally to be in recoined before it can be turned to account which is attended with considerable expense as well as much loss of time. The Government having now provided steamers to command the means of rapid conveyance its facilities of finance would be much increased by having the coin also everywhere the same. This needs not to be enlarged upon.

Fifth.But the difficulties merchants and especially small dealers experience in ordinary commerce from the difference of coins and the impossibility of rapidly transmitting bullion far exceed those of Government and from a great obstruction to trade.

*Second head: For the uniform currency the Arcot or Madras rupee is the preferable coin to select.*

First, because it weighs 180 grains and which has been fixed upon as the weight of the tola the unit of the pondcrary system of India according to which the man or maund exactly equals 100 pounds Troy, and weighs 3,200 Arcot Rupees – that is 80 Rupees to the seer.

Secondly, because of all the Government Rupees current it has the most extensive circulation being the rupee of the entire Madras Presidency and being of the same weight and value with the Farrukhabad Rupees which is current more than one-half of the Bengal Provinces, besides which it corresponds almost exactly with the old coin of Bombay, and the new coin there has been made to conform with it precisely so that it is convertible into all these currencies without any *batta* or difference of exchange.

Thirdly, because the Arcot rupee is so nearly equal in intrinsic value to two shillings English that in all British colonies it will pass as two shillings piece. Its intrinsic value relatively to the Calcutta Sicca Rupee would give it a *batta* of precisely one anna which would be equally convenient.[5]

Fourthly, because where the choice is between coins of different value which is to make the universal coin every motive of policy suggests that the selection of the less valuable. The coin first comes into notice through its issue from the Government treasury. In the Government were to choose a coin of high-value than usual everybody dependent on such issues for income and the means of living would receive so many fewer rupees in tale. They would be dissatisfied because for some time there bazar expenses and wages of their servants would not settle down into the due proportion for the new coin. Receiving therefore less than their 100 or 1,000 rupees they would still have to pay their servants the same 3-4-8 or 10 rupees without deduction for the difference of intrinsic value. Hence they would be general dissatisfaction and discontent and all that received salary or lived on the interest of the Public Debt in other words the influential classes of the community would be the first to raise the clamour. As applied to the Army the unpopularity of a measure fraught with reduction in the nominal pay of the troops may be conceived. The precise contrary effect is produced by commencing payments in a coin where the payees have the Batta to receive, and as the revenue payees continue at their option to make payments in the old coin until it disappears gradually from circulation which will not be for years to come they feel not the inconvenience of the Batta being against them in the Tale.

Fifthly, Because the pay of the Army is already fixed in the Sonat rupee and that of Civil Servants has been regulated by the same scale in proportion for the general adoption of this rupee for the coin of British India.

Sixthly, The issue of pay to both services would be with the new Rupee at par with the Sonat as is now the case with the Farrukhabad rupee which would be attended with a saving to Government of two per cent in all issues made from the Treasuries of Bengal and Behar on these accounts.

*Third head: If a general coin be established for British India the device should be different and easily distinguishable for any existing coin.*

Because first, if nearly corresponding in figure and appearance with any current coin or with any coin likely to be current a faithful source of imposition will be opened attended with gain to none but the money changers at the expense of the rest of the community.

Because secondly the existing confusion in out Ports like Singapore and Mauritius from the different value of the different rupees current can only be got over and removed by the substitution of a coin markedly different from anyone of those in use, all of which are depreciated and receive with distrust from their family likeness and known variety of intrinsic value.

Because thirdly the present coin is very defective being so thick and liable in consequent to be drilled and otherwise exfoliated and this is a defect, common to all the rupees of India.

Because fourthly the opportunity should be taken to improve the coin in all respects by making it of a device not easily imitated creditable in taste and workmanship, and ornamental as far as may be practicable.

Because fifthly by enlarging the size of the coin and making it proportionately thinner the means will be afforded of applying the common test of its ring or sound in vibration as a certain criterion of the goodness of the coin. This cannot be done with the existing currency the because the thickness of the rupee makes liable to be dum[b] in case of any blisters or other accident to break the continuity of the metal and because out of the coin now current as large a proportion as 10 per cent is stated in the recent letter of the Mint Master to be dumb that is yielding no sound in vibration.

*Fourth head: The device adopted should be pictorial and essentially English and for preference the head of the reigning King of England.*

First. The pictorial device is important as a security against imitation the commonest seal cutter of any Mofussil town of India could imitate without difficulty the Persian inscription upon the rupees hitherto coined at all three presidencies. The dies have indeed been cut by people of this description but of new dies of ingenious device be prepared by the most accomplished engravers of the day, the imitation of them will be beyond the art of ordinary practitioners more especially as from the abandonment of the Persian inscription the work will be no longer of the peculiar kind with which they are most familiar.

Second. That the King's head is the best device to adopt will be evident on consideration that it is and has been the practice in various parts of Asia as in Europe to strike on the coin a likeness of the reigning sovereign, a practice only discontinued after the Muhammadans conquest and within the track of country brought by the Muhammadans under subjection. If the Persian distich of Shah Alum and all other Persian inscriptions be abandoned than either the Sovereign's head or armorial bearings or some allegorical device must be adopted. The two last would be quite unintelligible to the great body of the people, and to the Muhammadans allegory is Idolatry. The natural and simple device therefore is the King's head and the adoption of this universal method of perpetuating the remembrance of each reign is of great advantage to History as has been experienced in many instances where the existence of Dynasties has been ascertained and the verification of dates and other important facts has been made through coins of the period discovered long after.

But thirdly the most obvious and important reason of stamping on the coin some emblems of the British sovereignty in India by preference the head of the reigning King is this, that whereas many petty rajas and all the Muhammadan courts have the privilege of coining, a privilege of which they could not justly be deprived it is necessary not only to adopt a coin that shall be entirely distinguished from any coin by these, but to adopt such a device as shall entitle us to forbid any but ourselves from striking it. It is the only other day that the Bombay Government represented the inconvenience and loss that had resulted from one of the petty chiefs of that side of India having adopted a device nearly similar to the Bombay Rupee; but of very inferior value, the consequence of which was that the base coin head effectually driven the Government currency out of use in the district and capital city of Poona. If the British coin bear the device of His Majesty's Head, all native courts or chiefs may be left in the free enjoyment of their privilege of coining after their own fashion, the pieces struck at their mints will have local circulation like the counters or copper coins of the British manufacturies but never can interfere with the general circulation established through India by means of the mints and Treasuries of the British Government all using one coin of British device.

*Fifth head: It is important nay necessary that the change of the coin if determined upon should be made immediately.*

Because first the sovereignty of the King of England over India has now been broadly declared by the act of Parliament and promulgated over the world, after which to continue striking coin with the unmeaning distich of Shah Alam is ridiculous if it been not less. Majesty Wooder is already expressed throughout India that the British Government has not yet coined in its own name, nay even in Kabool the first question to European traveller was whether this Government coin with its own device the answer in the negative led the questioners to doubt whether the dominions of India was yet really with the English nation.

Because secondly owing to the new discovery of a means of extracting Gold from silver through the agency of highly concentrated sulphuric acid it is desirable immediately to set a distinguishing mark on the coin of the Mint for it is worthwhile to subject silver to the process if there be mixed with it as much as 5 gr. in the lb. Troy and individuals will do this hereafter for the sake of the profit before importing their Bullion only a small proportion therefore of the silver that may hereafter be brought to be coined will be found to contain any gold at all, whereas all the coin that has been coined for these 50 years has such a proportion as to yield by its abstraction enough to pay the expense of recoinage. If the mint go on coining Rupees of the old device undistinguishable from the current and containing gold, these rupees being of disaureated silver will be so mixed with the currency as to destroy the profit that might be made by separating and subjecting to the new process those coined before its discovery. This is a very important circumstance deserving immediate consideration.

Because thirdly the only reason that restrains the Government from at once adopting the measure recommended is the positive order issued by the Court of Directors so far back as the year 1829[6] against making any alterations in the device of the coin without their approval and permission previously obtained. But these orders cannot be construed as a perpetual prohibition against taking a measure called for by a present exigency and more especially must they be considered as much qualified if not entirely superseded by the new legislative act which has conferred full powers of Legislation on the Supreme Council of India and has left to it so broadly the initiative in all measures of internal policy. The Government must take the step, if the exigency be such as to require something be done. If disapproved the home authorities may then, seeing what has been done, shape their instructions upon a full view of the circumstances, and with a better insight into the probable effects and consequences, then they would possess, if attempting to frame before hand in England a course of action for a case they must necessarily see but imperfectly.

There are many questions which it is desirable that the Home authorities should not commit themselves upon without very sure grounds. By the Government's taking the initiated the power is deserved to the Home authorities of stepping in to apply the remedy in case of the measure failing, or of dissatisfaction discontent or confusion following, such as to make it desirable to replace the step. There are reasons why reform of the coinage should be looked upon as one of these questions. It cannot be doubted that all in England would desire that a British coin should form the currency of India, the time and the mode, and the form in which the attempt should be made to effect this desirable and much desired object must surely be questions for determination in India.

But the specific grounds of objection urged by the Honourable Court the motives which induced the Court to hesitate upon in the adoption of the reform suggested when the plan was laid before them deserved to be more fully entered upon and discussed.

On this account an abstract of the entire dispatch of the 11th March 1829 is annexed.

It will be observe that the court, treating the question as a general one, and not being aware of any circumstances to call for a prompt decision or to require the step to be taken at one time rather than another, discussed fairly and very ably the relative advantage of the two methods of completing the desired uniformity of the coin, viz., either by raising other coins to the standard of the Calcutta Sicca Rupee, or reducing the latter to the standard of the Arcot, with which all others had been assimilated. The preferableness of the latter course being admitted, the following difficulties are stated in a complaint that neither the Government not the Mint Committee had considered the measure sufficiently in its general operation and its bearing on the financial transactions of the Government its receipts and payments. If the Calcutta Mint were to coin Arcot in lieu of siccas of the 19th Sun, the difference of intrinsic value being 6½ per cent one of two courses must be pursued. Either the new rupee must be received and issued at par with the Calcutta siccas or with a *batta* equivalent to the difference of value.

If received at par the Government would sacrifice permanently the difference of revenue, wherever its demand is settled forever at a fixed amount of Sicca Rupees for the land revenue in the lower provinces of Bengal.

If received with a *batta* zamindars would have to pay more than the tale amount of their tahoods or engagements and might complain that the perpetual settlement had been violated.

Issues again are the three great classes:

First to the Army whose pay is regulated in Sonats a nominal coin bearing to the Calcutta Sicca the proportion of 95.11 of the latter to 100 Sonats.

Second to civil servants and pensioners whose allowances were than regulated for the most part in Sicca Rupees, but some as the King's judges and members of Council by act of Parliament in pound sterling.

Thirdly on account of the debt which has been all constructed on Calcutta Siccas. The Army, the court remarked, might be paid in Arcots at par with Sonats without a murmur. The Farrukhabad Rupees having long being issued at par in such payments though deficient in value 2 per cent.

But the public officers whose salaries were fixed by the act of Parliament would be entitled to claim the full *batta* of the intrinsic value, and if given to them, it could not be refused to other public servants and pensioners, whose allowances had been fixed in Sicca Rupees. If given to civil officers, the Army would be discontented, and the court could see no means of getting over this embarrassment.

Again the interest and principal of the debt and Bills of Exchange, etc., must be discharged and adjusted at the intrinsic par value of the new rupee which would breed discontent if a different rate prevailed for them and for other payments.

These were the difficulties which appalled the Court of Directors, and led to the Government being prohibited from taking the step admitted to be so much desired to assimilate the currencies of India.

It is now proposed to issue and receive the new currency at par with Sonats in transactions with the Army.

To adjust Revenue engagements and the interest and principal of the Debt contracted for in Calcutta Siccas at the par of the intrinsic value, viz., 6½ per cent that is to establish the new Arcot Rupee as the equivalent of 15 annas of the sicca and to make it a legal tender at the rate.

But salaries, pensions and other payments and optional issues, that government can be considered to be entitled to regulate will be made at the rate of payments to the Army, viz., 114½ of the new rupees for 100 Calcutta Siccas.

It remains to be shown how the difficulties stated by the Court of Directors will be removed by this arrangement.

First for of the revenue Tahoods. As one will be under obligation to make payments in the new rupee and since many years must pass before all the coin that has been circulating for 50 years at least in Bengal will disappear no one will consider it a hardship or be entitled to complain if required to pay in the new rupees at their *batta* seeing that the option of being the old will always remain.[7] The zamindars will of course require the same *batta* from the under tenants and it is rightly they should do so. But these will have the same option of paying in old Calcutta Sicca so that while the new Rupees will be retained to perform the operations of the local currency the old will always be reserved for revenue payments and so come into the treasury for recoinage until they entirely disappear which for effecting the conversion is exactly what the Government will require. It is assumed that the recoinage will be paid for by the gold extracted and therefore that no new seignorage will be necessary to protect Government from loss in this operation and if it be desired further to expedite and force the conversion the Mint may be opened for the exchange of new coin for old at its par value without seignorage which would soon effect the object and would further entirely remove all objection to the increased tale by providing a ready means of exchange without fluctuation of *batta*.

If the new rupee to be received in payment of the land revenue at 4½ per cent which is the *batta* of the Farrukhabad Rupee it would be received above its par and all payments would be made in it instead of in Calcutta Sicca which is wanted for recoinage. The new rupee would in that case not penetrate into the petty dealings of the interior but would remain at the Sudder station to be gathered up every month by the Mahajans and money dealers for revenue payments and to be reissued again by the Collectors in salaries or in discharge of Calcutta Bills of Exchange to the same parties thus making a confined circuit that would defeat or much impede the success of the proposed measure.

But the Court remarked that the zamindars may appeal to the course followed at Benares when the value of that rupee was lowered to the standard of the Farrukhabad and no demand of *batta* made in consequence.[8]

The reply is that in that case the difference was only about one per cent and the rupees had always been received and issued at par relatively one to the other. It would have been therefore both invidious and unjust only to apply the *batta* where it made in favor of Government that is in the Revenue Demand. The difference of 6½ per cent, however, is much too great for the two coins ever to circulate or to be received and issued at par. In like manner therefore as the Government will pay the interest of its Bonds and engagements contracted in Sicca Rupees at the *batta* of intrinsic value so will it be entitled to require the same from the zamindars when they shall chose to make their payments in these rupees. The same rate will be fixed as the legal tender for the discharge of Bonds and obligations contracted by individuals in Sicca Rupees and the relative value of the two coins will at once be recognized and established. The Government will commence first by increasing to everyone the tale receipt of his interest on the public debt and this will effectually prevent any murmur at the increased tale demand for revenue more especially considering the option which will remain to all of paying in old rupees. This circumstance is never adverted to by the Court and seems eventually to meet the difficulty stated in respect to the Land Revenue Demand of the Lower Provinces.

Second, the issues to the Army to the civil service and to pensioners will be in the new coin at the rate of Sonats or relatively to the Sicca Rupee 104½ for 100. Public officers paid under the provisions of an act of Parliament will exclusively be entitled to the *batta* of intrinsic value, viz., 6½ per cent. These latter are few and it is well known that they have a legal demand on the Government similar to those who hold its Bonds. The distinction in their favor will therefore not be invidious while all others have been prepared by the measures already adopted to have the Farrukhabad Rupee recognized and proclaimed everywhere as the Sonat. The measure to these is precisely similar to adding two per cent to the seignorage on the coin as the salaries of civil servants have now been fixed in Sonats in order that there may be no invidious distinctions or difference in the mode of treating them and Army all the embarrassments so strongly dwelt upon by the Court of Directors and which appears to have been the principal motives of the court's hesitation to sanction the measure are effectually removed. To both classes and to all who depend for income upon issues from the public treasury it cannot but be both acceptable and popular that they should receive more than the usual tale amount of coin for their monthly expenses. To them it can be no hardship that the difference or Batta does not exactly equal the intrinsic value, for no account will for a longtime be taken of so small a percentage nor in ordinary Bazar dealings isn't difference of one or two per cent ever considered as will be apparent from observing the wide rates at which coins of various denominations and values fluctuate at different times in Bazars where they have currency, as in those of Central India.

The necessity therefore of any tale increased to the Army and to the civil service of Bengal in case of the adoption of the Arcot Rupee for the general coin of British India being obviated, the objections of the Honourable Court of Directors which in the para 35 of the letter cited and whereof an abstract is annexed, are stated to rest mainly on the apprehended necessity for this late increase will entirely disappear.

The measure must be judged separately upon its own merits as it may be thought desirable or the contrary to effect the object proposed proper or not so to make the attempt expedient or rather of urgent necessity to commence promptly and without further delay, or susceptible of reference for decision to the Home Authorities. The grounds of hesitation stated by the Honourable Court clearly do not exist at present. The question must be decided therefore as any other before Government and subject of course to the usual responsibilities and controlled and means of correction in case of an erroneous decision.

*Source:* NAI, Financial Department, Mint Proceedings (India), vol. 21, November 1834–23 December 1835, dated 12 January 1835, no. 3, pp. 56-68.

## Notes

1. Unfortunately that cracked in the process of hardening it but although thus materially injured, enough of the face remains to enable one experienced in such matters to judge of the execution.
2. It must be borne in mind that these two dies are just as they came from the engraver not even polished on the field the connectors would be improved on the punch die before taking up the working dies there from moreover the dotted edge is too much raised this was done at the Mint and Kasinath is therefore not responsible for these trifling blemishes.
3. Perhaps vessels of Earthen ware might be found to answer or even of Gold if Platina be found too costly. The Gold will always retain its value.
4. Vide separate paper.
5. The Farruckabad Rupee contains of pure silver 165 grains.
   The New English Shilling 80.70
   The first therefore equals 2,0322 or 3¼ hundredth more than twice of the second.
   Thus the intrinsic par compared with the new shillings makes the 1 Fd [Farrukhabad] Re –2[sh.]0[d.]½[p.] nearly but allowing for the seignorage in India and England and for the preference given to coin of the latter 2sh may be assumed as the commercial par in British colonies which used the coin of England. It is to be observed that gold being the measure of value in England. The real commercial par between the silver coin of that country and India or any other country that uses silver cannot be ascertained without reference to the price of gold at the time of enquiry.
6. 11 March 1829 and of para 36. We therefore positively direct that no measures be adopted in respect to the alteration proposed in any of its parts nor any other alteration of the currency without previous communication with us on the subject. See abstract annexed.

7. On this point see the Minute of the Governor-General dated 3rd November 1829 forwarded to Court of Directors 16th November of that year but not yet acknowledged or answered.
8. See the Governor-General's Minute above referred to for the observations on this point also.

# 5

# Acts, Proclamations, Declarations and Notifications of the Government of India Concerning the Coinage, Currency and its Legal Tender (1835-56)

## a. Act No. XVII of 1835

*Passed by the Honourable the Governor-General of India in Council on the 17th August* 1835

I. *Weight standard and denomination of silver coins*: BE it enacted, that from the 1st day of September, 1835, the undermentioned silver coins *only* shall be coined at the mints within the territories of the East India Company: a rupee, to be denominated the Company's rupee; a half-rupee, a quarter-rupee, and a double rupee; and the weight of the said rupee shall be 180 grains troy, and the standard shall be as follows:
$^{11}/_{12}$ or 165 grains of pure silver,
$^{1}/_{12}$ or 15 grains of alloy;
and the other coins shall be of proportionate weight and of the same standard.

II. *What impression to bear*: And be it enacted, that these coins shall bear on the obverse the head and the name of the *reigning* sovereign of the United Kingdom of Great Britain and Ireland, and on the reverse the designation of the coin in English and Persian, and the words 'East-India Company' in English, with such embellishment as shall from time to time be ordered by the Governor-General in Council.

III. *What may be a legal tender*: And be it enacted, that the Company's rupee, half-rupee, and double rupee, shall be a legal tender in satisfaction of all engagements, provided the coin shall not have lost more than two per cent. in weight, and provided it shall not have been clipped or filed, or have been defaced otherwise than by use.

IV. *Relative value of the Company's with other rupees*: And be it enacted, that the said rupee shall be received as equivalent to the Bombay, Madras, Furruckabad, and Sonat rupees, and to fifteen-sixteenths of the Calcutta sicca rupee; and the half and double rupee respectively shall be received as equivalent to the half and double of the above-mentioned Bombay, Madras, Furruckabad, and Sonat rupees, and to the half and double of fifteen-sixteenths of the Calcutta sicca rupee.

V. *How the quarter-rupee may be legally tendered*: And be it enacted, that the Company's quarter-rupee shall be a legal tender only in payment of the fraction of a rupee.

VI. *Provisos*: Provided, that if in any contract for the payment of Calcutta sicca rupees it shall have been specially stipulated, that if payment be made in the territories of the Madras, Bombay, or Agra presidency, it shall be made in the rupee now current in those presidencies respectively, at a different rate from that above provided with reference to the Calcutta sicca rupee, the contract shall be satisfied by payment within those presidencies of Company's rupees of the amount of Furruckabad, Madras, or Bombay rupees so especially stipulated.

Provided also, that if payment of the principal or interest of the public debt be made for the convenience of creditors at any public treasury other than as stipulated in the notes and engagement of the Government, it shall be competent to the Government to make such payments at the same exchange as heretofore.

VII. *Weight and standard of gold coins*: And be it enacted, that the undermentioned gold coins only shall henceforth be coined at the mints within the territories of the East India Company.

*First.* A gold mohur or 15-rupee piece of the weight of 180 grains troy, and of the following standard, viz.:

$^{11}/_{12}$ or 165 grains of pure gold,

$^{1}/_{12}$ or 15 grains of alloy.

*Second.* A five-rupee piece equal to a third of a gold mohur.
*Third.* A ten-rupee piece equal to two-thirds of a gold mohur.
*Fourth.* A thirty-rupee piece or double gold mohur; and the three last-mentioned coins shall be of the same standard with the gold mohur, and of proportionate weight.

VIII. *What impression to bear*: And be it enacted, that these gold coins shall bear on the obverse the head and name of the *reigning* sovereign of the United Kingdom of Great Britain and Ireland, and on the reverse the designation of the coin in English and Persian, and the word, 'East-India Company' in English, with such embellishment as shall from time to time be ordered by the Governor-General in Council, which shall be different from that of the silver coinage.

IX. *Gold coin not a legal tender*: And be it enacted that no gold coin shall henceforth be a legal tender of payment in any of the territories of the East India Company.

X. *Powers of the Governor-General in Council as to coinage and mints. Copper Coinage*: And be it enacted, that it shall be competent to the Governor-General in Council, in his executive capacity, to direct the coining and issuing of all coins authorized by this Act; to prescribe the devices and inscriptions of the copper coins issued from the mints in the said territories, and to establish, regulate, and abolish mints, any law hitherto in force to the contrary notwithstanding.

*Source*: *Calcutta Gazette*, 19 August 1835.

## b. Act No. XXI of 1835

*Passed by the Honourable the Governor-General of India in Council on the 7th December 1835*

I. *Weight of Copper coins in Bengal*: BE it enacted, that from the 20th day of December 1835, the following copper coins only shall be issued from any mint within the presidency of Bengal:

| | |
|---|---|
| 1. A pice, weighing | 100 grains troy |
| 2. A double pice | 200 grains troy |

3. A pie, or one-twelfth of an anna-piece 33 ⅓ grains troy with such devices as shall be fixed for the same by the Governor-General in Council, according to the provisions of Section X. of Act XVII of 1835.

II. *Value of Copper coins in Bengal*: And be it enacted, that from the said 20th day of December, 1835, the said pice shall be legal tender for 1/64 of the Company's rupee, and the said double pice for 1/32 of the Company's rupee, and the said pie for 1/192 of the Company's rupee.

III. *When Copper coins may be legally tendered*: Provided always, that after the said 20th day of December, 1835, no copper coin shall in any part of the territories of the East India Company be legal tender, except for fractions of a rupee.

*Source*: *Calcutta Gazette*, 19 August 1835.

## C. Act No. XIII of 1836

*Passed by the Right Honourable the Governor-General of India in Council on 23 May 1836*

I. It is hereby enacted, that from the 1st January 1838 the Calcutta sicca rupee shall cease to be a legal tender in discharge of any debt, but shall be received by the collectors of land revenue, and at all other public treasuries, by weight, and subject to a charge of one per cent, for re-coinage.

II. And it is hereby enacted, that from the 1st of June 1836, section 5, Regulation XXV. 1817, of the Bengal Code, which provides that 'the pice struck at the mints of Benares and Furruckabad, agreeably to the provisions of Regulation X. 1809, and Regulation VII 1814, and Regulation XXI 1816, shall be considered as circulating equally with the pice of Calcutta coinage throughout the provinces of Bengal, Behar, and Orissa., and shall in like manner be received as a legal tender in payment of the fractional parts of a rupee of the local currency, at the rate of sixty-four pice for each rupee,' shall be repealed, and the said pice shall be a legal tender only within the provinces and places for which they were respectively coined, as provided by Regulation X. 1809, Regulation VII 1814, and Regulation XXI 1816, respectively.

*Source: Calcutta Gazette*, 28 May 1836.

## d. Proclamation

*Fort William, Financial Department, 23 May 1836*

The Right Honourable the Governor-General of India in Council having this day passed an Act, whereby it is declared, that after the 1st January 1838 the Calcutta sicca rupee shall cease to be a legal tender in payment of any debt or demand, but shall be received at the public treasuries as bullion by weight, and subject to a seignorage duty of 1 per cent, to pay the expense of recoinage; notice is hereby given, that the holders of Calcutta sicca rupees shall be entitled until the said date to pay the same into the General Treasury of Calcutta, and to receive in exchange new or Company's rupees, coined under the provisions of the Act No. XVII of 1835, at the rate of 16 new or Company's rupees for every 15 Calcutta sicca rupees of due weight. The collectors of land revenue will he furnished with the means of similarly exchanging Calcutta sicca rupees for new rupees, and notice will be given by the collector in each district of the date from which the exchange will commence at his treasury; the period to be allowed being in no instance less than three months.

Published by order of the Right Honourable the Governor of Bengal.

(signed) H.T. Prinsep,
Secretary to the Government of Bengal.

*Source: Calcutta Gazette*, 28 May 1836.
*Note:* Republished in *Calcutta Gazette*, 30 December 1837.

## e. Notice

*Fort William, Financial Department, 23 May 1836*

The Right Honourable the Governor-General of India in Council having repealed section 5, Regulation XXV, 1817, under which the privilege of circulation in Bengal and Behar, at the rate of 64 pice to the local rupee, was given to the Trisoolee pice of Benares, it is hereby notified to the holders of pice of this description, that on the delivery of the same at the Calcutta mint, if of proper weight, and not manifestly spurious, they shall receive for every 720 pice paid in, 640 new Company's pice, coined under the Act XXI of 1835, until the 1st July next, but the mint officers will not receive pice in smaller quantities than above stated, that is, of the value of ten rupees for each exchange, and they shall be at liberty to reject as spurious any pice not of due weight and device, or manifestly not coined at a Government mint.

Published by order of the Right Honourable the Governor of Bengal.

(signed) H.T. Prinsep,
Secretary to the Government of Bengal.

*Source: Calcutta Gazette*, 28 May 1836.

## f. Act No. XXXI of 1837

*Passed by the Honourable the President of the Council of India in Council, on the 20th November 1837*

I. It is hereby enacted, that so much of Act No. XVII of 1835 as directs that certain coins issued from the mints within the territories of the East India Company, shall bear on the obverse the head of the reigning Sovereign of the United Kingdom of Great Britain and Ireland, shall be suspended till the Governor-General of India in Council shall, by an order in Council, declare those parts of the said Act to be again in force.

II. And it is hereby enacted, that till the said Governor-General in Council shall make such an order in Council as is aforesaid, the said coins shall bear on their obverse the head of his late Majesty William the Fourth.

*Source: Calcutta Gazette*, 22 November 1837.

## g. Notice to the Mint Master, Calcutta, 21 March 1838

*Fort William, Financial Department*

The Honourable the President in Council gives notice, that the Mint-master at Calcutta has been authorised to receive, until further orders, Madras rupees of full weight, at their intrinsic par, viz., as equal to Company's rupees, without any charge of seignorage for re-coinage.

By order of the Honourable the President in Council.

(signed) H.T. Prinsep,
Secretary to the Government of India.

*Source: Calcutta Gazette*, 28 March 1838.

## h. Public Notice, 9 May 1838

*Fort William, Financial Department, Mint Branch*

The public is hereby informed, that the Mint-master of Calcutta has been authorised, until further orders, to receive Bombay and Furruckabad rupees in like manner as Madras rupees, and generally the rupees issued from any mint of the British Government that may still be a legal tender in any part of India, for re-coinage, without demand of seignorage duty. Rupees of any such coinage will be received by weight, according to the forms of the mint for the receipt of bullion, and if of equal standard, a mint certificate will be granted, entitling the holder to Company's rupees of equal weight. If the coin brought be better than standard, the advantage will be given according to the tables; but counterfeit pieces, as well as drilled, plugged, and other bad coin, will, of course, be rejected. The mint of Calcutta will not, however, receive a less quantity of the coins above specified than 1,000 tolas; but, for the convenience of officers and soldiers, and other persons in public employ, less sums than 1,000 tolas will be exchanged on the same terms at the general treasury, the sub-treasurer having been authorised to collect them for transmission to the mint.

Published by order of the Honourable the President of India in Council.

(signed) H.T. Prinsep,
Secretary to the Government of India.

*Source: Calcutta Gazette*, 28 March 1838.

## i. Act No. XXI of 1838

*Passed by the Honourable the President of the Council of India in Council, on the 27th August 1838*

I. It is hereby enacted, that it shall be lawful for the Governor-General of India in Council, in his executive capacity, to direct the coinage and issuing of any silver coins of a value represented in even annas, or sixteenths of the Company's rupee, provided they be of the same standard as that prescribed for such rupee by the Act No. XVII of 1835, and of proportionate weight.

II. And it is hereby enacted, that the provisions of Act No. XVII of 1835, and of Act No. XXXI of 1837, applicable to the devices, inscriptions and embellishments of the coins coined and issued by virtue of the Act No. XVII of 1835, shall be applicable to the coins which may be coined and issued by virtue of this Act.

*Source: Calcutta Gazette*, 5 September 1838.

## j. Act No. XXXI of 1839

*Passed by the Honourable the President of the Council of India in Council, on the 23rd December 1839.*

An Act for remedying certain Defects in the Statute 9 Geo. 4, c. 74, relating to the Coin

I. Whereas it is expedient to remedy certain defects in the Statute 9 Geo. 4, c. 74, of which the inconvenience is particularly experienced relating to injuries to the coin;

It is hereby enacted, that if any person shall fraudulently clip, file, drill, deface, or debase any current gold or silver coin issued from any mint of the East India Company, or usually received as money in any part of the territories under the Government of the East India Company, with intent to make the coin so clipped, filed, drilled, defaced, or debased, pass for the current gold or silver coin so issued, or usually received as money as aforesaid, every such offender shall be guilty of felony, and shall be liable on conviction, at the discretion of the court, to be transported to such place as the court shall direct, for life, or any term of years, or to be imprisoned for any term not exceeding four years.

II. And it is hereby provided, that it shall not be lawful for any court under the authority of this Act to order the transportation of any person being a native of the East Indies, and not born of European parents, to the eastern coast of New South Wales, or any of the islands adjacent thereto.

III. And it is hereby enacted, that this Act shall extend to all persons and over all places over whom or which the criminal jurisdiction of any of Her Majesty's Courts of Justice within the territories under the Government of the East India Company extends, but not further or otherwise.

*Source: Calcutta Gazette*, 25 December 1838.

## k. Proclamation, 11 November 1840

*Fort William, Financial Department*

The Governor-General in Council is pleased to notify, that from and after the 11th day of November 1840 in respect to the Mint of Calcutta, and from and after the 1st day of April 1841 in respect to the Mints of Fort St. George and Bombay, those parts of Act No. XVII of 1835, which were suspended by Act No. XXXI of 1837, directing that certain silver coins issued from the mints within the territories of the East India Company, shall bear on the obverse the head of the reigning sovereign of the United Kingdom of Great Britain and Ireland, will be again in force; and that the device of the silver coins which shall be coined from and after the said dates respectively in the mints of India, in conformity with Acts XVII of 1835 and XXI of 1838, will be as Act No. XVII of 1835 requires, viz.:

*On the Obverse* – The head of Her Majesty Victoria, with the words, 'Victoria, Queen.'

*On the Reverse* – The denomination of the coin in English and Persian in the centre, encircled by a wreath, and around the margin the words 'East India Company, 1840.'

The coin will be milled on the edge, with a serrated or upright milling, like the rupee now current, bearing the head of his late Majesty William IV.

An engraving of the Victoria device is hereunto annexed, for the information of the public.

The Weight, Standard, Fineness, and Value of the Company's Rupees, as defined in the Act, are here repeated:

*Weight* – 180 grains troy, or one tolah.

*Standard Quality* – Eleven-twelfths silver, one-twelfth alloy.

*Value* – The same as the Company's rupee of 1835, the Madras, Bombay, Furrukabad, and Sonat rupee, and equal to fifteen-sixteenths of the late Sicca rupee.

The other silver coins authorised to be issued from the Government mints by Act No. XVII of 1835, and Act No. XXI of

1838, viz., double, half, and quarter rupees, and two anna pieces, will bear in all respects a due proportion to this rupee.

The Governor-General in Council hereby directs that all magistrates, collectors, and other public officers, will promulgate this proclamation throughout their respective districts, and that a translation of it be affixed in a conspicuous place at every public treasury.

Money changers, shroffs, podars, and others, should be required to take notice of the provision in Act No. XVII of 1835, against clipping, filing, punching, or otherwise defacing the legal coin. The silver coins issued from the mints of Government under Act XVII of 1835, if not cut, clipped, marked, or otherwise wilfully impaired, are legal tender for their full value, until by gradual wear they have lost two per cent, of their original weight.

Published by order of the Right Honourable the Governor-General of India in Council.

(signed) G.A. Bushby,
Secretary to the Government of India.

*Source: Calcutta Gazette*, 14 November 1838.

## l. Notice, 13 January 1841
*Fort William, Mint Department*

It is hereby notified, that officers in charge of treasuries are not to demand seignorage on silver coins of a Government mint because they are defaced by marking or punching, provided only they are of proper weight, or within the limit allowed for circulation.

By order of the Right Honourable the Governor-General of India in Council.

(signed) G.A. Bushby,
Secretary to the Government of India.

*Source: Calcutta Gazette*, 20 January 1841.

## m. Proclamation, 13 January 1841

*Fort William, Mint Department*

The Governor-General in Council is pleased to notify, that the gold coins henceforth to be issued from the Government mints at the different Presidencies in India, in conformity with Act No. XVII of 1835, shall bear the following device:

*On the Obverse* – The head of Her Majesty Queen Victoria, with the words 'Victoria, Queen, 1841'.

*On the Reverse* – A lion, and a palm tree in the centre, with the designation of the coin in English and Persian; below and around the margin the words 'East India Company'.

The coin will be milled on the edge, like the rupee.

An engraving of the device is hereunto annexed.

The weight and standard will be according to the Act as follows:

*Weight of the Gold* – Mohur, or 15 rupee piece, 180 grains troy.

*Standard of the Gold* – Eleven-twelfths, or 165 grains pure gold; 1/21 of 15 grains alloy.

The other gold coins, viz., the 5 rupee, 10 rupee, and 30 rupee or double gold mohur pieces, will be of the same standard as the gold mohur, or 15 rupee piece, and of proportionate weight.

Officers in charge of public treasuries are hereby authorized freely to receive these gold coins at the rates, until further orders, respectively denoted by the denomination of the pieces, until they shall have passed the limits of lightness allowed for wear, and laid down in the annexed table, when they will be only receivable as bullion, and be subject to a deduction of one per cent, for seignorage:

| | *30 Rs.*<br>*grs.* | *15 Rs.*<br>*grs.* | *10 Rs.*<br>*grs.* | *5 Rs.*<br>*grs.* |
|---|---|---|---|---|
| Standard Weight | 360 | 180 | 120 | 60 |
| Limit for Wearage | 3 | 1½ | 1 | –½ |
| Minimum Weight | 357 | 178½ | 119 | 59½ |

The gold coin received in public treasuries will be disposed of as may be ordered by the Accountant-General or the Accountant of the Presidency.

The Governor-General in Council directs that all magistrates, collectors, and other public officers will promulgate this proclamation throughout their respective districts, and that a translation of it be affixed in a conspicuous place at every public treasury.

Published by order of the Right Honourable the Governor-General of India in Council.

(signed) G.A. Bushby,
Secretary to the Government of India.

*Source: Calcutta Gazette*, 10 February 1841.

## n. Act No. XIII of 1844

### *An Act for making Trisoolee Pyce no longer a Legal Tender within the Province of Benares, and for their withdrawal from Circulation*

It is hereby enacted, that from and after the 1st day of August 1844 the Trisoolee pice struck for the province of Benares, under the provisions of Regulations X of 1809, and VII. of 1814, and at the Saugor Mint, shall cease to be a legal tender within the province of Benares.

II. And it is hereby enacted, that until the said 1st day of August 1844 such Trisoolee pice shall be received on account of the Government, and shall be exchanged by tael (that is to say, every Trisoolee pice paid in shall be received as one Company's pice, and one Company's pice shall be given for every Trisoolee pice presented for exchange) at such treasuries or other places within the province of Benares as shall be pointed out for that purpose in any Proclamation of the Lieutenant-Governor of the North Western Provinces.

III. And it is hereby enacted, that immediately after the passing of this Act, the said Lieutenant-Governor shall issue a Proclamation pointing out the treasuries or other places within the province of Benares at which such Trisoolee pice shall be so received and exchanged as aforesaid, and notifying any regulations respecting such receipt or exchange as the said Lieutenant-Governor may deem it expedient to establish for the carrying into effect of the same for the prevention of fraud therein, and especially for the rejection of such Trisoolee pice as may appear to the officer appointed to receive or exchange the same under this Act to be undoubtedly spurious.

IV. And it is hereby enacted, that it shall be lawful for the said Lieutenant-Governor, if he shall see fit, to order that in any case one Company's rupee shall be given for every 64 Trisoolee pice so presented for exchange, and that in every such case one Company's rupee shall be given for every 64 Trisoolee pice accordingly.

*Source: Calcutta Gazette*, 29 June 1844.

## o. Act No. XXII of 1844

*Passed by the Governor-General in Council,*
*on the 28th December 1844*

An Act for regulating the Copper Coinage of the Mints in the Territories of the East India Company.

I. It is hereby enacted, that from and after the passing of this Act, the following copper coins only shall be issued from any mint within the territories of the East India Company:

| | |
|---|---|
| 1. A pice, weighing | 100 grains troy, |
| 2. A double pice | 200 grains troy, |
| 3. A pie, of one-twelfth of an anna piece | 33⅓ grains troy, |

with such devices as shall be fixed for the same by the Governor-General in Council.

II. And it is hereby enacted, that from and after the passing of this Act, the said pice shall be a legal tender throughout the territories of the East India Company for 1/64 of the Company's rupee, and the said double pice for 1/32 of the Company's rupee, and the said pie for 1/192 of the Company's rupee.

III. And it is hereby enacted, that all copper coins of the weights specified in section 1 of this Act which may have been issued since the passing of Act XXI of 1835 from any mint within the

Presidency of Bombay, shall be legal tender respectively for the values specified in section 2 of this Act within that Presidency.

IV. Provided always, that none of the said copper coins shall be legal tender except for fractions of a rupee.

*Source: Calcutta Gazette*, 4 January 1845.

## p. Act No. VI of 1847

*Passed by the Honourable the President of the Council of India in Council, on the 1st May 1847.*

An Act for establishing a Copper Currency in the Settlements of Penang, Singapore, and Malacca.

I. It is hereby enacted, that from and after the date of the passing of this Act, the provisions of Acts XXI. of 1835 and XXII of 1844 shall not be deemed to apply to copper currency of the settlements of Penang, Singapore, and Malacca.

II. And it is hereby enacted, that from and after the 1st day of January 1848, the following copper coins only shall be received at or issued from any Government Treasury within the said settlements:

1. A cent, weighing 144 grains troy.
2. A half cent, weighing 72 grains.
3. A quarter cent, weighing 36 grains.

III. And it is hereby enacted, that from and after the date of the passing of this Act, the said cent shall be legal tender throughout the said settlement for $1/100$ of a dollar, and the said half cent for $1/200$ of a dollar, and the said quarter cent for $1/400$ of a dollar.

IV. Provided always, and it is hereby enacted, that none of the said coins shall be legal tender, except for fractions of a dollar.

V. And it is hereby enacted, that, after the 1st day of January 1848, no other copper coins or tokens than those specified in section 2 of this Act shall be legal tender of payment for the fractional parts of a dollar within the said settlements.

VI. And it is hereby enacted, that, with the exception of the copper coins specified in section 2 of this Act, the circulation in the said settlements, after the said day, of all copper coins or tokens not being the authorised legal coinage of any British or Foreign Government, is prohibited.

VII. And it is hereby enacted, that after the said day any person who shall circulate, or attempt to circulate, in the said settlements any copper coins or tokens other than those specified in section 2 of this Act, and not being the authorised legal coinage of any British or Foreign Government, shall, on summary conviction before a magistrate, be liable to a fine not exceeding ten rupees; and in default of payment, any person so convicted shall be subject to imprisonment for a term not exceeding one month.

VIII. And it is hereby enacted, that it shall be competent to the Governor-General in Council, in his executive capacity, to direct the coining and issuing, and tc prescribe the devices and inscriptions, of the coins to be issued under the authority of this Act.

*Source: Calcutta Gazette*, 1 May 1847.

(signed) *G.A. Bushby*,

Secretary to the Government of India.

## q. Notification, 22 December 1852

*Fort William, Financial Department*

By Section 9, Act XVII of 1835, of the Government of India, it was enacted, that thenceforward no gold coin should be a legal tender of payment in any of the territories of the East India Company, and accordingly gold ceased from the date of the passing of the Act to be a legal tender of payment in the Company's territories in India:

But by a Proclamation, issued on the 13th January 1841, officers in charge of public treasuries were authorised freely to receive gold coins struck in conformity with the provisions of the same Act (XVIL of 1835), at the rates indicated by the denomination of the pieces, until they should have passed certain limits of lightness, set forth in a table published with the Proclamation, or until further orders, and gold coins have been thus received in liquidation of public demands up to the present date;

Notice is now given, that so much of the Proclamation of the 13th January 1841 as authorised the receipt of gold coins into the public treasuries of Government, will be withdrawn, and cancelled from the 1st January 1853, and that on and after that date no gold coin will be received on account of payments due, or in any way to be made, to the Government in any public treasury within the territories of the East India Company. Gold will continue, as heretofore, to be received into any of the mints within the territories of the East India Company for coinage, under the Act and rules at present in force for the coinage of gold; but mint certificates for gold coins will be discharged in gold only, and no such certificate for gold will be accepted in any public treasury in liquidation of public demands, or on account of any payment to the Government whatever.

Published by order of the Most Noble the Governor-General of India in Council.

(signed) J.A. Dorin,
Secretary to the Government of India.

*Source: Calcutta Gazette*, 25 December 1852.

## r. Act No. XI of 1854

*Passed by the Governor-General of India in Council on the 3rd March 1854*

An Act to amend Act No. XXI of 1835, and Act No. XXII of 1844, and to authorise the Issue of Half Pice

Whereas it has been deemed expedient, with reference to the convenience of the public, that copper coins, to be called half pice, should be issued; it is enacted as follows:

I. So much OF Section 1, Act No. XXL of 1835, as enacts that the copper coins therein mentioned only shall be issued from any mint in the Presidency of Bengal, and so much of Section 1, Act

No. XXII of 1844, as enacts that the copper coins therein mentioned only shall he issued from any mint within the territories of the East India Company, are repealed.

II. After the passing of this Act, copper coins, to be called half pice, may be issued from any of the mints in the territories under the Government of the East India Company.

III. A half pice shall weigh 50 grains troy, and shall BE A legal tender in any part of the said territories for a part of the Company's rupee, but shall not be a legal tender, except for fractions of a rupee.

*Source: Calcutta Gazette*, 8 March 1854.

## s. Notification, 24 March 1854

*Fort William, Financial Department*

Notice is hereby given, that the following device has been approved, and ordered by the Most Noble the Governor-General of India in Council, for the half pice pieces to be coined and issued after the date of this notification, and under the provisions of Act XI of 1854, from the mints within the territories under the Government of the East India Company:

*On the Obverse* – The armorial bearings of the East India Company.

*On the Reverse* – The value of the coin in English, half pice, and encircled by a wreath, with the words 'East India Company' round the margin.

The above half pice, being a legal tender for any fraction of a Company's rupee, will be received and issued at the rate of 128 to the said rupee; and the Governor-General in Council further directs, that the said half pice shall be received by public officers, on account of the Government, in payment of any fraction of a Company's rupee, at the rate of 128 of the said half pice to the said Company's rupee.

Copper pice, double pice, and pies of the devices previously established by regulations, will remain current as heretofore.

By order of the Most Noble the Governor-General of India in Council.

(signed) C. Allen,
Officiating Secretary to the Government of India.

*Source: Calcutta Gazette*, 25 March 1854.

## t. Act No. XVII of 1855

*Passed by the Governor-General of India on the 29th May 1855 (communicated to the Legislative Council on the 23d June 1855).*

An Act to improve the Law relating to the Copper Currency in the Straits.

Preamble – Whereas the Company's rupee is by Act XVII of 1836 a legal tender, in Preamble, satisfaction of all engagements, in the settlement of Prince of Wales' Island, Singapore, and Malacca, but no copper coin, except the half pice, issued under Act XI. of 1854, is now by law legal tender for fractions of a rupee in that settlement, and it is expedient to remedy this defect in the law: and whereas, besides the rupee, the dollar is by custom current in the said settlement, and it is therefore expedient to provide that the copper currency, which will be legal tender in the said settlement for fractions of a rupee, shall also be legal tender in the said settlement for fractions of a dollar; it is enacted as follows:

Acts repealed – I. Sections 1, 2, and 5, of Act VI of 1847, are hereby repealed, in so far Acts repealed, as they relate to copper pice, double pice, and pies coined in accordance with Act XXII. of 1844, or Act XXI. of 1835; but in so far as they relate to all other copper coins, the said sections shall remain in full force. And the provisions of sections 1, 2, and 4, of Act XXII of 1844, so far as they are now in force, are hereby extended to the settlement of Prince of Wales' Island, Singapore, and Malacca, where they shall have effect, anything in Act VI of 1847 to the contrary notwithstanding.

Pice legal tender for dollars – II. From and after the first day of July 1855, within the said settlement a Pice legal tender pice, coined according to Act XXII of 1844, shall be legal tender for one one- for dollars, hundred-and-fortieth part of a dollar, and a double pice so coined shall be legal tender for one-seventieth part of a dollar; and a pie so coined shall be legal tender for one four-hundred-and-twentieth part of a dollar; also a half pice coined according to Act XI of 1854 shall *be* legal tender for one two-hundred-and-eightieth part of a dollar.

Proviso – III. Provided always, and it is hereby enacted, that no copper coins within Proviso, the said settlement shall be legal tender, except for fractions of a rupee, or fractions of a dollar.

*Source: Calcutta Gazette*, 27 June 1855.

## u. Notification , 17 March 1856
*Fort William, Financial Department*

It appears that it has hitherto been the practice in some treasuries to treat silver fractions of a rupee less than half a rupee as falling under the operation of section 3, Act XVII of 1835, which declares the rupee, half rupee, and double rupee to be legal tender in satisfaction of all engagements, provided the coin shall not have lost more than two per cent, in weight, and provided it shall not have been clipped or filed, or have been defaced otherwise than by use; but this practice is opposed to section 5 of the same Act, which refers to the quarter rupee, and provides that it shall be a legal tender in payment of the fractions of a rupee, without making any provision in regard to loss of weight of the coin; it is therefore notified, for general information, that four and two anna silver pieces will in future be allowed to pass current, so long as they have lost weight only by fair abrasion; but if they have lost weight from any other cause, they will be treated as bullion.

By order of the Right Honourable the Governor-General in Council.

(signed) C. Hugh Lushington,
Secretary to the Government of India.

*Source: Calcutta Gazette*, 19 March 1856.

# Bibliography


Acemoglu, Daron and James A. Robinson, *Why Nations Fail: The Origins of Power, Prosperity and Poverty* (London, 2012).

Ali, M. Athar, *The Mughal Nobility under Aurangzeb* (Bombay, 1968).

Ambedkar, B.R., *The Problems of the Indian Rupee: Its Origin and Solutions* (London, 1923).

______, *Evolution of Provincial Finance in British India: A Study in the Provincial Decentralisation of Imperial Finance* (Westminster, 1925).

Anderson, Gary M., Robert E. McCormick and Robert D. Tollison, 'The Economic Organization of the English East India Company', *Journal of Economic Behavior & Organization*, vol. 4.2-3 (1983), pp. 221-38.

Andrews, A., *Australasian Tokens & Coins* (Sydney, 1921).

Appadorai, A., *Economic Conditions in Southern India, 1000-1500 A.D.*, 2 vols. (Madras, 1936).

Atkins, J., *Coins and Tokens of the British Possessions and Colonies of the British Empire* (London, 1889).

Atkinson, Fred, 'Rupee Price in india', *JSS*, vol. 66 (1903), p. 116.

______, 'Silver Prices in India', *JSS*, vol. 60 (1897), p. 117.

______, *The Indian Currency Question* (Allahabad, 1894).

Atwell, William S., 'Notes on Silver, Foreign Trade, and the Late Ming Economy', *Chingshih Wen-t'i*, vol. 3.8 (1977), pp. 1-33.

Bagchi, Amiya Kumar, *Colonialism and Indian Economy* (Oxford, 2010).

Bagehot, Waller, *On the Depreciation of Silver* (London, 1877).

Banerji, A.K., *Finances in the Early Raj: Investments and the External Sector* (New Delhi, 1995).

Barbour, David, *The Standard of Value* (London, 1912).

Barrow, Ian, *The East India Company, 1600-1858: A Short History with Documents* (Indianapolis, 2017).

Bates, Crispin, *Subalterns and Raj: South Asia Since 1600* (New York, 2007).

Bernier, François, *The History of the Late Revolution of the Empire of the Great Mogol: Together with the Most Considerable Passages for 5 Years Following in That Empire: to Which Is Added a Letter to the Lord Colbert Touching the Extent of Indostan, the Circulation of the Gold and Silver of the World to Discharge Itself there, As Also the Riches, Forces, and Justice of the Same, and the Principal Cause of the Decay of the States of Asia*, 4 vols. (London, 1676).

Bhadra, Gautam, 'The Role of Pykars in the Silk Industry of Bengal *c.* 1767-1830', paper read at the Indian History Congress, 36th Session, Aligarh, 1975.

Bhandare, S. and P.J.E. Stevens, 'Bombay Billys, the British Coinage of the Malabar Coast: A Reappraisal', *ONS-NL*, Supplement, no. 172 (2002), pp. 1-22.

Bhattacharya, Sabyasachi, *The Financial Foundations of the British Raj: Ideas and Interests in the Reconstruction of Indian Public Finance, 1858-1872*, rev. edn. (Hyderabad, 2005).

Bidie, G., 'The Pagoda or Varaha Coins of Southern India', *JASB*, vol. 52.1 (1883), pp. 33-55.

Bolts, William, *Considerations on India Affairs; Particularly Respecting the Present State of Bengal and its Dependencies: To which is Prefixed, a Map of Those Countries, Chiefly from Actual Surveys, The Second Edition, Aith additions* (London, 1772).

Bowen, H.V., *The Business of Empire: The East India Company and Imperial Britain, 1756-1833* (Cambridge, 2006).

Broadberry, Stephen and Bishnupriya Gupta, 'The Early Modern Great Divergence: Wages, Prices and Economic Development in Europe and Asia, 1500-1800 – Super-1', *HER*, vol. 59.1 (2006), pp. 2-31.

Bruce, John, *Annals of the Honorable East-India Company, from Their Establishment by the Charter of Queen Elizabeth, 1600 to the Union of the London and English East-India Companies, 1707-8* (London, 1810).

Burbank, Jane and Frederick Cooper, *Empires in World History: Power and the Politics of Difference* (Princeton, 2010).

Buttrey, T.V., 'Cut Coins in Canada', *BNJ*, vol. 36 (1967), pp. 176-8.

Caldecott, J.B., 'Coins and tokens of the British Possessions and Colonies', *BNJ*, vol. 9 (1912), p. 419.

——, 'Coins of the Patna Mint Struck by the East India Company', *BNJ*, vol. 3 (1906), p. 61.

——, 'Countermarked Spanish Dollar for Old Canada', *BNJ*, vol. 1 (1904), pp. 353-8.

______, 'The Spanish Dollar as Adapted for Currency in our West Indian Colonies', *BNJ*, vol. 1 (1904), pp. 287-98.

Carus-Wilson, E.M. (ed.), *Essays in Economic History*, vol. III (London, 1902).

Cipolla, Carlo (ed.), *The Fontana Economic History of Europe: The Sixteenth & Seventeenth Centuries* (Glasgow, 1974).

Chakrabarti, Shubhra, 'Intransigent Shroffs and the East India Company's Currency Reforms in Bengal', *IESHR*, vol. 34.1 (1994), pp. 69-94.

Chalmers, Robert, *History of Colonist Currency,* [*sic.*] *A History of Currency in the British Colonies* (London, 1893).

Chapman, S.D., 'Industrial Capital before the Industrial Revolution: An Analysis of the Assets of a thousand Textile Enterprises, c. 1730-50', in Harte and Pointing (eds.), *Textile History and Economic History: Essays in Honour of Miss Julia de Lacy Mana* (Manchester, 1973), pp. 113-37.

Chatterjee, N.L., *Verelst's Rule in Bengal* (Allahabad, 1956).

Chaudhuri, K.N., 'Foreign Trade and Balance of Payments (1757-1947)', in *CEHI*, vol. II, pp. 804-77.

______, 'The Economic and Monetary Problem of European Trade with Asia during the Seventeenth and Eighteenth Centuries', *JEEH*, vol. 4 (1975), pp. 323-58.

______, *The Trading World of Asia and East India Company, 1660-1760* (Cambridge, 1978).

______, 'India's Foreign Trade and the Cessation of the East India Company's Trading Activities, 1828-40', *EHR*, vol. 19.2 (1966), pp. 345-63.

______, 'The East India Company and the Export of Treasure in the Early Seventeenth Century', *EHR* (Second Series), vol. 16.1 (1963), pp. 23-38.

Chitty, A., 'Early Australian Coins', *BNJ*, vol. 4 (1907), pp. 179-87.

______, 'The Australian Gold Coins struck at the Sydney, Melbourne and Perth Mints', *BNJ*, vol. 8 (1911), pp. 365-8.

Claessen, H. and P. Skolnik (eds.), *The Study of the State* (The Hague, 1981).

Coats, Warren L. and Deena R. Khatkhate, *Money and Monetary Policy in Less Developed Countries: A Survey of Issues and Evidence* (Oxford, 1983).

Coryate, Thomas, *Coryat's Crudities: Reprinted from the Edition of 1611. To which are now Added, his Letters from India, &c. and Extracts relating to him, from Various Authors: Being a More Particular*

*Account of his Travels (Mostly on Foot) in Different Parts of the Globe, than any Hitherto Published. Together with his Orations, Character, Death, &c. With Copper-Plates*, 3 vols. (London, 1776).

Coyajee, J.C., *The Indian Currency System, 1835-1926* (Madras, 1930).

Crawfurd, John, *Notes on the Settlement or Colonization of British Subjects in India: With an Appendix of Proofs and Illustrations* (London, 1833).

Cribb, J.E., 'Origins of the Hong Kong Coinage, 1841-1866', read at the Meeting of the British Numismatic Society, London, 27 September 1988.

______, *Money in the Bank: An Illustrated Introduction to the Money Collection of the Hong Kong & Shanghai Banking Corp*oration (London, 1987).

Crosby, Sylvester S., *The Early Coins of America, and the Laws Governing Their Issue: Comprising Also Descriptions of the Washington Pieces, the Anglo-American Tokens, Many Pieces of Unknown Origin of the Seventeenth and Eighteenth Centuries and the First Patterns of the United States Mint* (Boston, 1875).

Dalrymple, A., *Oriental Repertory*, 2 vols. (London, 1808).

Dalrymple, William, 'The East India Company: The Original Corporate Raiders', The Guardian, 4 March 2015. Online edition: https://www.theguardian.com/world/2015/mar/04/east-india-company-original-corporate-raiders. Last accessed: 18 March 2018.

Datta, P., 'Rise of the Calcutta Money Market in Relation to Public Borrowing and Public Credit', in *Calcutta Review*, vol. 46.2, 1933, pp. 171-204.

Davenport, H.J., *The Economies of Enterprise* (New York, 1913).

Dayal Das, 'First Uniform Currency for India', *PIHRC* (Bhubaneswar), vol. 32.1 (1958), pp. 65-76.

De Claremont, A. and J.D. Wheeler, *Spink's Catalogue of British Commonwealth Coins* (London, 1986).

De Leat, Johannes, *De Imperio Magni Mogolis, sive India vera. Commentarius ex variis auctoribus congestus. [Including a 'Fragmentum historiæ Indicæ', based on a Dutch MS. chronicle probably compiled by F. Pelsaert.]* (Lugduni Batavorum, 1631).

Desan, Christine, *Making Money: Coin, Currency, and the Coming of Capitalism* (Oxford, 2014).

Dodwell, H., 'Substitution of Silver for Gold in South India', *IJE*, vol. 3.2 (1921), pp. 183-204.

______, *Calendar of Madras Records: 1740-1744* (Madras, 1917).

Dolley, Michael, 'A Sesquicentennial Note on some Official Restrikes of the British Colonial 1/50 and 1/100 Dollar Patterns dated 1823', *Num. Cir.*, vol. 81 (1973), pp. 290-1.

Doty, R., *The Soho Mint and the Industrialisation of Money* (London, 1998).

Dutt, R.C., *The Economic History of India in the Victorian Age*, 7th edn. (London, 1956).

______, *The Economic History of India under Early British Rule*, 8th impr. (London, 1956).

Hawkins, Edward, *The Silver Coins of England* (London, 1841).

Thomas, Edward, *The Revenue Resources of the Mughal Empire* (London, 1871).

Elliot, H.M. and J. Dawson, *History of India as Told by Its Own Historians*, vol. 4 (Allahabad, 1964).

Elliot, Walter, 'Coins of Southern India', *The International Numismata Orientalia*, vol. 3.2 (London, 1886).

Erikson, Emily, *Between Monopoly and Free Trade: The English East India Company, 1600-1757* (Princeton, 2014). http://press.princeton.edu/titles/10262.html

Esteban, Javier Cuenca, 'The British Balance of Payments, 1772-1820: India Transfers and War Finance', *EHR*, vol. 54.1 (2001), pp. 58-86.

______, 'India's contribution to the British Balance of Payments, 1757-1812', Universidad Carlos III de Madrid, Departamento de Historia Económica e Instituciones, Working Papers in Economic History, No. WP 06-03 (March 2006). Online version: http://www.uc3m.es/uc3m/dpto/HISEC/working_papers/working_papers_general.html (last accessed: 10 February 2017).

Ferishta, Muhammad Q.H.S., *History of the Rise of Mahomedan Power in India, till the year A.D. 1612.* Translated from Original Persian by John Briggs, 4 vols. (Calcutta, 1908).

Ferishtah, Muhammad Qasim Hindu Shah Astarabadi, *Tarikh-i-Ferishtah*, Persian Text, Lithographed edn. (Bombay, 1831).

Foster, W[illiam], 'A Note on the First English Coinage at Bombay', *NC*, 4th series, vol. 4 (1906), pp. 351-7.

______, *English Factories in India*, 13 vols. (Oxford, 1906).

Freehill, M., 'On the Coinage of Australia', *BNJ*, vol. 34 (1965), p. 188.

Furber, Holder, *Rival Empires of Trade in the Orient 1600-1800* (Minneapolis, 1976).

FWIHC, *Fort-William India House Correspondence, 1748-1800*, 21 vols. (New Delhi, 1945-85):
*FWIHC*, vol. I, *Public, 1748-58*, ed. K.K. Datta (New Delhi, 1958).
*FWIHC*, vol. II, *Public, 1758-59*, ed. H.N. Sinha (New Delhi, 1957).
*FWIHC*, vol. III, *Public, 1760-63*, ed. R.R. Sethi (New Delhi, 1968).
*FWIHC*, vol. IV, *Public, 1764-66*, ed. C.S. Srinivasachari (New Delhi, 1962).
*FWIHC*, vol. V, *Public, 1767-69*, ed. N.K. Sinha (New Delhi, 1949).
*FWIHC*, vol. VI, *Public, 1770-72*, ed. Bisheswar Prasad (New Delhi, 1960).
*FWIHC*, vol. VII, *Public, 1773-76*, ed. R.P. Patwardhan (New Delhi, 1971).
*FWIHC*, vol. VIII, *Public, 1777-81*, ed. H.L. Gupta (New Delhi, 1981).
*FWIHC* vol. IX, *Public, 1782-85*, ed. B.A. Saletore (New Delhi, 1959).
*FWIHC*, vol. X, *Public, 1786-88*, ed. Raghubir Sinh (New Delhi, 1972).
*FWIHC*, vol. XI, *Public, 1789-92*, ed. I.B. Banerjee (New Delhi, 1974).
*FWIHC*, vol. XII, *Public, 1793-95*, ed. Amales Tripathi (New Delhi, 1978).
*FWIHC*, vol. XIII, *Public, 1795-1800*, ed. P.C. Gupta (New Delhi, 1959).
*FWIHC*, vol. XIV, *Secret and Secret Committee, 1752-81*, ed. Amba Prasad (New Delhi, 1985).
*FWIHC*, vol. XV, *Foreign and Secret Letters, 1782-86*, ed. C.H. Philips and B.B. Misra (New Delhi, 1963).
*FWIHC*, vol. XVI, *Foreign, Secret and Political, 1787-91*, ed. S.H. Askari (New Delhi, 1976).
*FWIHC*, vol. XVII, *Foreign, Political and Secret, 1792-95*, ed. Y.J. Taraporevala (New Delhi, 1955).
*FWIHC*, vol. XVIII, *Foreign, Political and Secret, 1798-1800*, ed. Fr. H. Heras (New Delhi, 1974).
*FWIHC*, vol. XIX, *Military, 1787-91*, ed. Bisheswar Prasad (New Delhi, 1975).
*FWIHC*, vol. XX, *Military, 1792-96*, ed. A.C. Banerjee (New Delhi, 1969).
*FWIHC*, vol. XXI, *Military, 1797-1800*, ed. S.R. Kohli (New Delhi, 1969).
Gardner, F., 'Some Notes Lin Australasian Currencies', *BNJ*, vol. 22 (1934/7), pp. 17-27.
Garg, Sanjay, *The Sikka and the Raj: A History of Currency Legislations of the East India Company, 1772-1835* (New Delhi, 2013).
———, 'Establishment of Calcutta Mint, 1757', *PIHC*, 51st Session, Calcutta (December 1990), pp. 383-92.

Geertz, Clifford, *Agricultural Involution: The Process of Ecological Change in Indonesia* (Berkeley, 1963).

Glamann, Kristof, *Dutch-Asiatic Trade, 1620-1740* (The Hague, 1958).

Gokhale, B.G., 'Broach and Baroda: Notes on the Economic History of Two Gujarat Cities in the XVIIth Century', *JASBom*, New Series, vols. 43-4 (1968/9), pp. 142-54.

______, 'Capital Accumulation in XVIIth Century India', *JBAS*, New Series, vol. 39-40 (1964/5), pp. 51-60.

Greenberg, Michael, *British Trade and the Opening of* China (Cambridge, 1969).

Guha, Amalendu, 'Raw Cotton of Western india 1750-1860', *IESHR*, vol. 9 (1972), pp. 1-42.

Gupta, A. Das, 'Trade and Politics in 18th Century India', in D.S. Richards (ed.), 1970, pp. 181-214.

Habib, Irfan, 'Potentialities of Capitalistic Development in the Economy of Mughal india', *JEH*, vol. 29 (1969), pp. 32-78.

______, 1961, 'The Currency System of the Mughal empire', *MIQ*, vol. 4.1-2 (1961), pp. 1-21.

Hamilton, C. J., *Trade Relations between England and India, 1600-1896* (Calcutta, 1919).

Harris, John, *Navigantium Atque Itinerantium Bibliotheca: Or, A Complete Collection of Voyages and Travels: Consisting of Above Six Hundred of the Most Authentic Writers . . .*, 2 vols. (London, 1764).

Harris, Joseph, *An Essay Upon Money and Coins* (London, 1757).

Harrison, F.C., 'The Past action of the Government of India with Regard to Gold', *EJ*, vol. 3.9 (1893), pp. 52-61.

Harrison, Joan, 'The Memoirs of John Norton of the Bombay Mint', *The Journal of the Families in British India Society* (*FIBIS*), no. 34 (2015), pp. 18-28.

Herbert, Thomas, *A Relation of Some Yeares Travaile, Begvnne Anno 1626: into Afrique and the Greater Asia, Especially the Territories of the Persian Monarchie, and Some Parts of the Oriental Indies and Iles Adjacent: Of their Religion, Language, Habit, Discent, Ceremonies and other Matters Concerning them : Together with the Proceedings and Death of the three late Ambassadours Sir D.C., Sir R.S. and the Persian Nogdibeg: As also the two Great Monarchs, the King of Persia, and the Great Mogul* (London, 1634).

Heyde, Gilbert C., *Renniks Unofficial Coins of Colonial Australia and New Zealand* (Unley, Adelaide, 1967).

Heywood, N., 'The Coins of the Ionian State', *BNJ*, vol. 4 (1907), pp. 189-92.

Hicks, John, *Critical Essays in Monetary Theory* (Oxford, 1967).

Hopkins, A.G., *An Economic History of West Africa* (London, 1973).

Hossain, Hameeda, 'The Alienation of Weavers: Impact of the Conflict between the Revenue and Commercial Interest of the East India Company, 1750-1800', *IESHR*, vol. 14 (1979), pp. 323-45.

Hume, David, *History of England: From the Invasion of Julius Caesar to the Revolution in 1688: To which is Prefixed, a Short Account of his Life, Written by Himself*, 8 vols. (London, 1822).

Hunter, H.H., *Annals of Rural Bengal* (Calcutta, 1865).

*[The] Imperial Gazetteer of India (1908-31)*, 26 vols. (Oxford, 1908-31), vol. IV: *The Indian Empire: Administrative* (Oxford, 1909).

Jackson, R.P., 'Some Copper Coins issued by the English East India Company and other European Powers in Southern India', *BNJ*, vol. 5 (1908), pp. 341-7.

______, 'The Dominions, Emblems and Coins of the South Indian Dynasties', *BNJ*, 9 (1912), pp. 296-396.

Jervis, Captain, *The Expediency and Facility of Establishing the Metrological and Monetary Systems throughout India on a Scientific and Permanent Basis, Grounded on an Analytical Review of the Weight, Measures and Coins of India . . .* (Bombay, 1836).

Jevons, William Stanley, *Money and Mechanism of Exchange* (New York, 1890).

Johnson, Marion, 'The Cowrie Currencies of West Africa', *JAH*, vol. 11 (1970), pp. 17-49 and 331-53.

Johnson, Marion, Jan Hogendorn and Joanne Lynch, 'The European Cowrie Trade', *Slavery and Abolition: A Journal of Slave and Post-Slave Studies*, vol. 2.3 (1981), pp. 263-75.

Joshi, G.V., *Writings and Speeches* (Poona, 1912).

Kamen, Henry, *The Iron Century: Social Change in Europe, 1560-1660*, revd. edn. (London, 1976).

Keay, J., *The Honourable Company: A History of the English East India Company* (London, 1991).

Kejariwal, O.P., 'James Prinsep: A Little Known Incident of his Life', *IMB*, vol. 32 (1997), pp. 157-63.

Kelly, P., *The Universal Cambist* (London, 1811).

Kerr, Robert, *A General History and Collection of Voyages and Travels, Arranged in Systematic Order: Forming a Complete History of the Origin and Progress of Navigation, Discovery, and Commerce, by*

*Sea and Land, from the Earliest Ages to the Present Time*, 18 vols. (Edinburgh, 1811-24).

Khan, Abdul Majed, *The Transition in Bengal* (London, 1969).

Kuiters, Willem G.J., *The British in Bengal, 1756-1773: A Society in Transition Seen Through the Biography of a Rebel: William Bolts (1739-1808)* (Paris, 2002).

Kumar, Dharma and Meghnad Desai (eds.), *The Cambridge Economic History of India*, vol. II: *c. 1751-c. 1970* (Cambridge, 1970).

Landow, George P., 'The British East India Company – the Company that Owned a Nation (or Two)', *The Victorian Web*, Online Edition: http://www.victorianweb.org/history/empire/india/eic.html. Last accessed: 18 March 2018.

Lane, Frederic C. (ed.), *Enterprise and Secular Change* (London, 1953).

Lane-Poole, Stanley, *The Coins of the Moghul Emperors of Hindustan in the British Museum* (London, 1892).

Lawrence, James, *Raj: The Making and Unmaking of British India* (London, 1997).

Leake, William Martin, *Journal of a Tour in Asia Minor; with Comparative Remarks on the Ancient and Modern Geography of that Country, etc.* (London, 1824).

Levine, David, *Family Formation in an Age of Nascent Capitalism* (New York, 1977).

Lipson, Ephraim, *The Economic History of England*, 3 vols. (London, 1959-61).

Liverpool, Charles, Earl of, *A Treatise on the Coins of Realm: In a Letter to the King* (Oxford, 1805).

Lockyer, Charles, *An Account of the Trade in India Containing Rules for Good Government in Trade, Price Courants, and Tables with Descriptions of Fort St. George, Acheen, Malacca, Condore, Canton, Anjengo, Muskat, Gombroon, Surat, Goa, Carwar, Telichery, Panola, Calicut, the Cape of Good-Hope, and St. Helena . . . : to Which is Added, an Account of the Management of the Dutch in Their Affairs in India* (London, 1711).

Love, H.D., *Vestiges of Old Madras, 1640-1800*, 4 vols. (London, 1913).

Luo, Yu, 'The Monetary Root of Financialisation', *Economic and Political Studies*, vol. 5.1 (2017) – Issue 1: A Special Issue on Financialisation of the Economy, pp. 41-59.

Lyall, Bob and David E. Schenkman, *The Tokens, Checks, Metallic Tickets, Passes, and Tallies of the British Caribbean & Bermuda* (Lake Mary, FL, 1988).

Lyall, R., 'Black Doggs and Silver Bitts: Cuts Plugs and Countermarks of the Caribbean', *BNJ*, vol. 66 (1996), p. 187.

Macleod, Henry Dunning, *Indian Currency* (London, 1898).

———, 'Indian Currency', *The Contemporary Review*, vol. 75 (1899), pp. 552-62.

Macpherson, David and Adam Anderson, *Annals of Commerce, Manufactures, Fisheries and Navigation: With Brief Notices of the Arts and Sciences Connected with Them, Containing the Commercial Transactions of the British Empire and Other Countries from the Earliest Accounts to the Meeting of the Union Parliament in January 1801 . . . with a Large Appendix . . . with a General Chronological Index*, 4 vols. (London, 1805).

Magalhaes-Godinho, Vitorio, *L'économie de l'empire Portugais aux XVe et XVIe Siecles* (Paris, 1969).

Maheshwari, K.K. and Biswajeet Rath (eds.), *Numismatic Panorama: Essays in Honour of Late Shri S.M. Shukla* (New Delhi, 1996).

Marsden, William, *Numismata Orientalia Illustrata: The Oriental Coins, Ancient and Modern, of His Collection Described and Historically Illustrated* (London, 1823).

Marshall, P.J., *East Indian Fortunes: The British in Bengal in the Eighteenth Century* (Oxford, 1976).

———, *Cambridge Illustrated History of the British Empire* (Cambridge, 1996).

Mayhew, Nicholas, *Sterling: The Rise and Fall of a Currency* (London, 1999).

Maynard, E.J., *Tokens of South Africa* (Johannesburg, 1966).

Medick, Hans, 'The Proto-Industrial Family Economy: The Structural Function of Household and Family during the Transition from Peasant Society to Industrial Capitalism', *Social History*, vol. 1 (1976), pp. 291-315.

Mendels, Franklin F., 'Proto-Industrialization: The First Phase of Industrialization', *JEH*, vol. 32 (1972), pp. 241-61.

Milburn, William and Thomas Thornton, *Oriental Commerce, or, The East India Trader's Complete Guide Containing a Geographical and Nautical Description of the Maritime Parts of India, China, Japan, and Neighbouring Countries, Including the Eastern Islands, and the Trading Stations on the Passage from Europe, with an Account of their Respective Commerce, Productions, Coins, Weights, and Measures, their Port Regulations, Duties, Rates, Charges &c.,*

*and a Description of the Commodities Imported from thence into Great Britain, and the Duties Payable Thereon, Together with a Mass of Miscellaneous Information, Collected during Many Years' Employment in the East India Service, and in the Course of Seven Voyages to India and China* (London, 1825) .

Mill, James, *The History of British India*, 3 vols. (London, 1817).

Mitchell, W.C., 'The Rationality of Economic Activity', *JPE*, vol. 18.2 (1910), pp. 97-113.

______, 'The Role of Money in Economic Theory', *AER* (Supplement), vol. 6.1 (1916), pp. 140-61.

Mitra, Debendra Bijoy, *The Cotton Weavers of Bengal, 1757-1833* (Calcutta, 1978).

______, *Monetary System in the Bengal Presidency, 1757-1835* (Calcutta, 1991).

Moosvi, Shireen, 'Money Supply and the Silver Influx in the Mughal Empire – a Fresh Attempt at Quantification', Indian History Congress, 41st Session (Bombay, 1980) (Papers on Medieval History, Presented by Aligarh Muslim University).

Moreland, W.H., *India at the Death of Akbar: An Economic Study* (London, 1920).

Nair, P.T., *James Prinsep: Life and Works*, vol. I (Calcutta, 1999).

Nelson, P., 'The Coinage of Ireland in Copper, Tin and Pewter', *BNJ*, vol. 1 (1904), p. 221.

______, 'The Coinage of William Wood for the American Colonies', *BNJ*, vol. 1 (1904), pp. 265-85.

______, 'The Pre-Revolutionary Coinage of America', *BNJ*, vol. 9 (1912), p. 417.

Om Prakash, 'On Coinage in Mughal India', *IESHR*, vol. 25.4 (1998), pp. 476-91.

Parker, Geoffrey, 'The Emergence of Modern Finance in Europe, 1500-1730', in Carlo Gippola (ed.), 1974, pp. 527-94.

Parsons, H.A., 'A Cut New England Three-pence attributed to the Leeward Islands', *BNJ*, vol. 15 (1919/20), pp. 225-7.

Parsons, H.A., 'The Bombay Pice struck by the English East India Company during the Reign of Charles II', *BNJ*, vol. 20 (1929/30), pp. 251-9.

______, *The Colonial Coinage of British West Africa with the Adjacent Islands* (London, 1950).

Perlin, Frank, 'The Pre-Colonial Indian State in History and Epistemology: A Reconstruction of Societal Formation in the Western

Deccan from the Fifteenth to the Early Nineteenth Centuries', in H. Claessen & P. Skolnik (eds.), 1981, pp. 275-302.

———, 'Proto-Industrialization and Pre-colonial South Asia', *Past and Present*, vol. 98 (1983), pp. 30-95.

———, 'Growth of Money Economy and Some Questions of Transition in Late Pre-colonial India', *The Journal of Peasant Studies*, vol. 11.3 (1984), pp. 96-107.

———, 'Money-use in Late Pre-colonial India and the International Trade in Currency Media', in Richards (ed.), 1987, pp. 232-373.

———, *The Invisible City: Monetary, Administrative and Popular Infrastructures in Asia and Europe, 1500-1900* (Aldershot, 1993).

———, *Unbroken Landscape: Commodity, Category, Sign and Identity: Their Production as Myth and Knowledge, from 1550* (Aldershot, 1994).

Pillai, Anantarankap, *The Private Diary of Ananda Ranga Pillai, Dubash to Joseph Francois Dupleix, Governor of Pondicherry: A Record of Matters Political, Historical, Social, and Personal, from 1736 to 1761*, 12 vols. (Madras, 1904).

Pinkerton, John, *A General Collection of the Best and Most Interesting Voyages and Travels in all Parts of the World: Many of which are now first Translated into English. Digested on a New Plan, by John Pinkerton . . . Illustrated with Plates* (London, 1811).

Pirenne, Henri, *Social and Economic History of Medieval Europe* (London, 1936).

Polanyi, Karl, Conrad M. Arensberg and Harry W. Pearson, *Trade & Market in Early Empires* (Glencoe, Illinois, 1957).

Polo, Marco, *The Travels of Marco Polo, the Venetian* (London, 1854).

Preston-Morley, P.J., 'The East India Company Portcullis Money of 1600', *BNJ*, vol. 63 (1993), p. 167.

Pridmore, F., 'The Officially Mutilated Coinage of British West Africa circa 1813 [1825-?]-1839', *Num. Cir.*, vol. 62 (1954), pp. 59-63.

———, *The Coins of the British Commonwealth of Nations to the End of the Reign of George VI, 1952*, 4 parts (London, 1960-80):

Pt. 1: *European Territories* (London, 1960).

Pt. 2: *Asian Territories* (London, 1965).

Pt. 3: *West Indies* (London, 1965).

Pt. 4: *India:*

Vol. 1: *East India Company Presidency Series, c.1642-1835* (London, 1975).

Vol. 2: *Uniform Coinage East India Company 1835-58, Imperial Period 1858-1947* (London, 1980).

______, 'The Cut Quarters of dollars Countermarked V.R.', *Num. Cir.*, vol. 69 (1961), pp. 242-3.

______, 'Notes on Colonial Coins: The British Protectorate of Egypt 18th December 1914-28th February 1922', *Num. Cir.*, vol. 72 (1964), pp. 196-7.

______, 'Notes on Colonial Coins, the Mint Letter G – A New Mint for the Coinage of British West Africa'. *Num. Cir.*, vol. 73 (1965), pp. 259-60.

______, 'The Coins of the Sierra Leone Company, 1791-1807', *Num. Cir.*, vol. 74 (1966), pp. 206-8, 237-9, and 277-9.

______, 'Mr A.P. Spencer, Artist/Engraver, His Majesty's Mint, Calcutta and the re-designed Coinages of King George VI British India 1938-1947', *BNJ*, vol. 37 (1968), pp. 158-74.

Pridmore, F. and St Helena, 'The East India Company's Coinages', *Num. Cir.*, vol. 70 (1972), pp. 410, 451-2.

Prinsep, James, *Essays on Indian Antiquities, Historic, Numismatic, and Palæographic, of the Late James Prinsep, to which are added his Useful Tables, Illustrative of Indian History, Chronology, Modern Coinages, Weights, Measures, etc.*, ed. Edward Thomas, 2 vols. (London, 1858).

______, *Useful Tables*, as an appendix to the *JASB*, vol. 4 (1835).

______, *Useful Tables, Illustrative of the Coins, Weights and Measures of the British India*, ed. Edward Thomas (London, 1858).

Purchas, Samuel, *Purchas his Pilgrimes, in Five Bookes. The First, Containing the Voyages . . . made by Ancient Kings, . . . and Others, to and Thorow the Remoter Parts of the Knowne World, etc.*, 4 vols. (London, 1625).

Raj, Kapil, 'The Historical Anatomy of a Contact Zone', *IESHR*, vol. 48.1 (2011), pp. 55-82.

Ranade, M.G., *Essays on Indian Economics* (Madras, 1920).

Rapson, E.J., *Sources of Indian History: Coins* (Strassburg, 1897).

Raychaudhuri, Tapan and Irfan Habib (eds.), *The Cambridge Economic History of India*, vol. I: *c. 1200-c. 1750* (Cambridge, 1982).

Reinhart, Carmen M. and Kenneth S. Rogoff, 'This Time is Different: A Panoramic View of Eight Centuries of Financial Crises', *Annals of Economics and Finance*, vol. 15.2 (2014), pp. 1065-1188.

Remick, J. et al., *The Guidebook and Catalogue of British Commonwealth Coins, 1694-1971*, 3rd edn. (Winnipeg, 1971).

Rich, E.E. and C.H. Wilson (eds.), *The Cambridge Economic History of Europe*, vol. V (Cambridge, 1977).

Richards, D.S. (ed.), *Islam & the Trade of Asia* (Oxford, 1970).

Richards, J.F. (ed.), *Imperial Monetary Systems in Mughal India* (New Delhi, 1987).

Richards, John F., 'The Finances of the East India Company in India, *c.* 1766-1859', London School of Economics and Political Science, Working Papers No. 153/11 (2011).

Robins, Nick, 'The Imperial Corporation: The English East India Company and the Lessons from the First Age of Globalization', *International Journal of Green Economics*, vol. 2.1 (2008), pp. 65-76.

Rodgers, Chas J., 'Couplets or "Baits" on the Coins of Shah Nuru-d-din Jahangir, the Son of Akbar', *JASB*, vol. 57.1 (1888), pp. 18-26.

Rothermund, Dietmar, *The Indian Economy under the British Rule: and other Essays* (New Delhi, 1983).

———, *An Economic History of India: From pre Colonial Times to 1986* (New York, 1988).

Roy, Kaushik, 'The Hybrid Military Establishment of the East India Company in South Asia: 1750-1849', *Journal of Global History*, vol. 6.2 (2011), pp. 195-218.

Ruding, Rogers, *Annals of the Coinage of Britain and Its Dependencies: From the Earliest Period of Authentick History to the End of the Fiftieth Year of the Reign of His Present Majesty King George III*, 6 vols. (London, 1819).

Ruggeri, Amanda, 'The East India Company was Vast and Powerful, Hiring Thousands across the World. But What was it Like to Work There? And are There Parallels with Today's Multinationals?', BBC, Capital, 30 March 2016. Online edition: http://www.bbc.com/capital/story/20160330-the-worlds-most-powerful-corporation. Last accessed 18 March 2018.

Sauerbeck, Augustus, 'Prices of Commodities and the Precious Metals', *JSS*, vol. 44 (1886); reprinted in Carus-Wilson (ed.), 1902, pp. 68-127.

Sealy, D.L.F., 'The Guernsey Eight Doubles of 1864', *BNJ*, vol. 33 (1964), pp. 164-7.

Sen, Sudipta, *Empire of Free Trade: The East India Company and the Making of the Colonial Marketplace* (Philadelphia, 1998).

Seth, Vijay K., 'The East India Company: A Case Study in Corporate Governance', *Global Business Review*, vol. 13.2 (2012), pp. 221-38.

Seton Karr, W.S., *Selections from Calcutta Gazette*, 5 vols. (Calcutta, 1864-9).

Sharma, G.D., 'Indigenous Banking and the State in Eastern Rajasthan during the Seventeenth Century'. *PIHC*, 40th Session (Waltair, 1979), pp. 332-441.

Sinha, J.C., 'Currency in Early British Days', *IJE*, vol. 7.3 (1927), pp. 168-70.

______, 'Earliest Currency Committee in India, 1787', *PIHRC* (Lahore), vol. 8 (1925), p. 183.

______, *Economic Annals of Bengal* (London, 1927).

Sivramkrishna, Sashi, 'From Merchant to Merchant-Ruler: A Structure-Conduct-Performance Perspective of the East India Company's History, 1600-1765', *Business History*, vol. 56.5 (2014), pp. 789-815.

Stern, Philip J., *The Company-State: Corporate Sovereignty and the Early Modern Foundations of the British Empire in India* (Oxford, 2011).

Steuart, James, *The Principles of Money Applied to the Present State of the Coin in Bengal: Being an Inquiry into the Methods to be Used for Correcting the Defects for Stopping the Drains which Carry off the Coin; and for Extending Circulation by Means of Paper Credit* (London, 1772).

Stevens, P[aul].J.E., 'An Indian Rarity of 1841', *BNJ*, vol. 54 (1984), p. 298.

______, 'The Reformation of the Coinage of Madras at the Beginning of the Nineteenth Century', *BNJ*, vol. 67 (1997), p. 172.

______, *The Coins of the Bengal Presidency*, The Coinage of the Hon. East India Company, pt. I (London, 2012).

Stewart, Charles, *The History of Bengal: From the First Mohammedan Invasion Until the Virtual Conquest of That Country by the English, A.D. 1757* (London, 1813).

Supple, B.E., *Commercial Crisis and Change in England 1600-1642: A Study in the Instability of a Mercantile Economy* (Cambridge, 1959).

Tavernier, Jean-Baptiste, *Les Six Voyages De Jean-Baptiste Tavernier, Ecuyer Baron D'aubonne, En Turquie, En Perse, Et Aux Indes, et aux Indes, Pendant l'espace de quaranteans, & par toutes les routes quel'onpeuttenir: Accompagnez d'observations particulieressur la qualité, la Religion, le Gouvernment, les Côutumes & le Commerce de chaquepais; avec les figures, le poids,& la valeur des monnoyes qui yontcours* (Paris, 1676).

———, *The Six Voyages of John Baptista Tavernier, a Noble Man of France Now Living, Through Turkey into Persia and the East-Indies, Finished in the Year 1670: Giving an Account of the State of Those Countries: Illustrated with Divers Sculptures; Together with a New Relation of the Present Grand Seignor's Seraglio, by the Same Author* (London, 1677, 1678).

Temple, R., 'General Monetary Practice in India', *JIB*, vol. 2 (1881), p. 406.

Theron, G.P., *Tokens of Southern Africa and their History* (Johannesburg, 1978).

Thomas, Edward, 'The Early Faith of Asoka', *JRAS*, New Series, vol. 9.2 (1877), pp. 155-234.

———, 'The Initial Coinage of Bengal', *JRAS*, New Series, vol. 2.1 (1866), pp. 145-224.

———, *Ancient Indian Weights* (London, 1874).

———, *Jainism: Or, the Early Faith of Asoka; with Illustrations of the Ancient Religions of the East, from the Pantheon of the Indo-Scythians . . . to which is Prefixed a Notice on Bactrian Coins and Indian Dates* (London, 1877).

———, *The Chronicles of the Pathan Kings of Dehli: Illustrated by Coins, Inscriptions, and Other Antiquarian Remains* (London, 1871).

———, *The Revenue Resources of the Mughal Empire in India, from A.D. 1593 to A.D. 1707: A Supplement to the Chronicles of the Pathan Kings of Dehli* (London, 1871).

Thomas, P.J. and B.N. Pillai, *Economic Depression in Madras Presidency from 1820 to 1854* (Madras, 1933).

Thompson, J.D.A., 'Documents Illustrating the Export of Counterfeit Currency to the West Indies', *BNJ*, vol. 27 (1952/4), pp. 80-7.

Thurston, Edgar, *History of the Coinage of the Territories of the East India Company in the Indian Peninsula and Catalogue of the Coins in the Madras Museum* (Madras, 1890).

Tripathi, A., *Trade and Finance in the Bengal Presidency* (Calcutta, 1956).

Tripathi, Dwijendra, 'The Silver Question: India and America', *JIH*, vol. 44.3 (1966), pp. 789-98.

Tucker, Henry St. George, *Memorials of Indian Government being a Selection from the Papers of Henry St. George Tucker . . .*, ed. John William Kaye (London, 1853).

Vakil, C.N. and S.K. Muranjan, *Currency and Prices in India* (Bombay, 1927).

Vakil, C.N., *Financial Development in Modern India, 1860-1921* (Bombay, 1924).
van Den Berg, N.P., *Munt Credieten Bankwezen, Hantel en Scheepvaart in Scheepvaari in Nederlandsch Indie* (The Hague, 1907).
Venkateswara, S.V., 'Mogul Currency and Coinage', *IJE*, vol. 2:2 (1918), pp. 169-79.
Verelst, Harry, *A View of the Rise, Progress, and Present State of the English Government in Bengal: Including a Reply to the Misrepresentations of Mr. Bolts, and Other Writers* (London, 1772).
Vice, D., 'A Pattern Cowrie Coinage for Bengal Presidency', *Format*, vol. 58 (1998), pp. 2-5.
______, *The Coinage of British West Africa & St Helena 1684-1958* (Birmingham, 1983).
*Vijayanagar Six-Centenary Commemoration Volume* (Dharwar, 1936).
Vilar, Pierre, *A History of Money and Gold, 1450-1920* (London, 1976).
Wallerstein, Immanuel, *The Modern World-System: Capitalist Agriculture and the Origin of the European World-Economy in the Sixteenth Century* (London, 1974).
______, *The Modern World-System: Mercantalism and the Consolidation of the European World-Economy, 1600-1750* (London, 1980).
Warring, John Scott, *Observations on the Present State of the East India Company and on the Measures to be Pursued for Ensuring its Permanency, and Augmenting its Commerce* (London, 1771).
Welch, James, 'The British Raj and India: British Colonial Influence: 1612-1948', Research Gate, Sept. 2011. Online Edition: https://www.researchgate.net/publication/272383606. Last accessed: 18 March 2018.
Wiggins, K.W., 'Acquisition of Indian Mints by the East India Company', in K.K. Maheshwari and Biswajeet Rath (eds.), 1996, pp. 327-44.
Wilks, Ivor, *Asante in the Nineteenth Century: The Structure and Evolution of a Political Order* (Cambridge, 1975).
Woolhouse, W.S.B., *Measures, Weights and Moneys*, Weale's series, 3rd edn. (London, 1867).
Wright, L.V.W., *Colonial and Commonwealth Coins* (London, 1959).

# Contributors

AMBEDKAR, Bhimrao Ramji (1891-1956), was a noted Indian jurist, politician and social reformer, who is widely known as the principal architect of the Constitution of India. He was Independent India's first law minister. As a student of economics, he received his postgraduate education at Columbia University, and at the London School of Economics. He was the first Indian to pursue a doctorate in economics abroad. In partial fulfilment of the requirements of the degree of Master of Arts, he submitted a dissertation on 'Administration and Finance of the East India Company' (1915). In 1923, he completed a D.Sc. in Economics. His thesis was on the 'The Problem of the Rupee: Its origin and its Solution'. His other well-known work on the economic and monetary history of the Raj includes, *Evolution of Provincial Finance in British India* (1925).

DALRYMPLE, Alexander (1737-1808) was a Scottish geographer and the first Hydrographer of the British Admiralty. He was born at Newhailes, near Edinburgh. He went to London in 1752 and was appointed a writer in the British East India Company. He arrived in Madras in 1753 and was soon involved in negotiating trading concessions for the Company in Manila and Canton. In 1765 he returned to London where was elected a fellow of the Royal Society. Apart from his hydrographic and navigational charts and surveys, Dalrymple also published a number of books and tracts on the economic activities of the East India Company. Apart from the tract on the coinage proposed for the Circars, included in this volume, these works on the East India Company include: *A Plan for Extending the Commerce of this Kingdom and of the East-India Company* (1769), *A General View of the East-India Company, written in January 1769; to which are added, some Observations on the Present State of their Affairs* (1772), and *A Retrospective view of the Antient [sic.] System of the East-India Company with a Plan of Regulation* (1784).

DAYAL DAS, served as Archivist in the National Archives of India. Though very knowledgeable about the archival collection of the East India Company, he sparingly contributed by way of academic writings. In his official capacity he was associated with the Indian Historical Records Commission (IHRC), and one of his papers that he presented at the Bhubaneswar Session of the IHRC (1958) has been included in this volume.

DODWELL, Henry Herbert (1879-1946), was educated at Thame Grammar School, then at St. John's College, University of Oxford. He entered the Indian Education Service in 1908 and was continued until 1922 when returned to Britain and held the first chair as the Professor of History and Culture of the British Dominions in Asia at the School of Oriental and African Studies (SOAS) from 1922-46. Dodwell edited two volumes of *The Cambridge History of India* (vols. 5 and 6), as well as *The Cambridge Shorter History of India* (1934).

GARG, Sanjay (b. 1965) – the Editor of this Series, and the present volume – is a numismatist and economic historian of international repute. He obtained his Ph.D. in History from the Jawaharlal Nehru University and Diploma in Archival Studies from the National Archives of India, New Delhi. He is an eminent researcher with extensive research experience in history of South Asia, with specialization on economic and monetary history, currency and coinage, architecture and archival studies. His research findings have been widely published in print and multimedia (for details, see: http://sanjaygarg.wikidot.com/). At present he is posted as the Director, Swami Vivekananda Cultural Centre, Astana (Kazakhstan).

MITRA, Debendra Bijoy, worked as a Postdoctoral Research Associate in the Department of History, University of Calcutta, on the monetary system of the Bengal Presidency under the supervision of Professor Binay Bhushan Chaudhuri, which was later published in a book form (1991). Earlier, he had published his research on the cotton weavers of Bengal (1978). Dr. Mitra taught at different government colleges of West Bengal, including at the Presidency College from 1983-9. He served as Reader in History at the Hooghly Mohsin College, Chinsurah (West Bengal). After his retirement he now lives in Kolkata.

PERLIN, Frank (b. 1939), is an historian of international repute who specializes in social, political and economic history, and monetary economy of pre-colonial India. Born in Liverpool, he completed his Masters at the School of Oriental and African Studies (SOAS), London (1972) and between 1979 and 2004 served as a lecturer Erasmus University Rotterdam (The Netherlands). He obtained his doctorate on 'Studies in Society and Economy in Late Pre-Colonial India', under the supervision of J.C. Heesterman, Leiden University (1983). Perlin retired in 2004. He has contributed scholarly papers in various international journals and edited works. His papers have also appeared in variorum editions, namely, *The Invisible City* (1993) and *Unbroken Landscape* (1994).

RAMACHANDRAN, C., has contributed several papers on coinage and currency as well as on economic history of the East India Company in the Madras Presidency. Most of his research papers appear in the journal, *Indo-British Review: A Journal of History*, published by the Indo-British Historical Society (estb. 1967), Madras (now Chennai), which now seem to have discontinued. No other information about the author is forthcoming.

ROTHERMUND, Dietmar (b. 1933), is a German historian best known for his research in the economy of India. Born in Kassel (Germany), he studied history and philosophy in Marburg and Munich, and received his PhD from the University of Pennsylvania in 1959. His doctoral dissertation cantered on the social history of America. Shortly thereafter, he travelled to India on a scholarship from the German Research Foundation. In 1963 Heidelberg

University offered him an appointment as a research assistant and in 1968 he received tenure and was given the Chair of South Asian History. Prof. Rothermund has authored several papers and books, including, *The Indian Economy under the British Rule* (1983), and *An Economic History of India: From Pre-Colonial Times to 1986* (1988).

SINHA, Jogish Chandra (1893-1954), was educated at the Presidency College (1909-15), Calcutta, after which he served as the Lecturer of Economics at the University of Calcutta from 1915-23. Thereafter, in 1923 he joined the Department of Economics at the University of Dacca and continued till 1932, when he joined the Presidency College, Calcutta as Senior Professor of Economics. Simultaneously, he also served as the Economic Advisor to the Government of Bengal. In 1948 he was elected President of the Indian Economic Congress held at Hyderabad. He retired in 1950. His *Economic Annals of Bengal* (1927), is a pioneering work in the field of monetary history of the Raj. Another work, *Indian Currency Problems of the Last Decade, 1926-1936* (1937), a collection of a series of lectures delivered at the University of Delhi in 1936, delineates a well-researched historical background of the economic problems faced by India as a result of the monetary policies of the successive British Governments.

STEVENS, Paul J.E. (b. 1952), is a well-known numismatist and a coin collector, and a qualified medical doctor. He began his working career as a research scientist looking for new medicines. During the 1970s and was particularly fascinated by the coins which were produced by the British for use in India. After taking early retirement in 2008, he fully concentrated on his numismatic interest and has since contributed several scholarly papers in reputed journals. In 2012, he has published a masterly work that explores the coins and mints of the Bengal Presidency from 1757, when the EIC first acquired the right to mint coins there, until 1835, when a uniform coinage was introduced into British India. This book is the first of a planned three part series covering the coins of the East India Company. The use of archival source materials for numismatic researches has been the hallmark of Dr Stevens academic contributions.

THOMAS, Edward (1813-86), an English civil servant of the East India Company, known for his writings on Indian antiquities. He was educated at the East India College at Haileybury, after which he went to India in 1832 as a writer in the Bengal service of the Company. After acting for a short time as judge at Delhi, Thomas was appointed Superintending Judge of the Saugor and Nerbudda Territory. He retired in 1857, and spent the rest of his life in scholarly pursuits. He is well-known for his masterly work – *Chronicles of the Pathan Kings of Delhi* (1847) as well as for his annotated edition of James Prinsep's *Essays on Indian Antiquities and Useful Tables* (2 vols. 1858). He made several scholarly contributions in numismatics, inscriptions, weights and measures, etc., including a masterly work on the revenue system of the Mughals (1871).

THURSTON, Edgar (1855-1935), was a resident of Kew, London and had received his school education at Eton College. Thereafter, he studied medicine at King's College, London, qualifying as L Royal College of Physicians in 1877. He worked as a medical officer in Kent County Lunatic Asylum and became a curator of the museum at King's College before joining the Madras Museum in 1885 as a Superintendent. Simultaneously, lectured in anatomy at the Madras Medical College. He contributed to the studies in the zoology, geology, botany and ethnology of India. His works on numismatics include four catalogues of different series of coins in the collection of the Madras Museum. His 'History of the Coinage of the East India Company…' (1890), included in this volume, was first detailed study of the subject which was based on authentic archival sources.

# Index

For Product Safety Concerns and Information please contact our EU representative GPSR@taylorandfrancis.com
Taylor & Francis Verlag GmbH, Kaufingerstraße 24, 80331 München, Germany

www.ingramcontent.com/pod-product-compliance
Ingram Content Group UK Ltd.
Pitfield, Milton Keynes, MK11 3LW, UK
UKHW022112190926
475702UK00013B/1394
*9781032652467*